# Thirteen Plays

# by

# Anton Chekhov

Cover Artwork: James Jebusa Shannon: In the spring time

ISBN: 978-1-78139-404-5

# Contents

## A TRAGEDIAN IN SPITE OF HIMSELF



## THE WEDDING



## THE PROPOSAL



## THE SEA-GULL



## UNCLE VANYA



## THE THREE SISTERS

# THE CHERRY ORCHARD

# ON THE HIGH ROAD

## Translated by Julius West

### CHARACTERS

TIHON EVSTIGNEYEV, the proprietor of a inn on the main road
SEMYON SERGEYEVITCH BORTSOV, a ruined landowner
MARIA EGOROVNA, his wife
SAVVA, an aged pilgrim
NAZAROVNA and EFIMOVNA, women pilgrims
FEDYA, a labourer
EGOR MERIK, a tramp
KUSMA, a driver
POSTMAN
BORTSOV'S WIFE'S COACHMAN
PILGRIMS, CATTLE-DEALERS, ETC.

# ON THE HIGH ROAD

The action takes place in one of the provinces of Southern Russia

*[The scene is laid in TIHON'S bar. On the right is the bar-counter and shelves with bottles. At the back is a door leading out of the house. Over it, on the outside, hangs a dirty red lantern. The floor and the forms, which stand against the wall, are closely occupied by pilgrims and passers-by. Many of them, for lack of space, are sleeping as they sit. It is late at night. As the curtain rises thunder is heard, and lightning is seen through the door.]*

*[TIHON is behind the counter. FEDYA is half-lying in a heap on one of the forms, and is quietly playing on a concertina. Next to him is BORTSOV, wearing a shabby summer overcoat. SAVVA, NAZAROVNA, and EFIMOVNA are stretched out on the floor by the benches.]*

EFIMOVNA. *[To NAZAROVNA]* Give the old man a nudge dear! Can't get any answer out of him.

NAZAROVNA. *[Lifting the corner of a cloth covering of SAVVA'S face]* Are you alive or are you dead, you holy man?

SAVVA. Why should I be dead? I'm alive, mother! *[Raises himself on his elbow]* Cover up my feet, there's a saint! That's it. A bit more on the right one. That's it, mother. God be good to us.

NAZAROVNA. *[Wrapping up SAVVA'S feet]* Sleep, little father.

SAVVA. What sleep can I have? If only I had the patience to endure this pain, mother; sleep's quite another matter. A sinner doesn't deserve to be given rest. What's that noise, pilgrim-woman?

NAZAROVNA. God is sending a storm. The wind is wailing, and the rain is pouring down, pouring down. All down the roof and into the windows like dried peas. Do you hear? The windows of heaven are opened... *[Thunder]* Holy, holy, holy...

FEDYA. And it roars and thunders, and rages, sad there's no end to it! Hoooo... it's like the noise of a forest.... Hoooo.... The wind is wailing like a dog.... *[Shrinking back]* It's cold! My clothes are wet, it's all coming in through the open door... you might put me through a wringer.... *[Plays softly]* My concertina's damp, and so there's no music for you, my Orthodox brethren, or else I'd give you such a concert, my word!—Something marvellous! You can have a quadrille, or a polka, if you like, or some Russian dance for two.... I can do them all. In the town, where I was an attendant at the Grand Hotel, I couldn't make any money, but I did wonders on my concertina. And, I can play the guitar.

A VOICE FROM THE CORNER. A silly speech from a silly fool.

FEDYA. I can hear another of them. *[Pause.]*

NAZAROVNA. *[To SAVVA]* If you'd only lie where it was warm now, old man, and warm your feet. *[Pause.]* Old man! Man of God! *[Shakes SAVVA]* Are you going to die?

FEDYA. You ought to drink a little vodka, grandfather. Drink, and it'll burn, burn in your stomach, and warm up your heart. Drink, do!

NAZAROVNA. Don't swank, young man! Perhaps the old man is giving back his soul to God, or repenting for his sins, and you talk like that, and play your concertina.... Put it down! You've no shame!

FEDYA. And what are you sticking to him for? He can't do anything and you... with your old women's talk... He can't say a word in reply, and you're glad, and happy because he's listening to your nonsense.... You go on sleeping, grandfather; never mind her! Let her talk, don't you take any notice of her. A woman's tongue is the devil's broom—it will sweep the good man and the clever man both out of the house. Don't you mind.... *[Waves his hands]* But it's thin you are, brother of mine! Terrible! Like a dead skeleton! No life in you! Are you really dying?

SAVVA. Why should I die? Save me, O Lord, from dying in vain.... I'll suffer a little, and then get up with God's help.... The Mother of God won't let me die in a strange land.... I'll die at home.

FEDYA. Are you from far off?

SAVVA. From Vologda. The town itself.... I live there.

FEDYA. And where is this Vologda?

TIHON. The other side of Moscow....

FEDYA. Well, well, well.... You have come a long way, old man! On foot?

SAVVA. On foot, young man. I've been to Tihon of the Don, and I'm going to the Holy Hills. *[Note: On the Donetz, south-east of Kharkov; a monastery containing a miraculous ikon.]*... From there, if God wills it, to Odessa.... They say you can get to Jerusalem cheap from there, for twenty-ones roubles, they say....

FEDYA. And have you been to Moscow?

SAVVA. Rather! Five times....

FEDYA. Is it a good town? *[Smokes]* Well-standing?

Sews. There are many holy places there, young man.... Where there are many holy places it's always a good town....

BORTSOV. *[Goes up to the counter, to TIHON]* Once more, please! For the sake of Christ, give it to me!

FEDYA. The chief thing about a town is that it should be clean. If it's dusty, it must be watered; if it's dirty, it must be cleaned. There ought to be big houses... a theatre... police... cabs, which... I've lived in a town myself, I understand.

BORTSOV. Just a little glass. I'll pay you for it later.

TIHON. That's enough now.

BORTSOV. I ask you! Do be kind to me!

TIHON. Get away!

BORTSOV. You don't understand me.... Understand me, you fool, if there's a drop of brain in your peasant's wooden head, that it isn't I who am asking you, but my inside, using the words you understand, that's what's asking! My illness is what's asking! Understand!

TIHON. We don't understand anything.... Get back!

BORTSOV. Because if I don't have a drink at once, just you understand this, if I don't satisfy my needs, I may commit some crime. God only knows what I might do! In the time you've kept this place, you rascal, haven't you seen a lot of drunkards, and haven't you yet got to understand what they're like? They're diseased! You can do anything you like to them, but you must give them vodka! Well, now, I implore you! Please! I humbly ask you! God only knows how humbly!

TIHON. You can have the vodka if you pay for it.

BORTSOV. Where am I to get the money? I've drunk it all! Down to the ground! What can I give you? I've only got this coat, but I can't give you that. I've nothing on underneath.... Would you like my cap? *[Takes it off and gives it to TIHON]*

TIHON. *[Looks it over]* Hm.... There are all sorts of caps.... It might be a sieve from the holes in it....

FEDYA. *[Laughs]* A gentleman's cap! You've got to take it off in front of the mam'selles. How do you do, good-bye! How are you?

TIHON. *[Returns the cap to BORTSOV]* I wouldn't give anything for it. It's muck.

BORTSOV. If you don't like it, then let me owe you for the drink! I'll bring in your five copecks on my way back from town. You can take it and choke yourself with it then! Choke yourself! I hope it sticks in your throat! *[Coughs]* I hate you!

TIHON. *[Banging the bar-counter with his fist]* Why do you keep on like that? What a man! What are you here for, you swindler?

BORTSOV. I want a drink! It's not I, it's my disease! Understand that!

TIHON. Don't you make me lose my temper, or you'll soon find yourself outside!

BORTSOV. What am I to do? *[Retires from the bar-counter]* What am I to do? *[Is thoughtful.]*

EFIMOVNA. It's the devil tormenting you. Don't you mind him, sir. The damned one keeps whispering, "Drink! Drink!" And you answer him, "I shan't drink! I shan't drink!" He'll go then.

FEDYA. It's drumming in his head.... His stomach's leading him on! *[Laughs]* Your honour's a happy man. Lie down and go to sleep! What's the use of standing like a scarecrow in the middle of the inn! This isn't an orchard!

BORTSOV. *[Angrily]* Shut up! Nobody spoke to you, you donkey.

FEDYA. Go on, go on! We've seen the like of you before! There's a lot like you tramping the high road! As to being a donkey, you wait till I've given you a clout on the ear and you'll howl worse than the wind. Donkey yourself! Fool! *[Pause]* Scum!

NAZAROVNA. The old man may be saying a prayer, or giving up his soul to God, and here are these unclean ones wrangling with one another and saying all sorts of... Have shame on yourselves!

FEDYA. Here, you cabbage-stalk, you keep quiet, even if you are in a public-house. Just you behave like everybody else.

BORTSOV. What am I to do? What will become of me? How can I make him understand? What else can I say to him? *[To TIHON]* The blood's boiling in my chest! Uncle Tihon! *[Weeps]* Uncle Tihon!

SAWA. *[Groans]* I've got shooting-pains in my leg, like bullets of fire.... Little mother, pilgrim.

EFIMOVNA. What is it, little father?

SAVVA. Who's that crying?

EFIMOVNA. The gentleman.

SAVVA. Ask him to shed a tear for me, that I might die in Vologda. Tearful prayers are heard.

BORTSOV. I'm not praying, grandfather! These aren't tears! Just juice! My soul is crushed; and the juice is running. *[Sits by SAVVA]* Juice! But you wouldn't understand! You, with your darkened brain, wouldn't understand. You people are all in the dark!

SAVVA. Where will you find those who live in the light?

BORTSOV. They do exist, grandfather.... They would understand!

SAVVA. Yes, yes, dear friend.... The saints lived in the light.... They understood all our griefs.... You needn't even tell them.... and they'll understand.... Just by looking at your eyes.... And then you'll have such peace, as if you were never in grief at all—it will all go!

FEDYA. And have you ever seen any saints?

SAVVA. It has happened, young man.... There are many of all sorts on this earth. Sinners, and servants of God.

BORTSOV. I don't understand all this.... *[Gets up quickly]* What's the use of talking when you don't understand, and what sort of a brain have I now? I've only an instinct, a thirst! *[Goes quickly to the counter]* Tihon, take my coat! Understand? *[Tries to take it off]* My coat...

TIHON. And what is there under your coat? *[Looks under it]* Your naked body? Don't take it off, I shan't have it.... I'm not going to burden my soul with a sin.

*[Enter MERIK.]*

BORTSOV. Very well, I'll take the sin on myself! Do you agree?

MERIK. *[In silence takes of his outer cloak and remains in a sleeveless jacket. He carries an axe in his belt]* A vagrant may sweat where a bear will freeze. I am hot. *[Puts his axe on the floor and takes off his jacket]* You get rid of a pailful of sweat while you drag one leg out of the mud. And while you are dragging it out, the other one goes farther in.

EFIMOVNA. Yes, that's true... is the rain stopping, dear?

MERIK. *[Glancing at EFIMOVNA]* I don't talk to old women. *[A pause.]*

BORTSOV. *[To TIHON]* I'll take the sin on myself. Do you hear me or don't you?

TIHON. I don't want to hear you, get away!

MERIK. It's as dark as if the sky was painted with pitch. You can't see your own nose. And the rain beats into your face like a snow-storm! *[Picks up his clothes and axe.]*

FEDYA. It's a good thing for the likes of us thieves. When the cat's away the mice will play.

MERIK. Who says that?

FEDYA. Look and see... before you forget.

MERIN. We'll make a note of it.... *[Goes up to TIHON]* How do you do, you with the large face! Don't you remember me.

TIHON. If I'm to remember every one of you drunkards that walks the high road, I reckon I'd need ten holes in my forehead.

MERIK. Just look at me.... *[A pause.]*

TIHON. Oh, yes; I remember. I knew you by your eyes! *[Gives him his hand]* Andrey Polikarpov?

MERIK. I used to be Andrey Polikarpov, but now I am Egor Merik.

TIHON. Why's that?

MERIK. I call myself after whatever passport God gives me. I've been Merik for two months. *[Thunder]* Rrrr.... Go on thundering, I'm not afraid! *[Looks round]* Any police here?

TIHON. What are you talking about, making mountains out of mole-hills?... The people here are all right... The police are fast asleep in their feather beds now.... *[Loudly]* Orthodox brothers, mind your pockets and your clothes, or you'll have to regret it. The man's a rascal! He'll rob you!

MERIK. They can look out for their money, but as to their clothes—I shan't touch them. I've nowhere to take them.

TIHON. Where's the devil taking you to?

MERIK. To Kuban.

TIHON. My word!

FEDYA. To Kuban? Really? *[Sitting up]* It's a fine place. You wouldn't see such a country, brother, if you were to fall asleep and dream for three years. They say the birds there, and the beasts are—my God! The grass grows all the year round, the people are good, and they've so much land they don't know what to do with it! The authorities, they say... a soldier was telling me the other day... give a hundred dessiatins ahead. There's happiness, God strike me!

MERIK. Happiness.... Happiness goes behind you.... You don't see it. It's as near as your elbow is, but you can't bite it. It's all silly.... *[Looking round at the benches and the people]* Like a lot of prisoners.... A poor lot.

EFIMOVNA. *[To MERIK]* What great, angry, eyes! There's an enemy in you, young man.... Don't you look at us!

MERIK. Yes, you're a poor lot here.

EFIMOVNA. Turn away! *[Nudges SAVVA]* Savva, darling, a wicked man is looking at us. He'll do us harm, dear. *[To MERIK]* Turn away, I tell you, you snake!

SAVVA. He won't touch us, mother, he won't touch us.... God won't let him.

MERIK. All right, Orthodox brothers! *[Shrugs his shoulders]* Be quiet! You aren't asleep, you bandy-legged fools! Why don't you say something?

EFIMOVNA. Take your great eyes away! Take away that devil's own pride!

MERIK. Be quiet, you crooked old woman! I didn't come with the devil's pride, but with kind words, wishing to honour your bitter lot! You're huddled together like flies because of the cold—I'd be sorry for you, speak kindly to you, pity your poverty, and here you go grumbling away! *[Goes up to FEDYA]* Where are you from?

FEDYA. I live in these parts. I work at the Khamonyevsky brickworks.

MERIK. Get up.

FEDYA. *[Raising himself]* Well?

MERIK. Get up, right up. I'm going to lie down here.

FEDYA. What's that.... It isn't your place, is it?

MERIK. Yes, mine. Go and lie on the ground!

FEDYA. You get out of this, you tramp. I'm not afraid of you.

MERIK. You're very quick with your tongue.... Get up, and don't talk about it! You'll be sorry for it, you silly.

TIHON. *[To FEDYA]* Don't contradict him, young man. Never mind.

FEDYA. What right have you? You stick out your fishy eyes and think I'm afraid! *[Picks up his belongings and stretches himself out on the ground]* You devil! *[Lies down and covers himself all over.]*

MERIK. *[Stretching himself out on the bench]* I don't expect you've ever seen a devil or you wouldn't call me one. Devils aren't like that. *[Lies down, putting his axe next to him.]* Lie down, little brother axe... let me cover you.

TIHON. Where did you get the axe from?

MERIK. Stole it.... Stole it, and now I've got to fuss over it like a child with a new toy; I don't like to throw it away, and I've nowhere to put it. Like a beastly wife.... Yes.... *[Covering himself over]* Devils aren't like that, brother.

FEDYA. *[Uncovering his head]* What are they like?

MERIK. Like steam, like air.... Just blow into the air. *[Blows]* They're like that, you can't see them.

A VOICE FROM THE CORNER. You can see them if you sit under a harrow.

MERIK. I've tried, but I didn't see any.... Old women's tales, and silly old men's, too.... You won't see a devil or a ghost or a corpse.... Our eyes weren't made so that we could see everything.... When I was a boy, I used to walk in the woods at night on purpose to see the demon of the woods.... I'd shout and shout, and there might be some spirit, I'd call for the demon of the woods and not blink my eyes: I'd see all sorts of little things moving about, but no demon. I used to go and walk about the churchyards at night, I wanted to see the ghosts—but the women lie. I saw all sorts of animals, but anything awful—not a sign. Our eyes weren't...

THE VOICE FROM THE CORNER. Never mind, it does happen that you do see.... In our village a man was gutting a wild boar... he was separating the tripe when... something jumped out at him!

SAVVA. *[Raising himself]* Little children, don't talk about these unclean things! It's a sin, dears!

MERIK. Aaa... greybeard! You skeleton! *[Laughs]* You needn't go to the churchyard to see ghosts, when they get up from under the floor to give advice to their relations.... A sin!... Don't you teach people your silly notions! You're an ignorant lot of people living in darkness.... *[Lights his pipe]* My father was peasant and used to be fond of teaching people. One night he stole a sack of apples from the village priest, and he brings them along and tells us, "Look, children, mind you don't eat any apples before Easter, it's a sin." You're like that.... You don't know what a devil is, but you go calling people devils.... Take this crooked old woman, for instance. *[Points to EFIMOVNA]* She sees an enemy in me, but is her time, for some woman's nonsense or other, she's given her soul to the devil five times.

EFIMOVNA. Hoo, hoo, hoo.... Gracious heavens! *[Covers her face]* Little Savva!

TIHON. What are you frightening them for? A great pleasure! *[The door slams in the wind]* Lord Jesus.... The wind, the wind!

MERIK. *[Stretching himself]* Eh, to show my strength! *[The door slams again]* If I could only measure myself against the wind! Shall I tear the door down, or suppose I tear up the inn by the roots! *[Gets up and lies down again]* How dull!

NAZAROVNA. You'd better pray, you heathen! Why are you so restless?

EFIMOVNA. Don't speak to him, leave him alone! He's looking at us again. *[To MERIK]* Don't look at us, evil man! Your eyes are like the eyes of a devil before cockcrow!

SAVVA. Let him look, pilgrims! You pray, and his eyes won't do you any harm.

BORTSOV. No, I can't. It's too much for my strength! *[Goes up to the counter]* Listen, Tihon, I ask you for the last time.... Just half a glass!

TIHON. *[Shakes his head]* The money!

BORTSOV. My God, haven't I told you! I've drunk it all! Where am I to get it? And you won't go broke even if you do let me have a drop of vodka on tick. A glass of it only costs you two copecks, and it will save me from suffering! I am suffering! Understand! I'm in misery, I'm suffering!

TIHON. Go and tell that to someone else, not to me.... Go and ask the Orthodox, perhaps they'll give you some for Christ's sake, if they feel like it, but I'll only give bread for Christ's sake.

BORTSOV. You can rob those wretches yourself, I shan't.... I won't do it! I won't! Understand? *[Hits the bar-counter with his fist]* I won't. *[A pause.]* Hm... just wait.... *[Turns to the pilgrim women]* It's an idea, all the same, Orthodox ones! Spare five copecks! My inside asks for it. I'm ill!

FEDYA. Oh, you swindler, with your "spare five copecks." Won't you have some water?

BORTSOV. How I am degrading myself! I don't want it! I don't want anything! I was joking!

MERIK. You won't get it out of him, sir.... He's a famous skinflint.... Wait, I've got a five-copeck piece somewhere.... We'll have a glass between us—half each *[Searches in his pockets]* The devil... it's lost somewhere.... Thought I heard it tinkling just now in my pocket.... No; no, it isn't there, brother, it's your luck! *[A pause.]*

BORTSOV. But if I can't drink, I'll commit a crime or I'll kill myself.... What shall I do, my God! *[Looks through the door]* Shall I go out, then? Out into this darkness, wherever my feet take me....

MERIK. Why don't you give him a sermon, you pilgrims? And you, Tihon, why don't you drive him out? He hasn't paid you for his night's accommodation. Chuck him out! Eh, the people are cruel nowadays. There's no gentleness or kindness in them.... A savage people! A man is drowning and they shout to him: "Hurry up and drown, we've got no time to look at you; we've got to go to work." As to throwing him a rope—there's no worry about that.... A rope would cost money.

SAVVA. Don't talk, kind man!

MERIK. Quiet, old wolf! You're a savage race! Herods! Sellers of your souls! *[To TIHON]* Come here, take off my boots! Look sharp now!

TIHON. Eh, he's let himself go I *[Laughs]* Awful, isn't it.

MERIK. Go on, do as you're told! Quick now! *[Pause]* Do you hear me, or don't you? Am I talking to you or the wall? *[Stands up]*

TIHON. Well... give over.

MERIK. I want you, you fleecer, to take the boots off me, a poor tramp.

TIHON. Well, well... don't get excited. Here have a glass.... Have a drink, now!

MERIK. People, what do I want? Do I want him to stand me vodka, or to take off my boots? Didn't I say it properly? *[To TIHON]* Didn't you hear me rightly? I'll wait a moment, perhaps you'll hear me then.

*[There is excitement among the pilgrims and tramps, who half-raise themselves in order to look at TIHON and MERIK They wait in silence.]*

TIHON. The devil brought you here! *[Comes out from behind the bar]* What a gentleman! Come on now. *[Takes off MERIK'S boots]* You child of Cain...

MERIK. That's right. Put them side by side.... Like that... you can go now!

TIHON. *[Returns to the bar-counter]* You're too fond of being clever. You do it again and I'll turn you out of the inn! Yes! *[To BORTSOV, who is approaching]* You, again?

BORTSOV. Look here, suppose I give you something made of gold.... I will give it to you.

TIHON. What are you shaking for? Talk sense!

BORTSOV. It may be mean and wicked on my part, but what am I to do? I'm doing this wicked thing, not reckoning on what's to come.... If I was tried for it, they'd let me off. Take it, only on condition that you return it later, when I come back from town. I give it to you in front of these witnesses. You will be my witnesses! *[Takes a gold medallion out from the breast of his coat]* Here it is.... I ought to take the portrait out, but I've nowhere to put it; I'm wet all over.... Well, take the portrait, too! Only mind this... don't let your fingers touch that face.... Please... I was rude to you, my dear fellow, I was a fool, but forgive me and... don't touch it with your fingers.... Don't look at that face with your eyes. *[Gives TIHON the medallion.]*

TIHON. *[Examining it]* Stolen property.... All right, then, drink.... *[Pours out vodka]* Confound you.

BORTSOV. Only don't you touch it... with your fingers. *[Drinks slowly, with feverish pauses.]*

TIHON. *[Opens the medallion]* Hm... a lady!... Where did you get hold of this?

MERIK. Let's have a look. *[Goes to the bar]* Let's see.

TIHON. *[Pushes his hand away]* Where are you going to? You look somewhere else!

FEDYA. *[Gets up and comes to TIHON]* I want to look too!

*[Several of the tramps, etc., approach the bar and form a group. MERIK grips TIHON's hand firmly with both his, looks at the portrait, in the medallion in silence. A pause.]*

MERIK. A pretty she-devil. A real lady....

FEDYA. A real lady.... Look at her cheeks, her eyes.... Open your hand, I can't see. Hair coming down to her waist.... It is lifelike! She might be going to say something.... *[Pause.]*

MERIK. It's destruction for a weak man. A woman like that gets a hold on one and... *[Waves his hand]* you're done for!

*[*KUSMA'S *voice is heard.* "Trrr.... Stop, you brutes!" *Enter KUSMA.]*

KUSMA. There stands an inn upon my way. Shall I drive or walk past it, say? You can pass your own father and not notice him, but you can see an inn in the dark a hundred versts away. Make way, if you believe in God! Hullo, there! *[Planks a five-copeck piece down on the counter]* A glass of real Madeira! Quick!

FEDYA. Oh, you devil!

TIHON. Don't wave your arms about, or you'll hit somebody.

KUSMA. God gave us arms to wave about. Poor sugary things, you're half-melted. You're frightened of the rain, poor delicate things. *[Drinks.]*

EFIMOVNA. You may well get frightened, good man, if you're caught on your way in a night like this. Now, thank God, it's all right, there are many villages and houses where you can shelter from the weather, but before that there weren't any. Oh, Lord, it was bad! You walk a hundred versts, and not only isn't there a village; or a house, but you don't even see a dry stick. So you sleep on the ground....

KUSMA. Have you been long on this earth, old woman?

EFIMOVNA. Over seventy years, little father.

KUSMA. Over seventy years! You'll soon come to crow's years. *[Looks at BORTSOV]* And what sort of a raisin is this? *[Staring at BORTSOV]* Sir! *[BORTSOV recognizes KUSMA and retires in confusion to a corner of the room, where he sits on a bench]* Semyon Sergeyevitch! Is that you, or isn't it? Eh? What are you doing in this place? It's not the sort of place for you, is it?

BORTSOV. Be quiet!

MERIK. *[To KUSMA]* Who is it?

KUSMA. A miserable sufferer. *[Paces irritably by the counter]* Eh? In an inn, my goodness! Tattered! Drunk! I'm upset, brothers... upset.... *[To MERIK, in an undertone]* It's my master... our landlord. Semyon Sergeyevitch and Mr. Bortsov.... Have you ever seen such a state? What does he look like? Just... it's the drink that brought him to this.... Give me some more! *[Drinks]* I come from his village, Bortsovka; you may have heard of it, it's 200 versts from here, in the Ergovsky district. We used to be his father's serfs.... What a shame!

MERIK. Was he rich?

KUSMA. Very.

MERIK. Did he drink it all?

KUSMA. No, my friend, it was something else.... He used to be great and rich and sober.... *[To TIHON]* Why you yourself used to see him riding, as he used to, past this inn, on his way to the town. Such bold and noble horses! A carriage on springs, of the best quality! He used to own five troikas, brother.... Five years ago, I remember, he came here driving two horses from Mikishinsky, and he paid with a five-rouble piece.... I haven't the time, he says, to wait for the change.... There!

MERIK. His brain's gone, I suppose.

KUSMA. His brain's all right.... It all happened because of his cowardice! From too much fat. First of all, children, because of a woman.... He fell in love with a woman of the town, and it seemed to him that there wasn't any more beautiful thing in the wide world. A fool may love as much as a wise man. The girl's people were all right.... But she wasn't exactly loose, but just... giddy... always changing her mind! Always winking at one! Always laughing and laughing.... No sense at all. The gentry like that, they think that's nice, but we moujiks would soon chuck her out.... Well, he fell in love, and his luck ran out. He began to keep company with her, one thing led to another... they used to go out in a boat all night, and play pianos....

BORTSOV. Don't tell them, Kusma! Why should you? What has my life got to do with them?

KUSMA. Forgive me, your honour, I'm only telling them a little... what does it matter, anyway.... I'm shaking all over. Pour out some more. *[Drinks.]*

MERIK. *[In a semitone]* And did she love him?

KUSMA. *[In a semitone which gradually becomes his ordinary voice]* How shouldn't she? He was a man of means.... Of course you'll fall in love when the man has a thousand dessiatins and money to burn.... He was a solid, dignified, sober gentleman... always the same, like this... give me your hand *[Takes MERIK'S hand]* "How do you do and good-bye, do me the favour." Well, I was going one evening past his garden—and what a garden, brother, versts of it—I was going along quietly, and I look and see the two of them sitting on a seat and kissing each other. *[Imitates the sound]* He kisses her once, and the snake gives him back two.... He was holding her white, little hand, and she was all fiery and kept on getting closer and closer, too.... "I love you," she says. And he, like one of the damned, walks about from one place to another and brags, the coward, about his happiness.... Gives one man a rouble, and two to another.... Gives me money for a horse. Let off everybody's debts....

BORTSOV. Oh, why tell them all about it? These people haven't any sympathy.... It hurts!

KUSMA. It's nothing, sir! They asked me! Why shouldn't I tell them? But if you are angry I won't... I won't.... What do I care for them.... *[Post-bells are heard.]*

FEDYA. Don't shout; tell us quietly....

KUSMA. I'll tell you quietly.... He doesn't want me to, but it can't be helped.... But there's nothing more to tell. They got married, that's all. There was nothing else. Pour out another drop for Kusma the stony! *[Drinks]* I don't like people getting drunk! Why the time the wedding took place, when the gentlefolk sat down to supper afterwards, she went off in a carriage... *[Whispers]* To the town, to her lover, a lawyer.... Eh? What do you think of her now? Just at the very moment! She would be let off lightly if she were killed for it!

MERIK. *[Thoughtfully]* Well... what happened then?

KUSMA. He went mad.... As you see, he started with a fly, as they say, and now it's grown to a bumble-bee. It was a fly then, and now—it's a bumble-bee.... And he still loves her. Look at him, he loves her! I expect he's walking now to the town to get a glimpse of her with one eye.... He'll get a glimpse of her, and go back....

*[The post has driven up to the in.. The POSTMAN enters and has a drink.]*

TIHON. The post's late to-day!

*[The POSTMAN pays in silence and goes out. The post drives off, the bells ringing.]*

A VOICE FROM THE CORNER. One could rob the post in weather like this—easy as spitting.

MERIK. I've been alive thirty-five years and I haven't robbed the post once.... *[Pause]* It's gone now... too late, too late....

KUSMA. Do you want to smell the inside of a prison?

MERIK. People rob and don't go to prison. And if I do go! *[Suddenly]* What else?

KUSMA. Do you mean that unfortunate?

MERIK. Who else?

KUSMA. The second reason, brothers, why he was ruined was because of his brother-in-law, his sister's husband.... He took it into his head to stand surety at the bank for 30,000 roubles for his brother-in-law. The brother-in-law's a thief.... The swindler knows which side his bread's buttered and won't budge an inch.... So he doesn't pay up.... So our man had to pay up the whole thirty thousand. *[Sighs]* The fool is suffering for his folly. His wife's got children now by the lawyer and the brother-in-law has bought an estate near Poltava, and our man goes round inns like a fool, and complains to the likes of us: "I've lost all faith, brothers! I can't believe in anybody now!" It's cowardly! Every man has his grief, a snake that sucks at his heart, and does that mean that he must drink? Take our village elder, for example. His wife plays about with the schoolmaster in broad daylight, and spends his money on drink, but the elder walks about smiling to himself. He's just a little thinner...

TIHON. *[Sighs]* When God gives a man strength....

KUSMA. There's all sorts of strength, that's true.... Well? How much does it come to? *[Pays]* Take your pound of flesh! Good-bye, children! Good-night and pleasant dreams! It's time I hurried off. I'm bringing my lady a midwife from the hospital.... She must be getting wet with waiting, poor thing.... *[Runs out. A pause.]*

TIHON. Oh, you! Unhappy man, come and drink this! *[Pours out.]*

BORTSOV. *[Comes up to the bar hesitatingly and drinks]* That means I now owe you for two glasses.

TIHON. You don't owe me anything? Just drink and drown your sorrows!

FEDYA. Drink mine, too, sir! Oh! *[Throws down a five-copeck piece]* If you drink, you die; if you don't drink, you die. It's good not to drink vodka, but by God you're easier when you've got some! Vodka takes grief away.... It is hot!

BORTSOV. Boo! The heat!

MERIK. Dive it here! *[Takes the medallion from TIHON and examines her portrait]* Hm. Ran off after the wedding. What a woman!

A VOICE FROM THE CORNER. Pour him out another glass, Tihon. Let him drink mine, too.

MERIK. *[Dashes the medallion to the ground]* Curse her! *[Goes quickly to his place and lies down, face to the wall. General excitement.]*

BORTSOV. Here, what's that? *[Picks up the medallion]* How dare you, you beast? What right have you? *[Tearfully]* Do you want me to kill you? You moujik! You boor!

TIHON. Don't be angry, sir.... It isn't glass, it isn't broken.... Have another drink and go to sleep. *[Pours out]* Here I've been listening to you all, and when I ought to have locked up long ago. *[Goes and looks door leading out.]*

BORTSOV. *[Drinks]* How dare he? The fool! *[to MERIK]* Do you understand? You're a fool, a donkey!

SAVVA. Children! If you please! Stop that talking! What's the good of making a noise? Let people go to sleep.

TIHON. Lie down, lie down... be quiet! *[Goes behind the counter and locks the till]* It's time to sleep.

FEDYA. It's time! *[Lies down]* Pleasant dreams, brothers!

MERIK. *[Gets up and spreads his short fur and coat the bench]* Come on, lie down, sir.

TIHON. And where will you sleep.

MERIK. Oh, anywhere.... The floor will do.... *[Spreads a coat on the floor]* It's all one to me *[Puts the axe by him]* It would be torture for him to sleep on the floor. He's used to silk and down....

TIHON. *[To BORTSOV]* Lie down, your honour! You've looked at that portrait long enough. *[Puts out a candle]* Throw it away!

BORTSOV. *[Swaying about]* Where can I lie down?

TIHON. In the tramp's place! Didn't you hear him giving it up to you?

BORTSOV. *[Going up to the vacant place]* I'm a bit... drunk... after all that.... Is this it?... Do I lie down here? Eh?

TIHON. Yes, yes, lie down, don't be afraid. *[Stretches himself out on the counter.]*

BORTSOV. *[Lying down]* I'm... drunk.... Everything's going round.... *[Opens the medallion]* Haven't you a little candle? *[Pause]* You're a queer little woman Masha.... Looking at me out of the frame and laughing.... *[Laughs]* I'm drunk! And should you laugh at a man because he's drunk? You look out, as Schastliv-tsev says, and... love the drunkard.

FEDYA. How the wind howls. It's dreary!

BORTSOV. *[Laughs]* What a woman.... Why do you keep on going round? I can't catch you!

MERIK. He's wandering. Looked too long at the portrait. *[Laughs]* What a business! Educated people go and invent all sorts of machines and medicines, but there hasn't yet been a man wise enough to invent a medicine against the female sex.... They try to cure every sort of disease, and it never occurs to them that more people die of women than of disease.... Sly, stingy, cruel, brainless.... The mother-in-law torments the bride and the bride makes things square by swindling the husband... and there's no end to it....

TIHON. The women have ruffled his hair for him, and so he's bristly.

MERIK. It isn't only I.... From the beginning of the ages, since the world has been in existence, people have complained.... It's not for nothing that in the songs and stories, the devil and the woman are put side by side.... Not for nothing! It's half true, at any rate... *[Pause]* Here's the gentleman playing the fool, but I had more sense, didn't I, when I left my father and mother, and became a tramp?

FEDYA. Because of women?

MERIK. Just like the gentleman... I walked about like one of the damned, bewitched, blessing my stars... on fire day and night, until at last my eyes were opened... It wasn't love, but just a fraud....

FEDYA. What did you do to her?

MERIK. Never you mind.... *[Pause]* Do you think I killed her?... I wouldn't do it.... If you kill, you are sorry for it.... She can live and be happy! If only I'd never set eyes on you, or if I could only forget you, you viper's brood! *[A knocking at the door.]*

TIHON. Whom have the devils brought.... Who's there? *[Knocking]* Who knocks? *[Gets up and goes to the door]* Who knocks? Go away, we've locked up!

A VOICE. Please let me in, Tihon. The carriage-spring's broken! Be a father to me and help me! If I only had a little string to tie it round with, we'd get there somehow or other.

TIHON. Who are you?

THE VOICE. My lady is going to Varsonofyev from the town.... It's only five versts farther on.... Do be a good man and help!

TIHON. Go and tell the lady that if she pays ten roubles she can have her string and we'll mend the spring.

THE VOICE. Have you gone mad, or what? Ten roubles! You mad dog! Profiting by our misfortunes!

TIHON. Just as you like.... You needn't if you don't want to.

THE VOICE. Very well, wait a bit. *[Pause]* She says, all right.

TIHON. Pleased to hear it!

*[Opens door. The COACHMAN enters.]*

COACHMAN. Good evening, Orthodox people! Well, give me the string! Quick! Who'll go and help us, children? There'll be something left over for your trouble!

TIHON. There won't be anything left over.... Let them sleep, the two of us can manage.

COACHMAN. Foo, I am tired! It's cold, and there's not a dry spot in all the mud.... Another thing, dear.... Have you got a little room in here for the lady to warm herself in? The carriage is all on one side, she can't stay in it....

TIHON. What does she want a room for? She can warm herself in here, if she's cold.... We'll find a place *[Clears a space next to BORTSOV]* Get up, get up! Just lie on the floor for an hour, and let the lady get warm. *[To BORTSOV]* Get up, your honour! Sit up! *[BORTSOV sits up]* Here's a place for you. *[Exit COACHMAN.]*

FEDYA. Here's a visitor for you, the devil's brought her! Now there'll be no sleep before daylight.

TIHON. I'm sorry I didn't ask for fifteen.... She'd have given them.... *[Stands expectantly before the door]* You're a delicate sort of people, I must say. *[Enter MARIA EGOROVNA, followed by the COACHMAN. TIHON bows.]* Please, your highness! Our room is very humble, full of blackbeetles! But don't disdain it!

MARIA EGOROVNA. I can't see anything.... Which way do I go?

TIHON. This way, your highness! *[Leads her to the place next to BORTSOV]* This way, please. *[Blows on the place]* I haven't any separate rooms, excuse me, but don't you be afraid, madam, the people here are good and quiet....

MARIA EGOROVNA. *[Sits next to BORTSOV]* How awfully stuffy! Open the door, at any rate!

TIHON. Yes, madam. *[Runs and opens the door wide.]*

MARIA. We're freezing, and you open the door! *[Gets up and slams it]* Who are you to be giving orders? *[Lies down]*

TIHON. Excuse me, your highness, but we've a little fool here... a bit cracked.... But don't you be frightened, he won't do you any harm.... Only you must excuse me, madam, I can't do this for ten roubles.... Make it fifteen.

MARIA EGOROVNA. Very well, only be quick.

TIHON. This minute... this very instant. *[Drags some string out from under the counter]* This minute. *[A pause.]*

BORTSOV. *[Looking at MARIA EGOROVNA]* Marie... Masha...

MARIA EGOROVNA. *[Looks at BORTSOV]* What's this?

BORTSOV. Marie... is it you? Where do you come from? *[MARIA EGOROVNA recognizes BORTSOV, screams and runs off into the centre of the floor. BORTSOV follows]* Marie, it is I... I *[Laughs loudly]* My wife! Marie! Where am I? People, a light!

MARIA EGOROVNA. Get away from me! You lie, it isn't you! It can't be! *[Covers her face with her hands]* It's a lie, it's all nonsense!

BORTSOV. Her voice, her movements.... Marie, it is I! I'll stop in a moment.... I was drunk.... My head's going round.... My God! Stop, stop.... I can't understand anything. *[Yells]* My wife! *[Falls at her feet and sobs. A group collects around the husband and wife.]*

MARIA EGOROVNA. Stand back! *[To the COACHMAN]* Denis, let's go! I can't stop here any longer!

MERIK. *[Jumps up and looks her steadily in the face]* The portrait! *[Grasps her hand]* It is she! Eh, people, she's the gentleman's wife!

MARIA EGOROVNA. Get away, fellow! *[Tries to tear her hand away from him]* Denis, why do you stand there staring? *[DENIS and TIHON run up to her and get hold of MERIK'S arms]* This thieves' kitchen! Let go my hand! I'm not afraid!... Get away from me!

MERIK. *[Note: Throughout this speech, in the original, Merik uses the familiar second person singular.]* Wait a bit, and I'll let go.... Just let me say one word to you.... One word, so that you may understand.... Just wait.... *[Turns to TIHON and DENIS]* Get away, you rogues, let go! I shan't let you go till I've had my say! Stop... one moment. *[Strikes his forehead with his fist]* No, God hasn't given me the wisdom! I can't think of the word for you!

MARIA EGOROVNA. *[Tears away her hand]* Get away! Drunkards... let's go, Denis!

*[She tries to go out, but MERIK blocks the door.]*

MERIK. Just throw a glance at him, with only one eye if you like! Or say only just one kind little word to him! God's own sake!

MARIA EGOROVNA. Take away this... fool.

MERIK. Then the devil take you, you accursed woman!

*[He swings his axe. General confusion. Everybody jumps up noisily and with cries of horror. SAVVA stands between MERIK and MARIA EGOROVNA. ... DENIS forces MERIK to one side and carries out his mistress. After this all stand as if turned to stone. A prolonged pause. BORTSOV suddenly waves his hands in the air.]*

BORTSOV. Marie... where are you, Marie!

NAZAROVNA. My God, my God! You've torn up my your murderers! What an accursed night!

MERIK. *[Lowering his hand; he still holds the axe]* Did I kill her or no?

TIHON. Thank God, your head is safe....

MERIK. Then I didn't kill her.... *[Totters to his bed]* Fate hasn't sent me to my death because of a stolen axe.... *[Falls down and sobs]* Woe! Woe is me! Have pity on me, Orthodox people!

**Curtain.**

# THE ANNIVERSARY

## Translated by Julius West

### CHARACTERS

ANDREY ANDREYEVITCH SHIPUCHIN, Chairman of the N—— Joint Stock Bank, a middle-aged man, with a monocle

TATIANA ALEXEYEVNA, his wife, aged 25

KUSMA NICOLAIEVITCH KHIRIN, the bank's aged book-keeper

NASTASYA FYODOROVNA MERCHUTKINA, an old woman wearing an old-fashioned cloak

DIRECTORS OF THE BANK

EMPLOYEES OF THE BANK

# THE ANNIVERSARY

The action takes place at the Bank

*[The private office of the Chairman of Directors. On the left is a door, leading into the public department. There are two desks. The furniture aims at a deliberately luxurious effect, with armchairs covered in velvet, flowers, statues, carpets, and a telephone. It is midday. KHIRIN is alone; he wears long felt boots, and is shouting through the door.]*

KHIRIN. Send out to the chemist for 15 copecks' worth of valerian drops, and tell them to bring some drinking water into the Directors' office! This is the hundredth time I've asked! *[Goes to a desk]* I'm absolutely tired out. This is the fourth day I've been working, without a chance of shutting my eyes. From morning to evening I work here, from evening to morning at home. *[Coughs]* And I've got an inflammation all over me. I'm hot and cold, and I cough, and my legs ache, and there's something dancing before my eyes. *[Sits]* Our scoundrel of a Chairman, the brute, is going to read a report at a general meeting. "Our Bank, its Present and Future." You'd think he was a Gambetta.... *[At work]* Two... one... one... six... nought... seven.... Next, six... nought... one... six.... He just wants to throw dust into people's eyes, and so I sit here and work for him like a galley-slave! This report of his is poetic fiction and nothing more, and here I've got to sit day after day and add figures, devil take his soul! *[Rattles on his counting-frame]* I can't stand it! *[Writing]* That is, one... three... seven... two... one... nought.... He promised to reward me for my work. If everything goes well to-day and the public is properly put into blinkers, he's promised me a gold charm and 300 roubles bonus.... We'll see. *[Works]* Yes, but if my work all goes for nothing, then you'd better look out.... I'm very excitable.... If I lose my temper I'm capable of committing some crime, so look out! Yes!

*[Noise and applause behind the scenes. SHIPUCHIN'S voice: "Thank you! Thank you! I am extremely grateful." Enter SHIPUCHIN. He wears a frockcoat and white tie; he carries an album which has been just presented to him.]*

SHIPUCHIN. *[At the door, addresses the outer office]* This present, my dear colleagues, will be preserved to the day of my death, as a memory of the happiest days of my life! Yes, gentlemen! Once more, I thank you! *[Throws a kiss into the air and turns to KHIRIN]* My dear, my respected Kusma Nicolaievitch!

*[All the time that SHIPUCHIN is on the stage, clerks intermittently come in with papers for his signature and go out.]*

KHIRIN. *[Standing up]* I have the honour to congratulate you, Andrey Andreyevitch, on the fiftieth anniversary of our Bank, and hope that...

SHIPUCHIN. *[Warmly shakes hands]* Thank you, my dear sir! Thank you! I think that in view of the unique character of the day, as it is an anniversary, we may kiss each other!... *[They kiss]* I am very, very glad! Thank you for your service... for everything! If, in the course of the time during which I have had the honour to be Chairman of this Bank anything useful has been done, the credit is due, more than to anybody else, to my colleagues. *[Sighs]* Yes, fifteen years! Fifteen years as my name's Shipuchin! *[Changes his tone]* Where's my report? Is it getting on?

KHIRIN. Yes; there's only five pages left.

SHIPUCHIN. Excellent. Then it will be ready by three?

KHIRIN. If nothing occurs to disturb me, I'll get it done. Nothing of any importance is now left.

SHIPUCHIN. Splendid. Splendid, as my name's Shipuchin! The general meeting will be at four. If you please, my dear fellow. Give me the first half, I'll peruse it.... Quick.... *[Takes the report]* I base enormous hopes on this report. It's my *profession de foi*, or, better still, my firework. *[Note: The actual word employed.]* My firework, as my name's Shipuchin! *[Sits and reads the report to himself]* I'm hellishly tired.... My gout kept on giving me trouble last night, all the morning I was running about, and then these excitements, ovations, agitations... I'm tired!

KHIRIN. Two... nought... nought... three... nine... two... nought. I can't see straight after all these figures.... Three... one... six... four... one... five.... *[Uses the counting-frame.]*

SHIPUCHIN. Another unpleasantness.... This morning your wife came to see me and complained about you once again. Said that last night you threatened her and her sister with a knife. Kusma Nicolaievitch, what do you mean by that? Oh, oh!

KHIRIN. *[Rudely]* As it's an anniversary, Andrey Andreyevitch, I'll ask for a special favour. Please, even if it's only out of respect for my toil, don't interfere in my family life. Please!

SHIPUCHIN. *[Sighs]* Yours is an impossible character, Kusma Nicolaievitch! You're an excellent and respected man, but you behave to women like some scoundrel. Yes, really. I don't understand why you hate them so?

KHIRIN. I wish I could understand why you love them so! *[Pause.]*

SHIPUCHIN. The employees have just presented me with an album; and the Directors, as I've heard, are going to give me an address and a silver loving-cup.... *[Playing with his monocle]* Very nice, as my name's Shipuchin! It isn't excessive. A certain pomp is essential to the reputation of the Bank, devil take it! You know everything, of course.... I composed the address myself, and I bought the cup myself, too.... Well, then there was 45 roubles for the cover of the address, but you can't do without that. They'd never have thought of it for themselves. *[Looks round]* Look at the furniture! Just look at it! They say I'm stingy, that all I want is that the locks on the doors should be polished, that the employees should wear fashionable ties, and that a fat hall-porter should stand by the door. No, no, sirs. Polished locks and a fat porter mean a good deal. I can behave as I like at home, eat and sleep like a pig, get drunk....

KHIRIN. Please don't make hints.

SHIPUCHIN. Nobody's making hints! What an impossible character yours is.... As I was saying, at home I can live like a tradesman, a *parvenu*, and be up to any games I like, but here everything must be *en grand*. This is a Bank! Here every detail must *imponiren*, so to speak, and have a majestic appearance. *[He picks up a paper from the floor and throws it into the fireplace]* My service to the Bank has been just this—I've raised its reputation. A thing of immense importance is tone! Immense, as my name's Shipuchin! *[Looks over KHIRIN]* My dear man, a deputation of shareholders may come here any moment, and there you are in felt boots, wearing a scarf... in some absurdly coloured jacket.... You might have put on a frock-coat, or at any rate a dark jacket....

KHIRIN. My health matters more to me than your shareholders. I've an inflammation all over me.

SHIPUCHIN. *[Excitedly]* But you will admit that it's untidy! You spoil the *ensemble*!

KHIRIN. If the deputation comes I can go and hide myself. It won't matter if... seven... one... seven... two... one... five... nought. I don't like untidiness myself.... Seven... two... nine... *[Uses the counting-frame]* I can't stand untidiness! It would have been wiser of you not to have invited ladies to to-day's anniversary dinner....

SHIPUCHIN. Oh, that's nothing.

KHIRIN. I know that you're going to have the hall filled with them to-night to make a good show, but you look out, or they'll spoil everything. They cause all sorts of mischief and disorder.

SHIPUCHIN. On the contrary, feminine society elevates!

KHIRIN. Yes.... Your wife seems intelligent, but on the Monday of last week she let something off that upset me for two days. In front of a lot of people she suddenly asks: "Is it true that at our Bank my husband bought up a lot of the shares of the Driazhsky-Priazhsky Bank, which have been falling on exchange? My husband is so annoyed about it!" This in front of people. Why do you tell them everything, I don't understand. Do you want them to get you into serious trouble?

SHIPUCHIN. Well, that's enough, enough! All that's too dull for an anniversary. Which reminds me, by the way. *[Looks at the time]* My wife ought to be here soon. I really ought to have gone to the station, to meet the poor little thing, but there's no time.... and I'm tired. I must say I'm not glad of her! That is to say, I am glad, but I'd be gladder if she only stayed another couple of days with her mother. She'll want me to spend the whole evening with her to-night, whereas we have arranged a little excursion for ourselves.... *[Shivers]* Oh, my nerves have already started dancing me about. They are so strained that I think the very smallest trifle would be enough to make me break into tears! No, I must be strong, as my name's Shipuchin!

*[Enter TATIANA ALEXEYEVNA SHIPUCHIN in a waterproof, with a little travelling satchel slung across her shoulder.]*

SHIPUCHIN. Ah! In the nick of time!

TATIANA ALEXEYEVNA. Darling!

*[Runs to her husband: a prolonged kiss.]*

SHIPUCHIN. We were only speaking of you just now! *[Looks at his watch.]*

TATIANA ALEXEYEVNA. *[Panting]* Were you very dull without me? Are you well? I haven't been home yet, I came here straight from the station. I've a lot, a lot to tell you.... I couldn't wait.... I shan't take off my clothes, I'll only stay a minute. *[To KHIRIN]* Good morning, Kusma Nicolaievitch! *[To her husband]* Is everything all right at home?

SHIPUCHIN. Yes, quite. And, you know, you've got to look plumper and better this week.... Well, what sort of a time did you have?

TATIANA ALEXEYEVNA. Splendid. Mamma and Katya send their regards. Vassili Andreitch sends you a kiss. *[Kisses him]* Aunt sends you a jar of jam, and is annoyed because you don't write. Zina sends you a kiss. *[Kisses.]* Oh, if you knew what's happened. If you only knew! I'm even frightened to tell you! Oh, if you only knew! But I see by your eyes that you're sorry I came!

SHIPUCHIN. On the contrary.... Darling.... *[Kisses her.]*

*[KHIRIN coughs angrily.]*

TATIANA ALEXEYEVNA. Oh, poor Katya, poor Katya! I'm so sorry for her, so sorry for her.

SHIPUCHIN. This is the Bank's anniversary to-day, darling, we may get a deputation of the shareholders at any moment, and you're not dressed.

TATIANA ALEXEYEVNA. Oh, yes, the anniversary! I congratulate you, gentlemen. I wish you.... So it means that to-day's the day of the meeting, the dinner.... That's good. And do you remember that beautiful address which you spent such a long time composing for the shareholders? Will it be read to-day?

*[KHIRIN coughs angrily.]*

SHIPUCHIN. *[Confused]* My dear, we don't talk about these things. You'd really better go home.

TATIANA ALEXEYEVNA. In a minute, in a minute. I'll tell you everything in one minute and go. I'll tell you from the very beginning. Well.... When you were seeing me off, you remember I was sitting next to that stout lady, and I began to read. I don't like to talk in the train. I read for three stations and didn't say a word to anyone.... Well, then the evening set in, and I felt so mournful, you know, with such sad thoughts! A young man was sitting opposite me—not a bad-looking fellow, a brunette.... Well, we fell into conversation.... A sailor came along then, then some student or other.... *[Laughs]* I told them that I wasn't married... and they did look after me! We chattered till midnight, the brunette kept on telling the most awfully funny stories, and the sailor kept on singing. My chest began to ache from laughing. And when the sailor—oh, those sailors!—when he got to know my name was TATIANA, you know what he sang? *[Sings in a bass voice]* "Onegin don't let me conceal it, I love Tatiana madly!" *[Note: From the Opera Evgeni Onegin—words by Pushkin.] [Roars with laughter.]*

*[KHIRIN coughs angrily.]*

SHIPUCHIN. Tania, dear, you're disturbing Kusma Nicolaievitch. Go home, dear.... Later on....

TATIANA ALEXEYEVNA. No, no, let him hear if he wants to, it's awfully interesting. I'll end in a minute. Serezha came to meet me at the station. Some young man or other turns up, an inspector of taxes, I think... quite handsome, especially his eyes.... Serezha introduced me, and the three of us rode off together.... It was lovely weather....

*[Voices behind the stage: "You can't, you can't! What do you want?" Enter MERCHUTKINA, waving her arms about.]*

MERCHUTKINA. What are you dragging at me for. What else! I want him himself! *[To SHIPUCHIN]* I have the honour, your excellency... I am the wife of a civil servant, Nastasya Fyodorovna Merchutkina.

SHIPUCHIN. What do you want?

MERCHUTKINA. Well, you see, your excellency, my husband has been ill for five months, and while he was at home, getting better, he was suddenly dismissed for no reason, your excellency, and when I went to get his salary, they, you see, deducted 24 roubles 36 copecks from it. What for? I ask. They said, "Well, he drew it from the employees' account, and the others had to make it up." How can that be? How could he draw anything without my permission? No, your excellency! I'm a poor woman... my lodgers are all I have to live on.... I'm weak and defenceless.... Everybody does me some harm, and nobody has a kind word for me.

SHIPUCHIN. Excuse me. *[Takes a petition from her and reads it standing.]*

TATIANA ALEXEYEVNA. *[To KHIRIN]* Yes, but first we.... Last week I suddenly received a letter from my mother. She writes that a certain Grendilevsky has proposed to my sister Katya. A nice, modest, young man, but with no means of his own, and no assured position. And, unfortunately, just think of it, Katya is absolutely gone on him. What's to be done? Mamma writes telling me to come at once and influence Katya....

KHIRIN. *[Angrily]* Excuse me, you've made me lose my place! You go talking about your mamma and Katya, and I understand nothing; and I've lost my place.

TATIANA ALEXEYEVNA. What does that matter? You listen when a lady is talking to you! Why are you so angry to-day? Are you in love? *[Laughs.]*

SHIPUCHIN. *[To MERCHUTKINA]* Excuse me, but what is this? I can't make head or tail of it.

TATIANA ALEXEYEVNA. Are you in love? Aha! You're blushing!

SHIPUCHIN. *[To his wife]* Tanya, dear, do go out into the public office for a moment. I shan't be long.

TATIANA ALEXEYEVNA. All right. *[Goes out.]*

SHIPUCHIN. I don't understand anything of this. You've obviously come to the wrong place, madam. Your petition doesn't concern us at all. You should go to the department in which your husband was employed.

MERCHUTKINA. I've been there a good many times these five months, and they wouldn't even look at my petition. I'd given up all hopes, but, thanks to my son-in-law, Boris Matveyitch, I thought of coming to you. "You go, mother," he says, "and apply to Mr. Shipuchin, he's an influential man and can do anything." Help me, your excellency!

SHIPUCHIN. We can't do anything for you, Mrs. Merchutkina. You must understand that your husband, so far as I can gather, was in the employ of the Army Medical Department, while this is a private, commercial concern, a bank. Don't you understand that?

MERCHUTKINA. Your excellency, I can produce a doctor's certificate of my husband's illness. Here it is, just look at it....

SHIPUCHIN. *[Irritated]* That's all right, I quite believe you, but it's not our business. *[Behind the scene, TATIANA ALEXEYEVNA'S laughter is heard, then a man's. SHIPUCHIN glances at the door]* She's disturbing the employees. *[To MERCHUTKINA]* It's strange and it's even silly. Surely your husband knows where you ought to apply?

MERCHUTKINA. Your excellency, I don't let him know anything. He just cried out: "It isn't your business! Get out of this!" And...

SHIPUCHIN. Madam, I repeat, your husband was in the employ of the Army Medical Department, and this is a bank, a private, commercial concern.

MERCHUTKINA. Yes, yes, yes.... I understand, my dear. In that case, your excellency, just order them to pay me 15 roubles! I don't mind taking that to be going on with.

SHIPUCHIN. *[Sighs]* Ouf!

KHIRIN. Andrey Andreyevitch, I'll never finish the report at this rate!

SHIPUCHIN. One moment. *[To MERCHUTKINA]* I can't get any sense out of you. But do understand that your taking this business here is as absurd as if you took a divorce petition to a chemist's or into a gold assay office. *[Knock at the door. The voice of TATIANA ALEXEYEVNA is heard, "Can I come in, Andrey?" SHIPUCHIN shouts]* Just wait one minute, dear! *[To MERCHUTKINA]* What has it got to do with us if you haven't been paid? As it happens, madam, this is an anniversary to-day, we're busy... and somebody may be coming here at any moment.... Excuse me....

MERCHUTKINA. Your excellency, have pity on me, an orphan! I'm a weak, defenceless woman.... I'm tired to death.... I'm having trouble with my lodgers, and on account of my husband, and I've got the house to look after, and my son-in-law is out of work....

SHIPUCHIN. Mrs. Merchutkina, I... No, excuse me, I can't talk to you! My head's even in a whirl.... You are disturbing us and making us waste our time. *[Sighs, aside]* What a business, as my name's Shipuchin! *[To KHIRIN]* Kusma Nicolaievitch, will you please explain to Mrs. Merchutkina. *[Waves his hand and goes out into public department.]*

KHIRIN. *[Approaching MERCHUTKINA, angrily]* What do you want?

MERCHUTKINA. I'm a weak, defenceless woman.... I may look all right, but if you were to take me to pieces you wouldn't find a single healthy bit in me! I can hardly stand on my legs, and I've lost my appetite. I drank my coffee to-day and got no pleasure out of it.

KHIRIN. I ask you, what do you want?

MERCHUTKINA. Tell them, my dear, to give me 15 roubles, and a month later will do for the rest.

KHIRIN. But haven't you been told perfectly plainly that this is a bank!

MERCHUTKINA. Yes, yes.... And if you like I can show you the doctor's certificate.

KHIRIN. Have you got a head on your shoulders, or what?

MERCHUTKINA. My dear, I'm asking for what's mine by law. I don't want what isn't mine.

KHIRIN. I ask you, madam, have you got a head on your shoulders, or what? Well, devil take me, I haven't any time to talk to you! I'm busy.... *[Points to the door]* That way, please!

MERCHUTKINA. *[Surprised]* And where's the money?

KHIRIN. You haven't a head, but this *[Taps the table and then points to his forehead.]*

MERCHUTKINA. *[Offended]* What? Well, never mind, never mind.... You can do that to your own wife, but I'm the wife of a civil servant.... You can't do that to me!

KHIRIN. *[Losing his temper]* Get out of this!

MERCHUTKINA. No, no, no... none of that!

KHIRIN. If you don't get out this second, I'll call for the hall-porter! Get out! *[Stamping.]*

MERCHUTKINA. Never mind, never mind! I'm not afraid! I've seen the like of you before! Miser!

KHIRIN. I don't think I've ever seen a more awful woman in my life.... Ouf! It's given me a headache.... *[Breathing heavily]* I tell you once more... do you hear me? If you don't get out of this, you old devil, I'll grind you into powder! I've got such a character that I'm perfectly capable of laming you for life! I can commit a crime!

MERCHUTKINA. I've heard barking dogs before. I'm not afraid. I've seen the like of you before.

KHIRIN. *[In despair]* I can't stand it! I'm ill! I can't! *[Sits down at his desk]* They've let the Bank get filled with women, and I can't finish my report! I can't.

MERCHUTKINA. I don't want anybody else's money, but my own, according to law. You ought to be ashamed of yourself! Sitting in a government office in felt boots....

*[Enter SHIPUCHIN and TATIANA ALEXEYEVNA.]*

TATIANA ALEXEYEVNA. *[Following her husband]* We spent the evening at the Berezhnitskys. Katya was wearing a sky-blue frock of foulard silk, cut low at the neck.... She looks very well with her hair done over her head, and I did her hair myself.... She was perfectly fascinating....

SHIPUCHIN. *[Who has had enough of it already]* Yes, yes... fascinating.... They may be here any moment....

MERCHUTKINA. Your excellency!

SHIPUCHIN. *[Dully]* What else? What do you want?

MERCHUTKINA. Your excellency! *[Points to KHIRIN]* This man... this man tapped the table with his finger, and then his head.... You told him to look after my affair, but he insults me and says all sorts of things. I'm a weak, defenceless woman....

SHIPUCHIN. All right, madam, I'll see to it... and take the necessary steps.... Go away now... later on! *[Aside]* My gout's coming on!

KHIRIN. *[In a low tone to SHIPUCHIN]* Andrey Andreyevitch, send for the hall-porter and have her turned out neck and crop! What else can we do?

SHIPUCHIN. *[Frightened]* No, no! She'll kick up a row and we aren't the only people in the building.

MERCHUTKINA. Your excellency.

KHIRIN. *[In a tearful voice]* But I've got to finish my report! I won't have time! I won't!

MERCHUTKINA. Your excellency, when shall I have the money? I want it now.

SHIPUCHIN. *[Aside, in dismay]* A re-mark-ab-ly beastly woman! *[Politely]* Madam, I've already told you, this is a bank, a private, commercial concern.

MERCHUTKINA. Be a father to me, your excellency.... If the doctor's certificate isn't enough, I can get you another from the police. Tell them to give me the money!

SHIPUCHIN. *[Panting]* Ouf!

TATIANA ALEXEYEVNA. *[To MERCHUTKINA]* Mother, haven't you already been told that you're disturbing them? What right have you?

MERCHUTKINA. Mother, beautiful one, nobody will help me. All I do is to eat and drink, and just now I didn't enjoy my coffee at all.

SHIPUCHIN. *[Exhausted]* How much do you want?

MERCHUTKINA. 24 roubles 36 copecks.

SHIPUCHIN. All right! *[Takes a 25-rouble note out of his pocket-book and gives it to her]* Here are 25 roubles. Take it and... go!

*[KHIRIN coughs angrily.]*

MERCHUTKINA. I thank you very humbly, your excellency. *[Hides the money.]*

TATIANA ALEXEYEVNA. *[Sits by her husband]* It's time I went home.... *[Looks at watch]* But I haven't done yet.... I'll finish in one minute and go away.... What a time we had! Yes, what a time! We went to spend the evening at the Berezhnitskys.... It was all right, quite fun, but nothing in particular.... Katya's devoted Grendilevsky was there, of course.... Well, I talked to Katya, cried, and induced her to talk to Grendilevsky and refuse him. Well, I thought, everything's, settled the best possible way; I've quieted mamma down, saved Katya, and can be quiet myself.... What do you think? Katya and I were going along the avenue, just before supper, and suddenly... *[Excitedly]* And suddenly we heard a shot.... No, I can't talk about it calmly! *[Waves her handkerchief]* No, I can't!

SHIPUCHIN. *[Sighs]* Ouf!

TATIANA ALEXEYEVNA. *[Weeps]* We ran to the summer-house, and there... there poor Grendilevsky was lying... with a pistol in his hand....

SHIPUCHIN. No, I can't stand this! I can't stand it! *[To MERCHUTKINA]* What else do you want?

MERCHUTKINA. Your excellency, can't my husband go back to his job?

TATIANA ALEXEYEVNA. *[Weeping]* He'd shot himself right in the heart... here.... And the poor man had fallen down senseless.... And he was awfully frightened, as he lay there... and asked for a doctor. A doctor came soon... and saved the unhappy man....

MERCHUTKINA. Your excellency, can't my husband go back to his job?

SHIPUCHIN. No, I can't stand this! *[Weeps]* I can't stand it! *[Stretches out both his hands in despair to KHIRIN]* Drive her away! Drive her away, I implore you!

KHIRIN. *[Goes up to TATIANA ALEXEYEVNA]* Get out of this!

SHIPUCHIN. Not her, but this one... this awful woman.... *[Points]* That one!

KHIRIN. *[Not understanding, to TATIANA ALEXEYEVNA]* Get out of this! *[Stamps]* Get out!

TATIANA ALEXEYEVNA. What? What are you doing? Have you taken leave of your senses?

SHIPUCHIN. It's awful? I'm a miserable man! Drive her out! Out with her!

KHIRIN. *[To TATIANA ALEXEYEVNA]* Out of it! I'll cripple you! I'll knock you out of shape! I'll break the law!

TATIANA ALEXEYEVNA. *[Running from him; he chases her]* How dare you! You impudent fellow! *[Shouts]* Andrey! Help! Andrey! *[Screams.]*

SHIPUCHIN. *[Chasing them]* Stop! I implore you! Not such a noise? Have pity on me!

KHIRIN. *[Chasing MERCHUTKINA]* Out of this! Catch her! Hit her! Cut her into pieces!

SHIPUCHIN. *[Shouts]* Stop! I ask you! I implore you!

MERCHUTKINA. Little fathers... little fathers! *[Screams]* Little fathers!...

TATIANA ALEXEYEVNA. *[Shouts]* Help! Help!... Oh, oh... I'm sick, I'm sick! *[Jumps on to a chair, then falls on to the sofa and groans as if in a faint.]*

KHIRIN. *[Chasing MERCHUTKINA]* Hit her! Beat her! Cut her to pieces!

MERCHUTKINA. Oh, oh... little fathers, it's all dark before me! Ah! *[Falls senseless into SHIPUCHIN'S arms. There is a knock at the door; a VOICE announces THE DEPUTATION]* The deputation... reputation... occupation...

KHIRIN. *[Stamps]* Get out of it, devil take me! *[Turns up his sleeves]* Give her to me: I may break the law!

*[A deputation of five men enters; they all wear frockcoats. One carries the velvet-covered address, another, the loving-cup. Employees look in at the door, from the public department. TATIANA ALEXEYEVNA on the sofa, and MERCHUTKINA in SHIPUCHIN'S arms are both groaning.]*

ONE OF THE DEPUTATION. *[Reads aloud]* "Deeply respected and dear Andrey Andreyevitch! Throwing a retrospective glance at the past history of our financial administration, and reviewing in our minds its gradual development, we receive an extremely satisfactory impression. It is true that in the first period of its existence, the inconsiderable amount of its capital, and the absence of serious operations of any description, and also the indefinite aims of this bank, made us attach an extreme importance to the question raised by Hamlet, 'To be or not to be,' and at one time there were even voices to be heard demanding our liquidation. But at that moment you become the head of our concern. Your knowledge, energies, and your native tact were the causes of extraordinary success and widespread extension. The reputation of the bank... *[Coughs]* reputation of the bank..."

MERCHUTKINA. *[Groans]* Oh! Oh!

TATIANA ALEXEYEVNA. *[Groans]* Water! Water!

THE MEMBER OF THE DEPUTATION. *[Continues]* The reputation *[Coughs]*... the reputation of the bank has been raised by you to such a height that we are now the rivals of the best foreign concerns.

SHIPUCHIN. Deputation... reputation... occupation.... Two friends that had a walk at night, held converse by the pale moonlight.... Oh tell me not, that youth is vain, that jealousy has turned my brain.

THE MEMBER OF THE DEPUTATION. *[Continues in confusion]* "Then, throwing an objective glance at the present condition of things, we, deeply respected and dear Andrey Andreyevitch... *[Lowering his voice]* In that case, we'll do it later on.... Yes, later on...." *[DEPUTATION goes out in confusion.]*

**Curtain.**

# ON THE HARMFUL EFFECTS OF TOBACCO

# ON THE HARMFUL EFFECTS OF TOBACCO

*[NYUKHIN enters the stage with great dignity, wearing long side whiskers and worn-out flock coat. He bows majestically to his audience, adjusts his waistcoat, and speaks.]*

NYUKHIN Ladies and ... so to speak... gentlemen. It was suggested to my wife that I give a public lecture here for charity. Well, if I must, I must. It's all the same to me. I am not a professor and I've never finished the university. And yet, nevertheless, over the past thirty years I have been ruining my health by constant, unceasing examination of matters of strictly scientific nature. I am a man of intellectual curiosity, and, if you can imagine, at times I write essays on scientific matters -- well, not exactly scientific, but, if you will pardon me, approximately scientific. Just the other day I finished a long article entitled:

"On the Harmfulness of Certain Insects." My daughters liked it immensely, especially the part about bedbugs. But I just read it over and tore it up. What difference does it make whether such things are written? You still have to have insect powder. We have bedbugs, even in our grand piano... For the subject of my lecture today I have taken, so to speak, the harm done to mankind by the use of tobacco. I myself smoke, but my wife told me to lecture on the harmfulness of tobacco, and so what's to be done? Tobacco it is. It's all the same to me; but, kind ladies and gentleman... I urge you to take my lecture with all due seriousness, or something awful may happen. If any of you are afraid of a dry, scientific lecture, cannot stomach that sort of thing, you needn't listen. You may leave.

*[He again adjusts his waistcoat.]*

Are there any doctors present? If so, I insist that you listen very carefully, for my lecture will contain much useful information, since tobacco, besides being harmful, contains certain medical properties. For example, if you take a fly and put him in a snuff box, he will die, probably from nervous exhaustion. Tobacco, strictly speaking, is a plant... Yes, I know, when I lecture I blink my right eye. Take no notice. It's simple nervousness. I am a very nervous man, generally speaking. I started blinking years ago, in

1889, to be precise, on September the thirteenth, the very day my wife gave birth, so to speak, to our fourth daughter, Varvara. All my daughters were born on the thirteenth. But...

*[He looks at his watch.]*

time at our disposal is strictly limited. I see I have digressed from the subject. I must tell you, by the way, that my wife runs a boarding school. Well, not exactly a boarding school, but something in the nature of one. Just between us, my wife likes to complain about hard times, but she has put away a little nest egg... some forty or fifty thousand rubles. As for me, I haven't a kopek to my name, not a penny... and, well, what's the use of dwelling on that? At her school, it is my lot to look after the housekeeping. I buy supplies, keep an eye on the servants, keep the books, stitch together the exercise books, exterminate bedbugs, take my wife's little dog for walks, catch mice. Last night, it fell to me to get the cook flour and butter for today's breakfast. Well, to make a long story short, today, when the pancakes were ready, my wife came to the kitchen and said that three of the students would not be eating pancakes, as they had swollen glands. So it seems we had a few too many pancakes. What to do with them? First my wife ordered them stored away, but then she thought awhile, and she said, "You eat those pancakes, you scarecrow." When she's out of humor, that's what she calls me: "scarecrow," or "viper," or "devil." What kind of devil am I? She's always in a bad mood. I didn't eat those pancakes; I wolfed them down. I am always hungry. Why yesterday, she gave me no dinner. She says, "What's the use feeding you, you scarecrow..." However...

*[He looks at his watch.]*

We have digressed from my subject. Let us continue. But some of you, I'm sure, would rather hear a romance, or a symphony, some aria...

*[He sings.]*

"We shall not shrink
In the heart of battle: Forward, be strong."

I forgot where that comes from... Oh, by the way, I should tell you that at my wife's school, apart from looking after the housekeeping, my duties include teaching mathematics, physics, chemistry, geography, history, vocal exercises, literature, and so forth. For dancing, singing, and drawing, my wife charges extra, although the singing and dancing master is yours truly. Our school is located at Dog Alley, number 1I suppose that's why my life has been so unlucky, living in house number thirteen. All my daughters were born on the thirteenth, I think I told you, and our house has thirteen windows, and, in short, what's the use? Appointments with my wife may be made for any hour, and the school's prospectus may be had for thirty kopeks from the porter.

*[He takes a few copies out of his pocket.]*

Ah, here you see, I've brought a few with me. Thirty kopecs a copy. Would anyone care for one?

*[NYUKIN pauses.]*

No one? Well, make it twenty kopecs. (Another pause.) What a shame! Yes, house number thirteen. I am a failure. I've grown old and stupid. Here I am, lecturing, and to all appearances enjoying myself, but I tell you I have such an urge to scream at the top of my lungs, to run away to the ends of the earth... There is no one to talk to. I want to weep. What about your daughters, you say, eh? Well, what about them? I try to talk to them, and they only laugh. My wife has seven daughters. Seven. No. Sorry, it's only six. Now, wait, it is seven. Anna, the eldest, is twenty-seven, the youngest is seventeen. Ladies and gentleman:

*[He looks around surreptitiously.]*

I am miserable: I have become a fool, a nonentity. But then, all in all, you see before you the happiest of fathers. Why shouldn't I be, and who am I to say that I am not? Oh, if you only knew: I have lived with my wife for thirty-three years, and, I can say they are the best years of my life... well, not the best, but approximately the best. They have passed, as it were, in a thrice, and, well, to hell with them.

*[Again, he looks around surreptitiously.]*

I don't think my wife has arrived yet. She is not here. So, I can say what I like. I am afraid... I am terribly afraid when she looks at me. Well, I was talking about our daughters. They don't get married, probably because they're so shy, and also because men can never get near them. My wife doesn't give parties. She never invites anyone to dinner. She's a stingy, shrewish, ill-tempered old biddy, and that's why no one comes to see us, but... I can tell you confidentially...

*[He comes down to the edge of his platform.]*

on holidays, my daughters can be seen at the home of their aunt, Natalia, the one who has rheumatism and always wears a yellow dress covered with black spots that look like cock-roaches. There you can eat. And if my wife happens not to be looking, then you'll see me...

*[He makes a drinking gesture.]*

Oh, you'll see I can get drunk on just one glass. Then I feel so happy and at the same time so sad, it's unimaginable. I think of my youth, and then somehow I long to run away, to clear out. Oh, if you only knew how I long to do it! To run away, to be free of everything, to run without ever looking back... Where? Anywhere, so long as it is away from that vile, mean, cheap life that has made me into a fool, a miserable idiot; to run away from that stupid, petty, hot headed, spiteful, nasty old miser, my wife, who has given me thirty-three years of torment; to run away from the music, the kitchen, my wife's bookkeeping ledgers, all those mundane, trivial affairs... To run away and then stop somewhere far, far away on a hill, and stand there like a tree, a pole, a scarecrow, under the great sky and the still, bright moon, and to forget, simply forget... Oh, how I long to forget! How I long to tear off this tail-coat that I wore thirty-three years ago at my wedding, and that I still wear for lectures for charity!

*[He tears off his coat.]*

Take that! And that!

*[Stamping on the coat.]*

I am a poor, shabby, tattered wretch, like the back of this waistcoat.

*[He turns his back showing his waistcoat.]*

I ask for nothing. I am better than that. I was young once; I went to the university, I had dreams, I thought of myself as a man, but now... now, I want nothing. Nothing but peace... peace.

*[He looks off stage. Quickly he pick up his flock coat and puts it on.]*

She is here. My wife is there in the wings waiting for me.

*[He looks at his watch.]*

I see our time is up. If she asks you, please, I beg you, tell her that her scarecrow husband, I mean, the lecturer, me, behaved with dignity. Oh, she is looking at me.

*[He resumes his dignity and raises his voice.]*

Given that tobacco contains a terrible poison, which I have had the pleasure of describing to you, smoking should at all costs be avoided, and permit me to add my hopes that these observations on the harmfulness of tobacco will have been of some profit to you. And so I conclude. Dixi et animan levavi![1] He bows majestically, and exits with grand dignity.

[1] "I have spoken and relieved my soul." Latin

# SWAN SONG

## CHARACTERS

VASILI SVIETLOVIDOFF, a comedian, 68 years old

NIKITA IVANITCH, a prompter, an old man

# SWAN SONG

*The scene is laid on the stage of a country theatre, at night, after the play. To the right a row of rough, unpainted doors leading into the dressing-rooms. To the left and in the background the stage is encumbered with all sorts of rubbish. In the middle of the stage is an overturned stool.*

SVIETLOVIDOFF. *[With a candle in his hand, comes out of a dressing-room and laughs]* Well, well, this is funny! Here's a good joke! I fell asleep in my dressing-room when the play was over, and there I was calmly snoring after everybody else had left the theatre. Ah! I'm a foolish old man, a poor old dodderer! I have been drinking again, and so I fell asleep in there, sitting up. That was clever! Good for you, old boy! *[Calls]* Yegorka! Petrushka! Where the devil are you? Petrushka! The scoundrels must be asleep, and an earthquake wouldn't wake them now! Yegorka! *[Picks up the stool, sits down, and puts the candle on the floor]* Not a sound! Only echoes answer me. I gave Yegorka and Petrushka each a tip to-day, and now they have disappeared without leaving a trace behind them. The rascals have gone off and have probably locked up the theatre. *[Turns his head about]* I'm drunk! Ugh! The play to-night was for my benefit, and it is disgusting to think how much beer and wine I have poured down my throat in honour of the occasion. Gracious! My body is burning all over, and I feel as if I had twenty tongues in my mouth. It is horrid! Idiotic! This poor old sinner is drunk again, and doesn't even know what he has been celebrating! Ugh! My head is splitting, I am shivering all over, and I feel as dark and cold inside as a cellar! Even if I don't mind ruining my health, I ought at least to remember my age, old idiot that I am! Yes, my old age! It's no use! I can play the fool, and brag, and pretend to be young, but my life is really over now, I kiss my hand to the sixty-eight years that have gone by; I'll never see them again! I have drained the bottle, only a few little drops are left at the bottom, nothing but the dregs. Yes,

yes, that's the case, Vasili, old boy. The time has come for you to rehearse the part of a mummy, whether you like it or not. Death is on its way to you. *[Stares ahead of him]* It is strange, though, that I have been on the stage now for forty-five years, and this is the first time I have seen a theatre at night, after the lights have been put out. The first time. *[Walks up to the footlights]* How dark it is! I can't see a thing. Oh, yes, I can just make out the prompter's box, and his desk; the rest is in pitch darkness, a black, bottomless pit, like a grave, in which death itself might be hiding.... Brr.... How cold it is! The wind blows out of the empty theatre as though out of a stone flue. What a place for ghosts! The shivers are running up and down my back. *[Calls]* Yegorka! Petrushka! Where are you both? What on earth makes me think of such gruesome things here? I must give up drinking; I'm an old man, I shan't live much longer. At sixty-eight people go to church and prepare for death, but here I am—heavens! A profane old drunkard in this fool's dress—I'm simply not fit to look at. I must go and change it at once.... This is a dreadful place, I should die of fright sitting here all night. *[Goes toward his dressing-room; at the same time NIKITA IVANITCH in a long white coat comes out of the dressing-room at the farthest end of the stage. SVIETLOVIDOFF sees IVANITCH—shrieks with terror and steps back]* Who are you? What? What do you want? *[Stamps his foot]* Who are you?

IVANITCH. It is I, sir.

SVIETLOVIDOFF. Who are you?

IVANITCH. *[Comes slowly toward him]* It is I, sir, the prompter, Nikita Ivanitch. It is I, master, it is I!

SVIETLOVIDOFF. *[Sinks helplessly onto the stool, breathes heavily and trembles violently]* Heavens! Who are you? It is you . . . you Nikitushka? What . . . what are you doing here?

IVANITCH. I spend my nights here in the dressing-rooms. Only please be good enough not to tell Alexi Fomitch, sir. I have nowhere else to spend the night; indeed, I haven't.

SVIETLOVIDOFF. Ah! It is you, Nikitushka, is it? Just think, the audience called me out sixteen times; they brought me three wreathes and lots of other things, too; they were all wild with enthusiasm, and yet not a soul came when it was all over to wake the poor, drunken old man and take him home. And I am an old man, Nikitushka! I am sixty-eight years old, and I am ill. I haven't the heart left to go on. *[Falls on IVANITCH'S neck and weeps]* Don't go away, Nikitushka; I am old and helpless, and I feel it is time for me to die. Oh, it is dreadful, dreadful!

IVANITCH. *[Tenderly and respectfully]* Dear master! it is time for you to go home, sir!

SVIETLOVIDOFF. I won't go home; I have no home—none! none!—none!

IVANITCH. Oh, dear! Have you forgotten where you live?

SVIETLOVIDOFF. I won't go there. I won't! I am all alone there. I have nobody, Nikitushka! No wife—no children. I am like the wind blowing across the lonely fields. I shall die, and no one will remember me. It is awful to be alone—no one to cheer me, no one to caress me, no one to help me to bed when I am drunk. Whom do I belong to? Who needs me? Who loves me? Not a soul, Nikitushka.

IVANITCH. *[Weeping]* Your audience loves you, master.

SVIETLOVIDOFF. My audience has gone home. They are all asleep, and have forgotten their old clown. No, nobody needs me, nobody loves me; I have no wife, no children.

IVANITCH. Oh, dear! Oh, dear! Don't be so unhappy about it.

SVIETLOVIDOFF. But I am a man, I am still alive. Warm, red blood is tingling in my veins, the blood of noble ancestors. I am an aristocrat, Nikitushka; I served in the army, in the artillery, before I fell as low as this, and what a fine young chap I was! Handsome, daring, eager! Where has it all gone? What has become of those old days? There's the pit that has swallowed them all! I remember it all now. Forty-five years of my life lie buried there, and what a life, Nikitushka! I can see it as clearly as I see your face: the ecstasy of youth, faith, passion, the love of women—women, Nikitushka!

IVANITCH. It is time you went to sleep, sir.

SVIETLOVIDOFF. When I first went on the stage, in the first glow of passionate youth, I remember a woman loved me for my acting. She was beautiful, graceful as a poplar, young, innocent, pure, and radiant as a summer dawn. Her smile could charm away the darkest night. I remember, I stood before her once, as I am now standing before you. She had never seemed so lovely to me as she did then, and she spoke to me so with her eyes—such a look! I shall never forget it, no, not even in the grave; so tender, so soft, so deep, so bright and young! Enraptured, intoxicated, I fell on my knees before her, I begged for my happiness, and she said: "Give up the stage!" Give up the stage!

Do you understand? She could love an actor, but marry him—never! I was acting that day, I remember—I had a foolish, clown's part, and as I acted, I felt my eyes being opened; I saw that the worship of the art I had held so sacred was a delusion and an empty dream; that I was a slave, a fool, the plaything of the idleness of strangers. I understood my audience at last, and since that day I have not believed in their applause, or in their wreathes, or in their enthusiasm. Yes, Nikitushka! The people applaud me, they buy my photograph, but I am a stranger to them. They don't know me, I am as the dirt beneath their feet. They are willing enough to meet me . . . but allow a daughter or a sister to marry me, an outcast, never! I have no faith in them, *[sinks onto the stool]* no faith in them.

IVANITCH. Oh, sir! you look dreadfully pale, you frighten me to death! Come, go home, have mercy on me!

SVIETLOVIDOFF. I saw through it all that day, and the knowledge was dearly bought. Nikitushka! After that . . . when that girl . . . well, I began to wander aimlessly about, living from day to day without looking ahead. I took the parts of buffoons and low comedians, letting my mind go to wreck. Ah! but I was a great artist once, till little by little I threw away my talents, played the motley fool, lost my looks, lost the power of expressing myself, and became in the end a Merry Andrew instead of a man. I have been swallowed up in that great black pit. I never felt it before, but to-night, when I woke up, I looked back, and there behind me lay sixty-eight years. I have just found out what it is to be old! It is all over . . . *[sobs]* . . . all over.

IVANITCH. There, there, dear master! Be quiet . . . gracious! *[Calls]* Petrushka! Yegorka!

SVIETLOVIDOFF. But what a genius I was! You cannot imagine what power I had, what eloquence; how graceful I was, how tender; how many strings *[beats his breast]* quivered in this breast! It chokes me to think of it! Listen now, wait, let me catch my breath, there; now listen to this:

"The shade of bloody Ivan now returning
Fans through my lips rebellion to a flame,
I am the dead Dimitri! In the burning
Boris shall perish on the throne I claim.
Enough! The heir of Czars shall not be seen

Kneeling to yonder haughty Polish Queen!"[1]

Is that bad, eh? *[Quickly]* Wait, now, here's something from King Lear. The sky is black, see? Rain is pouring down, thunder roars, lightning—zzz zzz zzz—splits the whole sky, and then, listen:

"Blow winds, and crack your cheeks! rage! blow!
You cataracts and hurricanoes spout
Till you have drench'd our steeples, drown'd the cocks!
You sulphurous thought-executing fires
Vaunt-couriers of oak-cleaving thunderbolts
Singe my white head! And thou, all shaking thunder,
Strike flat the thick rotundity o' the world!
Crack nature's moulds, all germons spill at once
That make ungrateful man!"

*[Impatiently]* Now, the part of the fool. *[Stamps his foot]* Come take the fool's part! Be quick, I can't wait!

IVANITCH. *[Takes the part of the fool]*

"O, Nuncle, court holy-water in a dry house is better than this rain-water out o' door. Good Nuncle, in; ask thy daughter's blessing: here's a night pities neither wise men nor fools."

SVIETLOVIDOFF.

"Rumble thy bellyful! spit, fire! spout, rain!
Nor rain, wind, thunder, fire, are my daughters;
I tax not you, you elements, with unkindness;
I never gave you kingdom, call'd you children."

Ah! there is strength, there is talent for you! I'm a great artist! Now, then, here's something else of the same kind, to bring back my youth to me. For instance, take this, from Hamlet, I'll begin . . . Let me see, how does it go? Oh, yes, this is it. *[Takes the part of Hamlet]*

"O! the recorders, let me see one.—To withdraw with you. Why do you go about to recover the wind of me, as if you would drive me into a toil?"

IVANITCH. "O, my lord, if my duty be too bold, my love is too unmannerly."

[1] From "Boris Godunoff," by Pushkin. [translator's note]

SVIETLOVIDOFF. "I do not well understand that. Will you play upon this pipe?"

IVANITCH. "My lord, I cannot."

SVIETLOVIDOFF. "I pray you."

IVANITCH. "Believe me, I cannot."

SVIETLOVIDOFF. "I do beseech you."

IVANITCH. "I know no touch of it, my lord."

SVIETLOVIDOFF. "'Tis as easy as lying: govern these vantages with your finger and thumb, give it breath with your mouth, and it will discourse most eloquent music. Look you, these are the stops."

IVANITCH. "But these I cannot command to any utterance of harmony: I have not the skill."

SVIETLOVIDOFF. "Why, look you, how unworthy a thing you make of me. You would play upon me; you would seem to know my stops; you would pluck out the heart of my mystery; you would sound me from my lowest note to the top of my compass; and there is much music, excellent voice, in this little organ, yet cannot you make it speak. S'blood! Do you think I am easier to be played on than a pipe? Call me what instrument you will, though you can fret me, you cannot play upon me!" *[laughs and clasps]* Bravo! Encore! Bravo! Where the devil is there any old age in that? I'm not old, that is all nonsense, a torrent of strength rushes over me; this is life, freshness, youth! Old age and genius can't exist together. You seem to be struck dumb, Nikitushka. Wait a second, let me come to my senses again. Oh! Good Lord! Now then, listen! Did you ever hear such tenderness, such music? Sh! Softly;

"The moon had set. There was not any light,
Save of the lonely legion'd watch-stars pale
In outer air, and what by fits made bright
Hot oleanders in a rosy vale
Searched by the lamping fly, whose little spark
Went in and out, like passion's bashful hope."

*[The noise of opening doors is heard]* What's that?

IVANITCH. There are Petrushka and Yegorka coming back. Yes, you have genius, genius, my master.

SVIETLOVIDOFF. *[Calls, turning toward the noise]* Come here to me, boys! *[To IVANITCH]* Let us go and get dressed. I'm not old! All that is foolishness, nonsense! *[laughs gaily]* What are you crying for? You poor old granny, you, what's the matter now? This won't do! There, there, this won't do at all! Come, come, old man, don't stare so! What makes you stare like that? There, there! *[Embraces him in tears]* Don't cry! Where there is art and genius there can never be such things as old age or loneliness or sickness . . . and death itself is half . . . *[Weeps]* No, no, Nikitushka! It is all over for us now! What sort of a genius am I? I'm like a squeezed lemon, a cracked bottle, and you—you are the old rat of the theatre . . . a prompter! Come on! *[They go]* I'm no genius, I'm only fit to be in the suite of Fortinbras, and even for that I am too old.... Yes.... Do you remember those lines from Othello, Nikitushka?

"Farewell the tranquil mind! Farewell content!
Farewell the plumed troops and the big wars
That make ambition virtue! O farewell!
Farewell the neighing steed and the shrill trump,
The spirit-stirring drum, the ear-piercing fife,
The royal banner, and all quality,
Pride, pomp and circumstance of glorious war!"

IVANITCH. Oh! You're a genius, a genius!

SVIETLOVIDOFF. And again this:

"Away! the moor is dark beneath the moon,
Rapid clouds have drunk the last pale beam of even:
Away! the gathering winds will call the darkness soon,
And profoundest midnight shroud the serene lights of heaven."

**They go out together, the curtain falls slowly.**

# IVANOFF

## CHARACTERS

NICHOLAS IVANOFF, perpetual member of the Council of Peasant Affairs

ANNA, his wife. Nee Sarah Abramson

MATTHEW SHABELSKI, a count, uncle of Ivanoff

PAUL LEBEDIEFF, President of the Board of the Zemstvo

ZINAIDA, his wife

SASHA, their daughter, twenty years old

LVOFF, a young government doctor

MARTHA BABAKINA, a young widow, owner of an estate and daughter of a rich merchant

KOSICH, an exciseman

MICHAEL BORKIN, a distant relative of Ivanoff, and manager of his estate

AVDOTIA NAZAROVNA, an old woman

GEORGE, lives with the Lebedieffs

FIRST GUEST SECOND GUEST THIRD GUEST FOURTH GUEST

PETER, a servant of Ivanoff

GABRIEL, a servant of Lebedieff

GUESTS OF BOTH SEXES

# ACT I

*The play takes place in one of the provinces of central Russia*

*The garden of IVANOFF'S country place. On the left is a terrace and the façade of the house. One window is open. Below the terrace is a broad semicircular lawn, from which paths lead to right and left into a garden. On the right are several garden benches and tables. A lamp is burning on one of the tables. It is evening. As the curtain rises sounds of the piano and violoncello are heard.*

*IVANOFF is sitting at a table reading.*

*BORKIN, in top-boots and carrying a gun, comes in from the rear of the garden. He is a little tipsy. As he sees IVANOFF he comes toward him on tiptoe, and when he comes opposite him he stops and points the gun at his face.*

IVANOFF. *[Catches sight of BORKIN. Shudders and jumps to his feet]* Misha! What are you doing? You frightened me! I can't stand your stupid jokes when I am so nervous as this. And having frightened me, you laugh! *[He sits down.]*

BORKIN. *[Laughing loudly]* There, I am sorry, really. I won't do it again. Indeed I won't. *[Take off his cap]* How hot it is! Just think, my dear boy, I have covered twelve miles in the last three hours. I am worn out. Just feel how my heart is beating.

IVANOFF. *[Goes on reading]* Oh, very well. I shall feel it later!

BORKIN. No, feel it now. *[He takes IVANOFF'S hand and presses it against his breast]* Can you feel it thumping? That means that it is weak and that I may die suddenly at any moment. Would you be sorry if I died?

IVANOFF. I am reading now. I shall attend to you later.

BORKIN. No, seriously, would you be sorry if I died? Nicholas, would you be sorry if I died?

IVANOFF. Leave me alone!

BORKIN. Come, tell me if you would be sorry or not.

IVANOFF. I am sorry that you smell so of vodka, Misha, it is disgusting.

BORKIN. Do I smell of vodka? How strange! And yet, it is not so strange after all. I met the magistrate on the road, and I must admit that we did drink about eight glasses together. Strictly speaking, of course, drinking is very harmful. Listen, it is harmful, isn't it? Is it? Is it?

IVANOFF. This is unendurable! Let me warn you, Misha, that you are going too far.

BORKIN. Well, well, excuse me. Sit here by yourself then, for heaven's sake, if it amuses you. *[Gets up and goes away]* What extraordinary people one meets in the world. They won't even allow themselves to be spoken to. *[He comes back]* Oh, yes, I nearly forgot. Please let me have eighty-two roubles.

IVANOFF. Why do you want eighty-two roubles?

BORKIN. To pay the workmen to-morrow.

IVANOFF. I haven't the money.

BORKIN. Many thanks. *[Angrily]* So you haven't the money! And yet the workmen must be paid, mustn't they?

IVANOFF. I don't know. Wait till my salary comes in on the first of the month.

BORKIN. How is it possible to discuss anything with a man like you? Can't you understand that the workmen are coming to-morrow morning and not on the first of the month?

IVANOFF. How can I help it? I'll be hanged if I can do anything about it now. And what do you mean by this irritating way you have of pestering me whenever I am trying to read or write or——

BORKIN. Must the workmen be paid or not, I ask you? But, good gracious! What is the use of talking to you! *[Waves his hand]* Do you think because you own an estate you can command the whole world? With your two thousand acres and your empty pockets you are like a man who has a cellar full of wine and no corkscrew. I have sold the oats as they stand in the field. Yes, sir! And to-morrow I shall sell the rye and the carriage horses. *[He stamps up and down]* Do you think I am going to stand upon ceremony with you? Certainly not! I am not that kind of a man!

ANNA appears at the open window.

ANNA. Whose voice did I hear just now? Was it yours, Misha? Why are you stamping up and down?

BORKIN. Anybody who had anything to do with your Nicholas would stamp up and down.

ANNA. Listen, Misha! Please have some hay carried onto the croquet lawn.

BORKIN. *[Waves his hand]* Leave me alone, please!

ANNA. Oh, what manners! They are not becoming to you at all. If you want to be liked by women you must never let them see you when you are angry or obstinate. *[To her husband]* Nicholas, let us go and play on the lawn in the hay!

IVANOFF. Don't you know it is bad for you to stand at the open window, Annie? *[Calls]* Shut the window, Uncle!

*[The window is shut from the inside.]*

BORKIN. Don't forget that the interest on the money you owe Lebedieff must be paid in two days.

IVANOFF. I haven't forgotten it. I am going over to see Lebedieff today and shall ask him to wait.

*[He looks at his watch.]*

BORKIN. When are you going?

IVANOFF. At once.

BORKIN. Wait! Wait! Isn't this Sasha's birthday? So it is! The idea of my forgetting it. What a memory I have. *[Jumps about]* I shall go with you! *[Sings]* I shall go, I shall go! Nicholas, old man, you are the joy of my life. If you were not always so nervous and cross and gloomy, you and I could do great things together. I would do anything for you. Shall I marry Martha Babakina and give you half her fortune? That is, not half, either, but all—take it all!

IVANOFF. Enough of this nonsense!

BORKIN. No, seriously, shan't I marry Martha and halve the money with you? But no, why should I propose it? How can you understand? *[Angrily]* You say to me: "Stop talking nonsense!" You are a good man and a clever one, but you haven't any red blood in your veins or any—well, enthusiasm. Why, if you wanted to, you and I could cut a dash together that would shame the devil himself. If you were a normal man instead of a morbid hypochondriac we would have a million in a year. For instance, if I had twenty-three hundred roubles now I could make twenty thousand in two weeks. You don't believe me? You think it is all nonsense? No, it isn't nonsense. Give me twenty-three hundred roubles and let me try. Ofsianoff is selling a strip of land across the river for that price. If we buy this, both banks will be ours, and we shall have the right to build a dam across the river. Isn't that so? We can say that we intend to build a mill, and when the people on the river below us hear that we mean to dam the river they will, of course, object violently and we shall say: If you don't want a dam here you will have to pay to get us away. Do you see the result? The factory would give us five thousand roubles, Korolkoff three thousand, the monastery five thousand more—

IVANOFF. All that is simply idiotic, Misha. If you don't want me to lose my temper you must keep your schemes to yourself.

BORKIN. *[Sits down at the table]* Of course! I knew how it would be! You never will act for yourself, and you tie my hands so that I am helpless.

Enter SHABELSKI and LVOFF.

SHABELSKI. The only difference between lawyers and doctors is that lawyers simply rob you, whereas doctors both rob you and kill you. I am not referring to any one present. *[Sits down on the bench]* They are all frauds and swindlers. Perhaps in Arcadia you might find an exception to the general rule and yet—I have treated thousands of sick people myself in my life, and I have never met a doctor who did not seem to me to be an unmistakable scoundrel.

BORKIN. *[To IVANOFF]* Yes, you tie my hands and never do anything for yourself, and that is why you have no money.

SHABELSKI. As I said before, I am not referring to any one here at present; there may be exceptions though, after all—*[He yawns.]*

IVANOFF. *[Shuts his book]* What have you to tell me, doctor?

LVOFF. *[Looks toward the window]* Exactly what I said this morning: she must go to the Crimea at once. *[Walks up and down.]*

SHABELSKI. *[Bursts out laughing]* To the Crimea! Why don't you and I set up as doctors, Misha? Then, if some Madame Angot or Ophelia finds the world tiresome and begins to cough and be consumptive, all we shall have to do will be to write out a prescription according to the laws of medicine: that is, first, we shall order her a young doctor, and then a journey to the Crimea. There some fascinating young Tartar——

IVANOFF. *[Interrupting]* Oh, don't be coarse! *[To LVOFF]* It takes money to go to the Crimea, and even if I could afford it, you know she has refused to go.

LVOFF. Yes, she has. *[A pause.]*

BORKIN. Look here, doctor, is Anna really so ill that she absolutely must go to the Crimea?

LVOFF. *[Looking toward the window]* Yes, she has consumption.

BORKIN. Whew! How sad! I have seen in her face for some time that she could not last much longer.

LVOFF. Can't you speak quietly? She can hear everything you say. *[A pause.]*

BORKIN. *[Sighing]* The life of man is like a flower, blooming so gaily in a field. Then, along comes a goat, he eats it, and the flower is gone!

SHABELSKI. Oh, nonsense, nonsense. *[Yawning]* Everything is a fraud and a swindle. *[A pause.]*

BORKIN. Gentlemen, I have been trying to tell Nicholas how he can make some money, and have submitted a brilliant plan to him, but my seed, as usual, has fallen on barren soil. Look what a sight he is now: dull, cross, bored, peevish——

SHABELSKI. *[Gets up and stretches himself]* You are always inventing schemes for everybody, you clever fellow, and telling them how to live; can't you tell me something? Give me some good advice, you ingenious young man. Show me a good move to make.

BORKIN. *[Getting up]* I am going to have a swim. Goodbye, gentlemen. *[To Shabelski]* There are at least twenty good moves you could make. If I were you I should have twenty thousand roubles in a week.

*[He goes out; SHABELSKI follows him.]*

SHABELSKI. How would you do it? Come, explain.

BORKIN. There is nothing to explain, it is so simple. *[Coming back]* Nicholas, give me a rouble.

*IVANOFF silently hands him the money*

BORKIN. Thanks. Shabelski, you still hold some trump cards.

*SHABELSKI follows him out.*

SHABELSKI. Well, what are they?

BORKIN. If I were you I should have thirty thousand roubles and more in a week. *[They go out together.]*

IVANOFF. *[After a pause]* Useless people, useless talk, and the necessity of answering stupid questions, have wearied me so, doctor, that I am ill. I have become so irritable and bitter that I don't know myself. My head aches for days at a time. I hear a ringing in my ears, I can't sleep, and yet there is no escape from it all, absolutely none.

LVOFF. Ivanoff, I have something serious to speak to you about.

IVANOFF. What is it?

LVOFF. It is about your wife. She refuses to go to the Crimea alone, but she would go with you.

IVANOFF. *[Thoughtfully]* It would cost a great deal for us both to go, and besides, I could not get leave to be away for so long. I have had one holiday already this year.

LVOFF. Very well, let us admit that. Now to proceed. The best cure for consumption is absolute peace of mind, and your wife has none whatever. She is forever excited by your behaviour to her. Forgive me, I am excited and am going to speak frankly. Your treatment of her is killing her. *[A pause]* Ivanoff, let me believe better things of you.

IVANOFF. What you say is true, true. I must be terribly guilty, but my mind is confused. My will seems to be paralysed by a kind of stupor; I can't understand myself or any one else. *[Looks toward the window]* Come, let us take a walk, we might be overheard here. *[They get up]* My dear friend, you should hear the whole story from the beginning if it were not so long and complicated that to tell it would take all night. *[They walk up and down]* Anna is a splendid, an exceptional woman. She has left her faith, her parents and her fortune for my sake. If I should demand a hundred other sacrifices, she would consent to every one without the quiver of an eyelid. Well, I am not a remarkable man in any way, and have sacrificed nothing. However, the story is a long one. In short, the whole point is, my dear doctor—*[Confused]* that I married her for love and promised to love her forever, and now after five years she loves me still and I—*[He waves his hand]* Now, when you tell me she is dying, I feel neither love nor pity, only a sort of loneliness and weariness. To all appearances this must seem horrible, and I cannot understand myself what is happening to me. *[They go out.]*

*[SHABELSKI comes in.]*

SHABELSKI. *[Laughing]* Upon my word, that man is no scoundrel, but a great thinker, a master-mind. He deserves a memorial. He is the essence of modern ingenuity, and combines in himself alone the genius of the lawyer, the doctor, and the financier. *[He sits down on the lowest step of the terrace]* And yet he has never finished a course of studies in any college; that is so surprising. What an ideal scoundrel he would have made if he had acquired a little culture and mastered the sciences! "You could make twenty thousand roubles in a week," he said. "You still hold the ace of trumps: it is your title." *[Laughing]* He said I might get a rich girl to marry me for it! *[ANNA opens the window and looks down]* "Let me make a match between you and Martha," says he. Who is this Martha? It must be that Balabalkina—Babakalkina woman, the one that looks like a laundress.

ANNA. Is that you, Count?

SHABELSKI. What do you want?

*[ANNA laughs.]*

SHABELSKI. *[With a Jewish accent]* Vy do you laugh?

ANNA. I was thinking of something you said at dinner, do you remember? How was it—a forgiven thief, a doctored horse.

SHABELSKI. A forgiven thief, a doctored horse, and a Christianised Jew are all worth the same price.

ANNA. *[Laughing]* You can't even repeat the simplest saying without ill-nature. You are a most malicious old man. *[Seriously]* Seriously, Count you are extremely disagreeable, and very tiresome and painful to live with. You are always grumbling and growling, and everybody to you is a blackguard and a scoundrel. Tell me honestly, Count, have you ever spoken well of any one?

SHABELSKI. Is this an inquisition?

ANNA. We have lived under this same roof now for five years, and I have never heard you speak kindly of people, or without bitterness and derision. What harm has the world done to you? Is it possible that you consider yourself better than any one else?

SHABELSKI. Not at all. I think we are all of us scoundrels and hypocrites. I myself am a degraded old man, and as useless as a cast-off shoe. I abuse myself as much as any one else. I was rich once, and free, and happy at times, but now I am a dependent, an object of charity, a joke to the world. When I am at last exasperated and defy them, they answer me with a laugh. When I laugh, they shake their heads sadly and say, "The old man has gone mad." But oftenest of all I am unheard and unnoticed by every one.

ANNA. *[Quietly]* Screaming again.

SHABELSKI. Who is screaming?

ANNA. The owl. It screams every evening.

SHABELSKI. Let it scream. Things are as bad as they can be already. *[Stretches himself]* Alas, my dear Sarah! If I could only win a thousand or two roubles, I should soon show you what I could do. I wish you could see me! I should get away out of this hole, and leave the bread of charity, and should not show my nose here again until the last judgment day.

ANNA. What would you do if you were to win so much money?

SHABELSKI. *[Thoughtfully]* First I would go to Moscow to hear the Gipsies play, and then—then I should fly to Paris and take an apartment and go to the Russian Church.

ANNA. And what else?

SHABELSKI. I would go and sit on my wife's grave for days and days and think. I would sit there until I died. My wife is buried in Paris. *[A pause.]*

ANNA. How terribly dull this is! Shall we play a duet?

SHABELSKI. As you like. Go and get the music ready. *[ANNA goes out.]*

*IVANOFF and LVOFF appear in one of the paths.*

IVANOFF. My dear friend, you left college last year, and you are still young and brave. Being thirty-five years old I have the right to advise you. Don't marry a Jewess or a bluestocking or a woman who is queer in any way. Choose some nice, common-place girl without any strange and startling points in her character. Plan your life for quiet; the greyer and more monotonous you can make the background, the better. My dear boy, do not try to fight alone against thousands; do not tilt with windmills; do not dash yourself against the rocks. And, above all, may you be spared the so-called rational life, all wild theories and impassioned talk. Everything is in the hands of God, so shut yourself up in your shell and do your best. That is the pleasant, honest, healthy way to live. But the life I have chosen has been so tiring, oh, so tiring! So full of mistakes, of injustice and stupidity! *[Catches sight of SHABELSKI, and speaks angrily]* There you are again, Uncle, always under foot, never letting one have a moment's quiet talk!

SHABELSKI. *[In a tearful voice]* Is there no refuge anywhere for a poor old devil like me? *[He jumps up and runs into the house.]*

IVANOFF. Now I have offended him! Yes, my nerves have certainly gone to pieces. I must do something about it, I must——

LVOFF. *[Excitedly]* Ivanoff, I have heard all you have to say and—and—I am going to speak frankly. You have shown me in your voice and manner, as well as in your words, the most heartless egotism and pitiless cruelty. Your nearest friend is dying simply because she is near you, her days are numbered, and you can feel such indifference that you go about giving advice and analysing your feelings. I cannot say all I should like to; I have not the gift of words, but—but I can at least say that you are deeply antipathetic to me.

IVANOFF. I suppose I am. As an onlooker, of course you see me more clearly than I see myself, and your judgment of me is probably right. No doubt I am terribly guilty. *[Listens]* I think I hear the carriage coming. I must get ready to go. *[He goes toward the house and then stops]* You dislike me, doctor, and you don't conceal it. Your sincerity does you credit. *[He goes into the house.]*

LVOFF. *[Alone]* What a confoundedly disagreeable character! I have let another opportunity slip without speaking to him as I meant to, but I simply cannot talk calmly to that man. The moment I open my mouth to speak I feel such a commotion and suffocation here *[He puts his hand on his breast]* that my tongue sticks to the roof of my mouth. Oh, I loathe that Tartuffe, that unmitigated rascal, with all my heart! There he is, preparing to go driving in spite of the entreaties of his unfortunate wife, who adores him and whose only happiness is his presence. She implores him to spend at least one evening with her, and he cannot even do that. Why, he might shoot himself in despair if he had to stay at home! Poor fellow, what he wants are new fields for his villainous schemes. Oh, I know why you go to Lebedieff's every evening, Ivanoff! I know.

*Enter IVANOFF, in hat and coat, ANNA and SHABELSKI*

SHABELSKI. Look here, Nicholas, this is simply barbarous You go away every evening and leave us here alone, and we get so bored that we have to go to bed at eight o'clock. It is a scandal, and no decent way of living. Why can you go driving if we can't? Why?

ANNA. Leave him alone, Count. Let him go if he wants to.

IVANOFF. How can a sick woman like you go anywhere? You know you have a cough and must not go out after sunset. Ask the doctor here. You are no child, Annie, you must be reasonable. And as for you, what would you do with yourself over there?

SHABELSKI. I am ready to go anywhere: into the jaws of a crocodile, or even into the jaws of hell, so long as I don't have to stay here. I am horribly bored. I am stupefied by this dullness. Every one here is tired of me. You leave me at home to entertain Anna, but I feel more like scratching and biting her.

ANNA. Leave him alone, Count. Leave him alone. Let him go if he enjoys himself there.

IVANOFF. What does this mean, Annie? You know I am not going for pleasure. I must see Lebedieff about the money I owe him.

ANNA. I don't see why you need justify yourself to me. Go ahead! Who is keeping you?

IVANOFF. Heavens! Don't let us bite one another's heads off. Is that really unavoidable?

SHABELSKI. *[Tearfully]* Nicholas, my dear boy, do please take me with you. I might possibly be amused a little by the sight of all the fools and scoundrels I should see there. You know I haven't been off this place since Easter.

IVANOFF. *[Exasperated]* Oh, very well! Come along then! How tiresome you all are!

SHABELSKI. I may go? Oh, thank you! *[Takes him gaily by the arm and leads him aside]* May I wear your straw hat?

IVANOFF. You may, only hurry, please.

*SHABELSKI runs into the house.*

IVANOFF. How tired I am of you all! But no, what am I saying? Annie, my manner to you is insufferable, and it never used to be. Well, good-bye, Annie. I shall be back by one.

ANNA. Nicholas! My dear husband, stay at home to-night!

IVANOFF. *[Excitedly]* Darling, sweetheart, my dear, unhappy one, I implore you to let me leave home in the evenings. I know it is cruel and unjust to ask this, but let me do you this injustice. It is such torture for me to stay. As soon as the sun goes down my soul is overwhelmed by the most horrible despair. Don't ask me why; I don't know; I swear I don't. This dreadful melancholy torments me here, it drives me to the Lebedieff's and there it grows worse than ever. I rush home; it still pursues me; and so I am tortured all through the night. It is breaking my heart.

ANNA. Nicholas, won't you stay? We will talk together as we used to. We will have supper together and read afterward. The old grumbler and I have learned so many duets to play to you. *[She kisses him. Then, after a pause]* I can't understand you any more. This has been going on for a year now. What has changed you so?

IVANOFF. I don't know.

ANNA. And why don't you want me to go driving with you in the evening?

IVANOFF. As you insist on knowing, I shall have to tell you. It is a little cruel, but you had best understand. When this melancholy fit is on me I begin to dislike you, Annie, and at such times I must escape from you. In short, I simply have to leave this house.

ANNA. Oh, you are sad, are you? I can understand that! Nicholas, let me tell you something: won't you try to sing and laugh and scold as you used to? Stay here, and we will drink some liqueur together, and laugh, and chase away this sadness of yours in no time. Shall I sing to you? Or shall we sit in your study in the twilight as we used to, while you tell me about your sadness? I can read such suffering in your eyes! Let me look into them and weep, and our hearts will both be lighter. *[She laughs and cries at once]* Or is it really true that the flowers return with every spring, but lost happiness never returns? Oh, is it? Well, go then, go!

IVANOFF. Pray for me, Annie! *[He goes; then stops and thinks for a moment]* No, I can't do it. *[IVANOFF goes out.]*

ANNA. Yes, go, go—*[Sits down at the table.]*

LVOFF. *[Walking up and down]* Make this a rule, Madam: as soon as the sun goes down you must go indoors and not come out again until morning. The damp evening air is bad for you.

ANNA. Yes, sir!

LVOFF. What do you mean by "Yes, sir"? I am speaking seriously.

ANNA. But I don't want to be serious. *[She coughs.]*

LVOFF. There now, you see, you are coughing already.

*SHABELSKI comes out of the house in his hat and coat.*

SHABELSKI. Where is Nicholas? Is the carriage here yet? *[Goes quickly to ANNA and kisses her hand]* Good-night, my darling! *[Makes a face and speaks with a Jewish accent]* I beg your bardon! *[He goes quickly out.]*

LVOFF. Idiot!

*A pause; the sounds of a concertina are heard in the distance.*

ANNA. Oh, how lonely it is! The coachman and the cook are having a little ball in there by themselves, and I—I am, as it were, abandoned. Why are you walking about, Doctor? Come and sit down here.

LVOFF. I can't sit down.

*[A pause.]*

ANNA. They are playing "The Sparrow" in the kitchen. *[She sings]*

"Sparrow, Sparrow, where are you?
On the mountain drinking dew."

*[A pause]* Are your father and mother living, Doctor?

LVOFF. My mother is living; my father is dead.

ANNA. Do you miss your mother very much?

LVOFF. I am too busy to miss any one.

ANNA. *[Laughing]* The flowers return with every spring, but lost happiness never returns. I wonder who taught me that? I think it was Nicholas himself. *[Listens]* The owl is hooting again.

LVOFF. Well, let it hoot.

ANNA. I have begun to think, Doctor, that fate has cheated me. Other people who, perhaps, are no better than I am are happy and have not had to pay for their happiness. But I have paid for it all, every moment of it, and such a price! Why should I have to pay so terribly? Dear friend, you are all too considerate and gentle with me to tell me the truth; but do you think I don't know what is the matter with me? I know perfectly well. However, this isn't a pleasant subject—*[With a Jewish accent]* "I beg your bardon!" Can you tell funny stories?

LVOFF. No, I can't.

ANNA. Nicholas can. I am beginning to be surprised, too, at the injustice of people. Why do they return hatred for love, and answer truth with lies? Can you tell me how much longer I shall be hated by my mother and father? They live fifty miles away, and yet I can feel their hatred day and night, even in my sleep. And how do you account for the sadness of Nicholas? He says that he only dislikes me in the evening, when the fit is on him. I understand that, and can tolerate it, but what if he should come to dislike me altogether? Of course that is impossible, and yet—no, no, I mustn't even imagine such a thing. *[Sings]*

"Sparrow, Sparrow, where are you?"

*[She shudders]* What fearful thoughts I have! You are not married, Doctor; there are many things that you cannot understand.

LVOFF. You say you are surprised, but—but it is you who surprise me. Tell me, explain to me how you, an honest and intelligent woman, almost a saint, could allow yourself to be so basely deceived and dragged into this den of bears? Why are you here? What have you in common with such a cold and heartless—but enough of your husband! What have you in common with these wicked and vulgar surroundings? With that eternal grumbler, the crazy and decrepit Count? With that swindler, that prince of rascals, Misha, with his fool's face? Tell me, I say, how did you get here?

ANNA. *[laughing]* That is what he used to say, long ago, oh, exactly! Only his eyes are larger than yours, and when he was excited they used to shine like coals—go on, go on!

LVOFF. *[Gets up and waves his hand]* There is nothing more to say. Go into the house.

ANNA. You say that Nicholas is not what he should be, that his faults are so and so. How can you possibly understand him? How can you learn to know any one in six months? He is a wonderful man, Doctor, and I am sorry you could not have known him as he was two or three years ago. He is depressed and silent now, and broods all day without doing anything, but he was splendid then. I fell in love with him at first sight. *[Laughing]* I gave one look and was caught like a mouse in a trap! So when he asked me to go with him I cut every tie that bound me to my old life as one snips the withered leaves from a plant. But things are different now. Now he goes to the Lebedieff's to amuse himself with other women, and I sit here in the garden and listen to the owls. *[The WATCHMAN'S rattle is heard]* Tell me, Doctor, have you any brothers and sisters?

LVOFF. No.

*ANNA sobs.*

LVOFF. What is it? What is the matter?

ANNA. I can't stand it, Doctor, I must go.

LVOFF. Where?

ANNA. To him. I am going. Have the horses harnessed. *[She runs into the house.]*

LVOFF. No, I certainly cannot go on treating any one under these conditions. I not only have to do it for nothing, but I am forced to endure this agony of mind besides. No, no, I can't stand it. I have had enough of it. *[He goes into the house.]*

**The curtain falls.**

# ACT II

*The drawing-room of LEBEDIEFFÕS house. In the centre is a door leading into a garden. Doors open out of the room to the right and left. The room is furnished with valuable old furniture, which is carefully protected by linen covers. The walls are hung with pictures. The room is lighted by candelabra. ZINAIDA is sitting on a sofa; the elderly guests are sitting in arm-chairs on either hand. The young guests are sitting about the room on small chairs. KOSICH, AVDOTIA NAZAROVNA, GEORGE, and others are playing cards in the background. GABRIEL is standing near the door on the right. The maid is passing sweetmeats about on a tray. During the entire act guests come and go from the garden, through the room, out of the door on the left, and back again. Enter MARTHA through the door on the right. She goes toward ZINAIDA.*

ZINAIDA. *[Gaily]* My dearest Martha!

MARTHA. How do you do, Zinaida? Let me congratulate you on your daughter's birthday.

ZINAIDA. Thank you, my dear; I am delighted to see you. How are you?

MARTHA. Very well indeed, thank you. *[She sits down on the sofa]* Good evening, young people!

*The younger guests get up and bow.*

FIRST GUEST. *[Laughing]* Young people indeed! Do you call yourself an old person?

MARTHA. *[Sighing]* How can I make any pretence to youth now?

FIRST GUEST. What nonsense! The fact that you are a widow means nothing. You could beat any pretty girl you chose at a canter.

*GABRIEL brings MARTHA some tea.*

ZINAIDA. Why do you bring the tea in like that? Go and fetch some jam to eat with it!

MARTHA. No thank you; none for me, don't trouble yourself. *[A pause.]*

FIRST GUEST. *[To MARTHA]* Did you come through Mushkine on your way here?

MARTHA. No, I came by way of Spassk. The road is better that way.

FIRST GUEST. Yes, so it is.

KOSICH. Two in spades.

GEORGE. Pass.

AVDOTIA. Pass.

SECOND GUEST. Pass.

MARTHA. The price of lottery tickets has gone up again, my dear. I have never known such a state of affairs. The first issue is already worth two hundred and seventy and the second nearly two hundred and fifty. This has never happened before.

ZINAIDA. How fortunate for those who have a great many tickets!

MARTHA. Don't say that, dear; even when the price of tickets is high it does not pay to put one's capital into them.

ZINAIDA. Quite true, and yet, my dear, one never can tell what may happen. Providence is sometimes kind.

THIRD GUEST. My impression is, ladies, that at present capital is exceedingly unproductive. Shares pay very small dividends, and speculating is exceedingly dangerous. As I understand it, the capitalist now finds himself in a more critical position than the man who——

MARTHA. Quite right.

*FIRST GUEST yawns.*

MARTHA. How dare you yawn in the presence of ladies?

FIRST GUEST. I beg your pardon! It was quite an accident.

*ZINAIDA gets up and goes out through the door on the right.*

GEORGE. Two in hearts.

SECOND GUEST. Pass.

KOSICH. Pass.

MARTHA. *[Aside]* Heavens! This is deadly! I shall die of ennui.

*Enter ZINAIDA and LEBEDIEFF through the door on the right.*

ZINAIDA. Why do you go off by yourself like a prima donna? Come and sit with our guests!

*[She sits down in her former place.]*

LEBEDIEFF. *[Yawning]* Oh, dear, our sins are heavy! *[He catches sight of MARTHA]* Why, there is my little sugar-plum! How is your most esteemed highness?

MARTHA. Very well, thank you.

LEBEDIEFF. Splendid, splendid! *[He sits down in an armchair]* Quite right—Oh, Gabriel!

*GABRIEL brings him a glass of vodka and a tumbler of water. He empties the glass of vodka and sips the water.*

FIRST GUEST. Good health to you!

LEBEDIEFF. Good health is too much to ask. I am content to keep death from the door. *[To his wife]* Where is the heroine of this occasion, Zuzu?

KOSICH. *[In a plaintive voice]* Look here, why haven't we taken any tricks yet? *[He jumps up]* Yes, why have we lost this game entirely, confound it?

AVDOTIA. *[Jumps up angrily]* Because, friend, you don't know how to play it, and have no right to be sitting here at all. What right had you to lead from another suit? Haven't you the ace left? *[They both leave the table and run forward.]*

KOSICH. *[In a tearful voice]* Ladies and gentlemen, let me explain! I had the ace, king, queen, and eight of diamonds, the ace of spades and one, just one, little heart, do you understand? Well, she, bad luck to her, she couldn't make a little slam. I said one in no-trumps——[1]

AVDOTIA. *[Interrupting him]* No, I said one in no-trumps; you said two in no-trumps——

KOSICH. This is unbearable! Allow me—you had—I had—you had— *[To LEBEDIEFF]* But you shall decide it, Paul: I had the ace, king, queen, and eight of diamonds——

LEBEDIEFF. *[Puts his fingers into his ears]* Stop, for heaven's sake, stop!

AVDOTIA. *[Yelling]* I said no-trumps, and not he!

KOSICH. *[Furiously]* I'll be damned if I ever sit down to another game of cards with that old cat!

[1] The game played is vint, the national card-game of Russia and the direct ancestor of auction bridge, with which it is almost identical. [translator's note]

*He rushes into the garden. The SECOND GUEST follows him. GEORGE is left alone at the table.*

AVDOTIA. Whew! He makes my blood boil! Old cat, indeed! You're an old cat yourself!

MARTHA. How angry you are, aunty!

AVDOTIA. *[Sees MARTHA and claps her hands]* Are you here, my darling? My beauty! And was I blind as a bat, and didn't see you? Darling child! *[She kisses her and sits down beside her]* How happy this makes me! Let me feast my eyes on you, my milk-white swan! Oh, oh, you have bewitched me!

LEBEDIEFF. Why don't you find her a husband instead of singing her praises?

AVDOTIA. He shall be found. I shall not go to my grave before I have found a husband for her, and one for Sasha too. I shall not go to my grave—*[She sighs]* But where to find these husbands nowadays? There sit some possible bridegrooms now, huddled together like a lot of half-drowned rats!

THIRD GUEST. A most unfortunate comparison! It is my belief, ladies, that if the young men of our day prefer to remain single, the fault lies not with them, but with the existing, social conditions!

LEBEDIEFF. Come, enough of that! Don't give us any more philosophy; I don't like it!

*Enter SASHA. She goes up to her father.*

SASHA. How can you endure the stuffy air of this room when the weather is so beautiful?

ZINAIDA. My dear Sasha, don't you see that Martha is here?

SASHA. I beg your pardon.

*[She goes up to MARTHA and shakes hands.]*

MARTHA. Yes, here I am, my dear little Sasha, and proud to congratulate you. *[They kiss each other]* Many happy returns of the day, dear!

SASHA. Thank you! *[She goes and sits down by her father.]*

LEBEDIEFF. As you were saying, Avdotia Nazarovna, husbands are hard to find. I don't want to be rude, but I must say that the young men of the present are a dull and poky lot, poor fellows! They can't dance or talk or drink as they should do.

AVDOTIA. Oh, as far as drinking goes, they are all experts. Just give them—give them——

LEBEDIEFF. Simply to drink is no art. A horse can drink. No, it must be done in the right way. In my young days we used to sit and cudgel our brains all day over our lessons, but as soon as evening came we would fly off on some spree and keep it up till dawn. How we used to dance and flirt, and drink, too! Or sometimes we would sit and chatter and discuss everything under the sun until we almost wagged our tongues off. But now—*[He waves his hand]* Boys are a puzzle to me. They are not willing either to give a candle to God or a pitchfork to the devil! There is only one young fellow in the country who is worth a penny, and he is married. *[Sighs]* They say, too, that he is going crazy.

MARTHA. Who is he?

LEBEDIEFF. Nicholas Ivanoff.

MARTHA. Yes, he is a fine fellow, only *[Makes a face]* he is very unhappy.

ZINAIDA. How could he be otherwise, poor boy! *[She sighs]* He made such a bad mistake. When he married that Jewess of his he thought of course that her parents would give away whole mountains of gold with her, but, on the contrary, on the day she became a Christian they disowned her, and Ivanoff has never seen a penny of the money. He has repented of his folly now, but it is too late.

SASHA. Mother, that is not true!

MARTHA. How can you say it is not true, Sasha, when we all know it to be a fact? Why did he have to marry a Jewess? He must have had some reason for doing it. Are Russian girls so scarce? No, he made a mistake, poor fellow, a sad mistake. *[Excitedly]* And what on earth can he do with her now? Where could she go if he were to come home some day and say: "Your parents have deceived me; leave my house at once!" Her parents wouldn't take her back. She might find a place as a house-maid if she had ever learned to work, which she hasn't. He worries and worries her now, but the Count interferes. If it had not been for the Count, he would have worried her to death long ago.

AVDOTIA. They say he shuts her up in a cellar and stuffs her with garlic, and she eats and eats until her very soul reeks of it. *[Laughter.]*

SASHA. But, father, you know that isn't true!

LEBEDIEFF. What if it isn't, Sasha? Let them spin yarns if it amuses them. *[He calls]* Gabriel!

*GABRIEL brings him another glass of vodka and a glass of water.*

ZINAIDA. His misfortunes have almost ruined him, poor man. His affairs are in a frightful condition. If Borkin did not take such good charge of his estate he and his Jewess would soon be starving to death. *[She sighs]* And what anxiety he has caused us! Heaven only knows how we have suffered. Do you realise, my dear, that for three years he has owed us nine thousand roubles?

MARTHA. *[Horrified]* Nine thousand!

ZINAIDA. Yes, that is the sum that my dear Paul has undertaken to lend him. He never knows to whom it is safe to lend money and to whom it is not. I don't worry about the principal, but he ought to pay the interest on his debt.

SASHA. *[Hotly]* Mamma, you have already discussed this subject at least a thousand times!

ZINAIDA. What difference does it make to you? Why should you interfere?

SASHA. What is this mania you all have for gossiping about a man who has never done any of you any harm? Tell me, what harm has he done you?

THIRD GUEST. Let me say two words, Miss Sasha. I esteem Ivanoff, and have always found him an honourable man, but, between ourselves, I also consider him an adventurer.

SASHA. I congratulate you on your opinion!

THIRD GUEST. In proof of its truth, permit me to present to you the following facts, as they were communicated to me by his secretary, or shall I say rather, by his factotum, Borkin. Two years ago, at the time of the cattle plague, he bought some cattle and had them insured—

ZINAIDA. Yes, I remember hearing' of that.

THIRD GUEST. He had them insured, as you understand, and then inoculated them with the disease and claimed the insurance.

SASHA. Oh, what nonsense, nonsense, nonsense! No one bought or inoculated any cattle! The story was invented by Borkin, who then went about boasting of his clever plan. Ivanoff would not forgive Borkin for two weeks after he heard of it. He is only guilty of a weak character and too great faith in humanity. He can't make up his mind to get rid of that Borkin, and so all his possessions have been tricked and stolen from him. Every one who has had anything to do with Ivanoff has taken advantage of his generosity to grow rich.

LEBEDIEFF. Sasha, you little firebrand, that will do!

SASHA. Why do you all talk like this? This eternal subject of Ivanoff, Ivanoff, and always Ivanoff has grown insufferable, and yet you never speak of anything else. *[She goes toward the door, then stops and comes back]* I am surprised, *[To the young men]* and utterly astonished at your patience, young men! How can you sit there like that? Aren't you bored? Why, the very air is as dull as ditchwater! Do, for heaven's sake say something; try to amuse the girls a little, move about! Or if you can't talk of anything except Ivanoff, you might laugh or sing or dance——

LEBEDIEFF. *[Laughing]* That's right, Sasha! Give them a good scolding.

SASHA. Look here, will you do me a favour? If you refuse to dance or sing or laugh, if all that is tedious, then let me beg you, implore you, to summon all your powers, if only for this once, and make one witty or clever remark. Let it be as impertinent and malicious as you like, so long as it is funny and original. Won't you perform this miracle, just once, to surprise us and make us laugh? Or else you might think of some little thing which you could all do together, something to make you stir about. Let the girls admire you for once in their lives! Listen to me! I suppose you want them to like you? Then why don't try to make them do it? Oh, dear! There is something wrong with you all! You are a lot of sleepy stick-in-the-muds! I have told you so a thousand times and shall always go on repeating it; there is something wrong with every one of you; something wrong, wrong, wrong!

*Enter IVANOFF and SHABELSKI through the door on the right.*

SHABELSKI. Who is making a speech here? Is it you, Sasha? *[He laughs and shakes hands with her]* Many happy returns of the day, my dear child. May you live as long as possible in this life, but never be born again!

ZINAIDA. *[Joyfully]* My dear Count!

LEBEDIEFF. Who can this be? Not you, Count?

SHABELSKI. *[Sees ZINAIDA and MARTHA sitting side by side]* Two gold mines side by side! What a pleasant picture it makes! *[He shakes hands with ZINAIDA]* Good evening, Zuzu! *[Shakes hands with MARTHA]* Good evening, Birdie!

ZINAIDA. I am charmed to see you, Count. You are a rare visitor here now. *[Calls]* Gabriel, bring some tea! Please sit down.

*She gets up and goes to the door and back, evidently much preoccupied. SASHA sits down in her former place. IVANOFF silently shakes hands with every one.*

LEBEDIEFF. *[To SHABELSKI]* What miracle has brought you here? You have given us a great surprise. Why, Count, you're a rascal, you haven't been treating us right at all. *[Leads him forward by the hand]* Tell me, why don't you ever come to see us now? Are you offended?

SHABELSKI. How can I get here to see you? Astride a broomstick? I have no horses of my own, and Nicholas won't take me with him when he goes out. He says I must stay at home to amuse Sarah. Send your horses for me and I shall come with pleasure.

LEBEDIEFF. *[With a wave of the hand]* Oh, that is easy to say! But Zuzu would rather have a fit than lend the horses to any one. My dear, dear old friend, you are more to me than any one I know! You and I are survivors of those good old days that are gone forever, and you alone bring back to my mind the love and longings of my lost youth. Of course I am only joking, and yet, do you know, I am almost in tears?

SHABELSKI. Stop, stop! You smell like the air of a wine cellar.

LEBEDIEFF. Dear friend, you cannot imagine how lonely I am without my old companions! I could hang myself! *[Whispers]* Zuzu has frightened all the decent men away with her stingy ways, and now we have only this riff-raff, as you see: Tom, Dick, and Harry. However, drink your tea.

ZINAIDA. *[Anxiously, to GABRIEL]* Don't bring it in like that! Go fetch some jam to eat with it!

SHABELSKI. *[Laughing loudly, to IVANOFF]* Didn't I tell you so? *[To LEBEDIEFF]* I bet him driving over, that as soon as we arrived Zuzu would want to feed us with jam!

ZINAIDA. Still joking, Count! *[She sits down.]*

LEBEDIEFF. She made twenty jars of it this year, and how else do you expect her to get rid of it?

SHABELSKI. *[Sits down near the table]* Are you still adding to the hoard, Zuzu? You will soon have a million, eh?

ZINAIDA. *[Sighing]* I know it seems as if no one could be richer than we, but where do they think the money comes from? It is all gossip.

SHABELSKI. Oh, yes, we all know that! We know how badly you play your cards! Tell me, Paul, honestly, have you saved up a million yet?

LEBEDIEFF. I don't know. Ask Zuzu.

SHABELSKI. *[To MARTHA]* And my plump little Birdie here will soon have a million too! She is getting prettier and plumper not only every day, but every hour. That means she has a nice little fortune.

MARTHA. Thank you very much, your highness, but I don't like such jokes.

SHABELSKI. My dear little gold mine, do you call that a joke? It was a wail of the soul, a cry from the heart, that burst through my lips. My love for you and Zuzu is immense. *[Gaily]* Oh, rapture! Oh, bliss! I cannot look at you two without a madly beating heart!

ZINAIDA. You are still the same, Count. *[To GEORGE]* Put out the candles please, George. *[GEORGE gives a start. He puts out the candles and sits down again]* How is your wife, Nicholas?

IVANOFF. She is very ill. The doctor said to-day that she certainly had consumption.

ZINAIDA. Really? Oh, how sad! *[She sighs]* And we are all so fond of her!

SHABELSKI. What trash you all talk! That story was invented by that sham doctor, and is nothing but a trick of his. He wants to masquerade as an Aesculapius, and so has started this consumption theory. Fortunately her husband isn't jealous. *[IVANOFF makes an inpatient gesture]* As for Sarah, I wouldn't trust a word or an action of hers. I have made a point all my life of mistrusting all doctors, lawyers, and women. They are shammers and deceivers.

LEBEDIEFF. *[To SHABELSKI]* You are an extraordinary person, Matthew! You have mounted this misanthropic hobby of yours, and you ride it through thick and thin like a lunatic You are a man like any other, and yet, from the way you talk one would imagine that you had the pip, or a cold in the head.

SHABELSKI. Would you have me go about kissing every rascal and scoundrel I meet?

LEBEDIEFF. Where do you find all these rascals and scoundrels?

SHABELSKI. Of course I am not talking of any one here present, nevertheless——-

LEBEDIEFF. There you are again with your "nevertheless." All this is simply a fancy of yours.

SHABELSKI. A fancy? It is lucky for you that you have no knowledge of the world!

LEBEDIEFF. My knowledge of the world is this: I must sit here prepared at any moment to have death come knocking at the door. That is my knowledge of the world. At our age, brother, you and I can't afford to worry about knowledge of the world. So then—*[He calls]* Oh, Gabriel!

SHABELSKI. You have had quite enough already. Look at your nose.

LEBEDIEFF. No matter, old boy. I am not going to be married to-day.

ZINAIDA. Doctor Lvoff has not been here for a long time. He seems to have forgotten us.

SASHA. That man is one of my aversions. I can't stand his icy sense of honour. He can't ask for a glass of water or smoke a cigarette without making a display of his remarkable honesty. Walking and talking, it is written on his brow: "I am an honest man." He is a great bore.

SHABELSKI. He is a narrow-minded, conceited medico. *[Angrily]* He shrieks like a parrot at every step: "Make way for honest endeavour!" and thinks himself another St. Francis. Everybody is a rascal who doesn't make as much noise as he does. As for his penetration, it is simply remarkable! If a peasant is well off and lives decently, he sees at once that he must be a thief and a scoundrel. If I wear a velvet coat and am dressed by my valet, I am a rascal and the valet is my slave. There is no place in this world for a man like him. I am actually afraid of him. Yes, indeed, he is likely, out of a sense of duty, to insult a man at any moment and to call him a knave.

IVANOFF. I am dreadfully tired of him, but I can't help liking him, too, he is so sincere.

SHABELSKI. Oh, yes, his sincerity is beautiful! He came up to me yesterday evening and remarked absolutely apropos of nothing: "Count, I have a deep aversion to you!" It isn't as if he said such things simply, but they are extremely pointed. His voice trembles, his eyes flash, his veins swell. Confound his infernal honesty! Supposing I am disgusting and odious to him? What is more natural? I know that I am, but I don't like to be told so to my face. I am a worthless old man, but he might have the decency to respect my grey hairs. Oh, what stupid, heartless honesty!

LEBEDIEFF. Come, come, you have been young yourself, and should make allowances for him.

SHABELSKI. Yes, I have been young and reckless; I have played the fool in my day and have seen plenty of knaves and scamps, but I have never called a thief a thief to his face, or talked of ropes in the house of a man who had been hung. I knew how to behave, but this idiotic doctor of yours would think himself in the seventh heaven of happiness if fate would allow him to pull my nose in public in the name of morality and human ideals.

LEBEDIEFF. Young men are all stubborn and restive. I had an uncle once who thought himself a philosopher. He would fill his house with guests, and after he had had a drink he would get up on a chair, like this, and begin: "You ignoramuses! You powers of darkness! This is the dawn of a new life!" And so on and so on; he would preach and preach——

SASHA. And the guests?

LEBEDIEFF. They would just sit and listen and go on drinking. Once, though, I challenged him to a duel, challenged my own uncle! It came out of a discussion about Sir Francis Bacon. I was sitting, I remember, where Matthew is, and my uncle and the late Gerasim Nilitch were standing over there, about where Nicholas is now. Well, Gerasim Nilitch propounded this question——

Enter BORKIN. He is dressed like a dandy and carries a parcel under his arm. He comes in singing and skipping through the door on the right. A murmur of approval is heard.

THE GIRLS. Oh, Michael Borkin!

LEBEDIEFF. Hallo, Misha!

SHABELSKI. The soul of the company!

BORKIN. Here we are! *[He runs up to SASHA]* Most noble Signorina, let me be so bold as to wish to the whole world many happy returns of the birthday of such an exquisite flower as you! As a token of my enthusiasm let me presume to present you with these fireworks and this Bengal fire of my own manufacture. *[He hands her the parcel]* May they illuminate the night as brightly as you illuminate the shadows of this dark world. *[He spreads them out theatrically before her.]*

SASHA. Thank you.

LEBEDIEFF. *[Laughing loudly, to IVANOFF]* Why don't you send this Judas packing?

BORKIN. *[To LEBEDIEFF]* My compliments to you, sir. *[To IVANOFF]* How are you, my patron? *[Sings]* Nicholas voila, hey ho hey! *[He greets everybody in turn]* Most highly honoured Zinaida! Oh, glorious Martha! Most ancient Avdotia! Noblest of Counts!

SHABELSKI. *[Laughing]* The life of the company! The moment he comes in the air feels livelier. Have you noticed it?

BORKIN. Whew! I am tired! I believe I have shaken hands with everybody. Well, ladies and gentlemen, haven't you some little tidbit to tell me; something spicy? *[Speaking quickly to ZINAIDA]* Oh, aunty! I have something to tell you. As I was on my way here—*[To GABRIEL]* Some tea, please Gabriel, but without jam—as I was on my way here I saw some peasants down on the river-bank pulling the bark off the trees. Why don't you lease that meadow?

LEBEDIEFF. *[To IVANOFF]* Why don't you send that Judas away?

ZINAIDA. *[Startled]* Why, that is quite true! I never thought of it.

BORKIN. *[Swinging his arms]* I can't sit still! What tricks shall we be up to next, aunty? I am all on edge, Martha, absolutely exalted. *[He sings]*

"Once more I stand before thee!"

ZINAIDA. Think of something to amuse us, Misha, we are all bored.

BORKIN. Yes, you look so. What is the matter with you all? Why are you sitting there as solemn as a jury? Come, let us play something; what shall it be? Forfeits? Hide-and-seek? Tag? Shall we dance, or have the fireworks?

THE GIRLS. *[Clapping their hands]* The fireworks! The fireworks! *[They run into the garden.]*

SASHA. *[To IVANOFF]* What makes you so depressed today?

IVANOFF. My head aches, little Sasha, and then I feel bored.

SASHA. Come into the sitting-room with me.

*They go out through the door on the right. All the guests go into the garden and ZINAIDA and LEBEDIEFF are left alone.*

ZINAIDA. That is what I like to see! A young man like Misha comes into the room and in a minute he has everybody laughing. *[She puts out the large lamp]* There is no reason the candles should burn for nothing so long as they are all in the garden. *[She blows out the candles.]*

LEBEDIEFF. *[Following her]* We really ought to give our guests something to eat, Zuzu!

ZINAIDA. What crowds of candles; no wonder we are thought rich.

LEBEDIEFF. *[Still following her]* Do let them have something to eat, Zuzu; they are young and must be hungry by now, poor things—Zuzu!

ZINAIDA. The Count did not finish his tea, and all that sugar has been wasted. *[Goes out through the door on the left.]*

LEBEDIEFF. Bah! *[Goes out into the garden.]*

*Enter IVANOFF and SASHA through the door on the right.*

IVANOFF. This is how it is, Sasha: I used to work hard and think hard, and never tire; now, I neither do anything nor think anything, and I am weary, body and soul. I feel I am terribly to blame, my conscience leaves me no peace day or night, and yet I can't see clearly exactly what my mistakes are. And now comes my wife's illness, our poverty, this eternal backbiting, gossiping, chattering, that foolish Borkin—My home has become unendurable to me, and to live there is worse than torture. Frankly, Sasha, the presence of my wife, who loves me, has become unbearable. You are an old friend, little Sasha, you will not be angry with me for speaking so openly. I came to you to be cheered, but I am bored here too, something urges me home again. Forgive me, I shall slip away at once.

SASHA. I can understand your trouble, Nicholas. You are unhappy because you are lonely. You need some one at your side whom you can love, someone who understands you.

IVANOFF. What an idea, Sasha! Fancy a crusty old badger like myself starting a love affair! Heaven preserve me from such misfortune! No, my little sage, this is not a case for romance. The fact is, I can endure all I have to suffer: sadness, sickness of mind, ruin, the loss of my wife, and my lonely, broken old age, but I cannot, I will not, endure the contempt I have for myself! I am nearly killed by shame when I think that a strong, healthy man like myself has become—oh, heaven only knows what—by no means a Manfred or a Hamlet! There are some unfortunates who feel flattered when people call them Hamlets and cynics, but to me it is an insult. It wounds my pride and I am tortured by shame and suffer agony.

SASHA. *[Laughing through her tears]* Nicholas, let us run away to America together!

IVANOFF. I haven't the energy to take such a step as that, and besides, in America you—*[They go toward the door into the garden]* As a matter of fact, Sasha, this is not a good place for you to live. When I look about at the men who surround you I am terrified for you; whom is there you could marry? Your only chance will be if some passing lieutenant or student steals your heart and carries you away.

*Enter ZINAIDA through the door on the right with a jar of jam.*

IVANOFF. Excuse me, Sasha, I shall join you in a minute.

*SASHA goes out into the garden.*

IVANOFF. *[To ZINAIDA]* Zinaida, may I ask you a favour?

ZINAIDA. What is it?

IVANOFF. The fact is, you know, that the interest on my note is due day after to-morrow, but I should be more than obliged to you if you will let me postpone the payment of it, or would let me add the interest to the capital. I simply cannot pay it now; I haven't the money.

ZINAIDA. Oh, Ivanoff, how could I do such a thing? Would it be business-like? No, no, don't ask it, don't torment an unfortunate old woman.

IVANOFF. I beg your pardon. *[He goes out into the garden.]*

ZINAIDA. Oh, dear! Oh, dear! What a fright he gave me! I am trembling all over. *[Goes out through the door on the right.]*

*Enter KOSICH through the door on the left. He walks across the stage.*

KOSICH. I had the ace, king, queen, and eight of diamonds, the ace of spades, and one, just one little heart, and she—may the foul fiend fly away with her,—she couldn't make a little slam!

*Goes out through the door on the right. Enter from the garden AVDOTIA and FIRST GUEST.*

AVDOTIA. Oh, how I should like to get my claws into her, the miserable old miser! How I should like it! Does she think it a joke to leave us sitting here since five o'clock without even offering us a crust to eat? What a house! What management!

FIRST GUEST. I am so bored that I feel like beating my head against the wall. Lord, what a queer lot of people! I shall soon be howling like a wolf and snapping at them from hunger and weariness.

AVDOTIA. How I should like to get my claws into her, the old sinner!

FIRST GUEST. I shall get a drink, old lady, and then home I go! I won't have anything to do with these belles of yours. How the devil can a man think of love who hasn't had a drop to drink since dinner?

AVDOTIA. Come on, we will go and find something.

FIRST GUEST. Sh! Softly! I think the brandy is in the sideboard in the dining-room. We will find George! Sh!

*They go out through the door on the left. Enter ANNA and LVOFF through the door on the right.*

ANNA. No, they will be glad to see us. Is no one here? Then they must be in the garden.

LVOFF. I should like to know why you have brought me into this den of wolves. This is no place for you and me; honourable people should not be subjected to such influences as these.

ANNA. Listen to me, Mr. Honourable Man. When you are escorting a lady it is very bad manners to talk to her the whole way about nothing but your own honesty. Such behaviour may be perfectly honest, but it is also tedious, to say the least. Never tell a woman how good you are; let her find it out herself. My Nicholas used only to sing and tell stories when he was young as you are, and yet every woman knew at once what kind of a man he was.

LVOFF. Don't talk to me of your Nicholas; I know all about him!

ANNA. You are a very worthy man, but you don't know anything at all. Come into the garden. He never said: "I am an honest man; these surroundings are too narrow for me." He never spoke of wolves' dens, called people bears or vultures. He left the animal kingdom alone, and the most I have ever heard him say when he was excited was: "Oh, how unjust I have been to-day!" or "Annie, I am sorry for that man." That's what he would say, but you—

*ANNA and LVOFF go out. Enter AVDOTIA and FIRST GUEST through the door on the left.*

FIRST GUEST. There isn't any in the dining-room, so it must be somewhere in the pantry. We must find George. Come this way, through the sitting-room.

AVDOTIA. Oh, how I should like to get my claws into her!

*They go out through the door on the right. MARTHA and BORKIN run in laughing from the garden. SHABELSK I comes mincing behind them, laughing and rubbing his hands.*

MARTHA. Oh, I am so bored! *[Laughs loudly]* This is deadly! Every one looks as if he had swallowed a poker. I am frozen to the marrow by this icy dullness. *[She skips about]* Let us do something!

*BORKIN catches her by the waist and kisses her cheek.*

SHABELSKI. *[Laughing and snapping his fingers]* Well, I'll be hanged! *[Cackling]* Really, you know!

MARTHA. Let go! Let go, you wretch! What will the Count think? Stop, I say!

BORKIN. Angel! Jewel! Lend me twenty-three hundred roubles.

MARTHA. Most certainly not! Do what you please, but I'll thank you to leave my money alone. No, no, no! Oh, let go, will you?

SHABELSKI. *[Mincing around them]* The little birdie has its charms! *[Seriously]* Come, that will do!

BORKIN. Let us come to the point, and consider my proposition frankly as a business arrangement. Answer me honestly, without tricks and equivocations, do you agree to do it or not? Listen to me; *[Pointing to Shabelski]* he needs money to the amount of at least three thousand a year; you need a husband. Do you want to be a Countess?

SHABELSKI. *[Laughing loudly]* Oh, the cynic!

BORKIN. Do you want to be a Countess or not?

MARTHA. *[Excitedly]* Wait a minute; really, Misha, these things aren't done in a second like this. If the Count wants to marry me, let him ask me himself, and—and—I don't see, I don't understand—all this is so sudden——

BORKIN. Come, don't let us beat about the bush; this is a business arrangement. Do you agree or not?

SHABELSKI. *[Chuckling and rubbing his hands]* Supposing I do marry her, eh? Hang it, why shouldn't I play her this shabby trick? What do you say, little puss? *[He kisses her cheek]* Dearest chick-a-biddy!

MARTHA. Stop! Stop! I hardly know what I am doing. Go away! No—don't go!

BORKIN. Answer at once: is it yes or no? We can't stand here forever.

MARTHA. Look here, Count, come and visit me for three or four days. It is gay at my house, not like this place. Come to-morrow. *[To BORKIN]* Or is this all a joke?

BORKIN. *[Angrily]* How could I joke on such a serious subject?

MARTHA. Wait! Stop! Oh, I feel faint! A Countess! I am fainting, I am falling!

*BORKIN and SHABELSKI laugh and catch her by the arms. They kiss her cheeks and lead her out through the door on the right. IVANOFF and SASHA run in from the garden.*

IVANOFF. *[Desperately clutching his head]* It can't be true! Don't Sasha, don't! Oh, I implore you not to!

SASHA. I love you madly. Without you my life can have no meaning, no happiness, no hope.

IVANOFF. Why, why do you say that? What do you mean? Little Sasha, don't say it!

SASHA. You were the only joy of my childhood; I loved you body and soul then, as myself, but now—Oh, I love you, Nicholas! Take me with you to the ends of the earth, wherever you wish; but for heaven's sake let us go at once, or I shall die.

IVANOFF. *[Shaking with wild laughter]* What is this? Is it the beginning for me of a new life? Is it, Sasha? Oh, my happiness, my joy! *[He draws her to him]* My freshness, my youth!

*Enter ANNA from the garden. She sees her husband and SASHA, and stops as if petrified.*

IVANOFF. Oh, then I shall live once more? And work?

IVANOFF and SASHA kiss each other. After the kiss they look around and see ANNA.

IVANOFF. *[With horror]* Sarah!

## The curtain falls

# ACT III

*Library in IVANOFF'S house. On the walls hang maps, pictures, guns, pistols, sickles, whips, etc. A writing-table. On it lie in disorder knick-knacks, papers, books, parcels, and several revolvers. Near the papers stand a lamp, a decanter of vodka, and a plate of salted herrings. Pieces of bread and cucumber are scattered about. SHABELSKI and LEBEDIEFF are sitting at the writing-table. BORKIN is sitting astride a chair in the middle of the room. PETER is standing near the door.*

LEBEDIEFF. The policy of France is clear and definite; the French know what they want: it is to skin those German sausages, but the Germans must sing another song; France is not the only thorn in their flesh.

SHABELSKI. Nonsense! In my opinion the Germans are cowards and the French are the same. They are showing their teeth at one another, but you can take my word for it, they will not do more than that; they'll never fight!

BORKIN. Why should they fight? Why all these congresses, this arming and expense? Do you know what I would do in their place? I would catch all the dogs in the kingdom and inoculate them with Pasteur's serum, then I would let them loose in the enemy's country, and the enemies would all go mad in a month.

LEBEDIEFF. *[Laughing]* His head is small, but the great ideas are hidden away in it like fish in the sea!

SHABELSKI. Oh, he is a genius.

LEBEDIEFF. Heaven help you, Misha, you are a funny chap. *[He stops laughing]* But how is this, gentlemen? Here we are talking Germany, Germany, and never a word about vodka! Repetatur! *[He fills three glasses]* Here's to you all! *[He drinks and eats]* This herring is the best of all relishes.

SHABELSKI. No, no, these cucumbers are better; every wise man since the creation of the world has been trying to invent something better than a salted cucumber, and not one has succeeded. *[To PETER]* Peter, go and fetch some more cucumbers. And Peter, tell the cook to make four little onion pasties, and see that we get them hot.

*PETER goes out.*

LEBEDIEFF. Caviar is good with vodka, but it must be prepared with skill. Take a quarter of a pound of pressed caviar, two little onions, and a little olive oil; mix them together and put a slice of lemon on top—so! Lord! The very perfume would drive you crazy!

BORKIN. Roast snipe are good too, but they must be cooked right. They should first be cleaned, then sprinkled with bread crumbs, and roasted until they will crackle between the teeth—crunch, crunch!

SHABELSKI. We had something good at Martha's yesterday: white mushrooms.

LEBEDIEFF. You don't say so!

SHABELSKI. And they were especially well prepared, too, with onions and bay-leaves and spices, you know. When the dish was opened, the odour that floated out was simply intoxicating!

LEBEDIEFF. What do you say, gentlemen? Repetatur! *[He drinks]* Good health to you! *[He looks at his watch]* I must be going. I can't wait for Nicholas. So you say Martha gave you mushrooms? We haven't seen one at home. Will you please tell me, Count, what plot you are hatching that takes you to Martha's so often?

SHABELSKI. *[Nodding at BORKIN]* He wants me to marry her.

LEBEDIEFF. Wants you to marry her! How old are you?

SHABELSKI. Sixty-two.

LEBEDIEFF. Really, you are just the age to marry, aren't you? And Martha is just suited to you!

BORKIN. This is not a question of Martha, but of Martha's money.

LEBEDIEFF. Aren't you moonstruck, and don't you want the moon too?

SHABELSKI. Borkin here is quite in earnest about it; the clever fellow is sure I shall obey orders, and marry Martha.

BORKIN. What do you mean? Aren't you sure yourself?

SHABELSKI. Are you mad? I never was sure of anything. Bah!

BORKIN. Many thanks! I am much obliged to you for the information. So you are trying to fool me, are you? First you say you will marry Martha and then you say you won't; the devil only knows which you really mean, but I have given her my word of honour that you will. So you have changed your mind, have you?

SHABELSKI. He is actually in earnest; what an extraordinary man!

BORKIN. *[losing his temper]* If that is how you feel about it, why have you turned an honest woman's head? Her heart is set on your title, and she can neither eat nor sleep for thinking of it. How can you make a jest of such things? Do you think such behaviour is honourable?

SHABELSKI. *[Snapping his fingers]* Well, why not play her this shabby trick, after all? Eh? Just out of spite? I shall certainly do it, upon my word I shall! What a joke it will be!

*Enter LVOFF.*

LEBEDIEFF. We bow before you, Aesculapius! *[He shakes hands with LVOFF and sings]*

"Doctor, doctor, save, oh, save me,
I am scared to death of dying!"

LVOFF. Hasn't Ivanoff come home yet?

LEBEDIEFF. Not yet. I have been waiting for him myself for over an hour.

*LVOFF walks impatiently up and down.*

LEBEDIEFF. How is Anna to-day?

LVOFF. Very ill.

LEBEDIEFF. *[Sighing]* May one go and pay one's respects to her?

LVOFF. No, please don't. She is asleep, I believe.

LEBEDIEFF. She is a lovely, charming woman. *[Sighing]* The day she fainted at our house, on Sasha's birthday, I saw that she had not much longer to live, poor thing. Let me see, why did she faint? When I ran up, she was lying on the floor, ashy white, with Nicholas on his knees beside her, and Sasha was standing by them in tears. Sasha and I went about almost crazy for a week after that.

SHABELSKI. *[To LVOFF]* Tell me, most honoured disciple of science, what scholar discovered that the frequent visits of a young doctor were beneficial to ladies suffering from affections of the chest?

It is a remarkable discovery, remarkable! Would you call such treatment Allopathic or Homeopathic?

*LVOFF tries to answer, but makes an impatient gesture instead, and walks out of the room.*

SHABELSKI. What a withering look he gave me!

LEBEDIEFF. Some fiend must prompt you to say such things! Why did you offend him?

SHABELSKI. *[Angrily]* Why does he tell such lies? Consumption! No hope! She is dying! It is nonsense, I can't abide him!

LEBEDIEFF. What makes you think he is lying?

SHABELSKI. *[Gets up and walks up and down]* I can't bear to think that a living person could die like that, suddenly, without any reason at all. Don't let us talk about it!

*KOSICH runs in panting.*

KOSICH. Is Ivanoff at home? How do you do? *[He shakes hands quickly all round]* Is he at home?

BORKIN. No, he isn't.

KOSICH. *[Sits down and jumps up again]* In that case I must say good-bye; I must be going. Business, you know. I am absolutely exhausted; run off my feet!

LEBEDIEFF. Where did you blow in from?

KOSICH. From Barabanoff's. He and I have been playing cards all night; we have only just stopped. I have been absolutely fleeced; that Barabanoff is a demon at cards. *[In a tearful voice]* Just listen to this: I had a heart and he *[He turns to BORKIN, who jumps away from him]* led a diamond, and I led a heart, and he led another diamond. Well, he didn't take the trick. *[To LEBEDIEFF]* We were playing three in clubs. I had the ace and queen, and the ace and ten of spades—

LEBEDIEFF. *[Stopping up his ears]* Spare me, for heaven's sake, spare me!

KOSICH. *[To SHABELSKI]* Do you understand? I had the ace and queen of clubs, the ace and ten of spades.

SHABELSKI. *[Pushes him away]* Go away, I don't want to listen to you!

KOSICH. When suddenly misfortune overtook me. My ace of spades took the first trick—

SHABELSKI. *[Snatching up a revolver]* Leave the room, or I shall shoot!

KOSICH. *[Waving his hands]* What does this mean? Is this the Australian bush, where no one has any interests in common? Where there is no public spirit, and each man lives for himself alone? However, I must be off. My time is precious. *[He shakes hands with LEBEDIEFF]* Pass!

*General laughter. KOSICH goes out. In the doorway he runs into AVDOTIA.*

AVDOTIA. *[Shrieks]* Bad luck to you, you nearly knocked me down.

ALL. Oh, she is always everywhere at once!

AVDOTIA. So this is where you all are? I have been looking for you all over the house. Good-day to you, boys!

*[She shakes hands with everybody.]*

LEBEDIEFF. What brings you here?

AVDOTIA. Business, my son. *[To SHABELSKI]* Business connected with your highness. She commanded me to bow. *[She bows]* And to inquire after your health. She told me to say, the little birdie, that if you did not come to see her this evening she would cry her eyes out. Take him aside, she said, and whisper in his ear. But why should I make a secret of her message? We are not stealing chickens, but arranging an affair of lawful love by mutual consent of both parties. And now, although I never drink, I shall take a drop under these circumstances.

LEBEDIEFF. So shall I. *[He pours out the vodka]* You must be immortal, you old magpie! You were an old woman when I first knew you, thirty years ago.

AVDOTIA. I have lost count of the years. I have buried three husbands, and would have married a fourth if any one had wanted a woman without a dowry. I have had eight children. *[She takes up the glass]* Well, we have begun a good work, may it come to a good end! They will live happily ever after, and we shall enjoy their happiness. Love and good luck to them both! *[She drinks]* This is strong vodka!

SHABELSKI. *[laughing loudly, to LEBEDIEFF]* The funny thing is, they actually think I am in earnest. How strange! *[He gets up]* And yet, Paul, why shouldn't I play her this shabby trick? Just out of spite? To give the devil something to do, eh, Paul?

LEBEDIEFF. You are talking nonsense, Count. You and I must fix our thoughts on dying now; we have left Martha's money far behind us; our day is over.

SHABELSKI. No, I shall certainly marry her; upon my word, I shall!

*Enter IVANOFF and LVOFF.*

LVOFF. Will you please spare me five minutes of your time?

LEBEDIEFF. Hallo, Nicholas! *[He goes to meet IVANOFF]* How are you, old friend? I have been waiting an hour for you.

AVDOTIA. *[Bows]* How do you do, my son?

IVANOFF. *[Bitterly]* So you have turned my library into a bar-room again, have you? And yet I have begged you all a thousand times not to do so! *[He goes up to the table]* There, you see, you have spilt vodka all over my papers and scattered crumbs and cucumbers everywhere! It is disgusting!

LEBEDIEFF. I beg your pardon, Nicholas. Please forgive me. I have something very important to speak to you about.

BORKIN. So have I.

LVOFF. May I have a word with you?

IVANOFF. *[Pointing to LEBEDIEFF]* He wants to speak to me; wait a minute. *[To LEBEDIEFF]* Well, what is it?

LEBEDIEFF. *[To the others]* Excuse me, ladies and gentlemen, I want to speak to him in private.

SHABELSKI goes out, followed by AVDOTIA, BORKIN, and LVOFF.

IVANOFF. Paul, you may drink yourself as much as you choose, it is your weakness, but I must ask you not to make my uncle tipsy. He never used to drink at all; it is bad for him.

LEBEDIEFF. *[Startled]* My dear boy, I didn't know that! I wasn't thinking of him at all.

IVANOFF. If this old baby should die on my hands the blame would be mine, not yours. Now, what do you want? *[A pause.]*

LEBEDIEFF. The fact is, Nicholas—I really don't know how I can put it to make it seem less brutal—Nicholas, I am ashamed of myself, I am blushing, my tongue sticks to the roof of my mouth. My dear boy, put yourself in my place; remember that I am not a free man, I am as putty in the hands of my wife, a slave—forgive me!

IVANOFF. What does this mean?

LEBEDIEFF. My wife has sent me to you; do me a favour, be a friend to me, pay her the interest on the money you owe her. Believe me, she has been tormenting me and going for me tooth and nail. For heaven's sake, free yourself from her clutches!

IVANOFF. You know, Paul, that I have no money now.

LEBEDIEFF. I know, I know, but what can I do? She won't wait. If she should sue you for the money, how could Sasha and I ever look you in the face again?

IVANOFF. I am ready to sink through the floor with shame, Paul, but where, where shall I get the money? Tell me, where? There is nothing I can do but to wait until I sell my wheat in the autumn.

LEBEDIEFF. *[Shrieks]* But she won't wait! *[A pause.]*

IVANOFF. Your position is very delicate and unpleasant, but mine is even worse. *[He walks up and down in deep thought]* I am at my wit's end, there is nothing I can sell now.

LEBEDIEFF. You might go to Mulbach and get some money from him; doesn't he owe you sixty thousand roubles?

*IVANOFF makes a despairing gesture.*

LEBEDIEFF. Listen to me, Nicholas, I know you will be angry, but you must forgive an old drunkard like me. This is between friends; remember I am your friend. We were students together, both Liberals; we had the same interests and ideals; we studied together at the University of Moscow. It is our Alma Mater. *[He takes out his purse]* I have a private fund here; not a soul at home knows of its existence. Let me lend it to you. *[He takes out the money and lays it on the table]* Forget your pride; this is between friends! I should take it from you, indeed I should! *[A pause]* There is the money, one hundred thousand roubles. Take it; go to her yourself and say: "Take the money, Zinaida, and may you choke on it." Only, for heaven's sake, don't let her see by your manner that you got it from me, or she would certainly go for me, with her old jam! *[He looks intently into IVANOFF'S face]* There, there, no matter. *[He quickly takes up the money and stuffs it back into his pocket]* Don't take it, I was only joking. Forgive me! Are you hurt?

*IVANOFF waves his hand.*

LEBEDIEFF. Yes, the truth is—*[He sighs]* This is a time of sorrow and pain for you. A man, brother, is like a samovar; he cannot always stand coolly on a shelf; hot coals will be dropped into him some day, and then—fizz! The comparison is idiotic, but it is the best I can think of. *[Sighing]* Misfortunes wring the soul, and yet I am not worried about you, brother. Wheat goes through the mill, and comes out as flour, and you will come safely through your troubles; but I am annoyed, Nicholas, and angry with the people around you. The whole countryside is buzzing with gossip; where does it all start? They say you will be soon arrested for your debts, that you are a bloodthirsty murderer, a monster of cruelty, a robber.

IVANOFF. All that is nothing to me; my head is aching.

LEBEDIEFF. Because you think so much.

IVANOFF. I never think.

LEBEDIEFF. Come, Nicholas, snap your fingers at the whole thing, and drive over to visit us. Sasha loves and understands you. She is a sweet, honest, lovely girl; too good to be the child of her mother and me! Sometimes, when I look at her, I cannot believe that such a treasure could belong to a fat old drunkard like me. Go to her, talk to her, and let her cheer you. She is a good, true-hearted girl.

IVANOFF. Paul, my dear friend, please go, and leave me alone.

LEBEDIEFF. I understand, I understand! *[He glances at his watch]* Yes, I understand. *[He kisses IVANOFF]* Good-bye, I must go to the blessing of the school now. *[He goes as far as the door, then stops]* She is so clever! Sasha and I were talking about gossiping yesterday, and she flashed out this epigram: "Father," she said, "fire-flies shine at night so that the night-birds may make them their prey, and good people are made to be preyed upon by gossips and slanderers." What do you think of that? She is a genius, another George Sand!

IVANOFF. *[Stopping him as he goes out]* Paul, what is the matter with me?

LEBEDIEFF. I have wanted to ask you that myself, but I must confess I was ashamed to. I don't know, old chap. Sometimes I think your troubles have been too heavy for you, and yet I know you are not the kind to give in to them; you would not be overcome by misfortune. It must be something else, Nicholas, but what it may be I can't imagine.

IVANOFF. I can't imagine either what the matter is, unless—and yet no— *[A pause]* Well, do you see, this is what I wanted to say. I used to have a workman called Simon, you remember him. Once, at threshing-time, to show the girls how strong he was, he loaded himself with two sacks of rye, and broke his back. He died soon after. I think I have broken my back also. First I went to school, then to the university, then came the cares of this estate, all my plans—I did not believe what others did; did not marry as others did; I worked passionately, risked everything; no one else, as you know, threw their money away to right and left as I did. So I heaped the burdens on my back, and it broke. We are all heroes at twenty, ready to attack anything, to do everything, and at thirty are worn-out, useless men. How, oh, how do you account for this weariness? However, I may be quite wrong; go away, Paul, I am boring you.

LEBEDIEFF. I know what is the matter with you, old man: you got out of bed on the wrong side this morning.

IVANOFF. That is stupid, Paul, and stale. Go away!

LEBEDIEFF. It is stupid, certainly. I see that myself now. I am going at once. *[LEBEDIEFF goes out.]*

IVANOFF. *[Alone]* I am a worthless, miserable, useless man. Only a man equally miserable and suffering, as Paul is, could love or esteem me now. Good God! How I loathe myself! How bitterly I hate my voice, my hands, my thoughts, these clothes, each step I take! How ridiculous it is, how disgusting! Less than a year ago I was healthy and strong, full of pride and energy and enthusiasm. I worked with these hands here, and my words could move the dullest man to tears. I could weep with sorrow, and grow indignant at the sight of wrong. I could feel the glow of inspiration, and understand the beauty and romance of the silent nights which I used to watch through from evening until dawn, sitting at my worktable, and giving up my soul to dreams. I believed in a bright future then, and looked into it as trustfully as a child looks into its mother's eyes. And now, oh, it is terrible! I am tired and without hope; I spend my days and nights in idleness; I have no control over my feet or brain. My estate is ruined, my woods are falling under the blows of the axe. *[He weeps]* My neglected land looks up at me as reproachfully as an orphan. I expect nothing, am sorry for nothing; my whole soul trembles at the thought of each new day. And what can I think of my treatment of Sarah? I promised her love and happiness forever; I opened her eyes to the promise of a future such as she had never even dreamed of. She believed me, and though for five years I have seen her sinking under the weight of her sacrifices to me, and losing her strength in her struggles with her conscience, God knows she has never given me one angry look, or uttered one word of reproach. What is the result? That I don't love her! Why? Is it possible? Can it be true? I can't understand. She is suffering; her days are numbered; yet I fly like a contemptible coward from her white face, her sunken chest, her pleading eyes. Oh, I am ashamed, ashamed! *[A pause]* Sasha, a young girl, is sorry for me in my misery. She confesses to me that she loves me; me, almost an old man! Whereupon I lose my head, and exalted as if by music, I yell: "Hurrah for a new life and new happiness!" Next day I believe in this new life and happiness as little as I believe in my happiness at home. What is the matter with me? What is this pit I am wallowing in? What is the cause of this weakness? What does this nervousness come from? If my sick wife wounds my pride, if a servant makes a mistake, if my gun misses fire, I lose my temper and get violent and altogether unlike myself. I can't, I can't understand it; the easiest way out would be a bullet through the head!

*Enter LVOFF.*

LVOFF. I must have an explanation with you, Ivanoff.

IVANOFF. If we are going to have an explanation every day, doctor, we shall neither of us have the strength to stand it.

LVOFF. Will you be good enough to hear me?

IVANOFF. I have heard all you have told me every day, and have failed to discover yet what you want me to do.

LVOFF. I have always spoken plainly enough, and only an utterly heartless and cruel man could fail to understand me.

IVANOFF. I know that my wife is dying; I know that I have sinned irreparably; I know that you are an honest man. What more can you tell me?

LVOFF. The sight of human cruelty maddens me. The woman is dying and she has a mother and father whom she loves, and longs to see once more before she dies. They know that she is dying and that she loves them still, but with diabolical cruelty, as if to flaunt their religious zeal, they refuse to see her and forgive her. You are the man for whom she has sacrificed her home, her peace of mind, everything. Yet you unblushingly go gadding to the Lebedieffs' every evening, for reasons that are absolutely unmistakable!

IVANOFF. Ah me, it is two weeks since I was there!

LVOFF. *[Not listening to him]* To men like yourself one must speak plainly, and if you don't want to hear what I have to say, you need not listen. I always call a spade a spade; the truth is, you want her to die so that the way may be cleared for your other schemes. Be it so; but can't you wait? If, instead of crushing the life out of your wife by your heartless egoism, you let her die naturally, do you think you would lose Sasha and Sasha's money? Such an absolute Tartuffe as you are could turn the girl's head and get her money a year from now as easily as you can to-day. Why are you in such a hurry? Why do you want your wife to die now, instead of in a month's time, or a year's?

IVANOFF. This is torture! You are a very bad doctor if you think a man can control himself forever. It is all I can do not to answer your insults.

LVOFF. Look here, whom are you trying to deceive? Throw off this disguise!

IVANOFF. You who are so clever, you think that nothing in the world is easier than to understand me, do you? I married Annie for her money, did I? And when her parents wouldn't give it to me, I changed my plans, and am now hustling her out of the world so that I may marry another woman, who will bring me what I want? You think so, do you? Oh, how easy and simple it all is! But you are mistaken, doctor; in each one of us there are too many springs, too many wheels and cogs for us to judge each other by first impressions or by two or three external indications. I can not understand you, you cannot understand me, and neither of us can understand himself. A man may be a splendid doctor, and at the same time a very bad judge of human nature; you will admit that, unless you are too self-confident.

LVOFF. Do you really think that your character is so mysterious, and that I am too stupid to tell vice from virtue?

IVANOFF. It is clear that we shall never agree, so let me beg you to answer me now without any more preamble: exactly what do you want me to do? *[Angrily]* What are you after anyway? And with whom have I the honour of speaking? With my lawyer, or with my wife's doctor?

LVOFF. I am a doctor, and as such I demand that you change your conduct toward your wife; it is killing her.

IVANOFF. What shall I do? Tell me! If you understand me so much better than I understand myself, for heaven's sake tell me exactly what to do!

LVOFF. In the first place, don't be so unguarded in your behaviour.

IVANOFF. Heaven help me, do you mean to say that you understand yourself? *[He drinks some water]* Now go away; I am guilty a thousand times over; I shall answer for my sins before God; but nothing has given you the right to torture me daily as you do.

LVOFF. Who has given you the right to insult my sense of honour? You have maddened and poisoned my soul. Before I came to this place I knew that stupid, crazy, deluded people existed, but I never imagined that any one could be so criminal as to turn his mind deliberately in the direction of wickedness. I loved and esteemed humanity then, but since I have known you—

IVANOFF. I have heard all that before.

LVOFF. You have, have you?

*He goes out, shrugging his shoulders. He sees SASHA, who comes in at this moment dressed for riding.*

LVOFF. Now, however, I hope that we can understand one another!

IVANOFF. *[Startled]* Oh, Sasha, is that you?

SASHA. Yes, it is I. How are you? You didn't expect me, did you? Why haven't you been to see us?

IVANOFF. Sasha, this is really imprudent of you! Your coming will have a terrible effect on my wife!

SASHA. She won't see me; I came in by the back entrance; I shall go in a minute. I am so anxious about you. Tell me, are you well? Why haven't you been to see us for such a long time?

IVANOFF. My wife is offended already, and almost dying, and now you come here; Sasha, Sasha, this is thoughtless and unkind of you.

SASHA. How could I help coming? It is two weeks since you were at our house, and you have not answered my letters. I imagined you suffering dreadfully, or ill, or dead. I have not slept for nights. I am going now, but first tell me that you are well.

IVANOFF. No, I am not well. I am a torment to myself, and every one torments me without end. I can't stand it! And now you come here. How morbid and unnatural it all is, Sasha. I am terribly guilty.

SASHA. What dreadful, pitiful speeches you make! So you are guilty, are you? Tell me, then, what is it you have done?

IVANOFF. I don't know; I don't know!

SASHA. That is no answer. Every sinner should know what he is guilty of. Perhaps you have been forging money?

IVANOFF. That is stupid.

SASHA. Or are you guilty because you no longer love your wife? Perhaps you are, but no one is master of his feelings, and you did not mean to stop loving her. Do you feel guilty because she saw me telling you that I love you? No, that cannot be, because you did not want her to see it—

IVANOFF. *[Interrupting her]* And so on, and so on! First you say I love, and then you say I don't; that I am not master of my feelings. All these are commonplace, worn-out sentiments, with which you cannot help me.

SASHA. It is impossible to talk to you. *[She looks at a picture on the wall]* How well those dogs are drawn! Were they done from life?

IVANOFF. Yes, from life. And this whole romance of ours is a tedious old story; a man loses heart and begins to go down in the world; a girl appears, brave and strong of heart, and gives him a hand to help him to rise again. Such situations are pretty, but they are only found in novels and not in real life.

SASHA. No, they are found in real life too.

IVANOFF. Now I see how well you understand real life! My sufferings seem noble to you; you imagine you have discovered in me a second Hamlet; but my state of mind in all its phases is only fit to furnish food for contempt and derision. My contortions are ridiculous enough to make any one die of laughter, and you want to play the guardian angel; you want to do a noble deed and save me. Oh, how I hate myself to-day! I feel that this tension must soon be relieved in some way. Either I shall break something, or else—

SASHA. That is exactly what you need. Let yourself go! Smash something; break it to pieces; give a yell! You are angry with me, it was foolish of me to come here. Very well, then, get excited about it; storm at me; stamp your feet! Well, aren't you getting angry?

IVANOFF. You ridiculous girl!

SASHA. Splendid! So we are smiling at last! Be kind, do me the favour of smiling once more!

IVANOFF. *[Laughing]* I have noticed that whenever you start reforming me and saving my soul, and teaching me how to be good, your face grows naive, oh so naive, and your eyes grow as wide as if you were looking at a comet. Wait a moment; your shoulder is covered with dust. *[He brushes her shoulder]* A naive man is nothing better than a fool, but you women contrive to be naive in such a way that in you it seems sweet, and gentle, and proper, and not as silly as it really is. What a strange way you have, though, of ignoring a man as long as he is well and happy, and fastening yourselves to him as soon as he begins to whine and go down-hill! Do you actually think it is worse to be the wife of a strong man than to nurse some whimpering invalid?

SASHA. Yes, it is worse.

IVANOFF. Why do you think so? *[Laughing loudly]* It is a good thing Darwin can't hear what you are saying! He would be furious with you for degrading the human race. Soon, thanks to your kindness, only invalids and hypochondriacs will be born into the world.

SASHA. There are a great many things a man cannot understand. Any girl would rather love an unfortunate man than a fortunate one, because every girl would like to do something by loving. A man has his work to do, and so for him love is kept in the background. To talk to his wife, to walk with her in the garden, to pass the time pleasantly with her, that is all that love means to a man. But for us, love means life. I love you; that means that I dream only of how I shall cure you of your sadness, how I shall go with you to the ends of the earth. If you are in heaven, I am in heaven; if you are in the pit, I am in the pit. For instance, it would be the greatest happiness for me to write all night for you, or to watch all night that no one should wake you. I remember that three years ago, at threshing time, you came to us all dusty and sunburnt and tired, and asked for a drink. When I brought you a glass of water you were already lying on the sofa and sleeping like a dead man. You slept there for half a day, and all that time I watched by the door that no one should disturb you. How happy I was! The more a girl can do, the greater her love will be; that is, I mean, the more she feels it.

IVANOFF. The love that accomplishes things—hm—that is a fairy tale, a girl's dream; and yet, perhaps it is as it should be. *[He shrugs his shoulders]* How can I tell? *[Gaily]* On my honour, Sasha, I really am quite a respectable man. Judge for yourself: I have always liked to discuss things, but I have never in my life said that our women were corrupt, or that such and such a woman was on the down-hill path. I have always been grateful, and nothing more. No, nothing more. Dear child, how comical you are! And what a ridiculous old stupid I am! I shock all good Christian folk, and go about complaining from morning to night. *[He laughs and then leaves her suddenly]* But you must go, Sasha; we have forgotten ourselves.

SASHA. Yes, it is time to go. Good-bye. I am afraid that that honest doctor of yours will have told Anna out of a sense of duty that I am here. Take my advice: go at once to your wife and stay with her. Stay, and stay, and stay, and if it should be for a year, you must still stay, or for ten years. It is your duty. You must repent, and ask her forgiveness, and weep. That is what you ought to do, and the great thing is not to forget to do right.

IVANOFF. Again I feel as if I were going crazy; again!

SASHA. Well, heaven help you! You must forget me entirely. In two weeks you must send me a line and I shall be content with that. But I shall write to you—

*BORKIN looks in at the door.*

BORKIN. Ivanoff, may I come in? *[He sees SASHA]* I beg your pardon, I did not see you. Bonjour! *[He bows.]*

SASHA. *[Embarrassed]* How do you do?

BORKIN. You are plumper and prettier than ever.

SASHA. *[To IVANOFF]* I must go, Nicholas, I must go. *[She goes out.]*

BORKIN. What a beautiful apparition! I came expecting prose and found poetry instead. *[Sings]*

"You showed yourself to the world as a bird——"

*IVANOFF walks excitedly up and down.*

BORKIN. *[Sits down]* There is something in her, Nicholas, that one doesn't find in other women, isn't there? An elfin strangeness. *[He sighs]* Although she is without doubt the richest girl in the country, her mother is so stingy that no one will have her. After her mother's death Sasha will have the whole fortune, but until then she will only give her ten thousand roubles and an old flat-iron, and to get that she will have to humble herself to the ground. *[He feels in his pockets]* Will you have a smoke? *[He offers IVANOFF his cigarette case]* These are very good.

IVANOFF. *[Comes toward BORKIN stifled with rage]* Leave my house this instant, and don't you ever dare to set foot in it again! Go this instant!

*BORKIN gets up and drops his cigarette.*

IVANOFF. Go at once!

BORKIN. Nicholas, what do you mean? Why are you so angry?

IVANOFF. Why! Where did you get those cigarettes? Where? You think perhaps that I don't know where you take the old man every day, and for what purpose?

BORKIN. *[Shrugs his shoulders]* What business is it of yours?

IVANOFF. You blackguard, you! The disgraceful rumours that you have been spreading about me have made me disreputable in the eyes of the whole countryside. You and I have nothing in common, and I ask you to leave my house this instant.

BORKIN. I know that you are saying all this in a moment of irritation, and so I am not angry with you. Insult me as much as you please. *[He picks up his cigarette]* It is time though, to shake off this melancholy of yours; you're not a schoolboy.

IVANOFF. What did I tell you? *[Shuddering]* Are you making fun of me?

*Enter ANNA.*

BORKIN. There now, there comes Anna! I shall go.

*IVANOFF stops near the table and stands with his head bowed.*

ANNA. *[After a pause]* What did she come here for? What did she come here for, I ask you?

IVANOFF. Don't ask me, Annie. *[A pause]* I am terribly guilty. Think of any punishment you want to inflict on me; I can stand anything, but don't, oh, don't ask questions!

ANNA. *[Angrily]* So that is the sort of man you are? Now I understand you, and can see how degraded, how dishonourable you are! Do you remember that you came to me once and lied to me about your love? I believed you, and left my mother, my father, and my faith to follow you. Yes, you lied to me of goodness and honour, of your noble aspirations and I believed every word——

IVANOFF. I have never lied to you, Annie.

ANNA. I have lived with you five years now, and I am tired and ill, but I have always loved you and have never left you for a moment. You have been my idol, and what have you done? All this time you have been deceiving me in the most dastardly way——

IVANOFF. Annie, don't say what isn't so. I have made mistakes, but I have never told a lie in my life. You dare not accuse me of that!

ANNA. It is all clear to me now. You married me because you expected my mother and father to forgive me and give you my money; that is what you expected.

IVANOFF. Good Lord, Annie! If I must suffer like this, I must have the patience to bear it. *[He begins to weep.]*

ANNA. Be quiet! When you found that I wasn't bringing you any money, you tried another game. Now I remember and understand everything. *[She begins to cry]* You have never loved me or been faithful to me—never!

IVANOFF. Sarah! That is a lie! Say what you want, but don't insult me with a lie!

ANNA. You dishonest, degraded man! You owe money to Lebedieff, and now, to escape paying your debts, you are trying to turn the head of his daughter and betray her as you have betrayed me. Can you deny it?

IVANOFF. *[Stifled with rage]* For heaven's sake, be quiet! I can't answer for what I may do! I am choking with rage and I—I might insult you!

ANNA. I am not the only one whom you have basely deceived. You have always blamed Borkin for all your dishonest tricks, but now I know whose they are.

IVANOFF. Sarah, stop at once and go away, or else I shall say something terrible. I long to say a dreadful, cruel thing *[He shrieks]* Hold your tongue, Jewess!

ANNA. I won't hold my tongue! You have deceived me too long for me to be silent now.

IVANOFF. So you won't be quiet? *[He struggles with himself]* Go, for heaven's sake!

ANNA. Go now, and betray Sasha!

IVANOFF. Know then that you—are dying! The doctor told me that you are dying.

ANNA. *[Sits down and speaks in a low voice]* When did he

IVANOFF. *[Clutches his head with both hands]* Oh, how guilty I am—how guilty! *[He sobs.]*

## The curtain falls.

# ACT IV

*About a year passes between the third and fourth acts.*

*A sitting-room in LEBEDIEFF'S house. In the middle of the wall at the back of the room is an arch dividing the sitting-room from the ballroom. To the right and left are doors. Some old bronzes are placed about the room; family portraits are hanging on the walls. Everything is arranged as if for some festivity. On the piano lies a violin; near it stands a violoncello. During the entire act guests, dressed as for a ball, are seen walking about in the ball-room.*

*Enter LVOFF, looking at his watch.*

LVOFF. It is five o'clock. The ceremony must have begun. First the priest will bless them, and then they will be led to the church to be married. Is this how virtue and justice triumph? Not being able to rob Sarah, he has tortured her to death; and now he has found another victim whom he will deceive until he has robbed her, and then he will get rid of her as he got rid of poor Sarah. It is the same old sordid story. *[A pause]* He will live to a fine old age in the seventh heaven of happiness, and will die with a clear conscience. No, Ivanoff, it shall not be! I shall drag your villainy to light! And when I tear off that accursed mask of yours and show you to the world as the blackguard you are, you shall come plunging down headfirst from your seventh heaven, into a pit so deep that the devil himself will not be able to drag you out of it! I am a man of honour; it is my duty to interfere in such cases as yours, and to open the eyes of the blind. I shall fulfil my mission, and to-morrow will find me far away from this accursed place. *[Thoughtfully]* But what shall I do? To have an explanation with Lebedieff would be a hopeless task. Shall I make a scandal, and challenge Ivanoff to a duel? I am as excited as a child, and have entirely lost the power of planning anything. What shall I do? Shall I fight a duel?

*Enter KOSICH. He goes gaily up to LVOFF.*

KOSICH. I declared a little slam in clubs yesterday, and made a grand slam! Only that man Barabanoff spoilt the whole game for me again. We were playing—well, I said "No trumps" and he said "Pass." "Two in clubs," he passed again. I made it two in hearts. He said "Three in clubs," and just imagine, can you, what happened? I declared a little slam and he never showed his ace! If he had showed his ace, the villain, I should have declared a grand slam in no trumps!

LVOFF. Excuse me, I don't play cards, and so it is impossible for me to share your enthusiasm. When does the ceremony begin?

KOSICH. At once, I think. They are now bringing Zuzu to herself again. She is bellowing like a bull; she can't bear to see the money go.

LVOFF. And what about the daughter?

KOSICH. No, it is the money. She doesn't like this affair anyway. He is marrying her daughter, and that means he won't pay his debts for a long time. One can't sue one's son-in-law.

*MARTHA, very much dressed up, struts across the stage past LVOFF and KOSICH. The latter bursts out laughing behind his hand. MARTHA looks around.*

MARTHA. Idiot!

*KOSICH digs her in the ribs and laughs loudly.*

MARTHA. Boor!

KOSICH. *[Laughing]* The woman's head has been turned. Before she fixed her eye on a title she was like any other woman, but there is no coming near her now! *[Angrily]* A boor, indeed!

LVOFF. *[Excitedly]* Listen to me; tell me honestly, what do you think of Ivanoff?

KOSICH. He's no good at all. He plays cards like a lunatic. This is what happened last year during Lent: I, the Count, Borkin and he, sat down to a game of cards. I led a——

LVOFF *[Interrupting him]* Is he a good man?

KOSICH. He? Yes, he's a good one! He and the Count are a pair of trumps. They have keen noses for a good game. First, Ivanoff set his heart on the Jewess, then, when his schemes failed in that quarter, he turned his thoughts toward Zuzu's money-bags. I'll wager you he'll ruin Zuzu in a year. He will ruin Zuzu, and the Count will ruin Martha. They will gather up all the money they can lay hands on, and live happily ever after! But, doctor, why are you so pale to-day? You look like a ghost.

LVOFF. Oh, it's nothing. I drank a little too much yesterday.

*Enter LEBEDIEFF with SASHA.*

LEBEDIEFF. We can have our talk here. *[To LVOFF and KOSICH]* Go into the ball-room, you two old fogies, and talk to the girls. Sasha and I want to talk alone here.

KOSICH. *[Snapping his fingers enthusiastically as he goes by SASHA]* What a picture! A queen of trumps!

LEBEDIEFF. Go along, you old cave-dweller; go along.

*KOSICH and LVOFF go out.*

LEBEDIEFF. Sit down, Sasha, there—*[He sits down and looks about him]* Listen to me attentively and with proper respect. The fact is, your mother has asked me to say this, do you understand? I am not speaking for myself. Your mother told me to speak to you.

SASHA. Papa, do say it briefly!

LEBEDIEFF. When you are married we mean to give you fifteen thousand roubles. Please don't let us have any discussion about it afterward. Wait, now! Be quiet! That is only the beginning. The best is yet to come. We have allotted you fifteen thousand roubles, but in consideration of the fact that Nicholas owes your mother nine thousand, that sum will have to be deducted from the amount we mean to give you. Very well. Now, beside that——

SASHA. Why do you tell me all this?

LEBEDIEFF. Your mother told me to.

SASHA. Leave me in peace! If you had any respect for yourself or me you could not permit yourself to speak to me in this way. I don't want your money! I have not asked for it, and never shall.

LEBEDIEFF. What are you attacking me for? The two rats in Gogol's fable sniffed first and then ran away, but you attack without even sniffing.

SASHA. Leave me in peace, and do not offend my ears with your twopenny calculations.

LEBEDIEFF. *[Losing his temper]* Bah! You all, every one of you, do all you can to make me cut my throat or kill somebody. One of you screeches and fusses all day and counts every penny, and the other is so clever and humane and emancipated that she cannot understand her own father! I offend your ears, do I? Don't you realise that before I came here to offend your ears I was being torn to pieces over there, *[He points to the door]* literally drawn and quartered? So you cannot understand? You two have addled my brain till I am utterly at my wits' end; indeed I am! *[He goes toward the door, and stops]* I don't like this business at all; I don't like any thing about you—

SASHA. What is it, especially, that you don't like?

LEBEDIEFF. Everything, everything!

SASHA. What do you mean by everything?

LEBEDIEFF. Let me explain exactly what I mean. Everything displeases me. As for your marriage, I simply can't abide it. *[He goes up to SASHA and speaks caressingly]* Forgive me, little Sasha, this marriage may be a wise one; it may be honest and not misguided, nevertheless, there is something about the whole affair that is not right; no, not right! You are not marrying as other girls do; you are young and fresh and pure as a drop of water, and he is a widower, battered and worn. Heaven help him. I don't understand him at all. *[He kisses his daughter]* Forgive me for saying so, Sasha, but I am sure there is something crooked about this affair; it is making a great deal of talk. It seems people are saying that first Sarah died, and then suddenly Ivanoff wanted to marry you. *[Quickly]* But, no, I am like an old woman; I am gossiping like a magpie. You must not listen to me or any one, only to your own heart.

SASHA. Papa, I feel myself that there is something wrong about my marriage. Something wrong, yes, wrong! Oh, if you only knew how heavy my heart is; this is unbearable! I am frightened and ashamed to confess this; Papa darling, you must help me, for heaven's sake. Oh, can't you tell me what I should do?

LEBEDIEFF. What is the matter, Sasha, what is it?

SASHA. I am so frightened, more frightened than I have ever been before. *[She glances around her]* I cannot understand him now, and I never shall. He has not smiled or looked straight into my eyes once since we have been engaged. He is forever complaining and apologising for something; hinting at some crime he is guilty of, and trembling. I am so tired! There are even moments when I think—I think—that I do not love him as I should, and when he comes to see us, or talks to me, I get so tired! What does it mean, dear father? I am afraid.

LEBEDIEFF. My darling, my only child, do as your old father advises you; give him up!

SASHA. *[Frightened]* Oh! How can you say that?

LEBEDIEFF. Yes, do it, little Sasha! It will make a scandal, all the tongues in the country will be wagging about it, but it is better to live down a scandal than to ruin one's life.

SASHA. Don't say that, father. Oh, don't. I refuse to listen! I must crush such gloomy thoughts. He is good and unhappy and misunderstood. I shall love him and learn to understand him. I shall set him on his feet again. I shall do my duty. That is settled.

LEBEDIEFF. This is not your duty, but a delusion—

SASHA. We have said enough. I have confessed things to you that I have not dared to admit even to myself. Don't speak about this to any one. Let us forget it.

LEBEDIEFF. I am hopelessly puzzled, and either my mind is going from old age or else you have all grown very clever, but I'll be hanged if I understand this business at all.

*Enter SHABELSKI.*

SHABELSKI. Confound you all and myself, too! This is maddening!

LEBEDIEFF. What do you want?

SHABELSKI Seriously, I must really do something horrid and rascally, so that not only I but everybody else will be disgusted by it. I certainly shall find something to do, upon my word I shall! I have already told Borkin to announce that I am to be married. *[He laughs]* Everybody is a scoundrel and I must be one too!

LEBEDIEFF. I am tired of you, Matthew. Look here, man you talk in such a way that, excuse my saying so, you will soon find yourself in a lunatic asylum!

SHABELSKI. Could a lunatic asylum possibly be worse than this house, or any other? Kindly take me there at once. Please do! Everybody is wicked and futile and worthless and stupid; I am an object of disgust to myself, I don't believe a word I say——-

LEBEDIEFF. Let me give you a piece of advice, old man; fill your mouth full of tow, light it, and blow at everybody. Or, better still, take your hat and go home. This is a wedding, we all want to enjoy ourselves and you are croaking like a raven. Yes, really.

*SHABELSKI leans on the piano and begins to sob.*

LEBEDIEFF. Good gracious, Matthew, Count! What is it, dear Matthew, old friend? Have I offended you? There, forgive me; I didn't mean to hurt you. Come, drink some water.

SHABELSKI. I don't want any water. *[Raises his head.]*

LEBEDIEFF. What are you crying about?

SHABELSKI. Nothing in particular; I was just crying.

LEBEDIEFF. Matthew, tell me the truth, what is it? What has happened?

SHABELSKI. I caught sight of that violoncello, and—and—I remembered the Jewess.

LEBEDIEFF. What an unfortunate moment you have chosen to remember her. Peace be with her! But don't think of her now.

SHABELSKI. We used to play duets together. She was a beautiful, a glorious woman.

*SASHA sobs.*

LEBEDIEFF. What, are you crying too? Stop, Sasha! Dear me, they are both howling now, and I—and I—Do go away; the guests will see you!

SHABELSKI. Paul, when the sun is shining, it is gay even in a cemetery. One can be cheerful even in old age if it is lighted by hope; but I have nothing to hope for—not a thing!

LEBEDIEFF. Yes, it is rather sad for you. You have no children, no money, no occupation. Well, but what is there to be done about it? *[To SASHA]* What is the matter with you, Sasha?

SHABELSKI. Paul, give me some money. I will repay you in the next world. I would go to Paris and see my wife's grave. I have given away a great deal of money in my life, half my fortune indeed, and I have a right to ask for some now. Besides, I am asking a friend.

LEBEDIEFF. *[Embarrassed]* My dear boy, I haven't a penny. All right though. That is to say, I can't promise anything, but you understand—very well, very well. *[Aside]* This is agony!

*Enter MARTHA.*

MARTHA. Where is my partner? Count, how dare you leave me alone? You are horrid! *[She taps SHABELSKI on the arm with her fan]*

SHABELSKI. *[Impatiently]* Leave me alone! I can't abide you!

MARTHA. *[Frightened]* How? What?

SHABELSKI. Go away!

MARTHA. *[Sinks into an arm-chair]* Oh! Oh! Oh! *[She bursts into tears.]*

*Enter ZINAIDA crying.*

ZINAIDA. Some one has just arrived; it must be one of the ushers. It is time for the ceremony to begin.

SASHA. *[Imploringly]* Mother!

LEBEDIEFF. Well, now you are all bawling. What a quartette! Come, come, don't let us have any more of this dampness! Matthew! Martha! If you go on like this, I—I—shall cry too. *[Bursts into tears]* Heavens!

ZINAIDA. If you don't need your mother any more, if you are determined not to obey her, I shall have to do as you want, and you have my blessing.

*Enter IVANOFF, dressed in a long coat, with gloves on.*

LEBEDIEFF This is the finishing touch! What do you want?

SHABELSKI. Why are you here?

IVANOFF. I beg your pardon, you must allow me to speak to Sasha alone.

LEBEDIEFF. The bridegroom must not come to see the bride before the wedding. It is time for you to go to the church.

IVANOFF. Paul, I implore you.

*LEBEDIEFF shrugs his shoulders. LEBEDIEFF, ZINAIDA, SHABELSKI, and MARTHA go out.*

SASHA. *[Sternly]* What do you want?

IVANOFF. I am choking with anger; I cannot speak calmly. Listen to me; as I was dressing just now for the wedding, I looked in the glass and saw how grey my temples were. Sasha, this must not be! Let us end this senseless comedy before it is too late. You are young and pure; you have all your life before you, but I——

SASHA. The same old story; I have heard it a thousand times and I am tired of it. Go quickly to the church and don't keep everybody waiting!

IVANOFF. I shall go straight home, and you must explain to your family somehow that there is to be no wedding. Explain it as you please. It is time we came to our senses. I have been playing the part of Hamlet and you have been playing the part of a noble and devoted girl. We have kept up the farce long enough.

SASHA. *[Losing her temper]* How can you speak to me like this? I won't have it.

IVANOFF. But I am speaking, and will continue to speak.

SASHA. What do you mean by coming to me like this? Your melancholy has become absolutely ridiculous!

IVANOFF. No, this is not melancholy. It is ridiculous, is it? Yes, I am laughing, and if it were possible for me to laugh at myself a thousand times more bitterly I should do so and set the whole world laughing, too, in derision. A fierce light has suddenly broken over my soul; as I looked into the glass just now, I laughed at myself, and nearly went mad with shame. *[He laughs]* Melancholy indeed! Noble grief! Uncontrollable sorrow! It only remains for me now to begin to write verses! Shall I mope and complain, sadden everybody I meet, confess that my manhood has gone forever, that I have decayed, outlived my purpose, that I have given myself up to cowardice and am bound hand and foot by this loathsome melancholy? Shall I confess all this when the sun is shining so brightly and when even the ants are carrying their little burdens in peaceful self-content? No, thanks. Can I endure the knowledge that one will look upon me as a fraud, while another pities me, a third lends me a helping hand, or worst of all, a fourth listens reverently to my sighs, looks upon me as a new Mahomet, and expects me to expound a new religion every moment? No, thank God for the pride and conscience he has left me still. On my way here I laughed at myself, and it seemed to me that the flowers and birds were laughing mockingly too.

SASHA. This is not anger, but madness!

IVANOFF. You think so, do you? No, I am not mad. I see things in their right light now, and my mind is as clear as your conscience. We love each other, but we shall never be married. It makes no difference how I rave and grow bitter by myself, but I have no right to drag another down with me. My melancholy robbed my wife of the last year of her life. Since you have been engaged to me you have forgotten how to laugh and have aged five years. Your father, to whom life was always simple and clear, thanks to me, is now unable to understand anybody. Wherever I go, whether hunting or visiting, it makes no difference, I carry depression, dulness, and discontent along with me. Wait! Don't interrupt me! I am bitter and harsh, I know, but I am stifled with rage. I cannot speak otherwise. I have never lied, and I never used to find fault with my lot, but since I have begun to complain of everything, I find fault with it involuntarily, and against my will. When I murmur at my fate every one who hears me is seized with the same disgust of life and begins to grumble too. And what a strange way I have of looking at things! Exactly as if I were doing the world a favour by living in it. Oh, I am contemptible.

SASHA. Wait a moment. From what you have just said, it is obvious that you are tired of your melancholy mood, and that the time has come for you to begin life afresh. How splendid!

IVANOFF. I don't see anything splendid about it. How can I lead a new life? I am lost forever. It is time we both understood that. A new life indeed!

SASHA. Nicholas, come to your senses. How can you say you are lost? What do you mean by such cynicism? No, I won't listen to you or talk with you. Go to the church!

IVANOFF. I am lost!

SASHA. Don't talk so loud; our guests will hear you!

IVANOFF. If an intelligent, educated, and healthy man begins to complain of his lot and go down-hill, there is nothing for him to do but to go on down until he reaches the bottom—there is no hope for him. Where could my salvation come from? How can I save myself? I cannot drink, because it makes my head ache. I never could write bad poetry. I cannot pray for strength and see anything lofty in the languor of my soul. Laziness is laziness and weakness weakness. I can find no other names for them. I am lost, I am lost; there is no doubt of that. *[Looking around]* Some one might come in; listen, Sasha, if you love me you must help me. Renounce me this minute; quickly!

SASHA. Oh, Nicholas! If you only knew how you are torturing me; what agony I have to endure for your sake! Good thoughtful friend, judge for yourself; can I possibly solve such a problem? Each day you put some horrible problem before me, each one more difficult than the last. I wanted to help you with my love, but this is martyrdom!

IVANOFF. And when you are my wife the problems will be harder than ever. Understand this: it is not love that is urging you to take this step, but the obstinacy of an honest nature. You have undertaken to reawaken the man in me and to save me in the face of every difficulty, and you are flattered by the hope of achieving your object. You are willing to give up now, but you are prevented from doing it by a feeling that is a false one. Understand yourself!

SASHA. What strange, wild reasoning! How can I give you up now? How can I? You have no mother, or sister, or friends. You are ruined; your estate has been destroyed; every one is speaking ill of you—

IVANOFF. It was foolish of me to come here; I should have done as I wanted to—

*Enter LEBEDIEFF.*

SASHA. *[Running to her father]* Father! He has rushed over here like a madman, and is torturing me! He insists that I should refuse to marry him; he says he doesn't want to drag me down with him. Tell him that I won't accept his generosity. I know what I am doing!

LEBEDIEFF. I can't understand a word of what you are saying. What generosity?

IVANOFF. This marriage is not going to take place.

SASHA. It is going to take place. Papa, tell him that it is going to take place.

LEBEDIEFF. Wait! Wait! What objection have you to the marriage?

IVANOFF. I have explained it all to her, but she refuses to understand me.

LEBEDIEFF. Don't explain it to her, but to me, and explain it so that I may understand. God forgive you, Nicholas, you have brought a great deal of darkness into our lives. I feel as if I were living in a museum; I look about me and don't understand anything I see. This is torture. What on earth can an old man like me do with you? Shall I challenge you to a duel?

IVANOFF. There is no need of a duel. All you need is a head on your shoulders and a knowledge of the Russian language.

SASHA. *[Walks up and down in great excitement]* This is dreadful, dreadful! Absolutely childish.

LEBEDIEFF. Listen to me, Nicholas; from your point of view what you are doing is quite right and proper, according to the rules of psychology, but I think this affair is a scandal and a great misfortune. I am an old man; hear me out for the last time. This is what I want to say to you: calm yourself; look at things simply, as every one else does; this is a simple world. The ceiling is white; your boots are black; sugar is sweet. You love Sasha and she loves you. If you love her, stay with her; if you don't, leave her. We shan't blame you. It is all perfectly simple. You are two healthy, intelligent, moral young people; thank God, you both have food and clothing—what more do you want? What if you have no money? That is no great misfortune—happiness is not bought with wealth. Of course your estate is mortgaged, Nicholas, as I know, and you have no money to pay the interest on the debt, but I am Sasha's father. I understand. Her mother can do as she likes—if she won't give any money, why, confound her, then she needn't, that's all! Sasha has just said that she does not want her part of it. As for your principles, Schopenhauer and all that, it is all folly. I have one hundred thousand roubles in the bank. *[Looking around him]* Not a soul in the house knows it; it was my grandmother's money. That shall be for you both. Take it, give Matthew two thousand—

*[The guests begin to collect in the ball-room].*

IVANOFF. It is no use discussing it any more, I must act as my conscience bids me.

SASHA. And I shall act as my conscience bids me—you may say what you please; I refuse to let you go! I am going to call my mother.

LEBEDIEFF. I am utterly puzzled.

IVANOFF. Listen to me, poor old friend. I shall not try to explain myself to you. I shall not tell you whether I am honest or a rascal, healthy or mad; you wouldn't understand me. I was young once; I have been eager and sincere and intelligent. I have loved and hated and believed as no one else has. I have worked and hoped and tilted against windmills with the strength of ten—not sparing my strength, not knowing what life was. I shouldered a load that broke my back. I drank, I worked, I excited myself, my energy knew no bounds. Tell me, could I have done otherwise? There are so few of us and so much to do, so much to do! And see how cruelly fate has revenged herself on me, who fought with her so bravely! I am a broken man. I am old at thirty. I have submitted myself to old age. With a heavy head and a sluggish mind, weary, used up, discouraged, without faith or love or an object in life, I wander like a shadow among other men, not knowing why I am alive or what it is that I want. Love seems to me to be folly, caresses false. I see no sense in working or playing, and all passionate speeches seem insipid and tiresome. So I carry my sadness with me wherever I go; a cold weariness, a discontent, a horror of life. Yes, I am lost for ever and ever. Before you stands a man who at thirty-five is disillusioned, wearied by fruitless efforts, burning with shame, and mocking at his own weakness. Oh, how my pride rebels against it all! What mad fury chokes me! *[He staggers]* I am staggering—my strength is failing me. Where is Matthew? Let him take me home.

*[Voices from the ball-room]* The best man has arrived!

*Enter SHABELSKI.*

SHABELSKI. In an old worn-out coat—without gloves! How many scornful glances I get for it! Such silly jokes and vulgar grins! Disgusting people.

*Enter BORKIN quickly. He is carrying a bunch of flowers and is in a dress-coat. He wears a flower in his buttonhole.*

BORKIN. This is dreadful! Where is he? *[To IVANOFF]* They have been waiting for you for a long time in the church, and here you are talking philosophy! What a funny chap you are. Don't you know you must not go to church with the bride, but alone, with me? I shall then come back for her. Is it possible you have not understood that? You certainly are an extraordinary man!

*Enter LVOFF.*

LVOFF. *[To IVANOFF]* Ah! So you are here? *[Loudly]* Nicholas Ivanoff, I denounce you to the world as a scoundrel!

IVANOFF. *[Coldly]* Many thanks!

BORKIN. *[To LVOFF]* Sir, this is dastardly! I challenge you to a duel!

LVOFF. Monsieur Borkin, I count it a disgrace not only to fight with you, but even to talk to you! Monsieur Ivanoff, however, can receive satisfaction from me whenever he chooses!

SHABELSKI. Sir, I shall fight you!

SASHA. *[To LVOFF]* Why, oh why, have you insulted him? Gentlemen, I beg you, let him tell me why he has insulted him.

LVOFF. Miss Sasha, I have not insulted him without cause. I came here as a man of honour, to open your eyes, and I beg you to listen to what I have to tell you.

SASHA. What can you possibly have to tell me? That you are a man of honour? The whole world knows it. You had better tell me on your honour whether you understand what you have done or not. You have come in here as a man of honour and have insulted him so terribly that you have nearly killed me. When you used to follow him like a shadow and almost keep him from living, you were convinced that you were doing your duty and that you were acting like a man of honour. When you interfered in his private affairs, maligned him and criticised him; when you sent me and whomever else you could, anonymous letters, you imagined yourself to be an honourable man! And, thinking that that too was honourable, you, a doctor, did not even spare his dying wife or give her a moment's peace from your suspicions. And no matter what violence, what cruel wrong you committed, you still imagined yourself to be an unusually honourable and clear-sighted man.

IVANOFF. *[Laughing]* This is not a wedding, but a parliament! Bravo! Bravo!

SASHA. *[To LVOFF]* Now, think it over! Do you see what sort of a man you are, or not? Oh, the stupid, heartless people! *[Takes IVANOFF by the hand]* Come away from here Nicholas! Come, father, let us go!

IVANOFF. Where shall we go? Wait a moment. I shall soon put an end to the whole thing. My youth is awake in me again; the former Ivanoff is here once more.

*[He takes out a revolver.]*

SASHA. *[Shrieking]* I know what he wants to do! Nicholas, for God's sake!

IVANOFF. I have been slipping down-hill long enough. Now, halt! It is time to know what honour is. Out of the way! Thank you, Sasha!

SASHA. *[Shrieking]* Nicholas! For God's sake hold him!

IVANOFF. Let go! *[He rushes aside, and shoots himself.]*

**The curtain falls.**

# THE BEAR

## Translated by Julius West

### CHARACTERS

ELENA IVANOVNA POPOVA, a landowning little widow, with dimples on her cheeks
GRIGORY STEPANOVITCH SMIRNOV, a middle-aged landowner
LUKA, Popova's aged footman

# THE BEAR

*[A drawing-room in POPOVA'S house.]*

*[POPOVA is in deep mourning and has her eyes fixed on a photograph. LUKA is haranguing her.]*

LUKA. It isn't right, madam.... You're just destroying yourself. The maid and the cook have gone off fruit picking, every living being is rejoicing, even the cat understands how to enjoy herself and walks about in the yard, catching midges; only you sit in this room all day, as if this was a convent, and don't take any pleasure. Yes, really! I reckon it's a whole year that you haven't left the house!

POPOVA. I shall never go out.... Why should I? My life is already at an end. He is in his grave, and I have buried myself between four walls.... We are both dead.

LUKA. Well, there you are! Nicolai Mihailovitch is dead, well, it's the will of God, and may his soul rest in peace.... You've mourned him—and quite right. But you can't go on weeping and wearing mourning for ever. My old woman died too, when her time came. Well? I grieved over her, I wept for a month, and that's enough for her, but if I've got to weep for a whole age, well, the old woman isn't worth it. *[Sighs]* You've forgotten all your neighbours. You don't go anywhere, and you see nobody. We live, so to speak, like spiders, and never see the light. The mice have eaten my livery. It isn't as if there were no good people around, for the district's full of them. There's a regiment quartered at Riblov, and the officers are such beauties—you can never gaze your fill at them. And, every Friday, there's a ball at the camp, and every day the soldier's band plays.... Eh, my lady! You're young and beautiful, with roses in your cheek—if you only took a little pleasure. Beauty won't last long, you know. In ten years' time you'll want to be a pea-hen yourself among the officers, but they won't look at you, it will be too late.

POPOVA. *[With determination]* I must ask you never to talk to me about it! You know that when Nicolai Mihailovitch died, life lost all its meaning for me. I vowed never to the end of my days to cease to wear mourning, or to see the light.... You hear? Let his ghost see how well I love him.... Yes, I know it's no secret to you that he was often unfair to me, cruel, and... and even unfaithful, but I shall be true till death, and show him how I can love. There, beyond the grave, he will see me as I was before his death....

LUKA. Instead of talking like that you ought to go and have a walk in the garden, or else order Toby or Giant to be harnessed, and then drive out to see some of the neighbours.

POPOVA. Oh! *[Weeps.]*

LUKA. Madam! Dear madam! What is it? Bless you!

POPOVA. He was so fond of Toby! He always used to ride on him to the Korchagins and Vlasovs. How well he could ride! What grace there was in his figure when he pulled at the reins with all his strength! Do you remember? Toby, Toby! Tell them to give him an extra feed of oats.

LUKA. Yes, madam. *[A bell rings noisily.]*

POPOVA. *[Shaking]* Who's that? Tell them that I receive nobody.

LUKA. Yes, madam. *[Exit.]*

POPOVA. *[Looks at the photograph]* You will see, Nicolas, how I can love and forgive.... My love will die out with me, only when this poor heart will cease to beat. *[Laughs through her tears]* And aren't you ashamed? I am a good and virtuous little wife. I've locked myself in, and will be true to you till the grave, and you... aren't you ashamed, you bad child? You deceived me, had rows with me, left me alone for weeks on end....

*[LUKA enters in consternation.]*

LUKA. Madam, somebody is asking for you. He wants to see you....

POPOVA. But didn't you tell him that since the death of my husband I've stopped receiving?

LUKA. I did, but he wouldn't even listen; says that it's a very pressing affair.

POPOVA. I do not receive!

LUKA. I told him so, but the... the devil... curses and pushes himself right in.... He's in the dining-room now.

POPOVA. *[Annoyed]* Very well, ask him in.... What manners! *[Exit LUKA]* How these people annoy me! What does he want of me? Why should he disturb my peace? *[Sighs]* No, I see that I shall have to go into a convent after all. *[Thoughtfully]* Yes, into a convent.... *[Enter LUKA with SMIRNOV.]*

SMIRNOV. *[To LUKA]* You fool, you're too fond of talking.... Ass! *[Sees POPOVA and speaks with respect]* Madam, I have the honour to present myself, I am Grigory Stepanovitch Smirnov, landowner and retired lieutenant of artillery! I am compelled to disturb you on a very pressing affair.

POPOVA. *[Not giving him her hand]* What do you want?

SMIRNOV. Your late husband, with whom I had the honour of being acquainted, died in my debt for one thousand two hundred roubles, on two bills of exchange. As I've got to pay the interest on a mortgage to-morrow, I've come to ask you, madam, to pay me the money to-day.

POPOVA. One thousand two hundred.... And what was my husband in debt to you for?

SMIRNOV. He used to buy oats from me.

POPOVA. *[Sighing, to LUKA]* So don't you forget, Luka, to give Toby an extra feed of oats. *[Exit LUKA]* If Nicolai Mihailovitch died in debt to you, then I shall certainly pay you, but you must excuse me to-day, as I haven't any spare cash. The day after to-morrow my steward will be back from town, and I'll give him instructions to settle your account, but at the moment I cannot do as you wish.... Moreover, it's exactly seven months to-day since the death of my husband, and I'm in a state of mind which absolutely prevents me from giving money matters my attention.

SMIRNOV. And I'm in a state of mind which, if I don't pay the interest due to-morrow, will force me to make a graceful exit from this life feet first. They'll take my estate!

POPOVA. You'll have your money the day after to-morrow.

SMIRNOV. I don't want the money the day after tomorrow, I want it to-day.

POPOVA. You must excuse me, I can't pay you.

SMIRNOV. And I can't wait till after to-morrow.

POPOVA. Well, what can I do, if I haven't the money now!

SMIRNOV. You mean to say, you can't pay me?

POPOVA. I can't.

SMIRNOV. Hm! Is that the last word you've got to say?

POPOVA. Yes, the last word.

SMIRNOV. The last word? Absolutely your last?

POPOVA. Absolutely.

SMIRNOV. Thank you so much. I'll make a note of it. *[Shrugs his shoulders]* And then people want me to keep calm! I meet a man on the road, and he asks me "Why are you always so angry, Grigory Stepanovitch?" But how on earth am I not to get angry? I want the money desperately. I rode out yesterday, early in the morning, and called on all my debtors, and not a single one of them paid up! I was just about dead-beat after it all, slept, goodness knows where, in some inn, kept by a Jew, with a vodka-barrel by my head. At last I get here, seventy versts from home, and hope to get something, and I am received by you with a "state of mind"! How shouldn't I get angry.

POPOVA. I thought I distinctly said my steward will pay you when he returns from town.

SMIRNOV. I didn't come to your steward, but to you! What the devil, excuse my saying so, have I to do with your steward!

POPOVA. Excuse me, sir, I am not accustomed to listen to such expressions or to such a tone of voice. I want to hear no more. *[Makes a rapid exit.]*

SMIRNOV. Well, there! "A state of mind."... "Husband died seven months ago!" Must I pay the interest, or mustn't I? I ask you: Must I pay, or must I not? Suppose your husband is dead, and you've got a state of mind, and nonsense of that sort.... And your steward's gone away somewhere, devil take him, what do you want me to do? Do you think I can fly away from my creditors in a balloon, or what? Or do you expect me to go and run my head into a brick wall? I go to Grusdev and he isn't at home, Yaroshevitch has hidden himself, I had a violent row with Kuritsin and nearly threw him out of the window, Mazugo has something the matter with his bowels, and this woman has "a state of mind." Not one of the swine wants to pay me! Just because I'm too gentle with them, because I'm a rag, just weak wax in their hands! I'm much too gentle with them! Well, just you wait! You'll find out what I'm like! I shan't let you play about with me, confound it! I shall jolly well stay here until she pays! Brr!... How angry I am to-day, how angry I am! All my inside is quivering with anger, and I can't even breathe.... Foo, my word, I even feel sick! *[Yells]* Waiter!

*[Enter LUKA.]*

LUKA. What is it?

SMIRNOV. Get me some kvass or water! *[Exit LUKA]* What a way to reason! A man is in desperate need of his money, and she won't pay it because, you see, she is not disposed to attend to money matters!... That's real silly feminine logic. That's why I never did like, and don't like now, to have to talk to women. I'd rather sit on a barrel of gunpowder than talk to a woman. Brr!... I feel quite chilly—and it's all on account of that little bit of fluff! I can't even see one of these poetic creatures from a distance without breaking out into a cold sweat out of sheer anger. I can't look at them. *[Enter LUKA with water.]*

LUKA. Madam is ill and will see nobody.

SMIRNOV. Get out! *[Exit LUKA]* Ill and will see nobody! No, it's all right, you don't see me.... I'm going to stay and will sit here till you give me the money. You can be ill for a week, if you like, and I'll stay here for a week.... If you're ill for a year—I'll stay for a year. I'm going to get my own, my dear! You don't get at me with your widow's weeds and your dimpled cheeks! I know those dimples! *[Shouts through the window]* Simeon, take them out! We aren't going away at once! I'm staying here! Tell them in the stable to give the horses some oats! You fool, you've let the near horse's leg get tied up in the reins again! *[Teasingly]* "Never mind...." I'll give it you. "Never mind." *[Goes away from the window]* Oh, it's bad.... The heat's frightful, nobody pays up. I slept badly, and on top of everything else here's a bit of fluff in mourning with "a state of mind."... My head's aching.... Shall I have some vodka, what? Yes, I think I will. *[Yells]* Waiter!

*[Enter LUKA.]*

LUKA. What is it?

SMIRNOV. A glass of vodka! *[Exit LUKA]* Ouf! *[Sits and inspects himself]* I must say I look well! Dust all over, boots dirty, unwashed, unkempt, straw on my waistcoat.... The dear lady may well have taken me for a brigand. *[Yawns]* It's rather impolite to come into a drawing-room in this state, but it can't be helped.... I am not here as a visitor, but as a creditor, and there's no dress specially prescribed for creditors....

*[Enter LUKA with the vodka.]*

LUKA. You allow yourself to go very far, sir....

SMIRNOV *[Angrily]* What?

LUKA. I... er... nothing... I really...

SMIRNOV. Whom are you talking to? Shut up!

LUKA. *[Aside]* The devil's come to stay.... Bad luck that brought him.... *[Exit.]*

SMIRNOV. Oh, how angry I am! So angry that I think I could grind the whole world to dust.... I even feel sick.... *[Yells]* Waiter!

*[Enter POPOVA.]*

POPOVA. *[Her eyes downcast]* Sir, in my solitude I have grown unaccustomed to the masculine voice, and I can't stand shouting. I must ask you not to disturb my peace.

SMIRNOV. Pay me the money, and I'll go.

POPOVA. I told you perfectly plainly; I haven't any money to spare; wait until the day after to-morrow.

SMIRNOV. And I told you perfectly plainly I don't want the money the day after to-morrow, but to-day. If you don't pay me to-day, I'll have to hang myself to-morrow.

POPOVA. But what can I do if I haven't got the money? You're so strange!

SMIRNOV. Then you won't pay me now? Eh?

POPOVA. I can't.

SMIRNOV. In that case I stay here and shall wait until I get it. *[Sits down]* You're going to pay me the day after to-morrow? Very well! I'll stay here until the day after to-morrow. I'll sit here all the time.... *[Jumps up]* I ask you: Have I got to pay the interest to-morrow, or haven't I? Or do you think I'm doing this for a joke?

POPOVA. Please don't shout! This isn't a stable!

SMIRNOV. I wasn't asking you about a stable, but whether I'd got my interest to pay to-morrow or not?

POPOVA. You don't know how to behave before women!

SMIRNOV. No, I do know how to behave before women!

POPOVA. No, you don't! You're a rude, ill-bred man! Decent people don't talk to a woman like that!

SMIRNOV. What a business! How do you want me to talk to you? In French, or what? *[Loses his temper and lisps] Madame, je vous prie*.... How happy I am that you don't pay me.... Ah, pardon. I have disturbed you! Such lovely weather to-day! And how well you look in mourning! *[Bows.]*

POPOVA. That's silly and rude.

SMIRNOV. *[Teasing her]* Silly and rude! I don't know how to behave before women! Madam, in my time I've seen more women than you've seen sparrows! Three times I've fought duels on account of women. I've refused twelve women, and nine have refused me! Yes! There was a time when I played the fool, scented myself, used honeyed words, wore jewellery, made beautiful bows. I used to love, to suffer, to sigh at the moon, to get sour, to thaw, to freeze.... I used to love passionately, madly, every blessed way, devil take me; I used to chatter like a magpie about emancipation, and wasted half my wealth on tender feelings, but now—you must excuse me! You won't get round me like that now! I've had enough! Black eyes, passionate eyes, ruby lips, dimpled cheeks, the moon, whispers, timid breathing—I wouldn't give a brass farthing for the lot, madam! Present company always excepted, all women, great or little, are insincere, crooked, backbiters, envious, liars to the marrow of their bones, vain, trivial, merciless, unreasonable, and, as far as this is concerned *[taps his forehead]* excuse my outspokenness, a sparrow can give ten points to any philosopher in petticoats you like to name! You look at one of these poetic creatures: all muslin, an ethereal demi-goddess, you have a million transports of joy, and you look into her soul—and see a common crocodile! *[He grips the back of a chair; the chair creaks and breaks]* But the most disgusting thing of all is that this crocodile for some reason or other imagines that its chef d'oeuvre, its privilege and monopoly, is its tender feelings. Why, confound it, hang me on that nail feet upwards, if you like, but have you met a woman who can love anybody except a lapdog? When she's in love, can she do anything but snivel and slobber? While a man is suffering and making sacrifices all her love expresses itself in her playing about with her scarf, and trying to hook him more firmly by the nose. You have the misfortune to be a woman, you know from yourself what is the nature of woman. Tell me truthfully, have you ever seen a woman who was sincere, faithful, and constant? You haven't! Only freaks and old women are faithful and constant! You'll meet a cat with a horn or a white woodcock sooner than a constant woman!

POPOVA. Then, according to you, who is faithful and constant in love? Is it the man?

SMIRNOV. Yes, the man!

POPOVA. The man! *[Laughs bitterly]* Men are faithful and constant in love! What an idea! *[With heat]* What right have you to talk like that? Men are faithful and constant! Since we are talking about it, I'll tell you that of all the men I knew and know, the best was my late husband.... I loved him passionately with all my being, as only a young and imaginative woman can love, I gave him my youth, my happiness, my life, my fortune, I breathed in him, I worshipped him as if I were a heathen, and... and what then? This best of men shamelessly deceived me at every step! After his death I found in his desk a whole drawerful of love-letters, and when he was alive—it's an awful thing to remember!—he used to leave me alone for weeks at a time, and make love to other women and betray me before my very eyes; he wasted my money, and made fun of my feelings.... And, in spite of all that, I loved him and was true to him. And not only that, but, now that he is dead, I am still true and constant to his memory. I have shut myself for ever within these four walls, and will wear these weeds to the very end....

SMIRNOV. *[Laughs contemptuously]* Weeds!... I don't understand what you take me for. As if I don't know why you wear that black domino and bury yourself between four walls! I should say I did! It's so mysterious, so poetic! When some junker *[Note: So in the original.]* or some tame poet goes past your windows he'll think: "There lives the mysterious Tamara who, for the love of her husband, buried herself between four walls." We know these games!

POPOVA. *[Exploding]* What? How dare you say all that to me?

SMIRNOV. You may have buried yourself alive, but you haven't forgotten to powder your face!

POPOVA. How dare you speak to me like that?

SMIRNOV. Please don't shout, I'm not your steward! You must allow me to call things by their real names. I'm not a woman, and I'm used to saying what I think straight out! Don't you shout, either!

POPOVA. I'm not shouting, it's you! Please leave me alone!

SMIRNOV. Pay me my money and I'll go.

POPOVA. I shan't give you any money!

SMIRNOV. Oh, no, you will.

POPOVA. I shan't give you a farthing, just to spite you. You leave me alone!

SMIRNOV. I have not the pleasure of being either your husband or your fiancé, so please don't make scenes. *[Sits]* I don't like it.

POPOVA. *[Choking with rage]* So you sit down?

SMIRNOV. I do.

POPOVA. I ask you to go away!

SMIRNOV. Give me my money.... *[Aside]* Oh, how angry I am! How angry I am!

POPOVA. I don't want to talk to impudent scoundrels! Get out of this! *[Pause]* Aren't you going? No?

SMIRNOV. No.

POPOVA. No?

SMIRNOV. No!

POPOVA. Very well then! *[Rings, enter LUKA]* Luka, show this gentleman out!

LUKA. *[Approaches SMIRNOV]* Would you mind going out, sir, as you're asked to! You needn't...

SMIRNOV. *[Jumps up]* Shut up! Who are you talking to? I'll chop you into pieces!

LUKA. *[Clutches at his heart]* Little fathers!... What people!... *[Falls into a chair]* Oh, I'm ill, I'm ill! I can't breathe!

POPOVA. Where's Dasha? Dasha! *[Shouts]* Dasha! Pelageya! Dasha! *[Rings.]*

LUKA. Oh! They've all gone out to pick fruit.... There's nobody at home! I'm ill! Water!

POPOVA. Get out of this, now.

SMIRNOV. Can't you be more polite?

POPOVA. *[Clenches her fists and stamps her foot]* You're a boor! A coarse bear! A Bourbon! A monster!

SMIRNOV. What? What did you say?

POPOVA. I said you are a bear, a monster!

SMIRNOV. *[Approaching her]* May I ask what right you have to insult me?

POPOVA. And suppose I am insulting you? Do you think I'm afraid of you?

SMIRNOV. And do you think that just because you're a poetic creature you can insult me with impunity? Eh? We'll fight it out!

LUKA. Little fathers!... What people!... Water!

SMIRNOV. Pistols!

POPOVA. Do you think I'm afraid of you just because you have large fists and a bull's throat? Eh? You Bourbon!

SMIRNOV. We'll fight it out! I'm not going to be insulted by anybody, and I don't care if you are a woman, one of the "softer sex," indeed!

POPOVA. *[Trying to interrupt him]* Bear! Bear! Bear!

SMIRNOV. It's about time we got rid of the prejudice that only men need pay for their insults. Devil take it, if you want equality of rights you can have it. We're going to fight it out!

POPOVA. With pistols? Very well!

SMIRNOV. This very minute.

POPOVA. This very minute! My husband had some pistols.... I'll bring them here. *[Is going, but turns back]* What pleasure it will give me to put a bullet into your thick head! Devil take you! *[Exit.]*

SMIRNOV. I'll bring her down like a chicken! I'm not a little boy or a sentimental puppy; I don't care about this "softer sex."

LUKA. Gracious little fathers!... *[Kneels]* Have pity on a poor old man, and go away from here! You've frightened her to death, and now you want to shoot her!

SMIRNOV. *[Not hearing him]* If she fights, well that's equality of rights, emancipation, and all that! Here the sexes are equal! I'll shoot her on principle! But what a woman! *[Parodying her]* "Devil take you! I'll put a bullet into your thick head." Eh? How she reddened, how her cheeks shone!... She accepted my challenge! My word, it's the first time in my life that I've seen....

LUKA. Go away, sir, and I'll always pray to God for you!

SMIRNOV. She is a woman! That's the sort I can understand! A real woman! Not a sour-faced jellybag, but fire, gunpowder, a rocket! I'm even sorry to have to kill her!

LUKA. *[Weeps]* Dear... dear sir, do go away!

SMIRNOV. I absolutely like her! Absolutely! Even though her cheeks are dimpled, I like her! I'm almost ready to let the debt go... and I'm not angry any longer.... Wonderful woman!

*[Enter POPOVA with pistols.]*

POPOVA. Here are the pistols.... But before we fight you must show me how to fire. I've never held a pistol in my hands before.

LUKA. Oh, Lord, have mercy and save her.... I'll go and find the coachman and the gardener.... Why has this infliction come on us.... *[Exit.]*

SMIRNOV. *[Examining the pistols]* You see, there are several sorts of pistols.... There are Mortimer pistols, specially made for duels, they fire a percussion-cap. These are Smith and Wesson revolvers, triple action, with extractors.... These are excellent pistols. They can't cost less than ninety roubles the pair.... You must hold the revolver like this.... *[Aside]* Her eyes, her eyes! What an inspiring woman!

POPOVA. Like this?

SMIRNOV. Yes, like this.... Then you cock the trigger, and take aim like this.... Put your head back a little! Hold your arm out properly.... Like that.... Then you press this thing with your finger—and that's all. The great thing is to keep cool and aim steadily.... Try not to jerk your arm.

POPOVA. Very well.... It's inconvenient to shoot in a room, let's go into the garden.

SMIRNOV. Come along then. But I warn you, I'm going to fire in the air.

POPOVA. That's the last straw! Why?

SMIRNOV. Because... because... it's my affair.

POPOVA. Are you afraid? Yes? Ah! No, sir, you don't get out of it! You come with me! I shan't have any peace until I've made a hole in your forehead... that forehead which I hate so much! Are you afraid?

SMIRNOV. Yes, I am afraid.

POPOVA. You lie! Why won't you fight?

SMIRNOV. Because... because you... because I like you.

POPOVA. *[Laughs]* He likes me! He dares to say that he likes me! *[Points to the door]* That's the way.

SMIRNOV. *[Loads the revolver in silence, takes his cap and goes to the door. There he stops for half a minute, while they look at each other in silence, then he hesitatingly approaches POPOVA]* Listen.... Are you still angry? I'm devilishly annoyed, too... but, do you understand... how can I express myself?... The fact is, you see, it's like this, so to speak.... *[Shouts]* Well, is it my fault that I like you? *[He snatches at the back of a chair; the chair creaks and breaks]* Devil take it, how I'm smashing up your furniture! I like you! Do you understand? I... I almost love you!

POPOVA. Get away from me—I hate you!

SMIRNOV. God, what a woman! I've never in my life seen one like her! I'm lost! Done for! Fallen into a mousetrap, like a mouse!

POPOVA. Stand back, or I'll fire!

SMIRNOV. Fire, then! You can't understand what happiness it would be to die before those beautiful eyes, to be shot by a revolver held in that little, velvet hand.... I'm out of my senses! Think, and make up your mind at once, because if I go out we shall never see each other again! Decide now.... I am a landowner, of respectable character, have an income of ten thousand a year. I can put a bullet through a coin tossed into the air as it comes down.... I own some fine horses.... Will you be my wife?

POPOVA. *[Indignantly shakes her revolver]* Let's fight! Let's go out!

SMIRNOV. I'm mad.... I understand nothing. *[Yells]* Waiter, water!

POPOVA. *[Yells]* Let's go out and fight!

SMIRNOV. I'm off my head, I'm in love like a boy, like a fool! *[Snatches her hand, she screams with pain]* I love you! *[Kneels]* I love you as I've never loved before! I've refused twelve women, nine have refused me, but I never loved one of them as I love you.... I'm weak, I'm wax, I've melted.... I'm on my knees like a fool, offering you my hand.... Shame, shame! I haven't been in love for five years, I'd taken a vow, and now all of a sudden I'm in love, like a fish out of water! I offer you my hand. Yes or no? You don't want me? Very well! *[Gets up and quickly goes to the door.]*

POPOVA. Stop.

SMIRNOV. *[Stops]* Well?

POPOVA. Nothing, go away.... No, stop.... No, go away, go away! I hate you! Or no.... Don't go away! Oh, if you knew how angry I am, how angry I am! *[Throws her revolver on the table]* My fingers have swollen because of all this.... *[Tears her handkerchief in temper]* What are you waiting for? Get out!

SMIRNOV. Good-bye.

POPOVA. Yes, yes, go away!... *[Yells]* Where are you going? Stop.... No, go away. Oh, how angry I am! Don't come near me, don't come near me!

SMIRNOV. *[Approaching her]* How angry I am with myself! I'm in love like a student, I've been on my knees.... *[Rudely]* I love you! What do I want to fall in love with you for? To-morrow I've got to pay the interest, and begin mowing, and here you.... *[Puts his arms around her]* I shall never forgive myself for this....

POPOVA. Get away from me! Take your hands away! I hate you! Let's go and fight!

*[A prolonged kiss. Enter LUKA with an axe, the GARDENER with a rake, the COACHMAN with a pitchfork, and WORKMEN with poles.]*

LUKA. *[Catches sight of the pair kissing]* Little fathers! *[Pause.]*

POPOVA. *[Lowering her eyes]* Luka, tell them in the stables that Toby isn't to have any oats at all to-day.

**Curtain.**

# A TRAGEDIAN IN SPITE OF HIMSELF

## Translated by Julius West

### CHARACTERS

IVAN IVANOVITCH TOLKACHOV, the father of a family
ALEXEY ALEXEYEVITCH MURASHKIN, his friend

# A TRAGEDIAN IN SPITE OF HIMSELF

*The scene is laid in St. Petersburg, in MURASHKIN'S flat*

*[MURASHKIN'S study. Comfortable furniture. MURASHKIN is seated at his desk. Enter TOLKACHOV holding in his hands a glass globe for a lamp, a toy bicycle, three hat-boxes, a large parcel containing a dress, a bin-case of beer, and several little parcels. He looks round stupidly and lets himself down on the sofa in exhaustion.]*

MURASHKIN. How do you do, Ivan Ivanovitch? Delighted to see you! What brings you here?

TOLKACHOV. *[Breathing heavily]* My dear good fellow... I want to ask you something.... I implore you lend me a revolver till to-morrow. Be a friend!

MURASHKIN. What do you want a revolver for?

TOLKACHOV. I must have it.... Oh, little fathers!... give me some water... water quickly!... I must have it... I've got to go through a dark wood to-night, so in case of accidents... do, please, lend it to me.

MURASHKIN. Oh, you liar, Ivan Ivanovitch! What the devil have you got to do in a dark wood? I expect you are up to something. I can see by your face that you are up to something. What's the matter with you? Are you ill?

TOLKACHOV. Wait a moment, let me breathe.... Oh little mothers! I am dog-tired. I've got a feeling all over me, and in my head as well, as if I've been roasted on a spit. I can't stand it any longer. Be a friend, and don't ask me any questions or insist on details; just give me the revolver! I beseech you!

MURASHKIN. Well, really! Ivan Ivanovitch, what cowardice is this? The father of a family and a Civil Servant holding a responsible post! For shame!

TOLKACHOV. What sort of a father of a family am I! I am a martyr. I am a beast of burden, a nigger, a slave, a rascal who keeps on waiting here for something to happen instead of starting off for the next world. I am a rag, a fool, an idiot. Why am I alive? What's the use? *[Jumps up]* Well now, tell me why am I alive? What's the purpose of this uninterrupted series of mental and physical sufferings? I understand being a martyr to an idea, yes! But to be a martyr to the devil knows what, skirts and lamp-globes, no! I humbly decline! No, no, no! I've had enough! Enough!

MURASHKIN. Don't shout, the neighbours will hear you!

TOLKACHOV. Let your neighbours hear; it's all the same to me! If you don't give me a revolver somebody else will, and there will be an end of me anyway! I've made up my mind!

MURASHKIN. Hold on, you've pulled off a button. Speak calmly. I still don't understand what's wrong with your life.

TOLKACHOV. What's wrong? You ask me what's wrong? Very well, I'll tell you! Very well! I'll tell you everything, and then perhaps my soul will be lighter. Let's sit down. Now listen... Oh, little mothers, I am out of breath!... Just let's take to-day as an instance. Let's take to-day. As you know, I've got to work at the Treasury from ten to four. It's hot, it's stuffy, there are flies, and, my dear fellow, the very dickens of a chaos. The Secretary is on leave, Khrapov has gone to get married, and the smaller fry is mostly in the country, making love or occupied with amateur theatricals. Everybody is so sleepy, tired, and done up that you can't get any sense out of them. The Secretary's duties are in the hands of an individual who is deaf in the left ear and in love; the public has lost its memory; everybody is running about angry and raging, and there is such a hullabaloo that you can't hear yourself speak. Confusion and smoke everywhere. And my work is deathly: always the same, always the same—first a correction, then a reference back, another correction, another reference back; it's all as monotonous as the waves of the sea. One's eyes, you understand, simply crawl out of one's head. Give me some water.... You come out a broken, exhausted man. You would like to dine and fall asleep, but you don't!—You remember that you live in the country—that is, you are a slave, a rag, a bit of string, a bit of limp flesh, and you've got to run round and do errands. Where we live a pleasant custom has grown up: when a man goes to town every wretched female inhabitant, not to mention one's own wife, has the power and the right to give him a crowd of commissions. The wife orders you to run into the modiste's and curse her for making a bodice too wide across the chest and too narrow across the shoulders; little Sonya wants a new pair of shoes; your sister-in-law wants some scarlet silk like the pattern at twenty copecks and three arshins long.... Just wait; I'll read you. *[Takes a note out of his pocket and reads]* A globe for the lamp; one pound of pork sausages; five copecks' worth of cloves and cinnamon; castor-oil for Misha; ten pounds of granulated sugar. To bring with you from home: a copper jar for the sugar; carbolic acid; insect powder, ten copecks' worth; twenty bottles of beer; vinegar; and corsets for Mlle. Shanceau at No. 82.... Ouf! And to bring home Misha's winter coat and goloshes. That is the order of my wife and family. Then there are the commissions of our dear friends and neighbours—devil take them! To-morrow is the name-day of Volodia Vlasin; I have to buy a bicycle for him. The wife of Lieutenant-Colonel Virkhin is in an interesting condition, and I am therefore bound to call in at the midwife's every day and invite her to come. And so on, and so on. There are five notes in my pocket and my handkerchief is all knots. And so, my dear fellow, you spend the time between your office and your train, running about the town like a dog with your tongue hanging out, running and running and cursing life. From the clothier's to the chemist's, from the chemist's to the modiste's, from the modiste's to the pork butcher's, and then back again to the chemist's. In one place you stumble, in a second you lose your money, in a third you forget to pay and they raise a hue and cry after you, in a fourth you tread on the train of a lady's dress.... Tfoo! You get so shaken up from all this that your bones ache all night and you dream of crocodiles. Well, you've made all your purchases, but how are you to pack all these things? For instance, how are you to put a heavy copper jar together with the lamp-globe or the carbolic acid with the tea? How are you to make a combination of beer-bottles and this bicycle? It's the labours of Hercules, a puzzle, a rebus! Whatever tricks you think of, in the long run you're bound to smash or scatter something, and at the station and in the train you have to stand with your arms apart, holding up some parcel or other under your chin, with parcels, cardboard boxes, and such-like rubbish all over you. The train starts, the passengers begin to throw your luggage about on all sides: you've got your things on somebody else's seat. They yell, they call for the conductor, they threaten to have you put out, but what can I do? I just stand and blink my eyes like a whacked donkey. Now listen to this. I get home. You think I'd like to have a nice little drink after my righteous labours and a good square meal—isn't that so?—but there is no chance of that. My spouse has been on the look-out for me for some time. You've hardly started on your soup when she has her claws into you, wretched slave that you are—and wouldn't you like to go to some amateur theatricals or to a dance? You can't protest. You are a husband, and the word husband when translated into the language of summer residents in the country means a dumb beast which you can load to any extent without fear of the interference of the Society for the Prevention of Cruelty to Animals. So you go and blink at "A Family Scandal" or something, you applaud when your wife tells you to, and you feel worse and worse and worse until you expect an apoplectic fit to happen any moment. If you go to a dance you have to find partners for your wife, and if there is a shortage of them then you dance the quadrilles yourself. You get back from the theatre or the dance after midnight, when you are no longer a man but a useless, limp rag. Well, at last you've got what you want; you unrobe and get into bed. It's excellent—you can close your eyes and sleep.... Everything is so nice, poetic, and warm, you understand; there are no children squealing behind the wall, and you've got rid of your wife, and your conscience is clear—what more can you want? You fall asleep—and suddenly... you hear a buzz!... Gnats! *[Jumps up]* Gnats! Be they triply accursed Gnats! *[Shakes his fist]* Gnats! It's one of the plagues of Egypt, one of the tortures of the Inquisition! Buzz! It sounds so pitiful, so pathetic, as if it's begging your pardon, but the villain stings so that you have to scratch yourself for an hour after. You smoke, and go for them, and cover yourself from head to foot, but it is no good! At last you have to sacrifice yourself and let the cursed things devour you. You've no sooner got used to the gnats when another plague begins: downstairs your wife begins practising sentimental songs with her two friends. They sleep by day and rehearse for amateur concerts by night. Oh, my God! Those tenors are a torture with which no gnats on earth can compare. *[He sings]* "Oh, tell me not my youth has ruined you." "Before thee do I stand enchanted." Oh, the beastly things! They've about killed me! So as to deafen myself a little I do this: I drum on my ears. This goes on till four o'clock. Oh, give me some more water, brother!... I can't... Well, not having slept, you get up at six o'clock in the morning and off you go to the station. You run so as not to be late, and it's muddy, foggy, cold—brr! Then you get to town and start all over again. So there, brother. It's a horrible life; I wouldn't wish one like it for my enemy. You understand—I'm ill! Got asthma, heartburn—I'm always afraid of something. I've got indigestion, everything is thick before me... I've become a regular psychopath.... *[Looking round]* Only, between ourselves, I want to go down to see Chechotte or Merzheyevsky. There's some devil in me, brother. In moments of despair and suffering, when the gnats are stinging or the tenors sing, everything suddenly grows dim; you jump up and race round the whole house like a lunatic and shout, "I want blood! Blood!" And really all the time you do want to let a knife into somebody or hit him over the head with a chair. That's what life in a summer villa leads to! And nobody has any sympathy for me, and everybody seems to think it's all as it should be. People even laugh. But understand, I am a living being and I want to live! This isn't farce, it's tragedy! I say, if you don't give me your revolver, you might at any rate sympathize.

MURASHKIN. I do sympathize.

TOLKACHOV. I see how much you sympathize.... Good-bye. I've got to buy some anchovies and some sausage... and some tooth-powder, and then to the station.

MURASHKIN. Where are you living?

TOLKACHOV. At Carrion River.

MURASHKIN. *[Delighted]* Really? Then you'll know Olga Pavlovna Finberg, who lives there?

TOLKACHOV. I know her. We are even acquainted.

MURASHKIN. How perfectly splendid! That's so convenient, and it would be so good of you...

TOLKACHOV. What's that?

MURASHKIN. My dear fellow, wouldn't you do one little thing for me? Be a friend! Promise me now.

TOLKACHOV. What's that?

MURASHKIN. It would be such a friendly action! I implore you, my dear man. In the first place, give Olga Pavlovna my very kind regards. In the second place, there's a little thing I'd like you to take down to her. She asked me to get a sewing-machine but I haven't anybody to send it down to her by.... You take it, my dear! And you might at the same time take down this canary in its cage... only be careful, or you'll break the door.... What are you looking at me like that for?

TOLKACHOV. A sewing-machine... a canary in a cage... siskins, chaffinches...

MURASHKIN. Ivan Ivanovitch, what's the matter with you? Why are you turning purple?

TOLKACHOV. *[Stamping]* Give me the sewing-machine! Where's the bird-cage? Now get on top yourself! Eat me! Tear me to pieces! Kill me! *[Clenching his fists]* I want blood! Blood! Blood!

MURASHKIN. You've gone mad!

TOLKACHOV. *[Treading on his feet]* I want blood! Blood!

MURASHKIN. *[In horror]* He's gone mad! *[Shouts]* Peter! Maria! Where are you? Help!

TOLKACHOV. *[Chasing him round the room]* I want blood! Blood!

**Curtain.**

# THE WEDDING

## Translated by Julius West

### CHARACTERS

EVDOKIM ZAHAROVITCH ZHIGALOV, a retired Civil Servant.
NASTASYA TIMOFEYEVNA, his wife
DASHENKA, their daughter
EPAMINOND MAXIMOVITCH APLOMBOV, Dashenka's bridegroom
FYODOR YAKOVLEVITCH REVUNOV-KARAULOV, a retired captain
ANDREY ANDREYEVITCH NUNIN, an insurance agent
ANNA MARTINOVNA ZMEYUKINA, a midwife, aged 30, in a brilliantly red dress
IVAN MIHAILOVITCH YATS, a telegraphist
HARLAMPI SPIRIDONOVITCII DIMBA, a Grcck confectioner
DMITRI STEPANOVITCH MOZGOVOY, a sailor of the Imperial Navy (Volunteer Fleet)
GROOMSMEN, GENTLEMEN, WAITERS, ETC.

# THE WEDDING

*The scene is laid in one of the rooms of Andronov's Restaurant*

*[A brilliantly illuminated room. A large table, laid for supper. Waiters in dress-jackets are fussing round the table. An orchestra behind the scene is playing the music of the last figure of a quadrille.]*

*[ANNA MARTINOVNA ZMEYUKINA, YATS, and a GROOMSMAN cross the stage.]*

ZMEYUKINA. No, no, no!

YATS. *[Following her]* Have pity on us! Have pity!

ZMEYUKINA. No, no, no!

GROOMSMAN. *[Chasing them]* You can't go on like this! Where are you off to? What about the *grand ronde? Grand ronde, s'il vous plait*! *[They all go off.]*

*[Enter NASTASYA TIMOFEYEVNA and APLOMBOV.]*

NASTASYA TIMOFEYEVNA. You had much better be dancing than upsetting me with your speeches.

APLOMBOV. I'm not a Spinosa or anybody of that sort, to go making figures-of-eight with my legs. I am a serious man, and I have a character, and I see no amusement in empty pleasures. But it isn't just a matter of dances. You must excuse me, maman, but there is a good deal in your behaviour which I am unable to understand. For instance, in addition to objects of domestic importance, you promised also to give me, with your daughter, two lottery tickets. Where are they?

NASTASYA TIMOFEYEVNA. My head's aching a little... I expect it's on account of the weather.... If only it thawed!

APLOMBOV. You won't get out of it like that. I only found out to-day that those tickets are in pawn. You must excuse me, *maman*, but it's only swindlers who behave like that. I'm not doing this out of egoisticism *[Note: So in the original]*—I don't want your tickets—but on principle; and I don't allow myself to be done by anybody. I have made your daughter happy, and if you don't give me the tickets to-day I'll make short work of her. I'm an honourable man!

NASTASYA TIMOFEYEVNA. *[Looks round the table and counts up the covers]* One, two, three, four, five...

A WAITER. The cook asks if you would like the ices served with rum, madeira, or by themselves?

APLOMBOV. With rum. And tell the manager that there's not enough wine. Tell him to prepare some more Haut Sauterne. *[To NASTASYA TIMOFEYEVNA]* You also promised and agreed that a general was to be here to supper. And where is he?

NASTASYA TIMOFEYEVNA. That isn't my fault, my dear.

APLOMBOV. Whose fault, then?

NASTASYA TIMOFEYEVNA. It's Andrey Andreyevitch's fault.... Yesterday he came to see us and promised to bring a perfectly real general. *[Sighs]* I suppose he couldn't find one anywhere, or he'd have brought him.... You think we don't mind? We'd begrudge our child nothing. A general, of course...

APLOMBOV. But there's more.... Everybody, including yourself, *maman*, is aware of the fact that Yats, that telegraphist, was after Dashenka before I proposed to her. Why did you invite him? Surely you knew it would be unpleasant for me?

NASTASYA TIMOFEYEVNA. Oh, how can you? Epaminond Maximovitch was married himself only the other day, and you've already tired me and Dashenka out with your talk. What will you be like in a year's time? You are horrid, really horrid.

APLOMBOV. Then you don't like to hear the truth? Aha! Oh, oh! Then behave honourably. I only want you to do one thing, be honourable!

*[Couples dancing the grand ronde come in at one door and out at the other end. The first couple are DASHENKA with one of the GROOMSMEN. The last are YATS and ZMEYUKINA. These two remain behind. ZHIGALOV and DIMBA enter and go up to the table.]*

GROOMSMAN. *[Shouting]* Promenade! Messieurs, promenade! *[Behind]* Promenade!

*[The dancers have all left the scene.]*

YATS. *[To ZMEYUKINA]* Have pity! Have pity, adorable Anna Martinovna.

ZMEYUKINA. Oh, what a man!... I've already told you that I've no voice to-day.

YATS. I implore you to sing! Just one note! Have pity! Just one note!

ZMEYUKINA. I'm tired of you.... *[Sits and fans herself.]*

YATS. No, you're simply heartless! To be so cruel—if I may express myself—and to have such a beautiful, beautiful voice! With such a voice, if you will forgive my using the word, you shouldn't be a midwife, but sing at concerts, at public gatherings! For example, how divinely you do that *fioritura*... that... *[Sings]* "I loved you; love was vain then...." Exquisite!

ZMEYUKINA. *[Sings]* "I loved you, and may love again." Is that it?

YATS. That's it! Beautiful!

ZMEYUKINA. No, I've no voice to-day.... There, wave this fan for me... it's hot! *[To APLOMBOV]* Epaminond Maximovitch, why are you so melancholy? A bridegroom shouldn't be! Aren't you ashamed of yourself, you wretch? Well, what are you so thoughtful about?

APLOMBOV. Marriage is a serious step! Everything must be considered from all sides, thoroughly.

ZMEYUKINA. What beastly sceptics you all are! I feel quite suffocated with you all around.... Give me atmosphere! Do you hear? Give me atmosphere! *[Sings a few notes.]*

YATS. Beautiful! Beautiful!

ZMEYUKINA. Fan me, fan me, or I feel I shall have a heart attack in a minute. Tell me, please, why do I feel so suffocated?

YATS. It's because you're sweating....

ZMEYUKINA. Foo, how vulgar you are! Don't dare to use such words!

YATS. Beg pardon! Of course, you're used, if I may say so, to aristocratic society and....

ZMEYUKINA. Oh, leave me alone! Give me poetry, delight! Fan me, fan me!

ZHIGALOV. *[To DIMBA]* Let's have another, what? *[Pours out]* One can always drink. So long only, Harlampi Spiridonovitch, as one doesn't forget one's business. Drink and be merry.... And if you can drink at somebody else's expense, then why not drink? You can drink.... Your health! *[They drink]* And do you have tigers in Greece?

DIMBA. Yes.

ZHIGALOV. And lions?

DIMBA. And lions too. In Russia zere's nussing, and in Greece zere's everysing—my fazer and uncle and brozeres—and here zere's nussing.

ZHIGALOV. H'm.... And are there whales in Greece?

DIMBA. Yes, everysing.

NASTASYA TIMOFEYEVNA. *[To her husband]* What are they all eating and drinking like that for? It's time for everybody to sit down to supper. Don't keep on shoving your fork into the lobsters.... They're for the general. He may come yet....

ZHIGALOV. And are there lobsters in Greece?

DIMBA. Yes... zere is everysing.

ZHIGALOV. Hm.... And Civil Servants.

ZMEYUKINA. I can imagine what the atmosphere is like in Greece!

ZHIGALOV. There must be a lot of swindling. The Greeks are just like the Armenians or gipsies. They sell you a sponge or a goldfish and all the time they are looking out for a chance of getting something extra out of you. Let's have another, what?

NASTASYA TIMOFEYEVNA. What do you want to go on having another for? It's time everybody sat down to supper. It's past eleven.

ZHIGALOV. If it's time, then it's time. Ladies and gentlemen, please! *[Shouts]* Supper! Young people!

NASTASYA TIMOFEYEVNA. Dear visitors, please be seated!

ZMEYUKINA. *[Sitting down at the table]* Give me poetry.

"And he, the rebel, seeks the storm,  
As if the storm can give him peace."

Give me the storm!

YATS. *[Aside]* Wonderful woman! I'm in love! Up to my ears!

*[Enter DASHENKA, MOZGOVOY, GROOMSMEN, various ladies and gentlemen, etc. They all noisily seat themselves at the table. There is a minute's pause, while the band plays a march.]*

MOZGOVOY. *[Rising]* Ladies and gentlemen! I must tell you this.... We are going to have a great many toasts and speeches. Don't let's wait, but begin at once. Ladies and gentlemen, the newly married!

*[The band plays a flourish. Cheers. Glasses are touched. APLOMBOV and DASHENKA kiss each other.]*

YATS. Beautiful! Beautiful! I must say, ladies and gentlemen, giving honour where it is due, that this room and the accommodation generally are splendid! Excellent, wonderful! Only you know, there's one thing we haven't got—electric light, if I may say so! Into every country electric light has already been introduced, only Russia lags behind.

ZHIGALOV. *[Meditatively]* Electricity... h'm.... In my opinion electric lighting is just a swindle.... They put a live coal in and think you don't see them! No, if you want a light, then you don't take a coal, but something real, something special, that you can get hold of! You must have a fire, you understand, which is natural, not just an invention!

YATS. If you'd ever seen an electric battery, and how it's made up, you'd think differently.

ZHIGALOV. Don't want to see one. It's a swindle, a fraud on the public.... They want to squeeze our last breath out of us.... We know then, these... And, young man, instead of defending a swindle, you would be much better occupied if you had another yourself and poured out some for other people—yes!

APLOMBOV. I entirely agree with you, papa. Why start a learned discussion? I myself have no objection to talking about every possible scientific discovery, but this isn't the time for all that! *[To DASHENKA]* What do you think, *ma chère*?

DASHENKA. They want to show how educated they are, and so they always talk about things we can't understand.

NASTASYA TIMOFEYEVNA. Thank God, we've lived our time without being educated, and here we are marrying off our third daughter to an honest man. And if you think we're uneducated, then what do you want to come here for? Go to your educated friends!

YATS. I, Nastasya Timofeyevna, have always held your family in respect, and if I did start talking about electric lighting it doesn't mean that I'm proud. I'll drink, to show you. I have always sincerely wished Daria Evdokimovna a good husband. In these days, Nastasya Timofeyevna, it is difficult to find a good husband. Nowadays everybody is on the look-out for a marriage where there is profit, money....

APLOMBOV. That's a hint!

YATS. *[His courage failing]* I wasn't hinting at anything.... Present company is always excepted.... I was only in general.... Please! Everybody knows that you're marrying for love... the dowry is quite trifling.

NASTASYA TIMOFEYEVNA. No, it isn't trifling! You be careful what you say. Besides a thousand roubles of good money, we're giving three dresses, the bed, and all the furniture. You won't find another dowry like that in a hurry!

YATS. I didn't mean... The furniture's splendid, of course, and... and the dresses, but I never hinted at what they are getting offended at.

NASTASYA TIMOFEYEVNA. Don't you go making hints. We respect you on account of your parents, and we've invited you to the wedding, and here you go talking. If you knew that Epaminond Maximovitch was marrying for profit, why didn't you say so before? *[Tearfully]* I brought her up, I fed her, I nursed her.... I cared for her more than if she was an emerald jewel, my little girl....

APLOMBOV. And you go and believe him? Thank you so much! I'm very grateful to you! *[To YATS]* And as for you, Mr. Yats, although you are acquainted with me, I shan't allow you to behave like this in another's house. Please get out of this!

YATS. What do you mean?

APLOMBOV. I want you to be as straightforward as I am! In short, please get out! *[Band plays a flourish]*

THE GENTLEMEN. Leave him alone! Sit down! Is it worth it! Let him be! Stop it now!

YATS. I never... I... I don't understand.... Please, I'll go.... Only you first give me the five roubles which you borrowed from me last year on the strength of a *piqué* waistcoat, if I may say so. Then I'll just have another drink and... go, only give me the money first.

VARIOUS GENTLEMEN. Sit down! That's enough! Is it worth it, just for such trifles?

A GROOMSMAN. *[Shouts]* The health of the bride's parents, Evdokim Zaharitch and Nastasya Timofeyevna! *[Band plays a flourish. Cheers.]*

ZHIGALOV. *[Bows in all directions, in great emotion]* I thank you! Dear guests! I am very grateful to you for not having forgotten and for having conferred this honour upon us without being standoffish And you must not think that I'm a rascal, or that I'm trying to swindle anybody. I'm speaking from my heart—from the purity of my soul! I wouldn't deny anything to good people! We thank you very humbly! *[Kisses.]*

DASHENKA. *[To her mother]* Mama, why are you crying? I'm so happy!

APLOMBOV. *Maman* is disturbed at your coming separation. But I should advise her rather to remember the last talk we had.

YATS. Don't cry, Nastasya Timofeyevna! Just think what are human tears, anyway? Just petty psychiatry, and nothing more!

ZMEYUKINA. And are there any red-haired men in Greece?

DIMBA. Yes, everysing is zere.

ZHIGALOV. But you don't have our kinds of mushroom.

DIMBA. Yes, we've got zem and everysing.

MOZGOVOY. Harlampi Spiridonovitch, it's your turn to speak! Ladies and gentlemen, a speech!

ALL. *[To DIMBA]* Speech! speech! Your turn!

DIMBA. Why? I don't understand.... What is it!

ZMEYUKINA. No, no! You can't refuse! It's you turn! Get up!

DIMBA. *[Gets up, confused]* I can't say what... Zere's Russia and zere's Greece. Zere's people in Russia and people in Greece.... And zere's people swimming the sea in karavs, which mean sips, and people on the land in railway trains. I understand. We are Greeks and you are Russians, and I want nussing.... I can tell you... zere's Russia and zere's Greece...

*[Enter NUNIN.]*

NUNIN. Wait, ladies and gentlemen, don't eat now! Wait! Just one minute, Nastasya Timofeyevna! Just come here, if you don't mind! *[Takes NASTASYA TIMOFEYEVNA aside, puffing]* Listen... The General's coming... I found one at last.... I'm simply worn out.... A real General, a solid one—old, you know, aged perhaps eighty, or even ninety.

NASTASYA TIMOFEYEVNA. When is he coming?

NUNIN. This minute. You'll be grateful to me all your life. *[Note: A few lines have been omitted: they refer to the "General's" rank and its civil equivalent in words for which the English language has no corresponding terms. The "General" is an ex-naval officer, a second-class captain.]*

NASTASYA TIMOFEYEVNA. You're not deceiving me, Andrey darling?

NUNIN. Well, now, am I a swindler? You needn't worry!

NASTASYA TIMOFEYEVNA. *[Sighs]* One doesn't like to spend money for nothing, Andrey darling!

NUNIN. Don't you worry! He's not a general, he's a dream! *[Raises his voice]* I said to him: "You've quite forgotten us, your Excellency! It isn't kind of your Excellency to forget your old friends! Nastasya Timofeyevna," I said to him, "she's very annoyed with you about it!" *[Goes and sits at the table]* And he says to me: "But, my friend, how can I go when I don't know the bridegroom?" "Oh, nonsense, your excellency, why stand on ceremony? The bridegroom," I said to him, "he's a fine fellow, very free and easy. He's a valuer," I said, "at the Law courts, and don't you think, your excellency, that he's some rascal, some knave of hearts. Nowadays," I said to him, "even decent women are employed at the Law courts." He slapped me on the shoulder, we smoked a Havana cigar each, and now he's coming.... Wait a little, ladies and gentlemen, don't eat....

APLOMBOV. When's he coming?

NUNIN. This minute. When I left him he was already putting on his goloshes. Wait a little, ladies and gentlemen, don't eat yet.

APLOMBOV. The band should be told to play a march.

NUNIN. *[Shouts]* Musicians! A march! *[The band plays a march for a minute.]*

A WAITER. Mr. Revunov-Karaulov!

*[ZHIGALOV, NASTASYA TIMOFEYEVNA, and NUNIN run to meet him. Enter REVUNOV-KARAULOV.]*

NASTASYA TIMOFEYEVNA. *[Bowing]* Please come in, your excellency! So glad you've come!

REVUNOV. Awfully!

ZHIGALOV. We, your excellency, aren't celebrities, we aren't important, but quite ordinary, but don't think on that account that there's any fraud. We put good people into the best place, we begrudge nothing. Please!

REVUNOV. Awfully glad!

NUNIN. Let me introduce to you, your excellency, the bridegroom, Epaminond Maximovitch Aplombov, with his newly born... I mean his newly married wife! Ivan Mihailovitch Yats, employed on the telegraph! A foreigner of Greek nationality, a confectioner by trade, Harlampi Spiridonovitch Dimba! Osip Lukitch Babelmandebsky! And so on, and so on.... The rest are just trash. Sit down, your excellency!

REVUNOV. Awfully! Excuse me, ladies and gentlemen, I just want to say two words to Andrey. *[Takes NUNIN aside]* I say, old man, I'm a little put out.... Why do you call me your excellency? I'm not a general! I don't rank as the equivalent of a colonel, even.

NUNIN. *[Whispers]* I know, only, Fyodor Yakovlevitch, be a good man and let us call you your excellency! The family here, you see, is patriarchal; it respects the aged, it likes rank.

REVUNOV. Oh, if it's like that, very well.... *[Goes to the table]* Awfully!

NASTASYA TIMOFEYEVNA. Sit down, your excellency! Be so good as to have some of this, your excellency! Only forgive us for not being used to etiquette; we're plain people!

REVUNOV. *[Not hearing]* What? Hm... yes. *[Pause]* Yes.... In the old days everybody used to live simply and was happy. In spite of my rank, I am a man who lives plainly. To-day Andrey comes to me and asks me to come here to the wedding. "How shall I go," I said, "when I don't know them? It's not good manners!" But he says: "They are good, simple, patriarchal people, glad to see anybody." Well, if that's the case... why not? Very glad to come. It's very dull for me at home by myself, and if my presence at a wedding can make anybody happy, then I'm delighted to be here....

ZHIGALOV. Then that's sincere, is it, your excellency? I respect that! I'm a plain man myself, without any deception, and I respect others who are like that. Eat, your excellency!

APLOMBOV. Is it long since you retired, your excellency?

REVUNOV. Eh? Yes, yes.... Quite true.... Yes. But, excuse me, what is this? The fish is sour... and the bread is sour. I can't eat this! *[APLOMBOV and DASHENKA kiss each other]* He, he, he... Your health! *[Pause]* Yes.... In the old days everything was simple and everybody was glad.... I love simplicity.... I'm an old man. I retired in 1865. I'm 72. Yes, of course, in my younger days it was different, but—*[Sees MOZGOVOY]* You there... a sailor, are you?

MOZGOVOY. Yes, just so.

REVUNOV. Aha, so... yes. The navy means hard work. There's a lot to think about and get a headache over. Every insignificant word has, so to speak, its special meaning! For instance, "Hoist her top-sheets and mainsail!" What's it mean? A sailor can tell! He, he!—With almost mathematical precision!

NUNIN. The health of his excellency Fyodor Yakovlevitch Revunov-Karaulov! *[Band plays a flourish. Cheers.]*

YATS. You, your excellency, have just expressed yourself on the subject of the hard work involved in a naval career. But is telegraphy any easier? Nowadays, your excellency, nobody is appointed to the telegraphs if he cannot read and write French and German. But the transmission of telegrams is the most difficult thing of all. Awfully difficult! Just listen.

*[Taps with his fork on the table, like a telegraphic transmitter.]*

REVUNOV. What does that mean?

YATS. It means, "I honour you, your excellency, for your virtues." You think it's easy? Listen now. *[Taps.]*

REVUNOV. Louder; I can't hear....

YATS. That means, "Madam, how happy I am to hold you in my embraces!"

REVUNOV. What madam are you talking about? Yes.... *[To MOZGOVOY]* Yes, if there's a head-wind you must... let's see... you must hoist your foretop halyards and topsail halyards! The order is: "On the cross-trees to the foretop halyards and topsail halyards" and at the same time, as the sails get loose, you take hold underneath of the foresail and fore-topsail halyards, stays and braces.

A GROOMSMAN. *[Rising]* Ladies and gentlemen...

REVUNOV. *[Cutting him short]* Yes... there are a great many orders to give. "Furl the fore-topsail and the foretop-gallant sail!!" Well, what does that mean? It's very simple! It means that if the top and top-gallant sails are lifting the halyards, they must level the foretop and foretop-gallant halyards on the hoist and at the same time the top-gallants braces, as needed, are loosened according to the direction of the wind...

NUNIN. *[To REVUNOV]* Fyodor Yakovlevitch, Mme. Zhigalov asks you to talk about something else. It's very dull for the guests, who can't understand....

REVUNOV. What? Who's dull? *[To MOZGOVOY]* Young man! Now suppose the ship is lying by the wind, on the starboard tack, under full sail, and you've got to bring her before the wind. What's the order? Well, first you whistle up above! He, he!

NUNIN. Fyodor Yakovlevitch, that's enough. Eat something.

REVUNOV. As soon as the men are on deck you give the order, "To your places!" What a life! You give orders, and at the same time you've got to keep your eyes on the sailors, who run about like flashes of lightning and get the sails and braces right. And at last you can't restrain yourself, and you shout, "Good children!" *[He chokes and coughs.]*

A GROOMSMAN. *[Making haste to use the ensuing pause to advantage]* On this occasion, so to speak, on the day on which we have met together to honour our dear...

REVUNOV. *[Interrupting]* Yes, you've got to remember all that! For instance, "Hoist the topsail halyards. Lower the topsail gallants!"

THE GROOMSMAN. *[Annoyed]* Why does he keep on interrupting? We shan't get through a single speech like that!

NASTASYA TIMOFEYEVNA.We are dull people, your excellency, and don't understand a word of all that, but if you were to tell us something appropriate...

REVUNOV. *[Not hearing]* I've already had supper, thank you. Did you say there was goose? Thanks... yes. I've remembered the old days.... It's pleasant, young man! You sail on the sea, you have no worries, and *[In an excited tone of voice]* do you remember the joy of tacking? Is there a sailor who doesn't glow at the memory of that manoeuvre? As soon as the word is given and the whistle blown and the crew begins to go up—it's as if an electric spark has run through them all. From the captain to the cabin-boy, everybody's excited.

ZMEYUKINA. How dull! How dull! *[General murmur.]*

REVUNOV. *[Who has not heard it properly]* Thank you, I've had supper. *[With enthusiasm]* Everybody's ready, and looks to the senior officer. He gives the command: "Stand by, gallants and topsail braces on the starboard side, main and counter-braces to port!" Everything's done in a twinkling. Top-sheets and jib-sheets are pulled... taken to starboard. *[Stands up]* The ship takes the wind and at last the sails fill out. The senior officer orders, "To the braces," and himself keeps his eye on the mainsail, and when at last this sail is filling out and the ship begins to turn, he yells at the top of his voice, "Let go the braces! Loose the main halyards!" Everything flies about, there's a general confusion for a moment—and everything is done without an error. The ship has been tacked!

NASTASYA TIMOFEYEVNA. *[Exploding]* General, your manners.... You ought to be ashamed of yourself, at your age!

REVUNOV. Did you say sausage? No, I haven't had any... thank you.

NASTASYA TIMOFEYEVNA. *[Loudly]* I say you ought to be ashamed of yourself at your age! General, your manners are awful!

NUNIN. *[Confused]* Ladies and gentlemen, is it worth it? Really...

REVUNOV. In the first place, I'm not a general, but a second-class naval captain, which, according to the table of precedence, corresponds to a lieutenant-colonel.

NASTASYA TIMOFEYEVNA. If you're not a general, then what did you go and take our money for? We never paid you money to behave like that!

REVUNOV. *[Upset]* What money?

NASTASYA TIMOFEYEVNA. You know what money. You know that you got 25 roubles from Andrey Andreyevitch.... *[To NUNIN]* And you look out, Andrey! I never asked you to hire a man like that!

NUNIN. There now... let it drop. Is it worth it?

REVUNOV. Paid... hired.... What is it?

APLOMBOV. Just let me ask you this. Did you receive 25 roubles from Andrey Andreyevitch?

REVUNOV. What 25 roubles? *[Suddenly realizing]* That's what it is! Now I understand it all.... How mean! How mean!

APLOMBOV. Did you take the money?

REVUNOV. I haven't taken any money! Get away from me! *[Leaves the table]* How mean! How low! To insult an old man, a sailor, an officer who has served long and faithfully! If you were decent people I could call somebody out, but what can I do now? *[Absently]* Where's the door? Which way do I go? Waiter, show me the way out! Waiter! *[Going]* How mean! How low! *[Exit.]*

NASTASYA TIMOFEYEVNA. Andrey, where are those 25 roubles?

NUNIN. Is it worth while bothering about such trifles? What does it matter! Everybody's happy here, and here you go.... *[Shouts]* The health of the bride and bridegroom! A march! A march!

*[The band plays a march]* The health of the bride and bride-groom!

ZMEYUKINA. I'm suffocating! Give me atmosphere! I'm suffocating with you all round me!

YATS. *[In a transport of delight]* My beauty! My beauty! *[Uproar.]*

A GROOMSMAN. *[Trying to shout everybody else down]* Ladies and gentlemen! On this occasion, if I may say so...

**Curtain.**

# THE PROPOSAL

## Translated by Julius West

### CHARACTERS

STEPAN STEPANOVITCH CHUBUKOV, a landowner
NATALYA STEPANOVNA, his daughter, twenty-five years old
IVAN VASSILEVITCH LOMOV, a neighbour of Chubukov, a large and hearty, but very suspicious landowner

# THE PROPOSAL

*The scene is laid at CHUBUKOV's country-house*

*A drawing-room in CHUBUKOV'S house.*

*[LOMOV enters, wearing a dress-jacket and white gloves. CHUBUKOV rises to meet him.]*

CHUBUKOV. My dear fellow, whom do I see! Ivan Vassilevitch! I am extremely glad! *[Squeezes his hand]* Now this is a surprise, my darling... How are you?

LOMOV. Thank you. And how may you be getting on?

CHUBUKOV. We just get along somehow, my angel, to your prayers, and so on. Sit down, please do.... Now, you know, you shouldn't forget all about your neighbours, my darling. My dear fellow, why are you so formal in your get-up? Evening dress, gloves, and so on. Can you be going anywhere, my treasure?

LOMOV. No, I've come only to see you, honoured Stepan Stepanovitch.

CHUBUKOV. Then why are you in evening dress, my precious? As if you're paying a New Year's Eve visit!

LOMOV. Well, you see, it's like this. *[Takes his arm]* I've come to you, honoured Stepan Stepanovitch, to trouble you with a request. Not once or twice have I already had the privilege of applying to you for help, and you have always, so to speak... I must ask your pardon, I am getting excited. I shall drink some water, honoured Stepan Stepanovitch. *[Drinks.]*

CHUBUKOV. *[Aside]* He's come to borrow money! Shan't give him any! *[Aloud]* What is it, my beauty?

LOMOV. You see, Honour Stepanitch... I beg pardon, Stepan Honouritch... I mean, I'm awfully excited, as you will please notice.... In short, you alone can help me, though I don't deserve it, of course... and haven't any right to count on your assistance....

CHUBUKOV. Oh, don't go round and round it, darling! Spit it out! Well?

LOMOV. One moment... this very minute. The fact is, I've come to ask the hand of your daughter, Natalya Stepanovna, in marriage.

CHUBUKOV. *[Joyfully]* By Jove! Ivan Vassilevitch! Say it again—I didn't hear it all!

LOMOV. I have the honour to ask...

CHUBUKOV. *[Interrupting]* My dear fellow... I'm so glad, and so on.... Yes, indeed, and all that sort of thing. *[Embraces and kisses LOMOV]* I've been hoping for it for a long time. It's been my continual desire. *[Sheds a tear]* And I've always loved you, my angel, as if you were my own son. May God give you both His help and His love and so on, and I did so much hope... What am I behaving in this idiotic way for? I'm off my balance with joy, absolutely off my balance! Oh, with all my soul... I'll go and call Natasha, and all that.

LOMOV. *[Greatly moved]* Honoured Stepan Stepanovitch, do you think I may count on her consent?

CHUBUKOV. Why, of course, my darling, and... as if she won't consent! She's in love; egad, she's like a love-sick cat, and so on.... Shan't be long! *[Exit.]*

LOMOV. It's cold... I'm trembling all over, just as if I'd got an examination before me. The great thing is, I must have my mind made up. If I give myself time to think, to hesitate, to talk a lot, to look for an ideal, or for real love, then I'll never get married.... Brr!... It's cold! Natalya Stepanovna is an excellent housekeeper, not bad-looking, well-educated.... What more do I want? But I'm getting a noise in my ears from excitement. *[Drinks]* And it's impossible for me not to marry.... In the first place, I'm already 35—a critical age, so to speak. In the second place, I ought to lead a quiet and regular life.... I suffer from palpitations, I'm excitable and always getting awfully upset.... At this very moment my lips are trembling, and there's a twitch in my right eyebrow.... But the very worst of all is the way I sleep. I no sooner get into bed and begin to go off when suddenly something in my left side—gives a pull, and I can feel it in my shoulder and head.... I jump up like a lunatic, walk about a bit, and lie down again, but as soon as I begin to get off to sleep there's another pull! And this may happen twenty times....

*[NATALYA STEPANOVNA comes in.]*

NATALYA STEPANOVNA. Well, there! It's you, and papa said, "Go; there's a merchant come for his goods." How do you do, Ivan Vassilevitch!

LOMOV. How do you do, honoured Natalya Stepanovna?

NATALYA STEPANOVNA. You must excuse my apron and négligé... we're shelling peas for drying. Why haven't you been here for such a long time? Sit down. *[They seat themselves]* Won't you have some lunch?

LOMOV. No, thank you, I've had some already.

NATALYA STEPANOVNA. Then smoke.... Here are the matches.... The weather is splendid now, but yesterday it was so wet that the workmen didn't do anything all day. How much hay have you stacked? Just think, I felt greedy and had a whole field cut, and now I'm not at all pleased about it because I'm afraid my hay may rot. I ought to have waited a bit. But what's this? Why, you're in evening dress! Well, I never! Are you going to a ball, or what?—though I must say you look better. Tell me, why are you got up like that?

LOMOV. *[Excited]* You see, honoured Natalya Stepanovna... the fact is, I've made up my mind to ask you to hear me out.... Of course you'll be surprised and perhaps even angry, but a... *[Aside]* It's awfully cold!

NATALYA STEPANOVNA. What's the matter? *[Pause]* Well?

LOMOV. I shall try to be brief. You must know, honoured Natalya Stepanovna, that I have long, since my childhood, in fact, had the privilege of knowing your family. My late aunt and her husband, from whom, as you know, I inherited my land, always had the greatest respect for your father and your late mother. The Lomovs and the Chubukovs have always had the most friendly, and I might almost say the most affectionate, regard for each other. And, as you know, my land is a near neighbour of yours. You will remember that my Oxen Meadows touch your birchwoods.

NATALYA STEPANOVNA. Excuse my interrupting you. You say, "my Oxen Meadows...." But are they yours?

LOMOV. Yes, mine.

NATALYA STEPANOVNA. What are you talking about? Oxen Meadows are ours, not yours!

LOMOV. No, mine, honoured Natalya Stepanovna.

NATALYA STEPANOVNA. Well, I never knew that before. How do you make that out?

LOMOV. How? I'm speaking of those Oxen Meadows which are wedged in between your birchwoods and the Burnt Marsh.

NATALYA STEPANOVNA. Yes, yes.... They're ours.

LOMOV. No, you're mistaken, honoured Natalya Stepanovna, they're mine.

NATALYA STEPANOVNA. Just think, Ivan Vassilevitch! How long have they been yours?

LOMOV. How long? As long as I can remember.

NATALYA STEPANOVNA. Really, you won't get me to believe that!

LOMOV. But you can see from the documents, honoured Natalya Stepanovna. Oxen Meadows, it's true, were once the subject of dispute, but now everybody knows that they are mine. There's nothing to argue about. You see, my aunt's grandmother gave the free use of these Meadows in perpetuity to the peasants of your father's grandfather, in return for which they were to make bricks for her. The peasants belonging to your father's grandfather had the free use of the Meadows for forty years, and had got into the habit of regarding them as their own, when it happened that...

NATALYA STEPANOVNA. No, it isn't at all like that! Both my grandfather and great-grandfather reckoned that their land extended to Burnt Marsh—which means that Oxen Meadows were ours. I don't see what there is to argue about. It's simply silly!

LOMOV. I'll show you the documents, Natalya Stepanovna!

NATALYA STEPANOVNA. No, you're simply joking, or making fun of me.... What a surprise! We've had the land for nearly three hundred years, and then we're suddenly told that it isn't ours! Ivan Vassilevitch, I can hardly believe my own ears.... These Meadows aren't worth much to me. They only come to five dessiatins *[Note: 13.5 acres]*, and are worth perhaps 300 roubles *[Note: £30.]*, but I can't stand unfairness. Say what you will, but I can't stand unfairness.

LOMOV. Hear me out, I implore you! The peasants of your father's grandfather, as I have already had the honour of explaining to you, used to bake bricks for my aunt's grandmother. Now my aunt's grandmother, wishing to make them a pleasant...

NATALYA STEPANOVNA. I can't make head or tail of all this about aunts and grandfathers and grandmothers! The Meadows are ours, and that's all.

LOMOV. Mine.

NATALYA STEPANOVNA. Ours! You can go on proving it for two days on end, you can go and put on fifteen dress-jackets, but I tell you they're ours, ours, ours! I don't want anything of yours and I don't want to give up anything of mine. So there!

LOMOV. Natalya Ivanovna, I don't want the Meadows, but I am acting on principle. If you like, I'll make you a present of them.

NATALYA STEPANOVNA. I can make you a present of them myself, because they're mine! Your behaviour, Ivan Vassilevitch, is strange, to say the least! Up to this we have always thought of you as a good neighbour, a friend: last year we lent you our threshing-machine, although on that account we had to put off our own threshing till November, but you behave to us as if we were gipsies. Giving me my own land, indeed! No, really, that's not at all neighbourly! In my opinion, it's even impudent, if you want to know....

LOMOV. Then you make out that I'm a land-grabber? Madam, never in my life have I grabbed anybody else's land, and I shan't allow anybody to accuse me of having done so.... *[Quickly steps to the carafe and drinks more water]* Oxen Meadows are mine!

NATALYA STEPANOVNA. It's not true, they're ours!

LOMOV. Mine!

NATALYA STEPANOVNA. It's not true! I'll prove it! I'll send my mowers out to the Meadows this very day!

LOMOV. What?

NATALYA STEPANOVNA. My mowers will be there this very day!

LOMOV. I'll give it to them in the neck!

NATALYA STEPANOVNA. You dare!

LOMOV. *[Clutches at his heart]* Oxen Meadows are mine! You understand? Mine!

NATALYA STEPANOVNA. Please don't shout! You can shout yourself hoarse in your own house, but here I must ask you to restrain yourself!

LOMOV. If it wasn't, madam, for this awful, excruciating palpitation, if my whole inside wasn't upset, I'd talk to you in a different way! *[Yells]* Oxen Meadows are mine!

NATALYA STEPANOVNA. Ours!

LOMOV. Mine!

NATALYA STEPANOVNA. Ours!

LOMOV. Mine!

*[Enter CHUBUKOV.]*

CHUBUKOV. What's the matter? What are you shouting at?

NATALYA STEPANOVNA. Papa, please tell to this gentleman who owns Oxen Meadows, we or he?

CHUBUKOV. *[To LOMOV]* Darling, the Meadows are ours!

LOMOV. But, please, Stepan Stepanitch, how can they be yours? Do be a reasonable man! My aunt's grandmother gave the Meadows for the temporary and free use of your grandfather's peasants. The peasants used the land for forty years and got as accustomed to it as if it was their own, when it happened that...

CHUBUKOV. Excuse me, my precious.... You forget just this, that the peasants didn't pay your grandmother and all that, because the Meadows were in dispute, and so on. And now everybody knows that they're ours. It means that you haven't seen the plan.

LOMOV. I'll prove to you that they're mine!

CHUBUKOV. You won't prove it, my darling.

LOMOV. I shall!

CHUBUKOV. Dear one, why yell like that? You won't prove anything just by yelling. I don't want anything of yours, and don't intend to give up what I have. Why should I? And you know, my beloved, that if you propose to go on arguing about it, I'd much sooner give up the meadows to the peasants than to you. There!

LOMOV. I don't understand! How have you the right to give away somebody else's property?

CHUBUKOV. You may take it that I know whether I have the right or not. Because, young man, I'm not used to being spoken to in that tone of voice, and so on: I, young man, am twice your age, and ask you to speak to me without agitating yourself, and all that.

LOMOV. No, you just think I'm a fool and want to have me on! You call my land yours, and then you want me to talk to you calmly and politely! Good neighbours don't behave like that, Stepan Stepanitch! You're not a neighbour, you're a grabber!

CHUBUKOV. What's that? What did you say?

NATALYA STEPANOVNA. Papa, send the mowers out to the Meadows at once!

CHUBUKOV. What did you say, sir?

NATALYA STEPANOVNA. Oxen Meadows are ours, and I shan't give them up, shan't give them up, shan't give them up!

LOMOV. We'll see! I'll have the matter taken to court, and then I'll show you!

CHUBUKOV. To court? You can take it to court, and all that! You can! I know you; you're just on the look-out for a chance to go to court, and all that.... You pettifogger! All your people were like that! All of them!

LOMOV. Never mind about my people! The Lomovs have all been honourable people, and not one has ever been tried for embezzlement, like your grandfather!

CHUBUKOV. You Lomovs have had lunacy in your family, all of you!

NATALYA STEPANOVNA. All, all, all!

CHUBUKOV. Your grandfather was a drunkard, and your younger aunt, Nastasya Mihailovna, ran away with an architect, and so on.

LOMOV. And your mother was hump-backed. *[Clutches at his heart]* Something pulling in my side.... My head.... Help! Water!

CHUBUKOV. Your father was a guzzling gambler!

NATALYA STEPANOVNA. And there haven't been many backbiters to equal your aunt!

LOMOV. My left foot has gone to sleep.... You're an intriguer.... Oh, my heart!... And it's an open secret that before the last elections you bri... I can see stars.... Where's my hat?

NATALYA STEPANOVNA. It's low! It's dishonest! It's mean!

CHUBUKOV. And you're just a malicious, double-faced intriguer! Yes!

LOMOV. Here's my hat.... My heart!... Which way? Where's the door? Oh!... I think I'm dying.... My foot's quite numb.... *[Goes to the door.]*

CHUBUKOV. *[Following him]* And don't set foot in my house again!

NATALYA STEPANOVNA. Take it to court! We'll see!

*[LOMOV staggers out.]*

CHUBUKOV. Devil take him! *[Walks about in excitement.]*

NATALYA STEPANOVNA. What a rascal! What trust can one have in one's neighbours after that!

CHUBUKOV. The villain! The scarecrow!

NATALYA STEPANOVNA. The monster! First he takes our land and then he has the impudence to abuse us.

CHUBUKOV. And that blind hen, yes, that turnip-ghost has the confounded cheek to make a proposal, and so on! What? A proposal!

NATALYA STEPANOVNA. What proposal?

CHUBUKOV. Why, he came here so as to propose to you.

NATALYA STEPANOVNA. To propose? To me? Why didn't you tell me so before?

CHUBUKOV. So he dresses up in evening clothes. The stuffed sausage! The wizen-faced frump!

NATALYA STEPANOVNA. To propose to me? Ah! *[Falls into an easy-chair and wails]* Bring him back! Back! Ah! Bring him here.

CHUBUKOV. Bring whom here?

NATALYA STEPANOVNA. Quick, quick! I'm ill! Fetch him! *[Hysterics.]*

CHUBUKOV. What's that? What's the matter with you? *[Clutches at his head]* Oh, unhappy man that I am! I'll shoot myself! I'll hang myself! We've done for her!

NATALYA STEPANOVNA. I'm dying! Fetch him!

CHUBUKOV. Tfoo! At once. Don't yell!

*[Runs out. A pause. NATALYA STEPANOVNA wails.]*

NATALYA STEPANOVNA. What have they done to me! Fetch him back! Fetch him! *[A pause.]*

*[CHUBUKOV runs in.]*

CHUBUKOV. He's coming, and so on, devil take him! Ouf! Talk to him yourself; I don't want to....

NATALYA STEPANOVNA. *[Wails]* Fetch him!

CHUBUKOV. *[Yells]* He's coming, I tell you. Oh, what a burden, Lord, to be the father of a grown-up daughter! I'll cut my throat! I will, indeed! We cursed him, abused him, drove him out, and it's all you... you!

NATALYA STEPANOVNA. No, it was you!

CHUBUKOV. I tell you it's not my fault. *[LOMOV appears at the door]* Now you talk to him yourself *[Exit.]*

*[LOMOV enters, exhausted.]*

LOMOV. My heart's palpitating awfully.... My foot's gone to sleep.... There's something keeps pulling in my side.

NATALYA STEPANOVNA. Forgive us, Ivan Vassilevitch, we were all a little heated.... I remember now: Oxen Meadows really are yours.

LOMOV. My heart's beating awfully.... My Meadows.... My eyebrows are both twitching....

NATALYA STEPANOVNA. The Meadows are yours, yes, yours.... Do sit down.... *[They sit]* We were wrong....

LOMOV. I did it on principle.... My land is worth little to me, but the principle...

NATALYA STEPANOVNA. Yes, the principle, just so.... Now let's talk of something else.

LOMOV. The more so as I have evidence. My aunt's grandmother gave the land to your father's grandfather's peasants...

NATALYA STEPANOVNA. Yes, yes, let that pass.... *[Aside]* I wish I knew how to get him started.... *[Aloud]* Are you going to start shooting soon?

LOMOV. I'm thinking of having a go at the blackcock, honoured Natalya Stepanovna, after the harvest. Oh, have you heard? Just think, what a misfortune I've had! My dog Guess, whom you know, has gone lame.

NATALYA STEPANOVNA. What a pity! Why?

LOMOV. I don't know.... Must have got twisted, or bitten by some other dog.... *[Sighs]* My very best dog, to say nothing of the expense. I gave Mironov 125 roubles for him.

NATALYA STEPANOVNA. It was too much, Ivan Vassilevitch.

LOMOV. I think it was very cheap. He's a first-rate dog.

NATALYA STEPANOVNA. Papa gave 85 roubles for his Squeezer, and Squeezer is heaps better than Guess!

LOMOV. Squeezer better than. Guess? What an idea! *[Laughs]* Squeezer better than Guess!

NATALYA STEPANOVNA. Of course he's better! Of course, Squeezer is young, he may develop a bit, but on points and pedigree he's better than anything that even Volchanetsky has got.

LOMOV. Excuse me, Natalya Stepanovna, but you forget that he is overshot, and an overshot always means the dog is a bad hunter!

NATALYA STEPANOVNA. Overshot, is he? The first time I hear it!

LOMOV. I assure you that his lower jaw is shorter than the upper.

NATALYA STEPANOVNA. Have you measured?

LOMOV. Yes. He's all right at following, of course, but if you want him to get hold of anything...

NATALYA STEPANOVNA. In the first place, our Squeezer is a thoroughbred animal, the son of Harness and Chisels, while there's no getting at the pedigree of your dog at all.... He's old and as ugly as a worn-out cab-horse.

LOMOV. He is old, but I wouldn't take five Squeezers for him.... Why, how can you?... Guess is a dog; as for Squeezer, well, it's too funny to argue.... Anybody you like has a dog as good as Squeezer... you may find them under every bush almost. Twenty-five roubles would be a handsome price to pay for him.

NATALYA STEPANOVNA. There's some demon of contradiction in you today, Ivan Vassilevitch. First you pretend that the Meadows are yours; now, that Guess is better than Squeezer. I don't like people who don't say what they mean, because you know perfectly well that Squeezer is a hundred times better than your silly Guess. Why do you want to say it isn't?

LOMOV. I see, Natalya Stepanovna, that you consider me either blind or a fool. You must realize that Squeezer is overshot!

NATALYA STEPANOVNA. It's not true.

LOMOV. He is!

NATALYA STEPANOVNA. It's not true!

LOMOV. Why shout, madam?

NATALYA STEPANOVNA. Why talk rot? It's awful! It's time your Guess was shot, and you compare him with Squeezer!

LOMOV. Excuse me; I cannot continue this discussion: my heart is palpitating.

NATALYA STEPANOVNA. I've noticed that those hunters argue most who know least.

LOMOV. Madam, please be silent.... My heart is going to pieces.... *[Shouts]* Shut up!

NATALYA STEPANOVNA. I shan't shut up until you acknowledge that Squeezer is a hundred times better than your Guess!

LOMOV. A hundred times worse! Be hanged to your Squeezer! His head... eyes... shoulder...

NATALYA STEPANOVNA. There's no need to hang your silly Guess; he's half-dead already!

LOMOV. *[Weeps]* Shut up! My heart's bursting!

NATALYA STEPANOVNA. I shan't shut up.

*[Enter CHUBUKOV.]*

CHUBUKOV. What's the matter now?

NATALYA STEPANOVNA. Papa, tell us truly, which is the better dog, our Squeezer or his Guess.

LOMOV. Stepan Stepanovitch, I implore you to tell me just one thing: is your Squeezer overshot or not? Yes or no?

CHUBUKOV. And suppose he is? What does it matter? He's the best dog in the district for all that, and so on.

LOMOV. But isn't my Guess better? Really, now?

CHUBUKOV. Don't excite yourself, my precious one.... Allow me.... Your Guess certainly has his good points.... He's pure-bred, firm on his feet, has well-sprung ribs, and all that. But, my dear man, if you want to know the truth, that dog has two defects: he's old and he's short in the muzzle.

LOMOV. Excuse me, my heart.... Let's take the facts.... You will remember that on the Marusinsky hunt my Guess ran neck-and-neck with the Count's dog, while your Squeezer was left a whole verst behind.

CHUBUKOV. He got left behind because the Count's whipper-in hit him with his whip.

LOMOV. And with good reason. The dogs are running after a fox, when Squeezer goes and starts worrying a sheep!

CHUBUKOV. It's not true!... My dear fellow, I'm very liable to lose my temper, and so, just because of that, let's stop arguing. You started because everybody is always jealous of everybody else's dogs. Yes, we're all like that! You too, sir, aren't blameless! You no sooner notice that some dog is better than your Guess than you begin with this, that... and the other... and all that.... I remember everything!

LOMOV. I remember too!

CHUBUKOV. *[Teasing him]* I remember, too.... What do you remember?

LOMOV. My heart... my foot's gone to sleep.... I can't...

NATALYA STEPANOVNA. *[Teasing]* My heart.... What sort of a hunter are you? You ought to go and lie on the kitchen oven and catch blackbeetles, not go after foxes! My heart!

CHUBUKOV. Yes really, what sort of a hunter are you, anyway? You ought to sit at home with your palpitations, and not go tracking animals. You could go hunting, but you only go to argue with people and interfere with their dogs and so on. Let's change the subject in case I lose my temper. You're not a hunter at all, anyway!

LOMOV. And are you a hunter? You only go hunting to get in with the Count and to intrigue.... Oh, my heart!... You're an intriguer!

CHUBUKOV. What? I an intriguer? *[Shouts]* Shut up!

LOMOV. Intriguer!

CHUBUKOV. Boy! Pup!

LOMOV. Old rat! Jesuit!

CHUBUKOV. Shut up or I'll shoot you like a partridge! You fool!

LOMOV. Everybody knows that—oh my heart!—your late wife used to beat you.... My feet... temples... sparks.... I fall, I fall!

CHUBUKOV. And you're under the slipper of your housekeeper!

LOMOV. There, there, there... my heart's burst! My shoulder's come off.... Where is my shoulder? I die. *[Falls into an armchair]* A doctor! *[Faints.]*

CHUBUKOV. Boy! Milksop! Fool! I'm sick! *[Drinks water]* Sick!

NATALYA STEPANOVNA. What sort of a hunter are you? You can't even sit on a horse! *[To her father]* Papa, what's the matter with him? Papa! Look, papa! *[Screams]* Ivan Vassilevitch! He's dead!

CHUBUKOV. I'm sick!... I can't breathe!... Air!

NATALYA STEPANOVNA. He's dead. *[Pulls LOMOV'S sleeve]* Ivan Vassilevitch! Ivan Vassilevitch! What have you done to me? He's dead. *[Falls into an armchair]* A doctor, a doctor! *[Hysterics.]*

CHUBUKOV. Oh!... What is it? What's the matter?

NATALYA STEPANOVNA. *[Wails]* He's dead... dead!

CHUBUKOV. Who's dead? *[Looks at LOMOV]* So he is! My word! Water! A doctor! *[Lifts a tumbler to LOMOV'S mouth]* Drink this!... No, he doesn't drink.... It means he's dead, and all that.... I'm the most unhappy of men! Why don't I put a bullet into my brain? Why haven't I cut my throat yet? What am I waiting for? Give me a knife! Give me a pistol! *[LOMOV moves]* He seems to be coming round.... Drink some water! That's right....

LOMOV. I see stars... mist.... Where am I?

CHUBUKOV. Hurry up and get married and—well, to the devil with you! She's willing! *[He puts LOMOV'S hand into his daughter's]* She's willing and all that. I give you my blessing and so on. Only leave me in peace!

LOMOV. *[Getting up]* Eh? What? To whom?

CHUBUKOV. She's willing! Well? Kiss and be damned to you!

NATALYA STEPANOVNA. *[Wails]* He's alive... Yes, yes, I'm willing....

CHUBUKOV. Kiss each other!

LOMOV. Eh? Kiss whom? *[They kiss]* Very nice, too. Excuse me, what's it all about? Oh, now I understand... my heart... stars... I'm happy. Natalya Stepanovna.... *[Kisses her hand]* My foot's gone to sleep....

NATALYA STEPANOVNA. I... I'm happy too....

CHUBUKOV. What a weight off my shoulders.... Ouf!

NATALYA STEPANOVNA. But... still you will admit now that Guess is worse than Squeezer.

LOMOV. Better!

NATALYA STEPANOVNA. Worse!

CHUBUKOV. Well, that's a way to start your family bliss! Have some champagne!

LOMOV. He's better!

NATALYA STEPANOVNA. Worse! worse! worse!

CHUBUKOV. *[Trying to shout her down]* Champagne! Champagne!

**Curtain.**

# THE SEA-GULL

## CHARACTERS

IRINA ABKADINA, an actress

CONSTANTINE TREPLIEFF, her son

PETER SORIN, her brother

NINA ZARIETCHNAYA, a young girl, the daughter of a rich landowner

ILIA SHAMRAEFF, the manager of SORIN'S estate

PAULINA, his wife

MASHA, their daughter

BORIS TRIGORIN, an author

EUGENE DORN, a doctor

SIMON MEDVIEDENKO, a schoolmaster

JACOB, a workman

A COOK

A MAIDSERVANT

# ACT I

*The scene is laid on SORIN'S estate. Two years elapse between the third and fourth acts.*

*The scene is laid in the park on SORIN'S estate. A broad avenue of trees leads away from the audience toward a lake which lies lost in the depths of the park. The avenue is obstructed by a rough stage, temporarily erected for the performance of amateur theatricals, and which screens the lake from view. There is a dense growth of bushes to the left and right of the stage. A few chairs and a little table are placed in front of the stage. The sun has just set. JACOB and some other workmen are heard hammering and coughing on the stage behind the lowered curtain.*

*MASHA and MEDVIEDENKO come in from the left, returning from a walk.*

MEDVIEDENKO. Why do you always wear mourning?

MASHA. I dress in black to match my life. I am unhappy.

MEDVIEDENKO. Why should you be unhappy? *[Thinking it over]* I don't understand it. You are healthy, and though your father is not rich, he has a good competency. My life is far harder than yours. I only have twenty-three roubles a month to live on, but I don't wear mourning. *[They sit down]*.

MASHA. Happiness does not depend on riches; poor men are often happy.

MEDVIEDENKO. In theory, yes, but not in reality. Take my case, for instance; my mother, my two sisters, my little brother and I must all live somehow on my salary of twenty-three roubles a month. We have to eat and drink, I take it. You wouldn't have us go without tea and sugar, would you? Or tobacco? Answer me that, if you can.

MASHA. *[Looking in the direction of the stage]* The play will soon begin.

MEDVIEDENKO. Yes, Nina Zarietchnaya is going to act in Treplieff's play. They love one another, and their two souls will unite to-night in the effort to interpret the same idea by different means. There is no ground on which your soul and mine can meet. I love you. Too restless and sad to stay at home, I tramp here every day, six miles and back, to be met only by your indifference. I am poor, my family is large, you can have no inducement to marry a man who cannot even find sufficient food for his own mouth.

MASHA. It is not that. *[She takes snuff]* I am touched by your affection, but I cannot return it, that is all. *[She offers him the snuff-box]* Will you take some?

MEDVIEDENKO. No, thank you. *[A pause.]*

MASHA. The air is sultry; a storm is brewing for to-night. You do nothing but moralise or else talk about money. To you, poverty is the greatest misfortune that can befall a man, but I think it is a thousand times easier to go begging in rags than to—You wouldn't understand that, though.

*SORIN leaning on a cane, and TREPLIEFF come in.*

SORIN. For some reason, my boy, country life doesn't suit me, and I am sure I shall never get used to it. Last night I went to bed at ten and woke at nine this morning, feeling as if, from oversleep, my brain had stuck to my skull. *[Laughing]* And yet I accidentally dropped off to sleep again after dinner, and feel utterly done up at this moment. It is like a nightmare.

TREPLIEFF. There is no doubt that you should live in town. *[He catches sight of MASHA and MEDVIEDENKO]* You shall be called when the play begins, my friends, but you must not stay here now. Go away, please.

SORIN. Miss Masha, will you kindly ask your father to leave the dog unchained? It howled so last night that my sister was unable to sleep.

MASHA. You must speak to my father yourself. Please excuse me; I can't do so. *[To MEDVIEDENKO]* Come, let us go.

MEDVIEDENKO. You will let us know when the play begins?

*MASHA and MEDVIEDENKO go out.*

SORIN. I foresee that that dog is going to howl all night again. It is always this way in the country; I have never been able to live as I like here. I come down for a month's holiday, to rest and all, and am plagued so by their nonsense that I long to escape after the first day. *[Laughing]* I have always been glad to get away from this place, but I have been retired now, and this was the only place I had to come to. Willy-nilly, one must live somewhere.

JACOB. *[To TREPLIEFF]* We are going to take a swim, Mr. Constantine.

TREPLIEFF. Very well, but you must be back in ten minutes.

JACOB. We will, sir.

TREPLIEFF. *[Looking at the stage]* Just like a real theatre! See, there we have the curtain, the foreground, the background, and all. No artificial scenery is needed. The eye travels direct to the lake, and rests on the horizon. The curtain will be raised as the moon rises at half-past eight.

SORIN. Splendid!

TREPLIEFF. Of course the whole effect will be ruined if Nina is late. She should be here by now, but her father and stepmother watch her so closely that it is like stealing her from a prison to get her away from home. *[He straightens SORIN'S collar]* Your hair and beard are all on end. Oughtn't you to have them trimmed?

SORIN. *[Smoothing his beard]* They are the tragedy of my existence. Even when I was young I always looked as if I were drunk, and all. Women have never liked me. *[Sitting down]* Why is my sister out of temper?

TREPLIEFF. Why? Because she is jealous and bored. *[Sitting down beside SORIN]* She is not acting this evening, but Nina is, and so she has set herself against me, and against the performance of the play, and against the play itself, which she hates without ever having read it.

SORIN. *[Laughing]* Does she, really?

TREPLIEFF. Yes, she is furious because Nina is going to have a success on this little stage. *[Looking at his watch]* My mother is a psychological curiosity. Without doubt brilliant and talented, capable of sobbing over a novel, of reciting all Nekrasoff's poetry by heart, and of nursing the sick like an angel of heaven, you should see what happens if any one begins praising Duse to her! She alone must be praised and written about, raved over, her marvellous acting in "La Dame aux Camelias" extolled to the skies. As she cannot get all that rubbish in the country, she grows peevish and cross, and thinks we are all against her, and to blame for it all. She is superstitious, too. She dreads burning three candles, and fears the thirteenth day of the month. Then she is stingy. I know for a fact that she has seventy thousand roubles in a bank at Odessa, but she is ready to burst into tears if you ask her to lend you a penny.

SORIN. You have taken it into your head that your mother dislikes your play, and the thought of it has excited you, and all. Keep calm; your mother adores you.

TREPLIEFF. *[Pulling a flower to pieces]* She loves me, loves me not; loves—loves me not; loves—loves me not! *[Laughing]* You see, she doesn't love me, and why should she? She likes life and love and gay clothes, and I am already twenty-five years old; a sufficient reminder to her that she is no longer young. When I am away she is only thirty-two, in my presence she is forty-three, and she hates me for it. She knows, too, that I despise the modern stage. She adores it, and imagines that she is working on it for the benefit of humanity and her sacred art, but to me the theatre is merely the vehicle of convention and prejudice. When the curtain rises on that little three-walled room, when those mighty geniuses, those high-priests of art, show us people in the act of eating, drinking, loving, walking, and wearing their coats, and attempt to extract a moral from their insipid talk; when playwrights give us under a thousand different guises the same, same, same old stuff, then I must needs run from it, as Maupassant ran from the Eiffel Tower that was about to crush him by its vulgarity.

SORIN. But we can't do without a theatre.

TREPLIEFF. No, but we must have it under a new form. If we can't do that, let us rather not have it at all. *[Looking at his watch]* I love my mother, I love her devotedly, but I think she leads a stupid life. She always has this man of letters of hers on her mind, and the newspapers are always frightening her to death, and I am tired of it. Plain, human egoism sometimes speaks in my heart, and I regret that my mother is a famous actress. If she were an ordinary woman I think I should be a happier man. What could be more intolerable and foolish than my position, Uncle, when I find myself the only nonentity among a crowd of her guests, all celebrated authors and artists? I feel that they only endure me because I am her son. Personally I am nothing, nobody. I pulled through my third year at college by the skin of my teeth, as they say. I have neither money nor brains, and on my passport you may read that I am simply a citizen of Kiev. So was my father, but he was a well-known actor. When the celebrities that frequent my mother's drawing-room deign to notice me at all, I know they only look at me to measure my insignificance; I read their thoughts, and suffer from humiliation.

SORIN. Tell me, by the way, what is Trigorin like? I can't understand him, he is always so silent.

TREPLIEFF. Trigorin is clever, simple, well-mannered, and a little, I might say, melancholic in disposition. Though still under forty, he is surfeited with praise. As for his stories, they are—how shall I put it?—pleasing, full of talent, but if you have read Tolstoi or Zola you somehow don't enjoy Trigorin.

SORIN. Do you know, my boy, I like literary men. I once passionately desired two things: to marry, and to become an author. I have succeeded in neither. It must be pleasant to be even an insignificant author.

TREPLIEFF. *[Listening]* I hear footsteps! *[He embraces his uncle]* I cannot live without her; even the sound of her footsteps is music to me. I am madly happy. *[He goes quickly to meet NINA, who comes in at that moment]* My enchantress! My girl of dreams!

NINA. *[Excitedly]* It can't be that I am late? No, I am not late.

TREPLIEFF. *[Kissing her hands]* No, no, no!

NINA. I have been in a fever all day, I was so afraid my father would prevent my coming, but he and my stepmother have just gone driving. The sky is clear, the moon is rising. How I hurried to get here! How I urged my horse to go faster and faster! *[Laughing]* I am *so* glad to see you! *[She shakes hands with SORIN.]*

SORIN. Oho! Your eyes look as if you had been crying. You mustn't do that.

NINA. It is nothing, nothing. Do let us hurry. I must go in half an hour. No, no, for heaven's sake do not urge me to stay. My father doesn't know I am here.

TREPLIEFF. As a matter of fact, it is time to begin now. I must call the audience.

SORIN. Let me call them—and all—I am going this minute. *[He goes toward the right, begins to sing "The Two Grenadiers," then stops.]* I was singing that once when a fellow-lawyer said to me: "You have a powerful voice, sir." Then he thought a moment and added, "But it is a disagreeable one!" *[He goes out laughing.]*

NINA. My father and his wife never will let me come here; they call this place Bohemia and are afraid I shall become an actress.

But this lake attracts me as it does the gulls. My heart is full of you. *[She glances about her.]*

TREPLIEFF. We are alone.

NINA. Isn't that some one over there?

TREPLIEFF. No. *[They kiss one another.]*

NINA. What is that tree?

TREPLIEFF. An elm.

NINA. Why does it look so dark?

TREPLIEFF. It is evening; everything looks dark now. Don't go away early, I implore you.

NINA. I must.

TREPLIEFF. What if I were to follow you, Nina? I shall stand in your garden all night with my eyes on your window.

NINA. That would be impossible; the watchman would see you, and Treasure is not used to you yet, and would bark.

TREPLIEFF. I love you.

NINA. Hush!

TREPLIEFF. *[Listening to approaching footsteps]* Who is that? Is it you, Jacob?

JACOB. *[On the stage]* Yes, sir.

TREPLIEFF. To your places then. The moon is rising; the play must commence.

NINA. Yes, sir.

TREPLIEFF. Is the alcohol ready? Is the sulphur ready? There must be fumes of sulphur in the air when the red eyes shine out. *[To NINA]* Go, now, everything is ready. Are you nervous?

NINA. Yes, very. I am not so much afraid of your mother as I am of Trigorin. I am terrified and ashamed to act before him; he is so famous. Is he young?

TREPLIEFF. Yes.

NINA. What beautiful stories he writes!

TREPLIEFF. *[Coldly]* I have never read any of them, so I can't say.

NINA. Your play is very hard to act; there are no living characters in it.

TREPLIEFF. Living characters! Life must be represented not as it is, but as it ought to be; as it appears in dreams.

NINA. There is so little action; it seems more like a recitation. I think love should always come into every play.

*NINA and TREPLIEFF go up onto the little stage; PAULINA and DORN come in.*

PAULINA. It is getting damp. Go back and put on your goloshes.

DORN. I am quite warm.

PAULINA. You never will take care of yourself; you are quite obstinate about it, and yet you are a doctor, and know quite well that damp air is bad for you. You like to see me suffer, that's what it is. You sat out on the terrace all yesterday evening on purpose.

DORN. *[Sings]*

"Oh, tell me not that youth is wasted."

PAULINA. You were so enchanted by the conversation of Madame Arkadina that you did not even notice the cold. Confess that you admire her.

DORN. I am fifty-five years old.

PAULINA. A trifle. That is not old for a man. You have kept your looks magnificently, and women still like you.

DORN. What are you trying to tell me?

PAULINA. You men are all ready to go down on your knees to an actress, all of you.

DORN. *[Sings]*

"Once more I stand before thee."

It is only right that artists should be made much of by society and treated differently from, let us say, merchants. It is a kind of idealism.

PAULINA. When women have loved you and thrown themselves at your head, has that been idealism?

DORN. *[Shrugging his shoulders]* I can't say. There has been a great deal that was admirable in my relations with women. In me they liked, above all, the superior doctor. Ten years ago, you remember, I was the only decent doctor they had in this part of the country—and then, I have always acted like a man of honour.

PAULINA. *[Seizes his hand]* Dearest!

DORN. Be quiet! Here they come.

*ARKADINA comes in on SORIN'S arm; also TRIGORIN, SHAMRAEFF, MEDVIEDENKO, and MASHA.*

SHAMRAEFF. She acted most beautifully at the Poltava Fair in 1873; she was really magnificent. But tell me, too, where Tchadin the comedian is now? He was inimitable as Rasplueff, better than Sadofski. Where is he now?

ARKADINA. Don't ask me where all those antediluvians are! I know nothing about them. *[She sits down.]*

SHAMRAEFF. *[Sighing]* Pashka Tchadin! There are none left like him. The stage is not what it was in his time. There were sturdy oaks growing on it then, where now but stumps remain.

DORN. It is true that we have few dazzling geniuses these days, but, on the other hand, the average of acting is much higher.

SHAMRAEFF. I cannot agree with you; however, that is a matter of taste, *de gustibus.*

*Enter TREPLIEFF from behind the stage.*

ARKADINA. When will the play begin, my dear boy?

TREPLIEFF. In a moment. I must ask you to have patience.

ARKADINA. *[Quoting from Hamlet]* My son,

"Thou turn'st mine eyes into my very soul;
And there I see such black grained spots
As will not leave their tinct."

*[A horn is blown behind the stage.]*

TREPLIEFF. Attention, ladies and gentlemen! The play is about to begin. *[A pause]* I shall commence. *[He taps the door with a stick, and speaks in a loud voice]* O, ye time-honoured, ancient mists that drive at night across the surface of this lake, blind you our eyes with sleep, and show us in our dreams that which will be in twice ten thousand years!

SORIN. There won't be anything in twice ten thousand years.

TREPLIEFF. Then let them now show us that nothingness.

ARKADINA. Yes, let them—we are asleep.

## ACT I

*The curtain rises. A vista opens across the lake. The moon hangs low above the horizon and is reflected in the water. NINA, dressed in white, is seen seated on a great rock.*

NINA. All men and beasts, lions, eagles, and quails, horned stags, geese, spiders, silent fish that inhabit the waves, starfish from the sea, and creatures invisible to the eye—in one word, life—all, all life, completing the dreary round imposed upon it, has died out at last. A thousand years have passed since the earth last bore a living creature on her breast, and the unhappy moon now lights her lamp in vain. No longer are the cries of storks heard in the meadows, or the drone of beetles in the groves of limes. All is cold, cold. All is void, void, void. All is terrible, terrible—*[A pause]* The bodies of all living creatures have dropped to dust, and eternal matter has transformed them into stones and water and clouds; but their spirits have flowed together into one, and that great world-soul am I! In me is the spirit of the great Alexander, the spirit of Napoleon, of Caesar, of Shakespeare, and of the tiniest leech that swims. In me the consciousness of man has joined hands with the instinct of the animal; I understand all, all, all, and each life lives again in me.

*[The will-o-the-wisps flicker out along the lake shore.]*

ARKADINA. *[Whispers]* What decadent rubbish is this?

TREPLIEFF. *[Imploringly]* Mother!

NINA. I am alone. Once in a hundred years my lips are opened, my voice echoes mournfully across the desert earth, and no one hears. And you, poor lights of the marsh, you do not hear me. You are engendered at sunset in the putrid mud, and flit wavering about the lake till dawn, unconscious, unreasoning, unwarmed by the breath of life. Satan, father of eternal matter, trembling lest the spark of life should glow in you, has ordered an unceasing movement of the atoms that compose you, and so you shift and change for ever. I, the spirit of the universe, I alone am immutable and eternal. *[A pause]* Like a captive in a dungeon deep and void, I know not where I am, nor what awaits me. One thing only is not hidden from me: in my fierce and obstinate battle with Satan, the source of the forces of matter, I am destined to be victorious in the end. Matter and spirit will then be one at last in glorious harmony, and the reign of freedom will begin on earth. But this can only come to pass by slow degrees, when after countless eons the moon and earth and shining Sirius himself shall fall to dust. Until that hour, oh, horror! horror! horror! *[A pause. Two glowing red points are seen shining across the lake]* Satan, my mighty foe, advances; I see his dread and lurid eyes.

ARKADINA. I smell sulphur. Is that done on purpose?

TREPLIEFF. Yes.

ARKADINA. Oh, I see; that is part of the effect.

TREPLIEFF. Mother!

NINA. He longs for man—

PAULINA. *[To DORN]* You have taken off your hat again! Put it on, you will catch cold.

ARKADINA. The doctor has taken off his hat to Satan father of eternal matter—

TREPLIEFF. *[Loudly and angrily]* Enough of this! There's an end to the performance. Down with the curtain!

ARKADINA. Why, what are you so angry about?

TREPLIEFF. *[Stamping his foot]* The curtain; down with it! *[The curtain falls]* Excuse me, I forgot that only a chosen few might write plays or act them. I have infringed the monopoly. I—I—-

*He would like to say more, but waves his hand instead, and goes out to the left.*

ARKADINA. What is the matter with him?

SORIN. You should not handle youthful egoism so roughly, sister.

ARKADINA. What did I say to him?

SORIN. You hurt his feelings.

ARKADINA. But he told me himself that this was all in fun, so I treated his play as if it were a comedy.

SORIN. Nevertheless—-

ARKADINA. Now it appears that he has produced a masterpiece, if you please! I suppose it was not meant to amuse us at all, but that he arranged the performance and fumigated us with sulphur to demonstrate to us how plays should be written, and what is worth acting. I am tired of him. No one could stand his constant thrusts and sallies. He is a wilful, egotistic boy.

SORIN. He had hoped to give you pleasure.

ARKADINA. Is that so? I notice, though, that he did not choose an ordinary play, but forced his decadent trash on us. I am willing to listen to any raving, so long as it is not meant seriously, but in showing us this, he pretended to be introducing us to a new form of art, and inaugurating a new era. In my opinion, there was nothing new about it, it was simply an exhibition of bad temper.

TRIGORIN. Everybody must write as he feels, and as best he may.

ARKADINA. Let him write as he feels and can, but let him spare me his nonsense.

DORN. Thou art angry, O Jove!

ARKADINA. I am a woman, not Jove. *[She lights a cigarette]* And I am not angry, I am only sorry to see a young man foolishly wasting his time. I did not mean to hurt him.

MEDVIEDENKO. No one has any ground for separating life from matter, as the spirit may well consist of the union of material atoms. *[Excitedly, to TRIGORIN]* Some day you should write a play, and put on the stage the life of a schoolmaster. It is a hard, hard life.

ARKADINA. I agree with you, but do not let us talk about plays or atoms now. This is such a lovely evening. Listen to the singing, friends, how sweet it sounds.

PAULINA. Yes, they are singing across the water. *[A pause.]*

ARKADINA. *[To TRIGORIN]* Sit down beside me here. Ten or fifteen years ago we had music and singing on this lake almost all night. There are six houses on its shores. All was noise and laughter and romance then, such romance! The young star and idol of them all in those days was this man here, *[Nods toward DORN]* Doctor Eugene Dorn. He is fascinating now, but he was irresistible then. But my conscience is beginning to prick me. Why did I hurt my poor boy? I am uneasy about him. *[Loudly]* Constantine! Constantine!

MASHA. Shall I go and find him?

ARKADINA. If you please, my dear.

MASHA. *[Goes off to the left, calling]* Mr. Constantine! Oh, Mr. Constantine!

NINA. *[Comes in from behind the stage]* I see that the play will never be finished, so now I can go home. Good evening. *[She kisses ARKADINA and PAULINA.]*

SORIN. Bravo! Bravo!

ARKADINA. Bravo! Bravo! We were quite charmed by your acting. With your looks and such a lovely voice it is a crime for you to hide yourself in the country. You must be very talented. It is your duty to go on the stage, do you hear me?

NINA. It is the dream of my life, which will never come true.

ARKADINA. Who knows? Perhaps it will. But let me present Monsieur Boris Trigorin.

NINA. I am delighted to meet you. *[Embarrassed]* I have read all your books.

ARKADINA. *[Drawing NINA down beside her]* Don't be afraid of him, dear. He is a simple, good-natured soul, even if he is a celebrity. See, he is embarrassed himself.

DORN. Couldn't the curtain be raised now? It is depressing to have it down.

SHAMRAEFF. *[Loudly]* Jacob, my man! Raise the curtain!

NINA. *[To TRIGORIN]* It was a curious play, wasn't it?

TRIGORIN. Very. I couldn't understand it at all, but I watched it with the greatest pleasure because you acted with such sincerity, and the setting was beautiful. *[A pause]* There must be a lot of fish in this lake.

NINA. Yes, there are.

TRIGORIN. I love fishing. I know of nothing pleasanter than to sit on a lake shore in the evening with one's eyes on a floating cork.

NINA. Why, I should think that for one who has tasted the joys of creation, no other pleasure could exist.

ARKADINA. Don't talk like that. He always begins to flounder when people say nice things to him.

SHAMRAEFF. I remember when the famous Silva was singing once in the Opera House at Moscow, how delighted we all were when he took the low C. Well, you can imagine our astonishment when one of the church cantors, who happened to be sitting in the gallery, suddenly boomed out: "Bravo, Silva!" a whole octave lower. Like this: *[In a deep bass voice]* "Bravo, Silva!" The audience was left breathless. *[A pause.]*

DORN. An angel of silence is flying over our heads.

NINA. I must go. Good-bye.

ARKADINA. Where to? Where must you go so early? We shan't allow it.

NINA. My father is waiting for me.

ARKADINA. How cruel he is, really. *[They kiss each other]* Then I suppose we can't keep you, but it is very hard indeed to let you go.

NINA. If you only knew how hard it is for me to leave you all.

ARKADINA. Somebody must see you home, my pet.

NINA. *[Startled]* No, no!

SORIN. *[Imploringly]* Don't go!

NINA. I must.

SORIN. Stay just one hour more, and all. Come now, really, you know.

NINA. *[Struggling against her desire to stay; through her tears]* No, no, I can't. *[She shakes hands with him and quickly goes out.]*

ARKADINA. An unlucky girl! They say that her mother left the whole of an immense fortune to her husband, and now the child is penniless because the father has already willed everything away to his second wife. It is pitiful.

DORN. Yes, her papa is a perfect beast, and I don't mind saying so—it is what he deserves.

SORIN. *[Rubbing his chilled hands]* Come, let us go in; the night is damp, and my legs are aching.

ARKADINA. Yes, you act as if they were turned to stone; you can hardly move them. Come, you unfortunate old man. *[She takes his arm.]*

SHAMRAEFF. *[Offering his arm to his wife]* Permit me, madame.

SORIN. I hear that dog howling again. Won't you please have it unchained, Shamraeff?

SHAMRAEFF. No, I really can't, sir. The granary is full of millet, and I am afraid thieves might break in if the dog were not there. *[Walking beside MEDVIEDENKO]* Yes, a whole octave lower: "Bravo, Silva!" and he wasn't a singer either, just a simple church cantor.

MEDVIEDENKO. What salary does the church pay its singers? *[All go out except DORN.]*

DORN. I may have lost my judgment and my wits, but I must confess I liked that play. There was something in it. When the girl spoke of her solitude and the Devil's eyes gleamed across the lake, I felt my hands shaking with excitement. It was so fresh and naive. But here he comes; let me say something pleasant to him.

*TREPLIEFF comes in.*

TREPLIEFF. All gone already?

DORN. I am here.

TREPLIEFF. Masha has been yelling for me all over the park. An insufferable creature.

DORN. Constantine, your play delighted me. It was strange, of course, and I did not hear the end, but it made a deep impression on me. You have a great deal of talent, and must persevere in your work.

*TREPLIEFF seizes his hand and squeezes it hard, then kisses him impetuously.*

DORN. Tut, tut! how excited you are. Your eyes are full of tears. Listen to me. You chose your subject in the realm of abstract thought, and you did quite right. A work of art should invariably embody some lofty idea. Only that which is seriously meant can ever be beautiful. How pale you are!

TREPLIEFF. So you advise me to persevere?

DORN. Yes, but use your talent to express only deep and eternal truths. I have led a quiet life, as you know, and am a contented man, but if I should ever experience the exaltation that an artist feels during his moments of creation, I think I should spurn this material envelope of my soul and everything connected with it, and should soar away into heights above this earth.

TREPLIEFF. I beg your pardon, but where is Nina?

DORN. And yet another thing: every work of art should have a definite object in view. You should know why you are writing, for if you follow the road of art without a goal before your eyes, you will lose yourself, and your genius will be your ruin.

TREPLIEFF. *[Impetuously]* Where is Nina?

DORN. She has gone home.

TREPLIEFF. *[In despair]* Gone home? What shall I do? I want to see her; I must see her! I shall follow her.

DORN. My dear boy, keep quiet.

TREPLIEFF. I am going. I must go.

*MASHA comes in.*

MASHA. Your mother wants you to come in, Mr. Constantine. She is waiting for you, and is very uneasy.

TREPLIEFF. Tell her I have gone away. And for heaven's sake, all of you, leave me alone! Go away! Don't follow me about!

DORN. Come, come, old chap, don't act like this; it isn't kind at all.

TREPLIEFF. *[Through his tears]* Good-bye, doctor, and thank you.

*TREPLIEFF goes out.*

DORN. *[Sighing]* Ah, youth, youth!

MASHA. It is always "Youth, youth," when there is nothing else to be said.

*She takes snuff. DORN takes the snuff-box out of her hands and flings it into the bushes.*

DORN. Don't do that, it is horrid. *[A pause]* I hear music in the house. I must go in.

MASHA. Wait a moment.

DORN. What do you want?

MASHA. Let me tell you again. I feel like talking. *[She grows more and more excited]* I do not love my father, but my heart turns to you. For some reason, I feel with all my soul that you are near to me. Help me! Help me, or I shall do something foolish and mock at my life, and ruin it. I am at the end of my strength.

DORN. What is the matter? How can I help you?

MASHA. I am in agony. No one, no one can imagine how I suffer. *[She lays her head on his shoulder and speaks softly]* I love Constantine.

DORN. Oh, how excitable you all are! And how much love there is about this lake of spells! *[Tenderly]* But what can I do for you, my child? What? What?

**The curtain falls.**

# ACT II

*The lawn in front of SORIN'S house. The house stands in the background, on a broad terrace. The lake, brightly reflecting the rays of the sun, lies to the left. There are flower-beds here and there. It is noon; the day is hot. ARKADINA, DORN, and MASHA are sitting on a bench on the lawn, in the shade of an old linden. An open book is lying on DORN'S knees.*

ARKADINA. *[To MASHA]* Come, get up. *[They both get up]* Stand beside me. You are twenty-two and I am almost twice your age. Tell me, Doctor, which of us is the younger looking?

DORN. You are, of course.

ARKADINA. You see! Now why is it? Because I work; my heart and mind are always busy, whereas you never move off the same spot. You don't live. It is a maxim of mine never to look into the future. I never admit the thought of old age or death, and just accept what comes to me.

MASHA. I feel as if I had been in the world a thousand years, and I trail my life behind me like an endless scarf. Often I have no desire to live at all. Of course that is foolish. One ought to pull oneself together and shake off such nonsense.

DORN. *[Sings softly]*

"Tell her, oh flowers—"

ARKADINA. And then I keep myself as correct-looking as an Englishman. I am always well-groomed, as the saying is, and carefully dressed, with my hair neatly arranged. Do you think I should ever permit myself to leave the house half-dressed, with untidy hair? Certainly not! I have kept my looks by never letting myself slump as some women do. *[She puts her arms akimbo, and walks up and down on the lawn]* See me, tripping on tiptoe like a fifteen-year-old girl.

DORN. I see. Nevertheless, I shall continue my reading. *[He takes up his book]* Let me see, we had come to the grain-dealer and the rats.

ARKADINA. And the rats. Go on. *[She sits down]* No, give me the book, it is my turn to read. *[She takes the book and looks for the place]* And the rats. Ah, here it is. *[She reads]* "It is as dangerous for society to attract and indulge authors as it is for grain-dealers to raise rats in their granaries. Yet society loves authors. And so, when a woman has found one whom she wishes to make her own, she lays siege to him by indulging and flattering him." That may be so in France, but it certainly is not so in Russia. We do not carry out a programme like that. With us, a woman is usually head over ears in love with an author before she attempts to lay siege to him. You have an example before your eyes, in me and Trigorin.

*SORIN comes in leaning on a cane, with NINA beside him. MEDVIEDENKO follows, pushing an arm-chair.*

SORIN. *[In a caressing voice, as if speaking to a child]* So we are happy now, eh? We are enjoying ourselves to-day, are we? Father and stepmother have gone away to Tver, and we are free for three whole days!

NINA. *[Sits down beside ARKADINA, and embraces her]* I am so happy. I belong to you now.

SORIN. *[Sits down in his arm-chair]* She looks lovely to-day.

ARKADINA. Yes, she has put on her prettiest dress, and looks sweet. That was nice of you. *[She kisses NINA]* But we mustn't praise her too much; we shall spoil her. Where is Trigorin?

NINA. He is fishing off the wharf.

ARKADINA. I wonder he isn't bored. *[She begins to read again.]*

NINA. What are you reading?

ARKADINA. "On the Water," by Maupassant. *[She reads a few lines to herself]* But the rest is neither true nor interesting. *[She lays down the book]* I am uneasy about my son. Tell me, what is the matter with him? Why is he so dull and depressed lately? He spends all his days on the lake, and I scarcely ever see him any more.

MASHA. His heart is heavy. *[Timidly, to NINA]* Please recite something from his play.

NINA. *[Shrugging her shoulders]* Shall I? Is it so interesting?

MASHA. *[With suppressed rapture]* When he recites, his eyes shine and his face grows pale. His voice is beautiful and sad, and he has the ways of a poet.

*SORIN begins to snore.*

DORN. Pleasant dreams!

ARKADINA. Peter!

SORIN. Eh?

ARKADINA. Are you asleep?

SORIN. Not a bit of it. *[A pause.]*

ARKADINA. You don't do a thing for your health, brother, but you really ought to.

DORN. The idea of doing anything for one's health at sixty-five!

SORIN. One still wants to live at sixty-five.

DORN. *[Crossly]* Ho! Take some camomile tea.

ARKADINA. I think a journey to some watering-place would be good for him.

DORN. Why, yes; he might go as well as not.

ARKADINA. You don't understand.

DORN. There is nothing to understand in this case; it is quite clear.

MEDVIEDENKO. He ought to give up smoking.

SORIN. What nonsense! *[A pause.]*

DORN. No, that is not nonsense. Wine and tobacco destroy the individuality. After a cigar or a glass of vodka you are no longer Peter Sorin, but Peter Sorin plus somebody else. Your ego breaks in two: you begin to think of yourself in the third person.

SORIN. It is easy for you to condemn smoking and drinking; you have known what life is, but what about me? I have served in the Department of Justice for twenty-eight years, but I have never lived, I have never had any experiences. You are satiated with life, and that is why you have an inclination for philosophy, but I want to live, and that is why I drink my wine for dinner and smoke cigars, and all.

DORN. One must take life seriously, and to take a cure at sixty-five and regret that one did not have more pleasure in youth is, forgive my saying so, trifling.

MASHA. It must be lunch-time. *[She walks away languidly, with a dragging step]* My foot has gone to sleep.

DORN. She is going to have a couple of drinks before lunch.

SORIN. The poor soul is unhappy.

DORN. That is a trifle, your honour.

SORIN. You judge her like a man who has obtained all he wants in life.

ARKADINA. Oh, what could be duller than this dear tedium of the country? The air is hot and still, nobody does anything but sit and philosophise about life. It is pleasant, my friends, to sit and listen to you here, but I had rather a thousand times sit alone in the room of a hotel learning a role by heart.

NINA. *[With enthusiasm]* You are quite right. I understand how you feel.

SORIN. Of course it is pleasanter to live in town. One can sit in one's library with a telephone at one's elbow, no one comes in without being first announced by the footman, the streets are full of cabs, and all—-

DORN. *[Sings]*

"Tell her, oh flowers—-"

SHAMRAEFF comes in, followed by PAULINA.

SHAMRAEFF. Here they are. How do you do? *[He kisses ARKADINA'S hand and then NINA'S]* I am delighted to see you looking so well. *[To ARKADINA]* My wife tells me that you mean to go to town with her to-day. Is that so?

ARKADINA. Yes, that is what I had planned to do.

SHAMRAEFF. Hm—that is splendid, but how do you intend to get there, madam? We are hauling rye to-day, and all the men are busy. What horses would you take?

ARKADINA. What horses? How do I know what horses we shall have?

SORIN. Why, we have the carriage horses.

SHAMRAEFF. The carriage horses! And where am I to find the harness for them? This is astonishing! My dear madam, I have the greatest respect for your talents, and would gladly sacrifice ten years of my life for you, but I cannot let you have any horses to-day.

ARKADINA. But if I must go to town? What an extraordinary state of affairs!

SHAMRAEFF. You do not know, madam, what it is to run a farm.

ARKADINA. *[In a burst of anger]* That is an old story! Under these circumstances I shall go back to Moscow this very day. Order a carriage for me from the village, or I shall go to the station on foot.

SHAMRAEFF. *[losing his temper]* Under these circumstances I resign my position. You must find yourself another manager. *[He goes out.]*

ARKADINA. It is like this every summer: every summer I am insulted here. I shall never set foot here again.

*She goes out to the left, in the direction of the wharf. In a few minutes she is seen entering the house, followed by TRIGORIN, who carries a bucket and fishing-rod.*

SORIN. *[Losing his temper]* What the deuce did he mean by his impudence? I want all the horses brought here at once!

NINA. *[To PAULINA]* How could he refuse anything to Madame Arkadina, the famous actress? Is not every wish, every caprice even, of hers, more important than any farm work? This is incredible.

PAULINA. *[In despair]* What can I do about it? Put yourself in my place and tell me what I can do.

SORIN. *[To NINA]* Let us go and find my sister, and all beg her not to go. *[He looks in the direction in which SHAMRAEFF went out]* That man is insufferable; a regular tyrant.

NINA. *[Preventing him from getting up]* Sit still, sit still, and let us wheel you. *[She and MEDVIEDENKO push the chair before them]* This is terrible!

SORIN. Yes, yes, it is terrible; but he won't leave. I shall have a talk with him in a moment. *[They go out. Only DORN and PAULINA are left.]*

DORN. How tiresome people are! Your husband deserves to be thrown out of here neck and crop, but it will all end by this old granny Sorin and his sister asking the man's pardon. See if it doesn't.

PAULINA. He has sent the carriage horses into the fields too. These misunderstandings occur every day. If you only knew how they excite me! I am ill; see! I am trembling all over! I cannot endure his rough ways. *[Imploringly]* Eugene, my darling, my beloved, take me to you. Our time is short; we are no longer young; let us end deception and concealment, even though it is only at the end of our lives. *[A pause.]*

DORN. I am fifty-five years old. It is too late now for me to change my ways of living.

PAULINA. I know that you refuse me because there are other women who are near to you, and you cannot take everybody. I understand. Excuse me—I see I am only bothering you.

*NINA is seen near the house picking a bunch of flowers.*

DORN. No, it is all right.

PAULINA. I am tortured by jealousy. Of course you are a doctor and cannot escape from women. I understand.

DORN. *[TO NINA, who comes toward him]* How are things in there?

NINA. Madame Arkadina is crying, and Sorin is having an attack of asthma.

DORN. Let us go and give them both some camomile tea.

NINA. *[Hands him the bunch of flowers]* Here are some flowers for you.

DORN. Thank you. *[He goes into the house.]*

PAULINA. *[Following him]* What pretty flowers! *[As they reach the house she says in a low voice]* Give me those flowers! Give them to me!

*DORN hands her the flowers; she tears them to pieces and flings them away. They both go into the house.*

NINA. *[Alone]* How strange to see a famous actress weeping, and for such a trifle! Is it not strange, too, that a famous author should sit fishing all day? He is the idol of the public, the papers are full of him, his photograph is for sale everywhere, his works have been translated into many foreign languages, and yet he is overjoyed if he catches a couple of minnows. I always thought famous people were distant and proud; I thought they despised the common crowd which exalts riches and birth, and avenged themselves on it by dazzling it with the inextinguishable honour and glory of their fame. But here I see them weeping and playing cards and flying into passions like everybody else.

*TREPLIEFF comes in without a hat on, carrying a gun and a dead seagull.*

TREPLIEFF. Are you alone here?

NINA. Yes.

*TREPLIEFF lays the sea-gull at her feet.*

NINA. What do you mean by this?

TREPLIEFF. I was base enough to-day to kill this gull. I lay it at your feet.

NINA. What is happening to you? *[She picks up the gull and stands looking at it.]*

TREPLIEFF. *[After a pause]* So shall I soon end my own life.

NINA. You have changed so that I fail to recognise you.

TREPLIEFF. Yes, I have changed since the time when I ceased to recognise you. You have failed me; your look is cold; you do not like to have me near you.

NINA. You have grown so irritable lately, and you talk so darkly and symbolically that you must forgive me if I fail to follow you. I am too simple to understand you.

TREPLIEFF. All this began when my play failed so dismally. A woman never can forgive failure. I have burnt the manuscript to the last page. Oh, if you could only fathom my unhappiness! Your estrangement is to me terrible, incredible; it is as if I had suddenly waked to find this lake dried up and sunk into the earth. You say you are too simple to understand me; but, oh, what is there to understand? You disliked my play, you have no faith in my powers, you already think of me as commonplace and worthless, as many are. *[Stamping his foot]* How well I can understand your feelings! And that understanding is to me like a dagger in the brain. May it be accursed, together with my stupidity, which sucks my life-blood like a snake! *[He sees TRIGORIN, who approaches reading a book]* There comes real genius, striding along like another Hamlet, and with a book, too. *[Mockingly]* "Words, words, words." You feel the warmth of that sun already, you smile, your eyes melt and glow liquid in its rays. I shall not disturb you. *[He goes out.]*

TRIGORIN. *[Making notes in his book]* Takes snuff and drinks vodka; always wears black dresses; is loved by a schoolteacher—

NINA. How do you do?

TRIGORIN. How are you, Miss Nina? Owing to an unforeseen development of circumstances, it seems that we are leaving here today. You and I shall probably never see each other again, and I am sorry for it. I seldom meet a young and pretty girl now; I can hardly remember how it feels to be nineteen, and the young girls in my books are seldom living characters. I should like to change places with you, if but for an hour, to look out at the world through your eyes, and so find out what sort of a little person you are.

NINA. And I should like to change places with you.

TRIGORIN. Why?

NINA. To find out how a famous genius feels. What is it like to be famous? What sensations does it give you?

TRIGORIN. What sensations? I don't believe it gives any. *[Thoughtfully]* Either you exaggerate my fame, or else, if it exists, all I can say is that one simply doesn't feel fame in any way.

NINA. But when you read about yourself in the papers?

TRIGORIN. If the critics praise me, I am happy; if they condemn me, I am out of sorts for the next two days.

NINA. This is a wonderful world. If you only knew how I envy you! Men are born to different destinies. Some dully drag a weary, useless life behind them, lost in the crowd, unhappy, while to one out of a million, as to you, for instance, comes a bright destiny full of interest and meaning. You are lucky.

TRIGORIN. I, lucky? *[He shrugs his shoulders]* H-m—I hear you talking about fame, and happiness, and bright destinies, and those fine words of yours mean as much to me—forgive my saying so—as sweetmeats do, which I never eat. You are very young, and very kind.

NINA. Your life is beautiful.

TRIGORIN. I see nothing especially lovely about it. *[He looks at his watch]* Excuse me, I must go at once, and begin writing again. I am in a hurry. *[He laughs]* You have stepped on my pet corn, as they say, and I am getting excited, and a little cross. Let us discuss this bright and beautiful life of mine, though. *[After a few moments' thought]* Violent obsessions sometimes lay hold of a man: he may, for instance, think day and night of nothing but the moon. I have such a moon. Day and night I am held in the grip of one besetting thought, to write, write, write! Hardly have I finished one book than something urges me to write another, and then a third, and then a fourth—I write ceaselessly. I am, as it were, on a treadmill. I hurry for ever from one story to another, and can't help myself. Do you see anything bright and beautiful in that? Oh, it is a wild life! Even now, thrilled as I am by talking to you, I do not forget for an instant that an unfinished story is awaiting me. My eye falls on that cloud there, which has the shape of a grand piano; I instantly make a mental note that I must remember to mention in my story a cloud floating by that looked like a grand piano. I smell heliotrope; I mutmutter to myself: a sickly smell, the colour worn by widows; I must remember that in writing my next description of a summer evening. I catch an idea in every sentence of yours or of my own, and hasten to lock all these treasures in my literary store-room, thinking that some day they may be useful to me. As soon as I stop working I rush off to the theatre or go fishing, in the hope that I may find oblivion there, but no! Some new subject for a story is sure to come rolling through my brain like an iron cannonball. I hear my desk calling, and have to go back to it and begin to write, write, write, once more. And so it goes for everlasting. I cannot escape myself, though I feel that I am consuming my life. To prepare the honey I feed to unknown crowds, I am doomed to brush the bloom from my dearest flowers, to tear them from their stems, and trample the roots that bore them under foot. Am I not a madman? Should I not be treated by those who know me as one mentally diseased? Yet it is always the same, same old story, till I begin to think that all this praise and admiration must be a deception, that I am being hoodwinked because they know I am crazy, and I sometimes tremble lest I should be grabbed from behind and whisked off to a lunatic asylum. The best years of my youth were made one continual agony for me by my writing. A young author, especially if at first he does not make a success, feels clumsy, ill-at-ease, and superfluous in the world. His nerves are all on edge and stretched to the point of breaking; he is irresistibly attracted to literary and artistic people, and hovers about them unknown and unnoticed, fearing to look them bravely in the eye, like a man with a passion for gambling, whose money is all gone. I did not know my readers, but for some reason I imagined they were distrustful and unfriendly; I was mortally afraid of the public, and when my first play appeared, it seemed to me as if all the dark eyes in the audience were looking at it with enmity, and all the blue ones with cold indifference. Oh, how terrible it was! What agony!

NINA. But don't your inspiration and the act of creation give you moments of lofty happiness?

TRIGORIN. Yes. Writing is a pleasure to me, and so is reading the proofs, but no sooner does a book leave the press than it becomes odious to me; it is not what I meant it to be; I made a mistake to write it at all; I am provoked and discouraged. Then the public reads it and says: "Yes, it is clever and pretty, but not nearly as good as Tolstoi," or "It is a lovely thing, but not as good as

Turgenieff's 'Fathers and Sons,'" and so it will always be. To my dying day I shall hear people say: "Clever and pretty; clever and pretty," and nothing more; and when I am gone, those that knew me will say as they pass my grave: "Here lies Trigorin, a clever writer, but he was not as good as Turgenieff."

NINA. You must excuse me, but I decline to understand what you are talking about. The fact is, you have been spoilt by your success.

TRIGORIN. What success have I had? I have never pleased myself; as a writer, I do not like myself at all. The trouble is that I am made giddy, as it were, by the fumes of my brain, and often hardly know what I am writing. I love this lake, these trees, the blue heaven; nature's voice speaks to me and wakes a feeling of passion in my heart, and I am overcome by an uncontrollable desire to write. But I am not only a painter of landscapes, I am a man of the city besides. I love my country, too, and her people; I feel that, as a writer, it is my duty to speak of their sorrows, of their future, also of science, of the rights of man, and so forth. So I write on every subject, and the public hounds me on all sides, sometimes in anger, and I race and dodge like a fox with a pack of hounds on his trail. I see life and knowledge flitting away before me. I am left behind them like a peasant who has missed his train at a station, and finally I come back to the conclusion that all I am fit for is to describe landscapes, and that whatever else I attempt rings abominably false.

NINA. You work too hard to realise the importance of your writings. What if you are discontented with yourself? To others you appear a great and splendid man. If I were a writer like you I should devote my whole life to the service of the Russian people, knowing at the same time that their welfare depended on their power to rise to the heights I had attained, and the people should send me before them in a chariot of triumph.

TRIGORIN. In a chariot? Do you think I am Agamemnon? *[They both smile.]*

NINA. For the bliss of being a writer or an actress I could endure want, and disillusionment, and the hatred of my friends, and the pangs of my own dissatisfaction with myself; but I should demand in return fame, real, resounding fame! *[She covers her face with her hands]* Whew! My head reels!

THE VOICE OF ARKADINA. *[From inside the house]* Boris! Boris!

TRIGORIN. She is calling me, probably to come and pack, but I don't want to leave this place. *[His eyes rest on the lake]* What a blessing such beauty is!

NINA. Do you see that house there, on the far shore?

TRIGORIN. Yes.

NINA. That was my dead mother's home. I was born there, and have lived all my life beside this lake. I know every little island in it.

TRIGORIN. This is a beautiful place to live. *[He catches sight of the dead sea-gull]* What is that?

NINA. A gull. Constantine shot it.

TRIGORIN. What a lovely bird! Really, I can't bear to go away. Can't you persuade Irina to stay? *[He writes something in his note-book.]*

NINA. What are you writing?

TRIGORIN. Nothing much, only an idea that occurred to me. *[He puts the book back in his pocket]* An idea for a short story. A young girl grows up on the shores of a lake, as you have. She loves the lake as the gulls do, and is as happy and free as they. But a man sees her who chances to come that way, and he destroys her out of idleness, as this gull here has been destroyed. *[A pause. ARKADINA appears at one of the windows.]*

ARKADINA. Boris! Where are you?

TRIGORIN. I am coming this minute.

He goes toward the house, looking back at NINA. ARKADINA remains at the window.

TRIGORIN. What do you want?

ARKADINA. We are not going away, after all.

TRIGORIN goes into the house. NINA comes forward and stands lost in thought.

NINA. It is a dream!

## The curtain falls.

# ACT III

*The dining-room of SORIN'S house. Doors open out of it to the right and left. A table stands in the centre of the room. Trunks and boxes encumber the floor, and preparations for departure are evident. TRIGORIN is sitting at a table eating his breakfast, and MASHA is standing beside him.*

MASHA. I am telling you all these things because you write books and they may be useful to you. I tell you honestly, I should not have lived another day if he had wounded himself fatally. Yet I am courageous; I have decided to tear this love of mine out of my heart by the roots.

TRIGORIN. How will you do it?

MASHA. By marrying Medviedenko.

TRIGORIN. The school-teacher?

MASHA. Yes.

TRIGORIN. I don't see the necessity for that.

MASHA. Oh, if you knew what it is to love without hope for years and years, to wait for ever for something that will never come! I shall not marry for love, but marriage will at least be a change, and will bring new cares to deaden the memories of the past. Shall we have another drink?

TRIGORIN. Haven't you had enough?

MASHA. Fiddlesticks! *[She fills a glass]* Don't look at me with that expression on your face. Women drink oftener than you imagine, but most of them do it in secret, and not openly, as I do. They do indeed, and it is always either vodka or brandy. *[They touch glasses]* To your good health! You are so easy to get on with that I am sorry to see you go. *[They drink.]*

TRIGORIN. And I am sorry to leave.

MASHA. You should ask her to stay.

TRIGORIN. She would not do that now. Her son has been behaving outrageously. First he attempted suicide, and now I hear he is going to challenge me to a duel, though what his provocation may be I can't imagine. He is always sulking and sneering and preaching about a new form of art, as if the field of art were not large enough to accommodate both old and new without the necessity of jostling.

MASHA. It is jealousy. However, that is none of my business. *[A pause. JACOB walks through the room carrying a trunk; NINA comes in and stands by the window]* That schoolteacher of mine is none too clever, but he is very good, poor man, and he loves me dearly, and I am sorry for him. However, let me say good-bye and wish you a pleasant journey. Remember me kindly in your thoughts. *[She shakes hands with him]* Thanks for your goodwill. Send me your books, and be sure to write something in them; nothing formal, but simply this: "To Masha, who, forgetful of her origin, for some unknown reason is living in this world." Good-bye. *[She goes out.]*

NINA. *[Holding out her closed hand to TRIGORIN]* Is it odd or even?

TRIGORIN. Even.

NINA. *[With a sigh]* No, it is odd. I had only one pea in my hand. I wanted to see whether I was to become an actress or not. If only some one would advise me what to do!

TRIGORIN. One cannot give advice in a case like this. *[A pause.]*

NINA. We shall soon part, perhaps never to meet again. I should like you to accept this little medallion as a remembrance of me. I have had your initials engraved on it, and on this side is the name of one of your books: "Days and Nights."

TRIGORIN. How sweet of you! *[He kisses the medallion]* It is a lovely present.

NINA. Think of me sometimes.

TRIGORIN. I shall never forget you. I shall always remember you as I saw you that bright day—do you recall it?—a week ago, when you wore your light dress, and we talked together, and the white seagull lay on the bench beside us.

NINA. *[Lost in thought]* Yes, the sea-gull. *[A pause]* I beg you to let me see you alone for two minutes before you go.

*She goes out to the left. At the same moment ARKADINA comes in from the right, followed by SORIN in a long coat, with his orders on his breast, and by JACOB, who is busy packing.*

ARKADINA. Stay here at home, you poor old man. How could you pay visits with that rheumatism of yours? *[To TRIGORIN]* Who left the room just now, was it Nina?

TRIGORIN. Yes.

ARKADINA. I beg your pardon; I am afraid we interrupted you. *[She sits down]* I think everything is packed. I am absolutely exhausted.

TRIGORIN. *[Reading the inscription on the medallion]* "Days and Nights, page 121, lines 11 and 12."

JACOB. *[Clearing the table]* Shall I pack your fishing-rods, too, sir?

TRIGORIN. Yes, I shall need them, but you can give my books away.

JACOB. Very well, sir.

TRIGORIN. *[To himself]* Page 121, lines 11 and 12. *[To ARKADINA]* Have we my books here in the house?

ARKADINA. Yes, they are in my brother's library, in the corner cupboard.

TRIGORIN. Page 121—*[He goes out.]*

SORIN. You are going away, and I shall be lonely without you.

ARKADINA. What would you do in town?

SORIN. Oh, nothing in particular, but somehow—*[He laughs]* They are soon to lay the corner-stone of the new court-house here. How I should like to leap out of this minnow-pond, if but for an hour or two! I am tired of lying here like an old cigarette stump. I have ordered the carriage for one o'clock. We can go away together.

ARKADINA. *[After a pause]* No, you must stay here. Don't be lonely, and don't catch cold. Keep an eye on my boy. Take good care of him; guide him along the proper paths. *[A pause]* I am going away, and so shall never find out why Constantine shot himself, but I think the chief reason was jealousy, and the sooner I take Trigorin away, the better.

SORIN. There were—how shall I explain it to you? other reasons besides jealousy for his act. Here is a clever young chap living in the depths of the country, without money or position, with no future ahead of him, and with nothing to do. He is ashamed and afraid of being so idle. I am devoted to him and he is fond of me, but nevertheless he feels that he is useless here, that he is little more than a dependent in this house. It is the pride in him.

ARKADINA. He is a misery to me! *[Thoughtfully]* He might possibly enter the army.

SORIN. *[Gives a whistle, and then speaks with hesitation]* It seems to me that the best thing for him would be if you were to let him have a little money. For one thing, he ought to be allowed to dress like a human being. See how he looks! Wearing the same little old coat that he has had for three years, and he doesn't even possess an overcoat! *[Laughing]* And it wouldn't hurt the youngster to sow a few wild oats; let him go abroad, say, for a time. It wouldn't cost much.

ARKADINA. Yes, but—However, I think I might manage about his clothes, but I couldn't let him go abroad. And no, I don't think I can let him have his clothes even, now. *[Decidedly]* I have no money at present.

*SORIN laughs.*

ARKADINA. I haven't indeed.

SORIN. *[Whistles]* Very well. Forgive me, darling; don't be angry. You are a noble, generous woman!

ARKADINA. *[Weeping]* I really haven't the money.

SORIN. If I had any money of course I should let him have some myself, but I haven't even a penny. The farm manager takes my pension from me and puts it all into the farm or into cattle or bees, and in that way it is always lost for ever. The bees die, the cows die, they never let me have a horse.

ARKADINA. Of course I have some money, but I am an actress and my expenses for dress alone are enough to bankrupt me.

SORIN. You are a dear, and I am very fond of you, indeed I am. But something is the matter with me again. *[He staggers]* I feel giddy. *[He leans against the table]* I feel faint, and all.

ARKADINA. *[Frightened ]* Peter! *[She tries to support him]* Peter! dearest! *[She calls]* Help! Help!

*TREPLIEFF and MEDVIEDENKO come in; TREPLIEFF has a bandage around his head.*

ARKADINA. He is fainting!

SORIN. I am all right. *[He smiles and drinks some water]* It is all over now.

TREPLIEFF. *[To his mother]* Don't be frightened, mother, these attacks are not dangerous; my uncle often has them now. *[To his uncle]* You must go and lie down, Uncle.

SORIN. Yes, I think I shall, for a few minutes. I am going to Moscow all the same, but I shall lie down a bit before I start. *[He goes out leaning on his cane.]*

MEDVIEDENKO. *[Giving him his arm]* Do you know this riddle? On four legs in the morning; on two legs at noon; and on three legs in the evening?

SORIN. *[Laughing]* Yes, exactly, and on one's back at night. Thank you, I can walk alone.

MEDVIEDENKO. Dear me, what formality! *[He and SORIN go out.]*

ARKADINA. He gave me a dreadful fright.

TREPLIEFF. It is not good for him to live in the country. Mother, if you would only untie your purse-strings for once, and lend him a thousand roubles! He could then spend a whole year in town.

ARKADINA. I have no money. I am an actress and not a banker. *[A pause.]*

TREPLIEFF. Please change my bandage for me, mother, you do it so gently.

*ARKADINA goes to the cupboard and takes out a box of bandages and a bottle of iodoform.*

ARKADINA. The doctor is late.

TREPLIEFF. Yes, he promised to be here at nine, and now it is noon already.

ARKADINA. Sit down. *[She takes the bandage off his head]* You look as if you had a turban on. A stranger that was in the kitchen yesterday asked to what nationality you belonged. Your wound is almost healed. *[She kisses his head]* You won't be up to any more of these silly tricks again, will you, when I am gone?

TREPLIEFF. No, mother. I did that in a moment of insane despair, when I had lost all control over myself. It will never happen again. *[He kisses her hand]* Your touch is golden. I remember when you were still acting at the State Theatre, long ago, when I was still a little chap, there was a fight one day in our court, and a poor washerwoman was almost beaten to death. She was picked up unconscious, and you nursed her till she was well, and bathed her children in the washtubs. Have you forgotten it?

ARKADINA. Yes, entirely. *[She puts on a new bandage.]*

TREPLIEFF. Two ballet dancers lived in the same house, and they used to come and drink coffee with you.

ARKADINA. I remember that.

TREPLIEFF. They were very pious. *[A pause]* I love you again, these last few days, as tenderly and trustingly as I did as a child. I have no one left me now but you. Why, why do you let yourself be controlled by that man?

ARKADINA. You don't understand him, Constantine. He has a wonderfully noble personality.

TREPLIEFF. Nevertheless, when he has been told that I wish to challenge him to a duel his nobility does not prevent him from playing the coward. He is about to beat an ignominious retreat.

ARKADINA. What nonsense! I have asked him myself to go.

TREPLIEFF. A noble personality indeed! Here we are almost quarrelling over him, and he is probably in the garden laughing at us at this very moment, or else enlightening Nina's mind and trying to persuade her into thinking him a man of genius.

ARKADINA. You enjoy saying unpleasant things to me. I have the greatest respect for that man, and I must ask you not to speak ill of him in my presence.

TREPLIEFF. I have no respect for him at all. You want me to think him a genius, as you do, but I refuse to lie: his books make me sick.

ARKADINA. You envy him. There is nothing left for people with no talent and mighty pretensions to do but to criticise those who are really gifted. I hope you enjoy the consolation it brings.

TREPLIEFF. *[With irony]* Those who are really gifted, indeed! *[Angrily]* I am cleverer than any of you, if it comes to that! *[He tears the bandage off his head]* You are the slaves of convention, you have seized the upper hand and now lay down as law everything that you do; all else you strangle and trample on. I refuse to accept your point of view, yours and his, I refuse!

ARKADINA. That is the talk of a decadent.

TREPLIEFF. Go back to your beloved stage and act the miserable ditchwater plays you so much admire!

ARKADINA. I never acted in a play like that in my life. You couldn't write even the trashiest music-hall farce, you idle good-for-nothing!

TREPLIEFF. Miser!

ARKADINA. Rag-bag!

*TREPLIEFF sits down and begins to cry softly.*

ARKADINA. *[Walking up and down in great excitement]* Don't cry! You mustn't cry! *[She bursts into tears]* You really mustn't. *[She kisses his forehead, his cheeks, his head]* My darling child, forgive me. Forgive your wicked mother.

TREPLIEFF. *[Embracing her]* Oh, if you could only know what it is to have lost everything under heaven! She does not love me. I see I shall never be able to write. Every hope has deserted me.

ARKADINA. Don't despair. This will all pass. He is going away to-day, and she will love you once more. *[She wipes away his tears]* Stop crying. We have made peace again.

TREPLIEFF. *[Kissing her hand]* Yes, mother.

ARKADINA. *[Tenderly]* Make your peace with him, too. Don't fight with him. You surely won't fight?

TREPLIEFF. I won't, but you must not insist on my seeing him again, mother, I couldn't stand it. *[TRIGORIN comes in]* There he is; I am going. *[He quickly puts the medicines away in the cupboard]* The doctor will attend to my head.

TRIGORIN. *[Looking through the pages of a book]* Page 121, lines 11 and 12; here it is. *[He reads]* "If at any time you should have need of my life, come and take it."

*TREPLIEFF picks up the bandage off the floor and goes out.*

ARKADINA. *[Looking at her watch]* The carriage will soon be here.

TRIGORIN. *[To himself]* If at any time you should have need of my life, come and take it.

ARKADINA. I hope your things are all packed.

TRIGORIN. *[Impatiently]* Yes, yes. *[In deep thought]* Why do I hear a note of sadness that wrings my heart in this cry of a pure soul? If at any time you should have need of my life, come and take it. *[To ARKADINA]* Let us stay here one more day!

*ARKADINA shakes her head.*

TRIGORIN. Do let us stay!

ARKADINA. I know, dearest, what keeps you here, but you must control yourself. Be sober; your emotions have intoxicated you a little.

TRIGORIN. You must be sober, too. Be sensible; look upon what has happened as a true friend would. *[Taking her hand]* You are capable of self-sacrifice. Be a friend to me and release me!

ARKADINA. *[In deep excitement]* Are you so much in love?

TRIGORIN. I am irresistibly impelled toward her. It may be that this is just what I need.

ARKADINA. What, the love of a country girl? Oh, how little you know yourself!

TRIGORIN. People sometimes walk in their sleep, and so I feel as if I were asleep, and dreaming of her as I stand here talking to you. My imagination is shaken by the sweetest and most glorious visions. Release me!

ARKADINA. *[Shuddering]* No, no! I am only an ordinary woman; you must not say such things to me. Do not torment me, Boris; you frighten me.

TRIGORIN. You could be an extraordinary woman if you only would. Love alone can bring happiness on earth, love the enchanting, the poetical love of youth, that sweeps away the sorrows of the world. I had no time for it when I was young and struggling with want and laying siege to the literary fortress, but now at last this love has come to me. I see it beckoning; why should I fly?

ARKADINA. *[With anger]* You are mad!

TRIGORIN. Release me.

ARKADINA. You have all conspired together to torture me to-day. *[She weeps.]*

TRIGORIN. *[Clutching his head desperately]* She doesn't understand me! She won't understand me!

ARKADINA. Am I then so old and ugly already that you can talk to me like this without any shame about another woman? *[She embraces and kisses him]* Oh, you have lost your senses! My splendid, my glorious friend, my love for you is the last chapter of my life. *[She falls on her knees]* You are my pride, my joy, my light. *[She embraces his knees]* I could never endure it should you desert me, if only for an hour; I should go mad. Oh, my wonder, my marvel, my king!

TRIGORIN. Some one might come in. *[He helps her to rise.]*

ARKADINA. Let them come! I am not ashamed of my love. *[She kisses his hands]* My jewel! My despair! You want to do a foolish thing, but I don't want you to do it. I shan't let you do it! *[She laughs]* You are mine, you are mine! This forehead is mine, these eyes are mine, this silky hair is mine. All your being is mine. You are so clever, so wise, the first of all living writers; you are the only hope of your country. You are so fresh, so simple, so deeply humourous. You can bring out every feature of a man or of a landscape in a single line, and your characters live and breathe. Do you think that these words are but the incense of flattery? Do you think I am not speaking the truth? Come, look into my eyes; look deep; do you find lies there? No, you see that I alone know how to treasure you. I alone tell you the truth. Oh, my very dear, you will go with me? You will? You will not forsake me?

TRIGORIN. I have no will of my own; I never had. I am too indolent, too submissive, too phlegmatic, to have any. Is it possible that women like that? Take me. Take me away with you, but do not let me stir a step from your side.

ARKADINA. *[To herself]* Now he is mine! *[Carelessly, as if nothing unusual had happened]* Of course you must stay here if you really want to. I shall go, and you can follow in a week's time. Yes, really, why should you hurry away?

TRIGORIN. Let us go together.

ARKADINA. As you like. Let us go together then. *[A pause. TRIGORIN writes something in his note-book]* What are you writing?

TRIGORIN. A happy expression I heard this morning: "A grove of maiden pines." It may be useful. *[He yawns]* So we are really off again, condemned once more to railway carriages, to stations and restaurants, to Hamburger steaks and endless arguments!

*SHAMRAEFF comes in.*

SHAMRAEFF. I am sorry to have to inform you that your carriage is at the door. It is time to start, honoured madam, the train leaves at two-five. Would you be kind enough, madam, to remember to inquire for me where Suzdaltzeff the actor is now? Is he still alive, I wonder? Is he well? He and I have had many a jolly time together. He was inimitable in "The Stolen Mail." A tragedian called Izmailoff was in the same company, I remember, who was also quite remarkable. Don't hurry, madam, you still have five minutes. They were both of them conspirators once, in the same melodrama, and one night when in the course of the play they were suddenly discovered, instead of saying "We have been trapped!" Izmailoff cried out: "We have been rapped!" *[He laughs]* Rapped!

While he has been talking JACOB has been busy with the trunks, and the maid has brought ARKADINA her hat, coat, parasol, and gloves. The cook looks hesitatingly through the door on the right, and finally comes into the room. PAULINA comes in. MEDVIEDENKO comes in.

PAULINA. *[Presenting ARKADINA with a little basket]* Here are some plums for the journey. They are very sweet ones. You may want to nibble something good on the way.

ARKADINA. You are very kind, Paulina.

PAULINA. Good-bye, my dearie. If things have not been quite as you could have wished, please forgive us. *[She weeps.]*

ARKADINA. It has been delightful, delightful. You mustn't cry.

*SORIN comes in through the door on the left, dressed in a long coat with a cape, and carrying his hat and cane. He crosses the room.*

SORIN. Come, sister, it is time to start, unless you want to miss the train. I am going to get into the carriage. *[He goes out.]*

MEDVIEDENKO. I shall walk quickly to the station and see you off there. *[He goes out.]*

ARKADINA. Good-bye, all! We shall meet again next summer if we live. *[The maid servant, JACOB, and the cook kiss her hand]* Don't forget me. *[She gives the cook a rouble]* There is a rouble for all three of you.

THE COOK. Thank you, mistress; a pleasant journey to you.

JACOB. God bless you, mistress.

SHAMRAEFF. Send us a line to cheer us up. *[TO TRIGORIN]* Good-bye, sir.

ARKADINA. Where is Constantine? Tell him I am starting. I must say good-bye to him. *[To JACOB]* I gave the cook a rouble for all three of you.

*All go out through the door on the right. The stage remains empty. Sounds of farewell are heard. The maid comes running back to fetch the basket of plums which has been forgotten. TRIGORIN comes back.*

TRIGORIN. I had forgotten my cane. I think I left it on the terrace. *[He goes toward the door on the right and meets NINA, who comes in at that moment]* Is that you? We are off.

NINA. I knew we should meet again. *[With emotion]* I have come to an irrevocable decision, the die is cast: I am going on the stage. I am deserting my father and abandoning everything. I am beginning life anew. I am going, as you are, to Moscow. We shall meet there.

TRIGORIN. *[Glancing about him]* Go to the Hotel Slavianski Bazar. Let me know as soon as you get there. I shall be at the Grosholski House in Moltchanofka Street. I must go now. *[A pause.]*

NINA. Just one more minute!

TRIGORIN. *[In a low voice]* You are so beautiful! What bliss to think that I shall see you again so soon! *[She sinks on his breast]* I shall see those glorious eyes again, that wonderful, ineffably tender smile, those gentle features with their expression of angelic purity! My darling! *[A prolonged kiss.]*

**The curtain falls.**

# ACT IV

*Two years elapse between the third and fourth acts.*

*A sitting-room in SORIN'S house, which has been converted into a writing-room for TREPLIEFF. To the right and left are doors leading into inner rooms, and in the centre is a glass door opening onto a terrace. Besides the usual furniture of a sitting-room there is a writing-desk in the right-hand corner of the room. There is a Turkish divan near the door on the left, and shelves full of books stand against the walls. Books are lying scattered about on the windowsills and chairs. It is evening. The room is dimly lighted by a shaded lamp on a table. The wind moans in the tree tops and whistles down the chimney. The watchman in the garden is heard sounding his rattle. MEDVIEDENKO and MASHA come in.*

MASHA. *[Calling TREPLIEFF]* Mr. Constantine, where are you? *[Looking about her]* There is no one here. His old uncle is forever asking for Constantine, and can't live without him for an instant.

MEDVIEDENKO. He dreads being left alone. *[Listening to the wind]* This is a wild night. We have had this storm for two days.

MASHA. *[Turning up the lamp]* The waves on the lake are enormous.

MEDVIEDENKO. It is very dark in the garden. Do you know, I think that old theatre ought to be knocked down. It is still standing there, naked and hideous as a skeleton, with the curtain flapping in the wind. I thought I heard a voice weeping in it as I passed there last night.

MASHA. What an idea! *[A pause.]*

MEDVIEDENKO. Come home with me, Masha.

MASHA. *[Shaking her head]* I shall spend the night here.

MEDVIEDENKO. *[Imploringly]* Do come, Masha. The baby must be hungry.

MASHA. Nonsense, Matriona will feed it. *[A pause.]*

MEDVIEDENKO. It is a pity to leave him three nights without his mother.

MASHA. You are getting too tiresome. You used sometimes to talk of other things besides home and the baby, home and the baby. That is all I ever hear from you now.

MEDVIEDENKO. Come home, Masha.

MASHA. You can go home if you want to.

MEDVIEDENKO. Your father won't give me a horse.

MASHA. Yes, he will; ask him.

MEDVIEDENKO. I think I shall. Are you coming home to-morrow?

MASHA. Yes, yes, to-morrow.

*She takes snuff. TREPLIEFF and PAULINA come in. TREPLIEFF is carrying some pillows and a blanket, and PAULINA is carrying sheets and pillow cases. They lay them on the divan, and TREPLIEFF goes and sits down at his desk.*

MASHA. Who is that for, mother?

PAULINA. Mr. Sorin asked to sleep in Constantine's room to-night.

MASHA. Let me make the bed.

*She makes the bed. PAULINA goes up to the desk and looks at the manuscripts lying on it. [A pause.]*

MEDVIEDENKO. Well, I am going. Good-bye, Masha. *[He kisses his wife's hand]* Good-bye, mother. *[He tries to kiss his mother-in-law's hand.]*

PAULINA. *[Crossly]* Be off, in God's name!

*TREPLIEFF shakes hands with him in silence, and MEDVIEDENKO goes out.*

PAULINA. *[Looking at the manuscripts]* No one ever dreamed, Constantine, that you would one day turn into a real author. The magazines pay you well for your stories. *[She strokes his hair.]* You have grown handsome, too. Dear, kind Constantine, be a little nicer to my Masha.

MASHA. *[Still making the bed]* Leave him alone, mother.

PAULINA. She is a sweet child. *[A pause]* A woman, Constantine, asks only for kind looks. I know that from experience.

*TREPLIEFF gets up from his desk and goes out without a word.*

MASHA. There now! You have vexed him. I told you not to bother him.

PAULINA. I am sorry for you, Masha.

MASHA. Much I need your pity!

PAULINA. My heart aches for you. I see how things are, and understand.

MASHA. You see what doesn't exist. Hopeless love is only found in novels. It is a trifle; all one has to do is to keep a tight rein on oneself, and keep one's head clear. Love must be plucked out the moment it springs up in the heart. My husband has been promised a school in another district, and when we have once left this place I shall forget it all. I shall tear my passion out by the roots. *[The notes of a melancholy waltz are heard in the distance.]*

PAULINA. Constantine is playing. That means he is sad.

*MASHA silently waltzes a few turns to the music.*

MASHA. The great thing, mother, is not to have him continually in sight. If my Simon could only get his remove I should forget it all in a month or two. It is a trifle.

*DORN and MEDVIEDENKO come in through the door on the left, wheeling SORIN in an arm-chair.*

MEDVIEDENKO. I have six mouths to feed now, and flour is at seventy kopecks.

DORN. A hard riddle to solve!

MEDVIEDENKO. It is easy for you to make light of it. You are rich enough to scatter money to your chickens, if you wanted to.

DORN. You think I am rich? My friend, after practising for thirty years, during which I could not call my soul my own for one minute of the night or day, I succeeded at last in scraping together one thousand roubles, all of which went, not long ago, in a trip which I took abroad. I haven't a penny.

MASHA. *[To her husband]* So you didn't go home after all?

MEDVIEDENKO. *[Apologetically]* How can I go home when they won't give me a horse?

MASHA. *[Under her breath, with bitter anger]* Would I might never see your face again!

*SORIN in his chair is wheeled to the left-hand side of the room. PAULINA, MASHA, and DORN sit down beside him. MEDVIEDENKO stands sadly aside.*

DORN. What a lot of changes you have made here! You have turned this sitting-room into a library.

MASHA. Constantine likes to work in this room, because from it he can step out into the garden to meditate whenever he feels like it. *[The watchman's rattle is heard.]*

SORIN. Where is my sister?

DORN. She has gone to the station to meet Trigorin. She will soon be back.

SORIN. I must be dangerously ill if you had to send for my sister. *[He falls silent for a moment]* A nice business this is! Here I am dangerously ill, and you won't even give me any medicine.

DORN. What shall I prescribe for you? Camomile tea? Soda? Quinine?

SORIN. Don't inflict any of your discussions on me again. *[He nods toward the sofa]* Is that bed for me?

PAULINA. Yes, for you, sir.

SORIN. Thank you.

DORN. *[Sings]* "The moon swims in the sky to-night."

SORIN. I am going to give Constantine an idea for a story. It shall be called "The Man Who Wished—L'Homme qui a voulu." When I was young, I wished to become an author; I failed. I wished to be an orator; I speak abominably, *[Exciting himself]* with my eternal "and all, and all," dragging each sentence on and on until I sometimes break out into a sweat all over. I wished to marry, and I didn't; I wished to live in the city, and here I am ending my days in the country, and all.

DORN. You wished to become State Councillor, and—you are one!

SORIN. *[Laughing]* I didn't try for that, it came of its own accord.

DORN. Come, you must admit that it is petty to cavil at life at sixty-two years of age.

SORIN. You are pig-headed! Can't you see I want to live?

DORN. That is futile. Nature has commanded that every life shall come to an end.

SORIN. You speak like a man who is satiated with life. Your thirst for it is quenched, and so you are calm and indifferent, but even you dread death.

DORN. The fear of death is an animal passion which must be overcome. Only those who believe in a future life and tremble for sins committed, can logically fear death; but you, for one thing, don't believe in a future life, and for another, you haven't committed any sins. You have served as a Councillor for twenty-five years, that is all.

SORIN. *[Laughing]* Twenty-eight years!

*TREPLIEFF comes in and sits down on a stool at SORIN'S feet. MASHA fixes her eyes on his face and never once tears them away.*

DORN. We are keeping Constantine from his work.

TREPLIEFF. No matter. *[A pause.]*

MEDVIEDENKO. Of all the cities you visited when you were abroad, Doctor, which one did you like the best?

DORN. Genoa.

TREPLIEFF. Why Genoa?

DORN. Because there is such a splendid crowd in its streets. When you leave the hotel in the evening, and throw yourself into the heart of that throng, and move with it without aim or object, swept along, hither and thither, their life seems to be yours, their soul flows into you, and you begin to believe at last in a great world spirit, like the one in your play that Nina Zarietchnaya acted. By the way, where is Nina now? Is she well?

TREPLIEFF. I believe so.

DORN. I hear she has led rather a strange life; what happened?

TREPLIEFF. It is a long story, Doctor.

DORN. Tell it shortly. *[A pause.]*

TREPLIEFF. She ran away from home and joined Trigorin; you know that?

DORN. Yes.

TREPLIEFF. She had a child that died. Trigorin soon tired of her and returned to his former ties, as might have been expected. He had never broken them, indeed, but out of weakness of character had always vacillated between the two. As far as I can make out from what I have heard, Nina's domestic life has not been altogether a success.

DORN. What about her acting?

TREPLIEFF. I believe she made an even worse failure of that. She made her debut on the stage of the Summer Theatre in Moscow, and afterward made a tour of the country towns. At that time I never let her out of my sight, and wherever she went I followed. She always attempted great and difficult parts, but her delivery was harsh and monotonous, and her gestures heavy and crude. She shrieked and died well at times, but those were but moments.

DORN. Then she really has a talent for acting?

TREPLIEFF. I never could make out. I believe she has. I saw her, but she refused to see me, and her servant would never admit me to her rooms. I appreciated her feelings, and did not insist upon a meeting. *[A pause]* What more can I tell you? She sometimes writes to me now that I have come home, such clever, sympathetic letters, full of warm feeling. She never complains, but I can tell that she is profoundly unhappy; not a line but speaks to me of an aching, breaking nerve. She has one strange fancy; she always signs herself "The Sea-gull." The miller in "Rusalka" called himself "The Crow," and so she repeats in all her letters that she is a sea-gull. She is here now.

DORN. What do you mean by "here?"

TREPLIEFF. In the village, at the inn. She has been there for five days. I should have gone to see her, but Masha here went, and she refuses to see any one. Some one told me she had been seen wandering in the fields a mile from here yesterday evening.

MEDVIEDENKO. Yes, I saw her. She was walking away from here in the direction of the village. I asked her why she had not been to see us. She said she would come.

TREPLIEFF. But she won't. *[A pause]* Her father and stepmother have disowned her. They have even put watchmen all around their estate to keep her away. *[He goes with the doctor toward the desk]* How easy it is, Doctor, to be a philosopher on paper, and how difficult in real life!

SORIN. She was a beautiful girl. Even the State Councillor himself was in love with her for a time.

DORN. You old Lovelace, you!

*SHAMRAEFF'S laugh is heard.*

PAULINA. They are coming back from the station.

TREPLIEFF. Yes, I hear my mother's voice.

ARKADINA and TRIGORIN come in, followed by SHAMRAEFF.

SHAMRAEFF. We all grow old and wither, my lady, while you alone, with your light dress, your gay spirits, and your grace, keep the secret of eternal youth.

ARKADINA. You are still trying to turn my head, you tiresome old man.

TRIGORIN. *[To SORIN]* How do you do, Peter? What, still ill? How silly of you! *[With evident pleasure, as he catches sight of MASHA]* How are you, Miss Masha?

MASHA. So you recognised me? *[She shakes hands with him.]*

TRIGORIN. Did you marry him?

MASHA. Long ago.

TRIGORIN. You are happy now? *[He bows to DORN and MEDVIEDENKO, and then goes hesitatingly toward TREPLIEFF]* Your mother says you have forgotten the past and are no longer angry with me.

*TREPLIEFF gives him his hand.*

ARKADINA. *[To her son]* Here is a magazine that Boris has brought you with your latest story in it.

TREPLIEFF. *[To TRIGORIN, as he takes the magazine]* Many thanks; you are very kind.

TRIGORIN. Your admirers all send you their regards. Every one in Moscow and St. Petersburg is interested in you, and all ply me with questions about you. They ask me what you look like, how old you are, whether you are fair or dark. For some reason they all think that you are no longer young, and no one knows who you are, as you always write under an assumed name. You are as great a mystery as the Man in the Iron Mask.

TREPLIEFF. Do you expect to be here long?

TRIGORIN. No, I must go back to Moscow to-morrow. I am finishing another novel, and have promised something to a magazine besides. In fact, it is the same old business.

*During their conversation ARKADINA and PAULINA have put up a card-table in the centre of the room; SHAMRAEFF lights the candles and arranges the chairs, then fetches a box of lotto from the cupboard.*

TRIGORIN. The weather has given me a rough welcome. The wind is frightful. If it goes down by morning I shall go fishing in the lake, and shall have a look at the garden and the spot—do you remember?—where your play was given. I remember the piece very well, but should like to see again where the scene was laid.

MASHA. *[To her father]* Father, do please let my husband have a horse. He ought to go home.

SHAMRAEFF. *[Angrily]* A horse to go home with! *[Sternly]* You know the horses have just been to the station. I can't send them out again.

MASHA. But there are other horses. *[Seeing that her father remains silent]* You are impossible!

MEDVIEDENKO. I shall go on foot, Masha.

PAULINA. *[With a sigh]* On foot in this weather? *[She takes a seat at the card-table]* Shall we begin?

MEDVIEDENKO. It is only six miles. Good-bye. *[He kisses his wife's hand;]* Good-bye, mother. *[His mother-in-law gives him her hand unwillingly]* I should not have troubled you all, but the baby—*[He bows to every one]* Good-bye. *[He goes out with an apologetic air.]*

SHAMRAEFF. He will get there all right, he is not a major-general.

PAULINA. Come, let us begin. Don't let us waste time, we shall soon be called to supper.

*SHAMRAEFF, MASHA, and DORN sit down at the card-table.*

ARKADINA. *[To TRIGORIN]* When the long autumn evenings descend on us we while away the time here by playing lotto. Look at this old set; we used it when our mother played with us as children. Don't you want to take a hand in the game with us until supper time? *[She and TRIGORIN sit down at the table]* It is a monotonous game, but it is all right when one gets used to it. *[She deals three cards to each of the players.]*

TREPLIEFF. *[Looking through the pages of the magazine]* He has read his own story, and hasn't even cut the pages of mine.

*He lays the magazine on his desk and goes toward the door on the right, stopping as he passes his mother to give her a kiss.*

ARKADINA. Won't you play, Constantine?

TREPLIEFF. No, excuse me please, I don't feel like it. I am going to take a turn through the rooms. *[He goes out.]*

MASHA. Are you all ready? I shall begin: twenty-two.

ARKADINA. Here it is.

MASHA. Three.

DORN. Right.

MASHA. Have you put down three? Eight. Eighty-one. Ten.

SHAMRAEFF. Don't go so fast.

ARKADINA. Could you believe it? I am still dazed by the reception they gave me in Kharkoff.

MASHA. Thirty-four. *[The notes of a melancholy waltz are heard.]*

ARKADINA. The students gave me an ovation; they sent me three baskets of flowers, a wreath, and this thing here.

*She unclasps a brooch from her breast and lays it on the table.*

SHAMRAEFF. There is something worth while!

MASHA. Fifty.

DORN. Fifty, did you say?

ARKADINA. I wore a perfectly magnificent dress; I am no fool when it comes to clothes.

PAULINA. Constantine is playing again; the poor boy is sad.

SHAMRAEFF. He has been severely criticised in the papers.

MASHA. Seventy-seven.

ARKADINA. They want to attract attention to him.

TRIGORIN. He doesn't seem able to make a success, he can't somehow strike the right note. There is an odd vagueness about his writings that sometimes verges on delirium. He has never created a single living character.

MASHA. Eleven.

ARKADINA. Are you bored, Peter? *[A pause]* He is asleep.

DORN. The Councillor is taking a nap.

MASHA. Seven. Ninety.

TRIGORIN. Do you think I should write if I lived in such a place as this, on the shore of this lake? Never! I should overcome my passion, and give my life up to the catching of fish.

MASHA. Twenty-eight.

TRIGORIN. And if I caught a perch or a bass, what bliss it would be!

DORN. I have great faith in Constantine. I know there is something in him. He thinks in images; his stories are vivid and full of colour, and always affect me deeply. It is only a pity that he has no definite object in view. He creates impressions, and nothing more, and one cannot go far on impressions alone. Are you glad, madam, that you have an author for a son?

ARKADINA. Just think, I have never read anything of his; I never have time.

MASHA. Twenty-six.

*TREPLIEFF comes in quietly and sits down at his table.*

SHAMRAEFF. *[To TRIGORIN]* We have something here that belongs to you, sir.

TRIGORIN. What is it?

SHAMRAEFF. You told me to have the sea-gull stuffed that Mr. Constantine killed some time ago.

TRIGORIN. Did I? *[Thoughtfully]* I don't remember.

MASHA. Sixty-one. One.

*TREPLIEFF throws open the window and stands listening.*

TREPLIEFF. How dark the night is! I wonder what makes me so restless.

ARKADINA. Shut the window, Constantine, there is a draught here.

*TREPLIEFF shuts the window.*

MASHA. Ninety-eight.

TRIGORIN. See, my card is full.

ARKADINA. *[Gaily]* Bravo! Bravo!

SHAMRAEFF. Bravo!

ARKADINA. Wherever he goes and whatever he does, that man always has good luck. *[She gets up]* And now, come to supper. Our renowned guest did not have any dinner to-day. We can continue our game later. *[To her son]* Come, Constantine, leave your writing and come to supper.

TREPLIEFF. I don't want anything to eat, mother; I am not hungry.

ARKADINA. As you please. *[She wakes SORIN]* Come to supper, Peter. *[She takes SHAMRAEFF'S arm]* Let me tell you about my reception in Kharkoff.

*PAULINA blows out the candles on the table, then she and DORN roll SORIN'S chair out of the room, and all go out through the door on the left, except TREPLIEFF, who is left alone. TREPLIEFF prepares to write. He runs his eye over what he has already written.*

TREPLIEFF. I have talked a great deal about new forms of art, but I feel myself gradually slipping into the beaten track. *[He reads]* "The placard cried it from the wall—a pale face in a frame of dusky hair"—cried—frame—that is stupid. *[He scratches out what he has written]* I shall begin again from the place where my hero is wakened by the noise of the rain, but what follows must go. This description of a moonlight night is long and stilted. Trigorin has worked out a process of his own, and descriptions are easy for him. He writes that the neck of a broken bottle lying on the bank glittered in the moonlight, and that the shadows lay black under the mill-wheel. There you have a moonlight night before your eyes, but I speak of the shimmering light, the twinkling stars, the distant sounds of a piano melting into the still and scented air, and the result is abominable. *[A pause]* The conviction is gradually forcing itself upon me that good literature is not a question of forms new or old, but of ideas that must pour freely from the author's heart, without his bothering his head about any forms whatsoever. *[A knock is heard at the window nearest the table]* What was that? *[He looks out of the window]* I can't see anything. *[He opens the glass door and looks out into the garden]* I heard some one run down the steps. *[He calls]* Who is there? *[He goes out, and is heard walking quickly along the terrace. In a few minutes he comes back with NINA ZARIETCHNAYA]* Oh, Nina, Nina!

*NINA lays her head on TREPLIEFF'S breast and stifles her sobs.*

TREPLIEFF. *[Deeply moved]* Nina, Nina! It is you—you! I felt you would come; all day my heart has been aching for you. *[He takes off her hat and cloak]* My darling, my beloved has come back to me! We mustn't cry, we mustn't cry.

NINA. There is some one here.

TREPLIEFF. No one is here.

NINA. Lock the door, some one might come.

TREPLIEFF. No one will come in.

NINA. I know your mother is here. Lock the door.

TREPLIEFF locks the door on the right and comes back to NINA.

TREPLIEFF. There is no lock on that one. I shall put a chair against it. *[He puts an arm-chair against the door]* Don't be frightened, no one shall come in.

NINA. *[Gazing intently into his face]* Let me look at you. *[She looks about her]* It is warm and comfortable in here. This used to be a sitting-room. Have I changed much?

TREPLIEFF. Yes, you have grown thinner, and your eyes are larger than they were. Nina, it seems so strange to see you! Why didn't you let me go to you? Why didn't you come sooner to me? You have been here nearly a week, I know. I have been several times each day to where you live, and have stood like a beggar beneath your window.

NINA. I was afraid you might hate me. I dream every night that you look at me without recognising me. I have been wandering about on the shores of the lake ever since I came back. I have often been near your house, but I have never had the courage to come in. Let us sit down. *[They sit down]* Let us sit down and talk our hearts out. It is so quiet and warm in here. Do you hear the wind whistling outside? As Turgenieff says, "Happy is he who can sit at night under the roof of his home, who has a warm corner in which to take refuge." I am a sea-gull—and yet—no. *[She passes her hand across her forehead]* What was I saying? Oh, yes, Turgenieff. He says, "and God help all houseless wanderers." *[She sobs.]*

TREPLIEFF. Nina! You are crying again, Nina!

NINA. It is all right. I shall feel better after this. I have not cried for two years. I went into the garden last night to see if our old theatre were still standing. I see it is. I wept there for the first time in two years, and my heart grew lighter, and my soul saw more clearly again. See, I am not crying now. *[She takes his hand in hers]* So you are an author now, and I am an actress. We have both been sucked into the whirlpool. My life used to be as happy as a child's; I used to wake singing in the morning; I loved you and dreamt of fame, and what is the reality? To-morrow morning early I must start for Eltz by train in a third-class carriage, with a lot of peasants, and at Eltz the educated tradespeople will pursue me with compliments. It is a rough life.

TREPLIEFF. Why are you going to Eltz?

NINA. I have accepted an engagement there for the winter. It is time for me to go.

TREPLIEFF. Nina, I have cursed you, and hated you, and torn up your photograph, and yet I have known every minute of my life that my heart and soul were yours for ever. To cease from loving you is beyond my power. I have suffered continually from the time I lost you and began to write, and my life has been almost unendurable. My youth was suddenly plucked from me then, and I seem now to have lived in this world for ninety years. I have called out to you, I have kissed the ground you walked on, wherever I looked I have seen your face before my eyes, and the smile that had illumined for me the best years of my life.

NINA. *[Despairingly]* Why, why does he talk to me like this?

TREPLIEFF. I am quite alone, unwarmed by any attachment. I am as cold as if I were living in a cave. Whatever I write is dry and gloomy and harsh. Stay here, Nina, I beseech you, or else let me go away with you.

*NINA quickly puts on her coat and hat.*

TREPLIEFF. Nina, why do you do that? For God's sake, Nina! *[He watches her as she dresses. A pause.]*

NINA. My carriage is at the gate. Do not come out to see me off. I shall find the way alone. *[Weeping]* Let me have some water.

*TREPLIEFF hands her a glass of water.*

TREPLIEFF. Where are you going?

NINA. Back to the village. Is your mother here?

TREPLIEFF. Yes, my uncle fell ill on Thursday, and we telegraphed for her to come.

NINA. Why do you say that you have kissed the ground I walked on? You should kill me rather. *[She bends over the table]* I am so tired. If I could only rest—rest. *[She raises her head]* I am a sea-gull—no—no, I am an actress. *[She hears ARKADINA and TRIGORIN laughing in the distance, runs to the door on the left and looks through the keyhole]* He is there too. *[She goes back to TREPLIEFF]* Ah, well—no matter. He does not believe in the theatre; he used to laugh at my dreams, so that little by little I became down-hearted and ceased to believe in it too. Then came all the cares of love, the continual anxiety about my little one, so that I soon grew trivial and spiritless, and played my parts without meaning. I never knew what to do with my hands, and I could not walk properly or control my voice. You cannot imagine the state of mind of one who knows as he goes through a play how terribly badly he is acting. I am a sea-gull—no—no, that is not what I meant to say. Do you remember how you shot a seagull once? A man chanced to pass that way and destroyed it out of idleness. That is an idea for a short story, but it is not what I meant to say. *[She passes her hand across her forehead]* What was I saying? Oh, yes, the stage. I have changed now. Now I am a real actress. I act with joy, with exaltation, I am intoxicated by it, and feel that I am superb. I have been walking and walking, and thinking and thinking, ever since I have been here, and I feel the strength of my spirit growing in me every day. I know now, I understand at last,

Constantine, that for us, whether we write or act, it is not the honour and glory of which I have dreamt that is important, it is the strength to endure. One must know how to bear one's cross, and one must have faith. I believe, and so do not suffer so much, and when I think of my calling I do not fear life.

TREPLIEFF. *[Sadly]* You have found your way, you know where you are going, but I am still groping in a chaos of phantoms and dreams, not knowing whom and what end I am serving by it all. I do not believe in anything, and I do not know what my calling is.

NINA. *[Listening]* Hush! I must go. Good-bye. When I have become a famous actress you must come and see me. Will you promise to come? But now—*[She takes his hand]* it is late. I can hardly stand. I am fainting. I am hungry.

TREPLIEFF. Stay, and let me bring you some supper.

NINA. No, no—and don't come out, I can find the way alone. My carriage is not far away. So she brought him back with her? However, what difference can that make to me? Don't tell Trigorin anything when you see him. I love him—I love him even more than I used to. It is an idea for a short story. I love him—I love him passionately—I love him to despair. Have you forgotten, Constantine, how pleasant the old times were? What a gay, bright, gentle, pure life we led? How a feeling as sweet and tender as a flower blossomed in our hearts? Do you remember, *[She recites]* "All men and beasts, lions, eagles, and quails, horned stags, geese, spiders, silent fish that inhabit the waves, starfish from the sea, and creatures invisible to the eye—in one word, life—all, all life, completing the dreary round set before it, has died out at last. A thousand years have passed since the earth last bore a living creature on its breast, and the unhappy moon now lights her lamp in vain. No longer are the cries of storks heard in the meadows, or the drone of beetles in the groves of limes——"

*She embraces TREPLIEFF impetuously and runs out onto the terrace.*

TREPLIEFF. *[After a pause]* It would be a pity if she were seen in the garden. My mother would be distressed.

*He stands for several minutes tearing up his manuscripts and throwing them under the table, then unlocks the door on the right and goes out.*

DORN. *[Trying to force open the door on the left]* Odd! This door seems to be locked. *[He comes in and puts the chair back in its former place]* This is like a hurdle race.

*ARKADINA and PAULINA come in, followed by JACOB carrying some bottles; then come MASHA, SHAMRAEFF, and TRIGORIN.*

ARKADINA. Put the claret and the beer here, on the table, so that we can drink while we are playing. Sit down, friends.

PAULINA. And bring the tea at once.

*She lights the candles and takes her seat at the card-table. SHAMRAEFF leads TRIGORIN to the cupboard.*

SHAMRAEFF. Here is the stuffed sea-gull I was telling you about. *[He takes the sea-gull out of the cupboard]* You told me to have it done.

TRIGORIN. *[looking at the bird]* I don't remember a thing about it, not a thing. *[A shot is heard. Every one jumps.]*

ARKADINA. *[Frightened]* What was that?

DORN. Nothing at all; probably one of my medicine bottles has blown up. Don't worry. *[He goes out through the door on the right, and comes back in a few moments]* It is as I thought, a flask of ether has exploded. *[He sings]*

"Spellbound once more I stand before thee."

ARKADINA. *[Sitting down at the table]* Heavens! I was really frightened. That noise reminded me of—*[She covers her face with her hands]* Everything is black before my eyes.

DORN. *[Looking through the pages of a magazine, to TRIGORIN]* There was an article from America in this magazine about two months ago that I wanted to ask you about, among other things. *[He leads TRIGORIN to the front of the stage]* I am very much interested in this question. *[He lowers his voice and whispers]* You must take Madame Arkadina away from here; what I wanted to say was, that Constantine has shot himself.

**The curtain falls.**

# UNCLE VANYA

## CHARACTERS

ALEXANDER SEREBRAKOFF, a retired professor

HELENA, his wife, twenty-seven years old

SONIA, his daughter by a former marriage

MME. VOITSKAYA, widow of a privy councillor, and mother of Serebrakoff's first wife

IVAN (VANYA) VOITSKI, her son

MICHAEL ASTROFF, a doctor

ILIA (WAFFLES) TELEGIN, an impoverished landowner

MARINA, an old nurse

A WORKMAN

# ACT I

*The scene is laid on SEREBRAKOFF'S country place*

A country house on a terrace. In front of it a garden. In an avenue of trees, under an old poplar, stands a table set for tea, with a samovar, etc. Some benches and chairs stand near the table. On one of them is lying a guitar. A hammock is swung near the table. It is three o'clock in the afternoon of a cloudy day.

*MARINA, a quiet, grey-haired, little old woman, is sitting at the table knitting a stocking.*

*ASTROFF is walking up and down near her.*

MARINA. *[Pouring some tea into a glass]* Take a little tea, my son.

ASTROFF. *[Takes the glass from her unwillingly]* Somehow, I don't seem to want any.

MARINA. Then will you have a little vodka instead?

ASTROFF. No, I don't drink vodka every day, and besides, it is too hot now. *[A pause]* Tell me, nurse, how long have we known each other?

MARINA. *[Thoughtfully]* Let me see, how long is it? Lord—help me to remember. You first came here, into our parts—let me think—when was it? Sonia's mother was still alive—it was two winters before she died; that was eleven years ago—*[thoughtfully]* perhaps more.

ASTROFF. Have I changed much since then?

MARINA. Oh, yes. You were handsome and young then, and now you are an old man and not handsome any more. You drink, too.

ASTROFF. Yes, ten years have made me another man. And why? Because I am overworked. Nurse, I am on my feet from dawn till dusk. I know no rest; at night I tremble under my blankets for fear of being dragged out to visit some one who is sick; I have toiled without repose or a day's freedom since I have known you; could I help growing old? And then, existence is tedious, anyway; it is a senseless, dirty business, this life, and goes heavily. Every one about here is silly, and after living with them for two or three years one grows silly oneself. It is inevitable. *[Twisting his moustache]* See what a long moustache I have grown. A foolish, long moustache. Yes, I am as silly as the rest, nurse, but not as stupid; no, I have not grown stupid. Thank God; my brain is not addled yet, though my feelings have grown numb. I ask nothing, I need nothing, I love no one, unless it is yourself alone. *[He kisses her head]* I had a nurse just like you when I was a child.

MARINA. Don't you want a bite of something to eat?

ASTROFF. No. During the third week of Lent I went to the epidemic at Malitskoi. It was eruptive typhoid. The peasants were all lying side by side in their huts, and the calves and pigs were running about the floor among the sick. Such dirt there was, and smoke! Unspeakable! I slaved among those people all day, not a crumb passed my lips, but when I got home there was still no rest for me; a switchman was carried in from the railroad; I laid him on the operating table and he went and died in my arms under chloroform, and then my feelings that should have been deadened awoke again, my conscience tortured me as if I had killed the man. I sat down and closed my eyes—like this—and thought: will our descendants two hundred years from now, for whom we are breaking the road, remember to give us a kind word? No, nurse, they will forget.

MARINA. Man is forgetful, but God remembers.

ASTROFF. Thank you for that. You have spoken the truth.

*Enter VOITSKI from the house. He has been asleep after dinner and looks rather dishevelled. He sits down on the bench and straightens his collar.*

VOITSKI. H'm. Yes. *[A pause]* Yes.

ASTROFF. Have you been asleep?

VOITSKI. Yes, very much so. *[He yawns]* Ever since the Professor and his wife have come, our daily life seems to have jumped the track. I sleep at the wrong time, drink wine, and eat all sorts of messes for luncheon and dinner. It isn't wholesome. Sonia and I used to work together and never had an idle moment, but now Sonia works alone and I only eat and drink and sleep. Something is wrong.

MARINA. [*Shaking her head*] Such a confusion in the house! The Professor gets up at twelve, the samovar is kept boiling all the morning, and everything has to wait for him. Before they came we used to have dinner at one o'clock, like everybody else, but now we have it at seven. The Professor sits up all night writing and reading, and suddenly, at two o'clock, there goes the bell! Heavens, what is that? The Professor wants some tea! Wake the servants, light the samovar! Lord, what disorder!

ASTROFF. Will they be here long?

VOITSKI. A hundred years! The Professor has decided to make his home here.

MARINA. Look at this now! The samovar has been on the table for two hours, and they are all out walking!

VOITSKI. All right, don't get excited; here they come.

*Voices are heard approaching. SEREBRAKOFF, HELENA, SONIA, and TELEGIN come in from the depths of the garden, returning from their walk.*

SEREBRAKOFF. Superb! Superb! What beautiful views!

TELEGIN. They are wonderful, your Excellency.

SONIA. To-morrow we shall go into the woods, shall we, papa?

VOITSKI. Ladies and gentlemen, tea is ready.

SEREBRAKOFF. Won't you please be good enough to send my tea into the library? I still have some work to finish.

SONIA. I am sure you will love the woods.

*HELENA, SEREBRAKOFF, and SONIA go into the house. TELEGIN sits down at the table beside MARINA.*

VOITSKI. There goes our learned scholar on a hot, sultry day like this, in his overcoat and goloshes and carrying an umbrella!

ASTROFF. He is trying to take good care of his health.

VOITSKI. How lovely she is! How lovely! I have never in my life seen a more beautiful woman.

TELEGIN. Do you know, Marina, that as I walk in the fields or in the shady garden, as I look at this table here, my heart swells with unbounded happiness. The weather is enchanting, the birds are singing, we are all living in peace and contentment—what more could the soul desire? [*Takes a glass of tea.*]

VOITSKI. [*Dreaming*] Such eyes—a glorious woman!

ASTROFF. Come, Ivan, tell us something.

VOITSKI. *[Indolently]* What shall I tell you?

ASTROFF. Haven't you any news for us?

VOITSKI. No, it is all stale. I am just the same as usual, or perhaps worse, because I have become lazy. I don't do anything now but croak like an old raven. My mother, the old magpie, is still chattering about the emancipation of woman, with one eye on her grave and the other on her learned books, in which she is always looking for the dawn of a new life.

ASTROFF. And the Professor?

VOITSKI. The Professor sits in his library from morning till night, as usual—

"Straining the mind, wrinkling the brow,
We write, write, write,
Without respite
Or hope of praise in the future or now."

Poor paper! He ought to write his autobiography; he would make a really splendid subject for a book! Imagine it, the life of a retired professor, as stale as a piece of hardtack, tortured by gout, headaches, and rheumatism, his liver bursting with jealousy and envy, living on the estate of his first wife, although he hates it, because he can't afford to live in town. He is everlastingly whining about his hard lot, though, as a matter of fact, he is extraordinarily lucky. He is the son of a common deacon and has attained the professor's chair, become the son-in-law of a senator, is called "your Excellency," and so on. But I'll tell you something; the man has been writing on art for twenty-five years, and he doesn't know the very first thing about it. For twenty-five years he has been chewing on other men's thoughts about realism, naturalism, and all such foolishness; for twenty-five years he has been reading and writing things that clever men have long known and stupid ones are not interested in; for twenty-five years he has been making his imaginary mountains out of molehills. And just think of the man's self-conceit and presumption all this time! For twenty-five years he has been masquerading in false clothes and has now retired absolutely unknown to any living soul; and yet see him! stalking across the earth like a demi-god!

ASTROFF. I believe you envy him.

VOITSKI. Yes, I do. Look at the success he has had with women! Don Juan himself was not more favoured. His first wife, who was my sister, was a beautiful, gentle being, as pure as the blue heaven there above us, noble, great-hearted, with more admirers than he has pupils, and she loved him as only beings of angelic purity can love those who are as pure and beautiful as themselves. His mother-in-law, my mother, adores him to this day, and he still inspires a sort of worshipful awe in her. His second wife is, as you see, a brilliant beauty; she married him in his old age and has surrendered all the glory of her beauty and freedom to him. Why? What for?

ASTROFF. Is she faithful to him?

VOITSKI. Yes, unfortunately she is.

ASTROFF. Why unfortunately?

VOITSKI. Because such fidelity is false and unnatural, root and branch. It sounds well, but there is no logic in it. It is thought immoral for a woman to deceive an old husband whom she hates, but quite moral for her to strangle her poor youth in her breast and banish every vital desire from her heart.

TELEGIN. *[In a tearful voice]* Vanya, I don't like to hear you talk so. Listen, Vanya; every one who betrays husband or wife is faithless, and could also betray his country.

VOITSKI. *[Crossly]* Turn off the tap, Waffles.

TELEGIN. No, allow me, Vanya. My wife ran away with a lover on the day after our wedding, because my exterior was unprepossessing. I have never failed in my duty since then. I love her and am true to her to this day. I help her all I can and have given my fortune to educate the daughter of herself and her lover. I have forfeited my happiness, but I have kept my pride. And she? Her youth has fled, her beauty has faded according to the laws of nature, and her lover is dead. What has she kept?

*HELENA and SONIA come in; after them comes MME. VOITSKAYA carrying a book. She sits down and begins to read. Some one hands her a glass of tea which she drinks without looking up.*

SONIA. *[Hurriedly, to the nurse]* There are some peasants waiting out there. Go and see what they want. I shall pour the tea. *[Pours out some glasses of tea.]*

*MARINA goes out. HELENA takes a glass and sits drinking in the hammock.*

ASTROFF. I have come to see your husband. You wrote me that he had rheumatism and I know not what else, and that he was very ill, but he appears to be as lively as a cricket.

HELENA. He had a fit of the blues yesterday evening and complained of pains in his legs, but he seems all right again to-day.

ASTROFF. And I galloped over here twenty miles at break-neck speed! No matter, though, it is not the first time. Once here, however, I am going to stay until to-morrow, and at any rate sleep *quantum satis.*

SONIA. Oh, splendid! You so seldom spend the night with us. Have you had dinner yet?

ASTROFF. No.

SONIA. Good. So you will have it with us. We dine at seven now. *[Drinks her tea]* This tea is cold!

TELEGIN. Yes, the samovar has grown cold.

HELENA. Don't mind, Monsieur Ivan, we will drink cold tea, then.

TELEGIN. I beg your pardon, my name is not Ivan, but Ilia, ma'am—Ilia Telegin, or Waffles, as I am sometimes called on account of my pock-marked face. I am Sonia's godfather, and his Excellency, your husband, knows me very well. I now live with you, ma'am, on this estate, and perhaps you will be so good as to notice that I dine with you every day.

SONIA. He is our great help, our right-hand man. *[Tenderly]* Dear godfather, let me pour you some tea.

MME. VOITSKAYA. Oh! Oh!

SONIA. What is it, grandmother?

MME. VOITSKAYA. I forgot to tell Alexander—I have lost my memory—I received a letter to-day from Paul Alexevitch in Kharkoff. He has sent me a new pamphlet.

ASTROFF. Is it interesting?

MME. VOITSKAYA. Yes, but strange. He refutes the very theories which he defended seven years ago. It is appalling!

VOITSKI. There is nothing appalling about it. Drink your tea, mamma.

MME. VOITSKAYA. It seems you never want to listen to what I have to say. Pardon me, Jean, but you have changed so in the last year that I hardly know you. You used to be a man of settled convictions and had an illuminating personality——

VOITSKI. Oh, yes. I had an illuminating personality, which illuminated no one. *[A pause]* I had an illuminating personality! You couldn't say anything more biting. I am forty-seven years old. Until last year I endeavoured, as you do now, to blind my eyes by your pedantry to the truths of life. But now—Oh, if you only knew! If you knew how I lie awake at night, heartsick and angry, to think how stupidly I have wasted my time when I might have been winning from life everything which my old age now forbids.

SONIA. Uncle Vanya, how dreary!

MME. VOITSKAYA. *[To her son]* You speak as if your former convictions were somehow to blame, but you yourself, not they, were at fault. You have forgotten that a conviction, in itself, is nothing but a dead letter. You should have done something.

VOITSKI. Done something! Not every man is capable of being a writer *perpetuum mobile* like your Herr Professor.

MME. VOITSKAYA. What do you mean by that?

SONIA. *[Imploringly]* Mother! Uncle Vanya! I entreat you!

VOITSKI. I am silent. I apologise and am silent. *[A pause.]*

HELENA. What a fine day! Not too hot. *[A pause.]*

VOITSKI. A fine day to hang oneself.

*TELEGIN tunes the guitar. MARINA appears near the house, calling the chickens.*

MARINA. Chick, chick, chick!

SONIA. What did the peasants want, nurse?

MARINA. The same old thing, the same old nonsense. Chick, chick, chick!

SONIA. Why are you calling the chickens?

MARINA. The speckled hen has disappeared with her chicks. I am afraid the crows have got her.

*TELEGIN plays a polka. All listen in silence. Enter WORKMAN.*

WORKMAN. Is the doctor here? *[To ASTROFF]* Excuse me, sir, but I have been sent to fetch you.

ASTROFF. Where are you from?

WORKMAN. The factory.

ASTROFF. *[Annoyed]* Thank you. There is nothing for it, then, but to go. *[Looking around him for his cap]* Damn it, this is annoying!

SONIA. Yes, it is too bad, really. You must come back to dinner from the factory.

ASTROFF. No, I won't be able to do that. It will be too late. Now where, where—*[To the WORKMAN]* Look here, my man, get me a glass of vodka, will you? *[The WORKMAN goes out]* Where—where—*[Finds his cap]* One of the characters in Ostroff's plays is a man with a long moustache and short wits, like me. However, let me bid you good-bye, ladies and gentlemen. *[To HELENA]* I should be really delighted if you would come to see me some day with Miss Sonia. My estate is small, but if you are interested in such things I should like to show you a nursery and seed-bed whose like you will not find within a thousand miles of here. My place is surrounded by government forests. The forester is old and always ailing, so I superintend almost all the work myself.

HELENA. I have always heard that you were very fond of the woods. Of course one can do a great deal of good by helping to preserve them, but does not that work interfere with your real calling?

ASTROFF. God alone knows what a man's real calling is.

HELENA. And do you find it interesting?

ASTROFF. Yes, very.

VOITSKI. *[Sarcastically]* Oh, extremely!

HELENA. You are still young, not over thirty-six or seven, I should say, and I suspect that the woods do not interest you as much as you say they do. I should think you would find them monotonous.

SONIA. No, the work is thrilling. Dr. Astroff watches over the old woods and sets out new plantations every year, and he has already received a diploma and a bronze medal. If you will listen to what he can tell you, you will agree with him entirely. He says that forests are the ornaments of the earth, that they teach mankind to understand beauty and attune his mind to lofty sentiments. Forests temper a stern climate, and in countries where the climate is milder, less strength is wasted in the battle with nature, and the people are kind and gentle. The inhabitants of such countries are handsome, tractable, sensitive, graceful in speech and gesture. Their philosophy is joyous, art and science blossom among them, their treatment of women is full of exquisite nobility——

VOITSKI. *[Laughing]* Bravo! Bravo! All that is very pretty, but it is also unconvincing. So, my friend *[To ASTROFF]* you must let me go on burning firewood in my stoves and building my sheds of planks.

ASTROFF. You can burn peat in your stoves and build your sheds of stone. Oh, I don't object, of course, to cutting wood from necessity, but why destroy the forests? The woods of Russia are trembling under the blows of the axe. Millions of trees have perished. The homes of the wild animals and birds have been desolated; the rivers are shrinking, and many beautiful landscapes are gone forever. And why? Because men are too lazy and stupid to stoop down and pick up their fuel from the ground. *[To HELENA]* Am I not right, Madame? Who but a stupid barbarian could burn so much beauty in his stove and destroy that which he cannot make? Man is endowed with reason and the power to create, so that he may increase that which has been given him, but until now he has not created, but demolished. The forests are disappearing, the rivers are running dry, the game is exterminated, the climate is spoiled, and the earth becomes poorer and uglier every day. *[To VOITSKI]* I read irony in your eye; you do not take what I am saying seriously, and—and—after all, it may very well be nonsense. But when I pass peasant-forests that I have preserved from the axe, or hear the rustling of the young plantations set out with my own hands, I feel as if I had had some small share in improving the climate, and that if mankind is happy a thousand years from now I will have been a little bit responsible for their happiness. When I plant a little birch tree and then see it budding into young green and swaying in the wind, my heart swells with pride and I— *[Sees the WORKMAN, who is bringing him a glass of vodka on a tray]* however—*[He drinks]* I must be off. Probably it is all nonsense, anyway. Good-bye.

*He goes toward the house. SONIA takes his arm and goes with him.*

SONIA. When are you coming to see us again?

ASTROFF. I can't say.

SONIA. In a month?

*ASTROFF and SONIA go into the house. HELENA and VOITSKI walk over to the terrace.*

HELENA. You have behaved shockingly again. Ivan, what sense was there in teasing your mother and talking about *perpetuum mo-*

*bile?* And at breakfast you quarrelled with Alexander again. Really, your behaviour is too petty.

VOITSKI. But if I hate him?

HELENA. You hate Alexander without reason; he is like every one else, and no worse than you are.

VOITSKI. If you could only see your face, your gestures! Oh, how tedious your life must be.

HELENA. It is tedious, yes, and dreary! You all abuse my husband and look on me with compassion; you think, "Poor woman, she is married to an old man." How well I understand your compassion! As Astroff said just now, see how you thoughtlessly destroy the forests, so that there will soon be none left. So you also destroy mankind, and soon fidelity and purity and self-sacrifice will have vanished with the woods. Why cannot you look calmly at a woman unless she is yours? Because, the doctor was right, you are all possessed by a devil of destruction; you have no mercy on the woods or the birds or on women or on one another.

VOITSKI. I don't like your philosophy.

HELENA. That doctor has a sensitive, weary face—an interesting face. Sonia evidently likes him, and she is in love with him, and I can understand it. This is the third time he has been here since I have come, and I have not had a real talk with him yet or made much of him. He thinks I am disagreeable. Do you know, Ivan, the reason you and I are such friends? I think it is because we are both lonely and unfortunate. Yes, unfortunate. Don't look at me in that way, I don't like it.

VOITSKI. How can I look at you otherwise when I love you? You are my joy, my life, and my youth. I know that my chances of being loved in return are infinitely small, do not exist, but I ask nothing of you. Only let me look at you, listen to your voice—

HELENA. Hush, some one will overhear you.

*[They go toward the house.]*

VOITSKI. *[Following her]* Let me speak to you of my love, do not drive me away, and this alone will be my greatest happiness!

HELENA. Ah! This is agony!

*TELEGIN strikes the strings of his guitar and plays a polka. MME. VOITSKAYA writes something on the leaves of her pamphlet.*

**The curtain falls.**

# ACT II

*The dining-room of SEREBRAKOFF'S house. It is night. The tapping of the WATCHMAN'S rattle is heard in the garden. SEREBRAKOFF is dozing in an arm-chair by an open window and HELENA is sitting beside him, also half asleep.*

SEREBRAKOFF. *[Rousing himself]* Who is here? Is it you, Sonia?

HELENA. It is I.

SEREBRAKOFF. Oh, it is you, Nelly. This pain is intolerable.

HELENA. Your shawl has slipped down. *[She wraps up his legs in the shawl]* Let me shut the window.

SEREBRAKOFF. No, leave it open; I am suffocating. I dreamt just now that my left leg belonged to some one else, and it hurt so that I woke. I don't believe this is gout, it is more like rheumatism. What time is it?

HELENA. Half past twelve. *[A pause.]*

SEREBRAKOFF. I want you to look for Batushka's works in the library to-morrow. I think we have him.

HELENA. What is that?

SEREBRAKOFF. Look for Batushka to-morrow morning; we used to have him, I remember. Why do I find it so hard to breathe?

HELENA. You are tired; this is the second night you have had no sleep.

SEREBRAKOFF. They say that Turgenieff got angina of the heart from gout. I am afraid I am getting angina too. Oh, damn this horrible, accursed old age! Ever since I have been old I have been hateful to myself, and I am sure, hateful to you all as well.

HELENA. You speak as if we were to blame for your being old.

SEREBRAKOFF. I am more hateful to you than to any one.

*HELENA gets up and walks away from him, sitting down at a distance.*

SEREBRAKOFF. You are quite right, of course. I am not an idiot; I can understand you. You are young and healthy and beautiful, and longing for life, and I am an old dotard, almost a dead man already. Don't I know it? Of course I see that it is foolish for me to live so long, but wait! I shall soon set you all free. My life cannot drag on much longer.

HELENA. You are overtaxing my powers of endurance. Be quiet, for God's sake!

SEREBRAKOFF. It appears that, thanks to me, everybody's power of endurance is being overtaxed; everybody is miserable, only I am blissfully triumphant. Oh, yes, of course!

HELENA. Be quiet! You are torturing me.

SEREBRAKOFF. I torture everybody. Of course.

HELENA. *[Weeping]* This is unbearable! Tell me, what is it you want me to do?

SEREBRAKOFF. Nothing.

HELENA. Then be quiet, please.

SEREBRAKOFF. It is funny that everybody listens to Ivan and his old idiot of a mother, but the moment I open my lips you all begin to feel ill-treated. You can't even stand the sound of my voice. Even if I am hateful, even if I am a selfish tyrant, haven't I the right to be one at my age? Haven't I deserved it? Haven't I, I ask you, the right to be respected, now that I am old?

HELENA. No one is disputing your rights. *[The window slams in the wind]* The wind is rising, I must shut the window. *[She shuts it]* We shall have rain in a moment. Your rights have never been questioned by anybody.

*The WATCHMAN in the garden sounds his rattle.*

SEREBRAKOFF. I have spent my life working in the interests of learning. I am used to my library and the lecture hall and to the esteem and admiration of my colleagues. Now I suddenly find myself plunged in this wilderness, condemned to see the same stupid people from morning till night and listen to their futile conversation. I want to live; I long for success and fame and the stir of the world, and here I am in exile! Oh, it is dreadful to spend every moment grieving for the lost past, to see the success of others and sit here with nothing to do but to fear death. I cannot stand it! It is more than I can bear. And you will not even forgive me for being old!

HELENA. Wait, have patience; I shall be old myself in four or five years.

*SONIA comes in.*

SONIA. Father, you sent for Dr. Astroff, and now when he comes you refuse to see him. It is not nice to give a man so much trouble for nothing.

SEREBRAKOFF. What do I care about your Astroff? He understands medicine about as well as I understand astronomy.

SONIA. We can't send for the whole medical faculty, can we, to treat your gout?

SEREBRAKOFF. I won't talk to that madman!

SONIA. Do as you please. It's all the same to me. *[She sits down.]*

SEREBRAKOFF. What time is it?

HELENA. One o'clock.

SEREBRAKOFF. It is stifling in here. Sonia, hand me that bottle on the table.

SONIA. Here it is. *[She hands him a bottle of medicine.]*

SEREBRAKOFF. *[Crossly]* No, not that one! Can't you understand me? Can't I ask you to do a thing?

SONIA. Please don't be captious with me. Some people may like it, but you must spare me, if you please, because I don't. Besides, I haven't the time; we are cutting the hay to-morrow and I must get up early.

*VOITSKI comes in dressed in a long gown and carrying a candle.*

VOITSKI. A thunderstorm is coming up. *[The lightning flashes]* There it is! Go to bed, Helena and Sonia. I have come to take your place.

SEREBRAKOFF. *[Frightened]* No, n-o, no! Don't leave me alone with him! Oh, don't. He will begin to lecture me.

VOITSKI. But you must give them a little rest. They have not slept for two nights.

SEREBRAKOFF. Then let them go to bed, but you go away too! Thank you. I implore you to go. For the sake of our former friendship do not protest against going. We will talk some other time——

VOITSKI. Our former friendship! Our former——

SONIA. Hush, Uncle Vanya!

SEREBRAKOFF. *[To his wife]* My darling, don't leave me alone with him. He will begin to lecture me.

VOITSKI. This is ridiculous.

*MARINA comes in carrying a candle.*

SONIA. You must go to bed, nurse, it is late.

MARINA. I haven't cleared away the tea things. Can't go to bed yet.

SEREBRAKOFF. No one can go to bed. They are all worn out, only I enjoy perfect happiness.

MARINA. *[Goes up to SEREBRAKOFF and speaks tenderly]* What's the matter, master? Does it hurt? My own legs are aching too, oh, so badly. *[Arranges his shawl about his legs]* You have had this illness such a long time. Sonia's dead mother used to stay awake with you too, and wear herself out for you. She loved you dearly. *[A pause]* Old people want to be pitied as much as young ones, but nobody cares about them somehow. *[She kisses SEREBRAKOFF'S shoulder]* Come, master, let me give you some linden-tea and warm your poor feet for you. I shall pray to God for you.

SEREBRAKOFF. *[Touched]* Let us go, Marina.

MARINA. My own feet are aching so badly, oh, so badly! *[She and SONIA lead SEREBRAKOFF out]* Sonia's mother used to wear herself out with sorrow and weeping. You were still little and foolish then, Sonia. Come, come, master.

*SEREBRAKOFF, SONIA and MARINA go out.*

HELENA. I am absolutely exhausted by him, and can hardly stand.

VOITSKI. You are exhausted by him, and I am exhausted by my own self. I have not slept for three nights.

HELENA. Something is wrong in this house. Your mother hates everything but her pamphlets and the professor; the professor is vexed, he won't trust me, and fears you; Sonia is angry with her father, and with me, and hasn't spoken to me for two weeks; I am at the end of my strength, and have come near bursting into tears at least twenty times to-day. Something is wrong in this house.

VOITSKI. Leave speculating alone.

HELENA. You are cultured and intelligent, Ivan, and you surely understand that the world is not destroyed by villains and conflagrations, but by hate and malice and all this spiteful tattling. It is your duty to make peace, and not to growl at every-everything.

VOITSKI. Help me first to make peace with myself. My darling! *[Seizes her hand.]*

HELENA. Let go! *[She drags her hand away]* Go away!

VOITSKI. Soon the rain will be over, and all nature will sigh and awake refreshed. Only I am not refreshed by the storm. Day and night the thought haunts me like a fiend, that my life is lost for ever. My past does not count, because I frittered it away on trifles, and the present has so terribly miscarried! What shall I do with my life and my love? What is to become of them? This wonderful feeling of mine will be wasted and lost as a ray of sunlight is lost that falls into a dark chasm, and my life will go with it.

HELENA. I am as it were benumbed when you speak to me of your love, and I don't know how to answer you. Forgive me, I have nothing to say to you. *[She tries to go out]* Good-night!

VOITSKI. *[Barring the way]* If you only knew how I am tortured by the thought that beside me in this house is another life that is being lost forever—it is yours! What are you waiting for? What accursed philosophy stands in your way? Oh, understand, understand——

HELENA. *[Looking at him intently]* Ivan, you are drunk!

VOITSKI. Perhaps. Perhaps.

HELENA. Where is the doctor?

VOITSKI. In there, spending the night with me. Perhaps I am drunk, perhaps I am; nothing is impossible.

HELENA. Have you just been drinking together? Why do you do that?

VOITSKI. Because in that way I get a taste of life. Let me do it, Helena!

HELENA. You never used to drink, and you never used to talk so much. Go to bed, I am tired of you.

VOITSKI. *[Falling on his knees before her]* My sweetheart, my beautiful one——

HELENA. *[Angrily]* Leave me alone! Really, this has become too disagreeable.

*HELENA goes out. A pause.*

VOITSKI *[Alone]* She is gone! I met her first ten years ago, at her sister's house, when she was seventeen and I was thirty-seven. Why did I not fall in love with her then and propose to her? It would have been so easy! And now she would have been my wife. Yes, we would both have been waked to-night by the thunderstorm, and she would have been frightened, but I would have held her in my arms and whispered: "Don't be afraid! I am here." Oh, enchanting dream, so sweet that I laugh to think of it. *[He laughs]* But my God! My head reels! Why am I so old? Why won't she understand me? I hate all that rhetoric of hers, that morality of indolence, that absurd talk about the destruction of the world——*[A pause]* Oh, how I have been deceived! For years I have worshipped that miserable gout-ridden professor. Sonia and I have squeezed this estate dry for his sake. We have bartered our butter and curds and peas like misers, and have never kept a morsel for ourselves, so that we could scrape enough pennies together to send to him. I was proud of him and of his learning; I received all his words and writings as inspired, and now? Now he has retired, and what is the total of his life? A blank! He is absolutely unknown, and his fame has burst like a soap-bubble. I have been deceived; I see that now, basely deceived.

*ASTROFF comes in. He has his coat on, but is without his waistcoat or collar, and is slightly drunk. TELEGIN follows him, carrying a guitar.*

ASTROFF. Play!

TELEGIN. But every one is asleep.

ASTROFF. Play!

*TELEGIN begins to play softly.*

ASTROFF. Are you alone here? No women about? *[Sings with his arms akimbo.]*

"The hut is cold, the fire is dead;  
Where shall the master lay his head?"

The thunderstorm woke me. It was a heavy shower. What time is it?

VOITSKI. The devil only knows.

ASTROFF. I thought I heard Helena's voice.

VOITSKI. She was here a moment ago.

ASTROFF. What a beautiful woman! *[Looking at the medicine bottles on the table]* Medicine, is it? What a variety we have; prescriptions from Moscow, from Kharkoff, from Tula! Why, he has been pestering all the towns of Russia with his gout! Is he ill, or simply shamming?

VOITSKI. He is really ill.

ASTROFF. What is the matter with you to-night? You seem sad. Is it because you are sorry for the professor?

VOITSKI. Leave me alone.

ASTROFF. Or in love with the professor's wife?

VOITSKI. She is my friend.

ASTROFF. Already?

VOITSKI. What do you mean by "already"?

ASTROFF. A woman can only become a man's friend after having first been his acquaintance and then his beloved—then she becomes his friend.

VOITSKI. What vulgar philosophy!

ASTROFF. What do you mean? Yes, I must confess I am getting vulgar, but then, you see, I am drunk. I usually only drink like this once a month. At such times my audacity and temerity know no bounds. I feel capable of anything. I attempt the most difficult operations and do them magnificently. The most brilliant plans for the future take shape in my head. I am no longer a poor fool of a doctor, but mankind's greatest benefactor. I evolve my own system of philosophy and all of you seem to crawl at my feet like so many insects or microbes. *[To TELEGIN]* Play, Waffles!

TELEGIN. My dear boy, I would with all my heart, but do listen to reason; everybody in the house is asleep.

ASTROFF. Play!

*TELEGIN plays softly.*

ASTROFF. I want a drink. Come, we still have some brandy left. And then, as soon as it is day, you will come home with me. *[He sees SONIA, who comes in at that moment.]*

ASTROFF. I beg your pardon, I have no collar on.

*[He goes out quickly, followed by TELEGIN. ]*

SONIA. Uncle Vanya, you and the doctor have been drinking! The good fellows have been getting together! It is all very well for him, he has always done it, but why do you follow his example? It looks dreadfully at your age.

VOITSKI. Age has nothing to do with it. When real life is wanting one must create an illusion. It is better than nothing.

SONIA. Our hay is all cut and rotting in these daily rains, and here you are busy creating illusions! You have given up the farm altogether. I have done all the work alone until I am at the end of my strength—*[Frightened]* Uncle! Your eyes are full of tears!

VOITSKI. Tears? Nonsense, there are no tears in my eyes. You looked at me then just as your dead mother used to, my darling—*[He eagerly kisses her face and hands]* My sister, my dearest sister, where are you now? Ah, if you only knew, if you only knew!

SONIA. If she only knew what, Uncle?

VOITSKI. My heart is bursting. It is awful. No matter, though. I must go. *[He goes out.]*

SONIA. *[Knocks at the door]* Dr. Astroff! Are you awake? Please come here for a minute.

ASTROFF. *[Behind the door]* In a moment.

*He appears in a few seconds. He has put on his collar and waistcoat.*

ASTROFF. What do you want?

SONIA. Drink as much as you please yourself if you don't find it revolting, but I implore you not to let my uncle do it. It is bad for him.

ASTROFF. Very well; we won't drink any more. I am going home at once. That is settled. It will be dawn by the time the horses are harnessed.

SONIA. It is still raining; wait till morning.

ASTROFF. The storm is blowing over. This is only the edge of it. I must go. And please don't ask me to come and see your father any more. I tell him he has gout, and he says it is rheumatism. I tell him to lie down, and he sits up. To-day he refused to see me at all.

SONIA. He has been spoilt. *[She looks in the sideboard]* Won't you have a bite to eat?

ASTROFF. Yes, please. I believe I will.

SONIA. I love to eat at night. I am sure we shall find something in here. They say that he has made a great many conquests in his life, and that the women have spoiled him. Here is some cheese for you.

*[They stand eating by the sideboard.]*

ASTROFF. I haven't eaten anything to-day. Your father has a very difficult nature. *[He takes a bottle out of the sideboard]* May I? *[He pours himself a glass of vodka]* We are alone here, and I can speak frankly. Do you know, I could not stand living in this house for even a month? This atmosphere would stifle me. There is your father, entirely absorbed in his books, and his gout; there is your Uncle Vanya with his hypochondria, your grandmother, and finally, your step-mother—

SONIA. What about her?

ASTROFF. A human being should be entirely beautiful: the face, the clothes, the mind, the thoughts. Your step-mother is, of course, beautiful to look at, but don't you see? She does nothing but sleep and eat and walk and bewitch us, and that is all. She has no responsibilities, everything is done for her—am I not right? And an idle life can never be a pure one. *[A pause]* However, I may be judging her too severely. Like your Uncle Vanya, I am discontented, and so we are both grumblers.

SONIA. Aren't you satisfied with life?

ASTROFF. I like life as life, but I hate and despise it in a little Russian country village, and as far as my own personal life goes, by heaven! there is absolutely no redeeming feature about it. Haven't you noticed if you are riding through a dark wood at night and see a little light shining ahead, how you forget your fatigue and the darkness and the sharp twigs that whip your face? I work, that you know—as no one else in the country works. Fate beats me on without rest; at times I suffer unendurably and I see no light ahead. I have no hope; I do not like people. It is long since I have loved any one.

SONIA. You love no one?

ASTROFF. Not a soul. I only feel a sort of tenderness for your old nurse for old-times' sake. The peasants are all alike; they are stupid and live in dirt, and the educated people are hard to get along with. One gets tired of them. All our good friends are petty and shallow and see no farther than their own noses; in one word, they are dull. Those that have brains are hysterical, devoured with a mania for self-analysis. They whine, they hate, they pick faults everywhere with unhealthy sharpness. They sneak up to me sideways, look at me out of a corner of the eye, and say: "That man is a lunatic," "That man is a wind-bag." Or, if they don't know what else to label me with, they say I am strange. I like the woods; that is strange. I don't eat meat; that is strange, too. Simple, natural relations between man and man or man and nature do not exist. *[He tries to go out; SONIA prevents him.]*

SONIA. I beg you, I implore you, not to drink any more!

ASTROFF. Why not?

SONIA. It is so unworthy of you. You are well-bred, your voice is sweet, you are even—more than any one I know—handsome. Why do you want to resemble the common people that drink and play cards? Oh, don't, I beg you! You always say that people do not create anything, but only destroy what heaven has given them. Why, oh, why, do you destroy yourself? Oh, don't, I implore you not to! I entreat you!

ASTROFF. *[Gives her his hand]* I won't drink any more.

SONIA. Promise me.

ASTROFF. I give you my word of honour.

SONIA. *[Squeezing his hand]* Thank you.

ASTROFF. I have done with it. You see, I am perfectly sober again, and so I shall stay till the end of my life. *[He looks his watch]* But, as I was saying, life holds nothing for me; my race is run. I am old, I am tired, I am trivial; my sensibilities are dead. I could never attach myself to any one again. I love no one, and never shall! Beauty alone has the power to touch me still. I am deeply moved by it. Helena could turn my head in a day if she wanted to, but that is not love, that is not affection—

*[He shudders and covers his face with his hands.]*

SONIA. What is it?

ASTROFF. Nothing. During Lent one of my patients died under chloroform.

SONIA. It is time to forget that. *[A pause]* Tell me, doctor, if I had a friend or a younger sister, and if you knew that she, well—loved you, what would you do?

ASTROFF. *[Shrugging his shoulders]* I don't know. I don't think I should do anything. I should make her understand that I could not return her love—however, my mind is not bothered about those things now. I must start at once if I am ever to get off. Good-bye, my dear girl. At this rate we shall stand here talking till morning. *[He shakes hands with her]* I shall go out through the sitting-room, because I am afraid your uncle might detain me. *[He goes out.]*

SONIA. *[Alone]* Not a word! His heart and soul are still locked from me, and yet for some reason I am strangely happy. I wonder why? *[She laughs with pleasure]* I told him that he was well-bred and handsome and that his voice was sweet. Was that a mistake? I can still feel his voice vibrating in the air; it caresses me. *[Wringing her hands]* Oh! how terrible it is to be plain! I am plain, I know it. As I came out of church last Sunday I overheard a woman say, "She is a dear, noble girl, but what a pity she is so ugly!" So ugly!

*HELENA comes in and throws open the window.*

HELENA. The storm is over. What delicious air! *[A pause]* Where is the doctor?

SONIA. He has gone. *[A pause.]*

HELENA. Sonia!

SONIA. Yes?

HELENA. How much longer are you going to sulk at me? We have not hurt each other. Why not be friends? We have had enough of this.

SONIA. I myself—*[She embraces HELENA]* Let us make peace.

HELENA. With all my heart. *[They are both moved.]*

SONIA. Has papa gone to bed?

HELENA. No, he is sitting up in the drawing-room. Heaven knows what reason you and I had for not speaking to each other for weeks. *[Sees the open sideboard]* Who left the sideboard open?

SONIA. Dr. Astroff has just had supper.

HELENA. There is some wine. Let us seal our friendship.

SONIA. Yes, let us.

HELENA. Out of one glass. *[She fills a wine-glass]* So, we are friends, are we?

SONIA. Yes. *[They drink and kiss each other]* I have long wanted to make friends, but somehow, I was ashamed to. *[She weeps.]*

HELENA. Why are you crying?

SONIA. I don't know. It is nothing.

HELENA. There, there, don't cry. *[She weeps]* Silly! Now I am crying too. *[A pause]* You are angry with me because I seem to have married your father for his money, but don't believe the gossip you hear. I swear to you I married him for love. I was fascinated by his fame and learning. I know now that it was not real love, but it seemed real at the time. I am innocent, and yet your clever, suspicious eyes have been punishing me for an imaginary crime ever since my marriage.

SONIA. Peace, peace! Let us forget the past.

HELENA. You must not look so at people. It is not becoming to you. You must trust people, or life becomes impossible.

SONIA. Tell me truly, as a friend, are you happy?

HELENA. Truly, no.

SONIA. I knew it. One more question: do you wish your husband were young?

HELENA. What a child you are! Of course I do. Go on, ask something else.

SONIA. Do you like the doctor?

HELENA. Yes, very much indeed.

SONIA. *[Laughing]* I have a stupid face, haven't I? He has just gone out, and his voice is still in my ears; I hear his step; I see his face in the dark window. Let me say all I have in my heart! But no, I cannot speak of it so loudly. I am ashamed. Come to my room and let me tell you there. I seem foolish to you, don't I? Talk to me of him.

HELENA. What can I say?

SONIA. He is clever. He can do everything. He can cure the sick, and plant woods.

HELENA. It is not a question of medicine and woods, my dear, he is a man of genius. Do you know what that means? It means he is brave, profound, and of clear insight. He plants a tree and his mind travels a thousand years into the future, and he sees visions of the happiness of the human race. People like him are rare and should be loved. What if he does drink and act roughly at times? A man of genius cannot be a saint in Russia. There he lives, cut off from the world by cold and storm and endless roads of bottomless mud, surrounded by a rough people who are crushed by poverty and disease, his life one continuous struggle, with never a day's respite; how can a man live like that for forty years and keep himself sober and unspotted? *[Kissing SONIA]* I wish you happiness with all my heart; you deserve it. *[She gets up]* As for me, I am a worthless, futile woman. I have always been futile; in music, in love, in my husband's house—in a word, in everything. When you come to think of it, Sonia, I am really very, very unhappy. *[Walks excitedly up and down]* Happiness can never exist for me in this world. Never. Why do you laugh?

SONIA. *[Laughing and covering her face with her hands]* I am so happy, so happy!

HELENA. I want to hear music. I might play a little.

SONIA. Oh, do, do! *[She embraces her]* I could not possibly go to sleep now. Do play!

HELENA. Yes, I will. Your father is still awake. Music irritates him when he is ill, but if he says I may, then I shall play a little. Go, Sonia, and ask him.

SONIA. Very well.

*[She goes out. The WATCHMAN'S rattle is heard in the garden.]*

HELENA. It is long since I have heard music. And now, I shall sit and play, and weep like a fool. *[Speaking out of the window]* Is that you rattling out there, Ephim?

VOICE OF THE WATCHMAN. It is I.

HELENA. Don't make such a noise. Your master is ill.

VOICE OF THE WATCHMAN. I am going away this minute. *[Whistles a tune.]*

SONIA. *[Comes back]* He says, no.

**The curtain falls.**

# ACT III

*The drawing-room of SEREBRAKOFF'S house. There are three doors: one to the right, one to the left, and one in the centre of the room. VOITSKI and SONIA are sitting down. HELENA is walking up and down, absorbed in thought.*

VOITSKI. We were asked by the professor to be here at one o'clock. *[Looks at his watch]* It is now a quarter to one. It seems he has some communication to make to the world.

HELENA. Probably a matter of business.

VOITSKI. He never had any business. He writes twaddle, grumbles, and eats his heart out with jealousy; that's all he does.

SONIA. *[Reproachfully]* Uncle!

VOITSKI. All right. I beg your pardon. *[He points to HELENA]* Look at her. Wandering up and down from sheer idleness. A sweet picture, really.

HELENA. I wonder you are not bored, droning on in the same key from morning till night. *[Despairingly]* I am dying of this tedium. What shall I do?

SONIA. *[Shrugging her shoulders]* There is plenty to do if you would.

HELENA. For instance?

SONIA. You could help run this place, teach the children, care for the sick—isn't that enough? Before you and papa came, Uncle Vanya and I used to go to market ourselves to deal in flour.

HELENA. I don't know anything about such things, and besides, they don't interest me. It is only in novels that women go out and teach and heal the peasants; how can I suddenly begin to do it?

SONIA. How can you live here and not do it? Wait awhile, you will get used to it all. *[Embraces her]* Don't be sad, dearest. *[Laughing]* You feel miserable and restless, and can't seem to fit into this life, and your restlessness is catching. Look at Uncle Vanya, he does nothing now but haunt you like a shadow, and I have left my work to-day to come here and talk with you. I am getting lazy, and don't want to go on with it. Dr. Astroff hardly ever used to come here; it was all we could do to persuade him to visit us once a month, and now he has abandoned his forestry and his practice, and comes every day. You must be a witch.

VOITSKI. Why should you languish here? Come, my dearest, my beauty, be sensible! The blood of a Nixey runs in your veins. Oh, won't you let yourself be one? Give your nature the reins for once in your life; fall head over ears in love with some other water sprite and plunge down head first into a deep pool, so that the Herr Professor and all of us may have our hands free again.

HELENA. *[Angrily]* Leave me alone! How cruel you are! *[She tries to go out.]*

VOITSKI. *[Preventing her]* There, there, my beauty, I apologise. *[He kisses her hand]* Forgive me.

HELENA. Confess that you would try the patience of an angel.

VOITSKI. As a peace offering I am going to fetch some flowers which I picked for you this morning: some autumn roses, beautiful, sorrowful roses. *[He goes out.]*

SONIA. Autumn roses, beautiful, sorrowful roses!

*[She and HELENA stand looking out of the window.]*

HELENA. September already! How shall we live through the long winter here? *[A pause]* Where is the doctor?

SONIA. He is writing in Uncle Vanya's room. I am glad Uncle Vanya has gone out, I want to talk to you about something.

HELENA. About what?

SONIA. About what?

*[She lays her head on HELENA'S breast.]*

HELENA. *[Stroking her hair]* There, there, that will do. Don't, Sonia.

SONIA. I am ugly!

HELENA. You have lovely hair.

SONIA. Don't say that! *[She turns to look at herself in the glass]* No, when a woman is ugly they always say she has beautiful hair or eyes. I have loved him now for six years, I have loved him more than one loves one's mother. I seem to hear him beside me every moment of the day. I feel the pressure of his hand on mine. If I look up, I seem to see him coming, and as you see, I run to you to talk of him. He is here every day now, but he never looks at me, he does not notice my presence. It is agony. I have absolutely no hope, no, no hope. Oh, my God! Give me strength to endure. I prayed all last night. I often go up to him and speak to him and look into his eyes. My pride is gone. I am not mistress of myself. Yesterday I told Uncle Vanya I couldn't control myself, and all the servants know it. Every one knows that I love him.

HELENA. Does he?

SONIA. No, he never notices me.

HELENA. *[Thoughtfully]* He is a strange man. Listen, Sonia, will you allow me to speak to him? I shall be careful, only hint. *[A pause]* Really, to be in uncertainty all these years! Let me do it!

*SONIA nods an affirmative.*

HELENA. Splendid! It will be easy to find out whether he loves you or not. Don't be ashamed, sweetheart, don't worry. I shall be careful; he will not notice a thing. We only want to find out whether it is yes or no, don't we? *[A pause]* And if it is no, then he must keep away from here, is that so?

*SONIA nods.*

HELENA. It will be easier not to see him any more. We won't put off the examination an instant. He said he had a sketch to show me. Go and tell him at once that I want to see him.

SONIA. *[In great excitement]* Will you tell me the whole truth?

HELENA. Of course I will. I am sure that no matter what it is, it will be easier for you to bear than this uncertainty. Trust to me, dearest.

SONIA. Yes, yes. I shall say that you want to see his sketch. *[She starts out, but stops near the door and looks back]* No, it is better not to know—and yet—there may be hope.

HELENA. What do you say?

SONIA. Nothing. *[She goes out.]*

HELENA. *[Alone]* There is no greater sorrow than to know another's secret when you cannot help them. *[In deep thought]* He is obviously not in love with her, but why shouldn't he marry her? She is not pretty, but she is so clever and pure and good, she would make a splendid wife for a country doctor of his years. *[A pause]* I can understand how the poor child feels. She lives here in this desperate loneliness with no one around her except these colourless shadows that go mooning about talking non-sense and knowing nothing except that they eat, drink, and sleep. Among them appears from time to time this Dr. Astroff, so different, so handsome, so interesting, so charming. It is like seeing the moon rise on a dark night. Oh, to surrender oneself to his embrace! To lose oneself in his arms! I am a little in love with him myself! Yes, I am lonely without him, and when I think of him I smile. That Uncle Vanya says I have the blood of a Nixey in my veins: "Give rein to your nature for once in your life!" Perhaps it is right that I should. Oh, to be free as a bird, to fly away from all your sleepy faces and your talk and forget that you have existed at all! But I am a coward, I am afraid; my conscience torments me. He comes here every day now. I can guess why, and feel guilty already; I should like to fall on my knees at Sonia's feet and beg her forgiveness, and weep.

*ASTROFF comes in carrying a portfolio.*

ASTROFF. How do you do? *[Shakes hands with her]* Do you want to see my sketch?

HELENA. Yes, you promised to show me what you had been doing. Have you time now?

ASTROFF. Of course I have!

*He lays the portfolio on the table, takes out the sketch and fastens it to the table with thumb-tacks.*

ASTROFF. Where were you born?

HELENA. *[Helping him]* In St. Petersburg.

ASTROFF. And educated?

HELENA. At the Conservatory there.

ASTROFF. You don't find this life very interesting, I dare say?

HELENA. Oh, why not? It is true I don't know the country very well, but I have read a great deal about it.

ASTROFF. I have my own desk there in Ivan's room. When I am absolutely too exhausted to go on I drop everything and rush over here to forget myself in this work for an hour or two. Ivan and Miss Sonia sit rattling at their counting-boards, the cricket chirps, and I sit beside them and paint, feeling warm and peaceful. But I don't permit myself this luxury very often, only once a month.

*[Pointing to the picture]* Look there! That is a map of our country as it was fifty years ago. The green tints, both dark and light, represent forests. Half the map, as you see, is covered with it. Where the green is striped with red the forests were inhabited by elk and wild goats. Here on this lake, lived great flocks of swans and geese and ducks; as the old men say, there was a power of birds of every kind. Now they have vanished like a cloud. Beside the hamlets and villages, you see, I have dotted down here and there the various settlements, farms, hermit's caves, and water-mills. This country carried a great many cattle and horses, as you can see by the quantity of blue paint. For instance, see how thickly it lies in this part; there were great herds of them here, an average of three horses to every house. *[A pause]* Now, look lower down. This is the country as it was twenty-five years ago. Only a third of the map is green now with forests. There are no goats left and no elk. The blue paint is lighter, and so on, and so on. Now we come to the third part; our country as it appears to-day. We still see spots of green, but not much. The elk, the swans, the black-cock have disappeared. It is, on the whole, the picture of a regular and slow decline which it will evidently only take about ten or fifteen more years to complete. You may perhaps object that it is the march of progress, that the old order must give place to the new, and you might be right if roads had been run through these ruined woods, or if factories and schools had taken their place. The people then would have become better educated and healthier and richer, but as it is, we have nothing of the sort. We have the same swamps and mosquitoes; the same disease and want; the typhoid, the diphtheria, the burning villages. We are confronted by the degradation of our country, brought on by the fierce struggle for existence of the human race. It is the consequence of the ignorance and unconsciousness of starving, shivering, sick humanity that, to save its children, instinctively snatches at everything that can warm it and still its hunger. So it destroys everything it can lay its hands on, without a thought for the morrow. And almost everything has gone, and nothing has been created to take its place. *[Coldly]* But I see by your face that I am not interesting you.

HELENA. I know so little about such things!

ASTROFF. There is nothing to know. It simply isn't interesting, that's all.

HELENA. Frankly, my thoughts were elsewhere. Forgive me! I want to submit you to a little examination, but I am embarrassed and don't know how to begin.

ASTROFF. An examination?

HELENA. Yes, but quite an innocent one. Sit down. *[They sit down]* It is about a certain young girl I know. Let us discuss it like honest people, like friends, and then forget what has passed between us, shall we?

ASTROFF. Very well.

HELENA. It is about my step-daughter, Sonia. Do you like her?

ASTROFF. Yes, I respect her.

HELENA. Do you like her—as a woman?

ASTROFF. *[Slowly]* No.

HELENA. One more word, and that will be the last. You have not noticed anything?

ASTROFF. No, nothing.

HELENA. *[Taking his hand]* You do not love her. I see that in your eyes. She is suffering. You must realise that, and not come here any more.

ASTROFF. My sun has set, yes, and then I haven't the time. *[Shrugging his shoulders]* Where shall I find time for such things? *[He is embarrassed.]*

HELENA. Bah! What an unpleasant conversation! I am as out of breath as if I had been running three miles uphill. Thank heaven, that is over! Now let us forget everything as if nothing had been said. You are sensible. You understand. *[A pause]* I am actually blushing.

ASTROFF. If you had spoken a month ago I might perhaps have considered it, but now—*[He shrugs his shoulders]* Of course, if she is suffering—but I cannot understand why you had to put me through this examination. *[He searches her face with his eyes, and shakes his finger at her]* Oho, you are wily!

HELENA. What does this mean?

ASTROFF. *[Laughing]* You are a wily one! I admit that Sonia is suffering, but what does this examination of yours mean? *[He prevents her from retorting, and goes on quickly]* Please don't put on such a look of surprise; you know perfectly well why I come here every day. Yes, you know perfectly why and for whose sake I come! Oh, my sweet tigress! don't look at me in that way; I am an old bird!

HELENA. *[Perplexed]* A tigress? I don't understand you.

ASTROFF. Beautiful, sleek tigress, you must have your victims! For a whole month I have done nothing but seek you eagerly. I have thrown over everything for you, and you love to see it. Now then, I am sure you knew all this without putting me through your examination. *[Crossing his arms and bowing his head]* I surrender. Here you have me—now, eat me.

HELENA. You have gone mad!

ASTROFF. You are afraid!

HELENA. I am a better and stronger woman than you think me. Good-bye. *[She tries to leave the room.]*

ASTROFF. Why good-bye? Don't say good-bye, don't waste words. Oh, how lovely you are—what hands! *[He kisses her hands.]*

HELENA. Enough of this! *[She frees her hands]* Leave the room! You have forgotten yourself.

ASTROFF. Tell me, tell me, where can we meet to-morrow? *[He puts his arm around her]* Don't you see that we must meet, that it is inevitable?

*He kisses her. VOITSKI comes in carrying a bunch of roses, and stops in the doorway.*

HELENA. *[Without seeing VOITSKI]* Have pity! Leave me, *[lays her head on ASTROFF'S shoulder]* Don't! *[She tries to break away from him.]*

ASTROFF. *[Holding her by the waist]* Be in the forest tomorrow at two o'clock. Will you? Will you?

HELENA. *[Sees VOITSKI]* Let me go! *[Goes to the window deeply embarrassed]* This is appalling!

VOITSKI. *[Throws the flowers on a chair, and speaks in great excitement, wiping his face with his handkerchief]* Nothing—yes, yes, nothing.

ASTROFF. The weather is fine to-day, my dear Ivan; the morning was overcast and looked like rain, but now the sun is shining again. Honestly, we have had a very fine autumn, and the wheat is looking fairly well. *[Puts his map back into the portfolio]* But the days are growing short.

HELENA. *[Goes quickly up to VOITSKI]* You must do your best; you must use all your power to get my husband and myself away from here to-day! Do you hear? I say, this very day!

VOITSKI. *[Wiping his face]* Oh! Ah! Oh! All right! I—Helena, I saw everything!

HELENA. *[In great agitation]* Do you hear me? I must leave here this very day!

*SEREBRAKOFF, SONIA, MARINA, and TELEGIN come in.*

TELEGIN. I am not very well myself, your Excellency. I have been limping for two days, and my head—

SEREBRAKOFF. Where are the others? I hate this house. It is a regular labyrinth. Every one is always scattered through the twenty-six enormous rooms; one never can find a soul. *[Rings]* Ask my wife and Madame Voitskaya to come here!

HELENA. I am here already.

SEREBRAKOFF. Please, all of you, sit down.

SONIA. *[Goes up to HELENA and asks anxiously]* What did he say?

HELENA. I'll tell you later.

SONIA. You are moved. *[looking quickly and inquiringly into her face]* I understand; he said he would not come here any more. *[A pause]* Tell me, did he?

*HELENA nods.*

SEREBRAKOFF. *[To TELEGIN]* One can, after all, become reconciled to being an invalid, but not to this country life. The ways of it stick in my throat and I feel exactly as if I had been whirled off the earth and landed on a strange planet. Please be seated, ladies and gentlemen. Sonia! *[SONIA does not hear. She is standing with her head bowed sadly forward on her breast]* Sonia! *[A pause]* She does not hear me. *[To MARINA]* Sit down too, nurse. *[MARINA sits down and begins to knit her stocking]* I crave your indulgence, ladies and gentlemen; hang your ears, if I may say so, on the peg of attention. *[He laughs.]*

VOITSKI. *[Agitated]* Perhaps you do not need me—may I be excused?

SEREBRAKOFF. No, you are needed now more than any one.

VOITSKI. What is it you want of me?

SEREBRAKOFF. You—but what are you angry about? If it is anything I have done, I ask you to forgive me.

VOITSKI. Oh, drop that and come to business; what do you want?

*MME. VOITSKAYA comes in.*

SEREBRAKOFF. Here is mother. Ladies and gentlemen, I shall begin. I have asked you to assemble here, my friends, in order to discuss a very important matter. I want to ask you for your assistance and advice, and knowing your unfailing amiability I think I can count on both. I am a book-worm and a scholar, and am unfamiliar with practical affairs. I cannot, I find, dispense with the help of well-informed people such as you, Ivan, and you, Telegin, and you, mother. The truth is, *manet omnes una nox,* that is to say, our lives are in the hands of God, and as I am old and ill, I realise that the time has come for me to dispose of my property in regard to the interests of my family. My life is nearly over, and I am not thinking of myself, but I have a young wife and daughter. *[A pause]* I cannot continue to live in the country; we were not made for country life, and yet we cannot afford to live in town on the income derived from this estate. We might sell the woods, but that would be an expedient we could not resort to every year. We must find some means of guaranteeing to ourselves a certain more or less fixed yearly income. With this object in view, a plan has occurred to me which I now have the honour of presenting to you for your consideration. I shall only give you a rough outline, avoiding all details. Our estate does not pay on an average more than two per cent on the money invested in it. I propose to sell it. If we then invest our capital in bonds, it will earn us four to five per cent, and we should probably have a surplus over of several thousand roubles, with which we could buy a summer cottage in Finland—

VOITSKI. Hold on! Repeat what you just said; I don't think I heard you quite right.

SEREBRAKOFF. I said we would invest the money in bonds and buy a cottage in Finland with the surplus.

VOITSKI. No, not Finland—you said something else.

SEREBRAKOFF. I propose to sell this place.

VOITSKI. Aha! That was it! So you are going to sell the place? Splendid. The idea is a rich one. And what do you propose to do with my old mother and me and with Sonia here?

SEREBRAKOFF. That will be decided in due time. We can't do everything at once.

VOITSKI. Wait! It is clear that until this moment I have never had a grain of sense in my head. I have always been stupid enough to think that the estate belonged to Sonia. My father bought it as a wedding present for my sister, and I foolishly imagined that as our laws were made for Russians and not Turks, my sister's estate would come down to her child.

SEREBRAKOFF. Of course it is Sonia's. Has any one denied it? I don't want to sell it without Sonia's consent; on the contrary, what I am doing is for Sonia's good.

VOITSKI. This is absolutely incomprehensible. Either I have gone mad or—or—

MME. VOITSKAYA. Jean, don't contradict Alexander. Trust to him; he knows better than we do what is right and what is wrong.

VOITSKI. I shan't. Give me some water. *[He drinks]* Go ahead! Say anything you please—anything!

SEREBRAKOFF. I can't imagine why you are so upset. I don't pretend that my scheme is an ideal one, and if you all object to it I shall not insist. *[A pause.]*

TELEGIN. *[With embarrassment]* I not only nourish feelings of respect toward learning, your Excellency, but I am also drawn to it by family ties. My brother Gregory's wife's brother, whom you may know; his name is Constantine Lakedemonoff, and he used to be a magistrate—

VOITSKI. Stop, Waffles. This is business; wait a bit, we will talk of that later. *[To SEREBRAKOFF]* There now, ask him what he thinks; this estate was bought from his uncle.

SEREBRAKOFF. Ah! Why should I ask questions? What good would it do?

VOITSKI. The price was ninety-five thousand roubles. My father paid seventy and left a debt of twenty-five. Now listen! This place could never have been bought had I not renounced my inheritance in favour of my sister, whom I deeply loved—and what is more, I worked for ten years like an ox, and paid off the debt.

SEREBRAKOFF. I regret ever having started this conversation.

VOITSKI. Thanks entirely to my own personal efforts, the place is entirely clear of debts, and now, when I have grown old, you want to throw me out, neck and crop!

SEREBRAKOFF. I can't imagine what you are driving at.

VOITSKI. For twenty-five years I have managed this place, and have sent you the returns from it like the most honest of servants, and you have never given me one single word of thanks for my work, not one—neither in my youth nor now. You allowed me a meagre salary of five hundred roubles a year, a beggar's pittance, and have never even thought of adding a rouble to it.

SEREBRAKOFF. What did I know about such things, Ivan? I am not a practical man and don't understand them. You might have helped yourself to all you wanted.

VOITSKI. Yes, why did I not steal? Don't you all despise me for not stealing, when it would have been only justice? And I should not now have been a beggar!

MME. VOITSKAYA. *[Sternly]* Jean!

TELEGIN. *[Agitated]* Vanya, old man, don't talk in that way. Why spoil such pleasant relations? *[He embraces him]* Do stop!

VOITSKI. For twenty-five years I have been sitting here with my mother like a mole in a burrow. Our every thought and hope was yours and yours only. By day we talked with pride of you and your work, and spoke your name with veneration; our nights we wasted reading the books and papers which my soul now loathes.

TELEGIN. Don't, Vanya, don't. I can't stand it.

SEREBRAKOFF. *[Wrathfully]* What under heaven do you want, anyway?

VOITSKI. We used to think of you as almost superhuman, but now the scales have fallen from my eyes and I see you as you are! You write on art without knowing anything about it. Those books of yours which I used to admire are not worth one copper kopeck. You are a hoax!

SEREBRAKOFF. Can't any one make him stop? I am going!

HELENA. Ivan, I command you to stop this instant! Do you hear me?

VOITSKI. I refuse! *[SEREBRAKOFF tries to get out of the room, but VOITSKI bars the door]* Wait! I have not done yet! You have wrecked my life. I have never lived. My best years have gone for nothing, have been ruined, thanks to you. You are my most bitter enemy!

TELEGIN. I can't stand it; I can't stand it. I am going. *[He goes out in great excitement.]*

SEREBRAKOFF. But what do you want? What earthly right have you to use such language to me? Ruination! If this estate is yours, then take it, and let me be ruined!

HELENA. I am going away out of this hell this minute. *[Shrieks]* This is too much!

VOITSKI. My life has been a failure. I am clever and brave and strong. If I had lived a normal life I might have become another Schopenhauer or Dostoieffski. I am losing my head! I am going crazy! Mother, I am in despair! Oh, mother!

MME. VOITSKAYA. *[Sternly]* Listen, Alexander!

*SONIA falls on her knees beside the nurse and nestles against her.*

SONIA. Oh, nurse, nurse!

VOITSKI. Mother! What shall I do? But no, don't speak! I know what to do. *[To SEREBRAKOFF]* And you will understand me!

*He goes out through the door in the centre of the room and MME. VOITSKAYA follows him.*

SEREBRAKOFF. Tell me, what on earth is the matter? Take this lunatic out of my sight! I cannot possibly live under the same roof with him. His room *[He points to the centre door]* is almost next door to mine. Let him take himself off into the village or into the wing of the house, or I shall leave here at once. I cannot stay in the same house with him.

HELENA. *[To her husband]* We are leaving to-day; we must get ready at once for our departure.

SEREBRAKOFF. What a perfectly dreadful man!

SONIA. *[On her knees beside the nurse and turning to her father. She speaks with emotion]* You must be kind to us, papa. Uncle Vanya and I are so unhappy! *[Controlling her despair]* Have pity on us. Remember how Uncle Vanya and Granny used to copy and translate your books for you every night—every, every night. Uncle Vanya has toiled without rest; he would never spend a penny on us, we sent it all to you. We have not eaten the bread of idleness. I am not saying this as I should like to, but you must understand us, papa, you must be merciful to us.

HELENA. *[Very excited, to her husband]* For heaven's sake, Alexander, go and have a talk with him—explain!

SEREBRAKOFF. Very well, I shall have a talk with him, but I won't apologise for a thing. I am not angry with him, but you must confess that his behaviour has been strange, to say the least. Excuse me, I shall go to him.

*[He goes out through the centre door.]*

HELENA. Be gentle with him; try to quiet him. *[She follows him out.]*

SONIA. *[Nestling nearer to MARINA]* Nurse, oh, nurse!

MARINA. It's all right, my baby. When the geese have cackled they will be still again. First they cackle and then they stop.

SONIA. Nurse!

MARINA. You are trembling all over, as if you were freezing. There, there, little orphan baby, God is merciful. A little linden-tea, and it will all pass away. Don't cry, my sweetest. *[Looking angrily at the door in the centre of the room]* See, the geese have all gone now. The devil take them!

*A shot is heard. HELENA screams behind the scenes. SONIA shudders.*

MARINA. Bang! What's that?

SEREBRAKOFF. *[Comes in reeling with terror]* Hold him! hold him! He has gone mad!

*HELENA and VOITSKI are seen struggling in the doorway.*

HELENA. *[Trying to wrest the revolver from him]* Give it to me; give it to me, I tell you!

VOITSKI. Let me go, Helena, let me go! *[He frees himself and rushes in, looking everywhere for SEREBRAKOFF]* Where is he? Ah, there he is! *[He shoots at him. A pause]* I didn't get him? I missed again? *[Furiously]* Damnation! Damnation! To hell with him!

*He flings the revolver on the floor, and drops helpless into a chair. SEREBRAKOFF stands as if stupefied. HELENA leans against the wall, almost fainting.*

HELENA. Take me away! Take me away! I can't stay here—I can't!

VOITSKI. *[In despair]* Oh, what shall I do? What shall I do?

SONIA. *[Softly]* Oh, nurse, nurse!

**The curtain falls.**

# ACT IV

*VOITSKI'S bedroom, which is also his office. A table stands near the window; on it are ledgers, letter scales, and papers of every description. Near by stands a smaller table belonging to ASTROFF, with his paints and drawing materials. On the wall hangs a cage containing a starling. There is also a map of Africa on the wall, obviously of no use to anybody. There is a large sofa covered with buckram. A door to the left leads into an inner room; one to the right leads into the front hall, and before this door lies a mat for the peasants with their muddy boots to stand on. It is an autumn evening. The silence is profound. TELEGIN and MARINA are sitting facing one another, winding wool.*

TELEGIN. Be quick, Marina, or we shall be called away to say good-bye before you have finished. The carriage has already been ordered.

MARINA. *[Trying to wind more quickly]* I am a little tired.

TELEGIN. They are going to Kharkoff to live.

MARINA. They do well to go.

TELEGIN. They have been frightened. The professor's wife won't stay here an hour longer. "If we are going at all, let's be off," says she, "we shall go to Kharkoff and look about us, and then we can send for our things." They are travelling light. It seems, Marina, that fate has decreed for them not to live here.

MARINA. And quite rightly. What a storm they have just raised! It was shameful!

TELEGIN. It was indeed. The scene was worthy of the brush of Aibazofski.

MARINA. I wish I'd never laid eyes on them. *[A pause]* Now we shall have things as they were again: tea at eight, dinner at one, and supper in the evening; everything in order as decent folks, as Christians like to have it. *[Sighs]* It is a long time since I have eaten noodles.

TELEGIN. Yes, we haven't had noodles for ages. *[A pause]* Not for ages. As I was going through the village this morning, Marina, one of the shop-keepers called after me, "Hi! you hanger-on!" I felt it bitterly.

MARINA. Don't pay the least attention to them, master; we are all dependents on God. You and Sonia and all of us. Every one must work, no one can sit idle. Where is Sonia?

TELEGIN. In the garden with the doctor, looking for Ivan. They fear he may lay violent hands on himself.

MARINA. Where is his pistol?

TELEGIN. *[Whispers]* I hid it in the cellar.

*VOITSKI and ASTROFF come in.*

VOITSKI. Leave me alone! *[To MARINA and TELEGIN]* Go away! Go away and leave me to myself, if but for an hour. I won't have you watching me like this!

TELEGIN. Yes, yes, Vanya. *[He goes out on tiptoe.]*

MARINA. The gander cackles; ho! ho! ho!

*[She gathers up her wool and goes out.]*

VOITSKI. Leave me by myself!

ASTROFF. I would, with the greatest pleasure. I ought to have gone long ago, but I shan't leave you until you have returned what you took from me.

VOITSKI. I took nothing from you.

ASTROFF. I am not jesting, don't detain me, I really must go.

VOITSKI. I took nothing of yours.

ASTROFF. You didn't? Very well, I shall have to wait a little longer, and then you will have to forgive me if I resort to force. We shall have to bind you and search you. I mean what I say.

VOITSKI. Do as you please. *[A pause]* Oh, to make such a fool of myself! To shoot twice and miss him both times! I shall never forgive myself.

ASTROFF. When the impulse came to shoot, it would have been as well had you put a bullet through your own head.

VOITSKI. *[Shrugging his shoulders]* Strange! I attempted murder, and am not going to be arrested or brought to trial. That means they think me mad. *[With a bitter laugh]* Me! I am mad, and those who hide their worthlessness, their dullness, their crying heartlessness behind a professor's mask, are sane! Those who marry old men and then deceive them under the noses of all, are sane! I saw you kiss her; I saw you in each other's arms!

ASTROFF. Yes, sir, I did kiss her; so there. *[He puts his thumb to his nose.]*

VOITSKI. *[His eyes on the door]* No, it is the earth that is mad, because she still bears us on her breast.

ASTROFF. That is nonsense.

VOITSKI. Well? Am I not a madman, and therefore irresponsible? Haven't I the right to talk nonsense?

ASTROFF. This is a farce! You are not mad; you are simply a ridiculous fool. I used to think every fool was out of his senses, but now I see that lack of sense is a man's normal state, and you are perfectly normal.

VOITSKI. *[Covers his face with his hands]* Oh! If you knew how ashamed I am! These piercing pangs of shame are like nothing on earth. *[In an agonised voice]* I can't endure them! *[He leans against the table]* What can I do? What can I do?

ASTROFF. Nothing.

VOITSKI. You must tell me something! Oh, my God! I am forty-seven years old. I may live to sixty; I still have thirteen years before me; an eternity! How shall I be able to endure life for thirteen years? What shall I do? How can I fill them? Oh, don't you see? *[He presses ASTROFF'S hand convulsively]* Don't you see, if only I could live the rest of my life in some new way! If I could only wake some still, bright morning and feel that life had begun again; that the past was forgotten and had vanished like smoke. *[He weeps]* Oh, to begin life anew! Tell me, tell me how to begin.

ASTROFF. *[Crossly]* What nonsense! What sort of a new life can you and I look forward to? We can have no hope.

VOITSKI. None?

ASTROFF. None. Of that I am convinced.

VOITSKI. Tell me what to do. *[He puts his hand to his heart]* I feel such a burning pain here.

ASTROFF. *[Shouts angrily]* Stop! *[Then, more gently]* It may be that posterity, which will despise us for our blind and stupid lives, will find some road to happiness; but we—you and I—have but one hope, the hope that we may be visited by visions, perhaps by pleasant ones, as we lie resting in our graves. *[Sighing]* Yes, brother, there were only two respectable, intelligent men in this county, you and I. Ten years or so of this life of ours, this miserable life, have sucked us under, and we have become as contemptible and petty as the rest. But don't try to talk me out of my purpose! Give me what you took from me, will you?

VOITSKI. I took nothing from you.

ASTROFF. You took a little bottle of morphine out of my medicine-case. *[A pause]* Listen! If you are positively determined to make an end to yourself, go into the woods and shoot yourself there. Give up the morphine, or there will be a lot of talk and guesswork; people will think I gave it to you. I don't fancy having to perform a post-mortem on you. Do you think I should find it interesting?

*SONIA comes in.*

VOITSKI. Leave me alone.

ASTROFF. *[To SONIA]* Sonia, your uncle has stolen a bottle of morphine out of my medicine-case and won't give it up. Tell him that his behaviour is—well, unwise. I haven't time, I must be going.

SONIA. Uncle Vanya, did you take the morphine?

ASTROFF. Yes, he took it. *[A pause]* I am absolutely sure.

SONIA. Give it up! Why do you want to frighten us? *[Tenderly]* Give it up, Uncle Vanya! My misfortune is perhaps even greater than yours, but I am not plunged in despair. I endure my sorrow, and shall endure it until my life comes to a natural end. You must endure yours, too. *[A pause]* Give it up! Dear, darling Uncle Vanya. Give it up! *[She weeps]* You are so good, I am sure you will have pity on us and give it up. You must endure your sorrow, Uncle Vanya; you must endure it.

*VOITSKI takes a bottle from the drawer of the table and hands it to ASTROFF.*

VOITSKI. There it is! *[To SONIA]* And now, we must get to work at once; we must do something, or else I shall not be able to endure it.

SONIA. Yes, yes, to work! As soon as we have seen them off we shall go to work. *[She nervously straightens out the papers on the table]* Everything is in a muddle!

ASTROFF. *[Putting the bottle in his case, which he straps together]* Now I can be off.

*HELENA comes in.*

HELENA. Are you here, Ivan? We are starting in a moment. Go to Alexander, he wants to speak to you.

SONIA. Go, Uncle Vanya. *[She takes VOITSKI 'S arm]* Come, you and papa must make peace; that is absolutely necessary.

*SONIA and VOITSKI go out.*

HELENA. I am going away. *[She gives ASTROFF her hand]* Good-bye.

ASTROFF. So soon?

HELENA. The carriage is waiting.

ASTROFF. Good-bye.

HELENA. You promised me you would go away yourself to-day.

ASTROFF. I have not forgotten. I am going at once. *[A pause]* Were you frightened? Was it so terrible?

HELENA. Yes.

ASTROFF. Couldn't you stay? Couldn't you? To-morrow—in the forest—

HELENA. No. It is all settled, and that is why I can look you so bravely in the face. Our departure is fixed. One thing I must ask of you: don't think too badly of me; I should like you to respect me.

ASTROFF. Ah! *[With an impatient gesture]* Stay, I implore you! Confess that there is nothing for you to do in this world. You have no object in life; there is nothing to occupy your attention, and sooner or later your feelings must master you. It is inevitable. It would be better if it happened not in Kharkoff or in Kursk, but here, in nature's lap. It would then at least be poetical, even beautiful. Here you have the forests, the houses half in ruins that Turgenieff writes of.

HELENA. How comical you are! I am angry with you and yet I shall always remember you with pleasure. You are interesting and original. You and I will never meet again, and so I shall tell you—why should I conceal it?—that I am just a little in love with you. Come, one more last pressure of our hands, and then let us part good friends. Let us not bear each other any ill will.

ASTROFF. *[Pressing her hand]* Yes, go. *[Thoughtfully]* You seem to be sincere and good, and yet there is something strangely disquieting about all your personality. No sooner did you arrive here with your husband than every one whom you found busy and actively creating something was forced to drop his work and give himself up for the whole summer to your husband's gout and yourself. You and he have infected us with your idleness. I have been swept off my feet; I have not put my hand to a thing for weeks, during which sickness has been running its course unchecked among the people, and the peasants have been pasturing their cattle in my woods and young plantations. Go where you will, you and your husband will always carry destruction in your train. I am joking of course, and yet I am strangely sure that had you stayed here we should have been overtaken by the most immense desolation. I would have gone to my ruin, and you—you would not have prospered. So go! E finita la comedia!

HELENA. *[Snatching a pencil off ASTROFF'S table, and hiding it with a quick movement]* I shall take this pencil for memory!

ASTROFF. How strange it is. We meet, and then suddenly it seems that we must part forever. That is the way in this world. As long as we are alone, before Uncle Vanya comes in with a bouquet—allow me—to kiss you good-bye—may I? *[He kisses her on the cheek]* So! Splendid!

HELENA. I wish you every happiness. *[She glances about her]* For once in my life, I shall! and scorn the consequences! *[She kisses him impetuously, and they quickly part]* I must go.

ASTROFF. Yes, go. If the carriage is there, then start at once. *[They stand listening.]*

ASTROFF. E finita!

VOITSKI, SEREBRAKOFF, MME. VOITSKAYA with her book, TELEGIN, and SONIA come in.

SEREBRAKOFF. *[To VOITSKI]* Shame on him who bears malice for the past. I have gone through so much in the last few hours that I feel capable of writing a whole treatise on the conduct of life for the instruction of posterity. I gladly accept your apology, and myself ask your forgiveness. *[He kisses VOITSKI three times.]*

*HELENA embraces SONIA.*

SEREBRAKOFF. *[Kissing MME. VOITSKAYA'S hand]* Mother!

MME. VOITSKAYA. *[Kissing him]* Have your picture taken, Alexander, and send me one. You know how dear you are to me.

TELEGIN. Good-bye, your Excellency. Don't forget us.

SEREBRAKOFF. *[Kissing his daughter]* Good-bye, good-bye all. *[Shaking hands with ASTROFF]* Many thanks for your pleasant company. I have a deep regard for your opinions and your enthusiasm, but let me, as an old man, give one word of advice at parting: do something, my friend! Work! Do something! *[They all bow]* Good luck to you all. *[He goes out followed by MME. VOITSKAYA and SONIA.]*

VOITSKI *[Kissing HELENA'S hand fervently]* Good-bye—forgive me. I shall never see you again!

HELENA. *[Touched]* Good-bye, dear boy.

*She lightly kisses his head as he bends over her hand, and goes out.*

ASTROFF. Tell them to bring my carriage around too, Waffles.

TELEGIN. All right, old man.

*ASTROFF and VOITSKI are left behind alone. ASTROFF collects his paints and drawing materials on the table and packs them away in a box.*

ASTROFF. Why don't you go to see them off?

VOITSKI. Let them go! I—I can't go out there. I feel too sad. I must go to work on something at once. To work! To work!

*He rummages through his papers on the table. A pause. The tinkling of bells is heard as the horses trot away.*

ASTROFF. They have gone! The professor, I suppose, is glad to go. He couldn't be tempted back now by a fortune.

*MARINA comes in.*

MARINA. They have gone. *[She sits down in an arm-chair and knits her stocking.]*

*SONIA comes in wiping her eyes.*

SONIA. They have gone. God be with them. *[To her uncle]* And now, Uncle Vanya, let us do something!

VOITSKI. To work! To work!

SONIA. It is long, long, since you and I have sat together at this table. *[She lights a lamp on the table]* No ink! *[She takes the inkstand to the cupboard and fills it from an ink-bottle]* How sad it is to see them go!

*MME. VOITSKAYA comes slowly in.*

MME. VOITSKAYA. They have gone.

*She sits down and at once becomes absorbed in her book. SONIA sits down at the table and looks through an account book.*

SONIA. First, Uncle Vanya, let us write up the accounts. They are in a dreadful state. Come, begin. You take one and I will take the other.

VOITSKI. In account with *[They sit silently writing.]*

MARINA. *[Yawning]* The sand-man has come.

ASTROFF. How still it is. Their pens scratch, the cricket sings; it is so warm and comfortable. I hate to go. *[The tinkling of bells is heard.]*

ASTROFF. My carriage has come. There now remains but to say good-bye to you, my friends, and to my table here, and then—away! *[He puts the map into the portfolio.]*

MARINA. Don't hurry away; sit a little longer with us.

ASTROFF. Impossible.

VOITSKI. *[Writing]* And carry forward from the old debt two seventy-five—

*WORKMAN comes in.*

WORKMAN. Your carriage is waiting, sir.

ASTROFF. All right. *[He hands the WORKMAN his medicine-case, portfolio, and box]* Look out, don't crush the portfolio!

WORKMAN. Very well, sir.

SONIA. When shall we see you again?

ASTROFF. Hardly before next summer. Probably not this winter, though, of course, if anything should happen you will let me know. *[He shakes hands with them]* Thank you for your kindness, for your hospitality, for everything! *[He goes up to MARINA and kisses her head]* Good-bye, old nurse!

MARINA. Are you going without your tea?

ASTROFF. I don't want any, nurse.

MARINA. Won't you have a drop of vodka?

ASTROFF. *[Hesitatingly]* Yes, I might.

*MARINA goes out.*

ASTROFF. *[After a pause]* My off-wheeler has gone lame for some reason. I noticed it yesterday when Peter was taking him to water.

VOITSKI. You should have him re-shod.

ASTROFF. I shall have to go around by the blacksmith's on my way home. It can't be avoided. *[He stands looking up at the map of Africa hanging on the wall]* I suppose it is roasting hot in Africa now.

VOITSKI. Yes, I suppose it is.

*MARINA comes back carrying a tray on which are a glass of vodka and a piece of bread.*

MARINA. Help yourself.

*ASTROFF drinks*

MARINA. To your good health! *[She bows deeply]* Eat your bread with it.

ASTROFF. No, I like it so. And now, good-bye. *[To MARINA]* You needn't come out to see me off, nurse.

*He goes out. SONIA follows him with a candle to light him to the carriage. MARINA sits down in her armchair.*

VOITSKI. *[Writing]* On the 2d of February, twenty pounds of butter; on the 16th, twenty pounds of butter again. Buckwheat flour—*[A pause. Bells are heard tinkling.]*

MARINA. He has gone. *[A pause.]*

*SONIA comes in and sets the candle stick on the table.*

SONIA. He has gone.

VOITSKI. *[Adding and writing]* Total, fifteen—twenty-five—

*SONIA sits down and begins to write.*

*[Yawning]* Oh, ho! The Lord have mercy.

*TELEGIN comes in on tiptoe, sits down near the door, and begins to tune his guitar.*

VOITSKI. *[To SONIA, stroking her hair]* Oh, my child, I am miserable; if you only knew how miserable I am!

SONIA. What can we do? We must live our lives. *[A pause]* Yes, we shall live, Uncle Vanya. We shall live through the long procession of days before us, and through the long evenings; we shall patiently bear the trials that fate imposes on us; we shall work for others without rest, both now and when we are old; and when our last hour comes we shall meet it humbly, and there, beyond the grave, we shall say that we have suffered and wept, that our life was bitter, and God will have pity on us. Ah, then dear, dear Uncle, we shall see that bright and beautiful life; we shall rejoice and look back upon our sorrow here; a tender smile—and—we shall rest. I have faith, Uncle, fervent, passionate faith. *[SONIA kneels down before her uncle and lays her head on his hands. She speaks in a weary voice]* We shall rest. *[TELEGIN plays softly on the guitar]* We shall rest. We shall hear the angels. We shall see heaven shining like a jewel. We shall see all evil and all our pain sink away in the great compassion that shall enfold the world. Our life will be as peaceful and tender and sweet as a caress. I have faith; I have faith. *[She wipes away her tears]* My poor, poor Uncle Vanya, you are crying! *[Weeping]* You have never known what happiness was, but wait, Uncle Vanya, wait! We shall rest. *[She embraces him]* We shall rest. *[The WATCHMAN'S rattle is heard in the garden; TELEGIN plays softly; MME. VOITSKAYA writes something on the margin of her pamphlet; MARINA knits her stocking]* We shall rest.

**The curtain slowly falls.**

# THE THREE SISTERS

## Translated by Julius West

### CHARACTERS

ANDREY SERGEYEVITCH PROSOROV
NATALIA IVANOVA (NATASHA), his fiancée, later his wife (28)
His sisters:
OLGA
MASHA
IRINA
FEODOR ILITCH KULIGIN, high school teacher, married to MASHA (20)
ALEXANDER IGNATEYEVITCH VERSHININ, lieutenant-colonel in charge of a battery (42)
ICOLAI LVOVITCH TUZENBACH, baron, lieutenant in the army (30)
VASSILI VASSILEVITCH SOLENI, captain
IVAN ROMANOVITCH CHEBUTIKIN, army doctor (60)
ALEXEY PETROVITCH FEDOTIK, sub-lieutenant
VLADIMIR CARLOVITCH RODE, sub-lieutenant
FERAPONT, door-keeper at local council offices, an old man
ANFISA, nurse (80)

The action takes place in a provincial town.

*[Ages are stated in brackets.]*

# ACT I

*[In PROSOROV'S house. A sitting-room with pillars; behind is seen a large dining-room. It is midday, the sun is shining brightly outside. In the dining-room the table is being laid for lunch.]*

*[OLGA, in the regulation blue dress of a teacher at a girl's high school, is walking about correcting exercise books; MASHA, in a black dress, with a hat on her knees, sits and reads a book; IRINA, in white, stands about, with a thoughtful expression.]*

OLGA. It's just a year since father died last May the fifth, on your name-day, Irina. It was very cold then, and snowing. I thought I would never survive it, and you were in a dead faint. And now a year has gone by and we are already thinking about it without pain, and you are wearing a white dress and your face is happy. *[Clock strikes twelve]* And the clock struck just the same way then. *[Pause]* I remember that there was music at the funeral, and they fired a volley in the cemetery. He was a general in command of a brigade but there were few people present. Of course, it was raining then, raining hard, and snowing.

IRINA. Why think about it!

*[BARON TUZENBACH, CHEBUTIKIN and SOLENI appear by the table in the dining-room, behind the pillars.]*

OLGA. It's so warm to-day that we can keep the windows open, though the birches are not yet in flower. Father was put in command of a brigade, and he rode out of Moscow with us eleven years ago. I remember perfectly that it was early in May and that everything in Moscow was flowering then. It was warm too, everything was bathed in sunshine. Eleven years have gone, and I remember everything as if we rode out only yesterday. Oh, God! When I awoke this morning and saw all the light and the spring, joy entered my heart, and I longed passionately to go home.

CHEBUTIKIN. Will you take a bet on it?

TUZENBACH. Oh, nonsense.

*[MASHA, lost in a reverie over her book, whistles softly.]*

OLGA. Don't whistle, Masha. How can you! *[Pause]* I'm always having headaches from having to go to the High School every day and then teach till evening. Strange thoughts come to me, as if I were already an old woman. And really, during these four years that I have been working here, I have been feeling as if every day my strength and youth have been squeezed out of me, drop by drop. And only one desire grows and gains in strength...

IRINA. To go away to Moscow. To sell the house, drop everything here, and go to Moscow...

OLGA. Yes! To Moscow, and as soon as possible.

*[CHEBUTIKIN and TUZENBACH laugh.]*

IRINA. I expect Andrey will become a professor, but still, he won't want to live here. Only poor Masha must go on living here.

OLGA. Masha can come to Moscow every year, for the whole summer.

*[MASHA is whistling gently.]*

IRINA. Everything will be arranged, please God. *[Looks out of the window]* It's nice out to-day. I don't know why I'm so happy: I remembered this morning that it was my name-day, and I suddenly felt glad and remembered my childhood, when mother was still with us. What beautiful thoughts I had, what thoughts!

OLGA. You're all radiance to-day, I've never seen you look so lovely. And Masha is pretty, too. Andrey wouldn't be bad-looking, if he wasn't so stout; it does spoil his appearance. But I've grown old and very thin, I suppose it's because I get angry with the girls at school. To-day I'm free. I'm at home. I haven't got a headache, and I feel younger than I was yesterday. I'm only twenty-eight.... All's well, God is everywhere, but it seems to me that if only I were married and could stay at home all day, it would be even better. *[Pause]* I should love my husband.

TUZENBACH. *[To SOLENI]* I'm tired of listening to the rot you talk. *[Entering the sitting-room]* I forgot to say that Vershinin, our new lieutenant-colonel of artillery, is coming to see us to-day. *[Sits down to the piano.]*

OLGA. That's good. I'm glad.

IRINA. Is he old?

TUZENBACH. Oh, no. Forty or forty-five, at the very outside. *[Plays softly]* He seems rather a good sort. He's certainly no fool, only he likes to hear himself speak.

IRINA. Is he interesting?

TUZENBACH. Oh, he's all right, but there's his wife, his mother-in-law, and two daughters. This is his second wife. He pays calls and tells everybody that he's got a wife and two daughters. He'll tell you so here. The wife isn't all there, she does her hair like a flapper and gushes extremely. She talks philosophy and tries to commit suicide every now and again, apparently in order to annoy her husband. I should have left her long ago, but he bears up patiently, and just grumbles.

SOLENI. *[Enters with CHEBUTIKIN from the dining-room]* With one hand I can only lift fifty-four pounds, but with both hands I can lift 180, or even 200 pounds. From this I conclude that two men are not twice as strong as one, but three times, perhaps even more....

CHEBUTIKIN. *[Reads a newspaper as he walks]* If your hair is coming out... take an ounce of naphthaline and hail a bottle of spirit... dissolve and use daily.... *[Makes a note in his pocket diary]* When found make a note of! Not that I want it though.... *[Crosses it out]* It doesn't matter.

IRINA. Ivan Romanovitch, dear Ivan Romanovitch!

CHEBUTIKIN. What does my own little girl want?

IRINA. Ivan Romanovitch, dear Ivan Romanovitch! I feel as if I were sailing under the broad blue sky with great white birds around me. Why is that? Why?

CHEBUTIKIN. *[Kisses her hands, tenderly]* My white bird....

IRINA. When I woke up to-day and got up and dressed myself, I suddenly began to feel as if everything in this life was open to me, and that I knew how I must live. Dear Ivan Romanovitch, I know everything. A man must work, toil in the sweat of his brow, whoever he may be, for that is the meaning and object of his life, his happiness, his enthusiasm. How fine it is to be a workman who gets up at daybreak and breaks stones in the street, or a shepherd, or a schoolmaster, who teaches children, or an engine-driver on the railway.... My God, let alone a man, it's better to be an ox, or just a horse, so long as it can work, than a young woman who wakes up at twelve o'clock, has her coffee in bed, and then spends two hours dressing.... Oh it's awful! Sometimes when it's hot, your thirst can be just as tiresome as my need for work. And if I don't get up early in future and work, Ivan Romanovitch, then you may refuse me your friendship.

CHEBUTIKIN. *[Tenderly]* I'll refuse, I'll refuse....

OLGA. Father used to make us get up at seven. Now Irina wakes at seven and lies and meditates about something till nine at least. And she looks so serious! *[Laughs.]*

IRINA. You're so used to seeing me as a little girl that it seems queer to you when my face is serious. I'm twenty!

TUZENBACH. How well I can understand that craving for work, oh God! I've never worked once in my life. I was born in Petersburg, a chilly, lazy place, in a family which never knew what work or worry meant. I remember that when I used to come home from my regiment, a footman used to have to pull off my boots while I fidgeted and my mother looked on in adoration and wondered why other people didn't see me in the same light. They shielded me from work; but only just in time! A new age is dawning, the people are marching on us all, a powerful, health-giving storm is gathering, it is drawing near, soon it will be upon us and it will drive away laziness, indifference, the prejudice against labour, and rotten dullness from our society. I shall work, and in twenty-five or thirty years, every man will have to work. Every one!

CHEBUTIKIN. I shan't work.

TUZENBACH. You don't matter.

SOLENI. In twenty-five years' time, we shall all be dead, thank the Lord. In two or three years' time apoplexy will carry you off, or else I'll blow your brains out, my pet. *[Takes a scent-bottle out of his pocket and sprinkles his chest and hands.]*

CHEBUTIKIN. *[Laughs]* It's quite true, I never have worked. After I came down from the university I never stirred a finger or opened a book, I just read the papers.... *[Takes another newspaper out of his pocket]* Here we are.... I've learnt from the papers that there used to be one, Dobrolubov *[Note: Dobroluboy (1836-81), in spite of the shortness of his career, established himself as one of the classic literary critics of Russia]*, for instance, but what he wrote—I don't know... God only knows.... *[Somebody is heard tapping on the floor from below]* There.... They're calling me downstairs, somebody's come to see me. I'll be back in a minute... won't be long.... *[Exit hurriedly, scratching his beard.]*

IRINA. He's up to something.

TUZENBACH. Yes, he looked so pleased as he went out that I'm pretty certain he'll bring you a present in a moment.

IRINA. How unpleasant!

OLGA. Yes, it's awful. He's always doing silly things.

MASHA. *[Gets up and sings softly.]*

"There stands a green oak by the sea.
And a chain of bright gold is around it...
And a chain of bright gold is around it...."

OLGA. You're not very bright to-day, Masha. *[MASHA sings, putting on her hat]* Where are you off to?

MASHA. Home.

IRINA. That's odd....

TUZENBACH. On a name-day, too!

MASHA. It doesn't matter. I'll come in the evening. Good-bye, dear. *[Kisses MASHA]* Many happy returns, though I've said it before. In the old days when father was alive, every time we had a name-day, thirty or forty officers used to come, and there was lots of noise and fun, and to-day there's only a man and a half, and it's as quiet as a desert... I'm off... I've got the hump to-day, and am not at all cheerful, so don't you mind me. *[Laughs through her tears]* We'll have a talk later on, but good-bye for the present, my dear; I'll go somewhere.

IRINA. *[Displeased]* You are queer....

OLGA. *[Crying]* I understand you, Masha.

SOLENI. When a man talks philosophy, well, it is philosophy or at any rate sophistry; but when a woman, or two women, talk philosophy—it's all my eye.

MASHA. What do you mean by that, you very awful man?

SOLENI. Oh, nothing. You came down on me before I could say... help! *[Pause.]*

MASHA. *[Angrily, to OLGA]* Don't cry!

*[Enter ANFISA and FERAPONT with a cake.]*

ANFISA. This way, my dear. Come in, your feet are clean. *[To IRINA]* From the District Council, from Mihail Ivanitch Protopopov... a cake.

IRINA. Thank you. Please thank him. *[Takes the cake.]*

FERAPONT. What?

IRINA. *[Louder]* Please thank him.

OLGA. Give him a pie, nurse. Ferapont, go, she'll give you a pie.

FERAPONT. What?

ANFISA. Come on, gran'fer, Ferapont Spiridonitch. Come on. *[Exeunt.]*

MASHA. I don't like this Mihail Potapitch or Ivanitch, Protopopov. We oughtn't to invite him here.

IRINA. I never asked him.

MASHA. That's all right.

*[Enter CHEBUTIKIN followed by a soldier with a silver samovar; there is a rumble of dissatisfied surprise.]*

OLGA. *[Covers her face with her hands]* A samovar! That's awful! *[Exit into the dining-room, to the table.]*

IRINA. My dear Ivan Romanovitch, what are you doing!

TUZENBACH. *[Laughs]* I told you so!

MASHA. Ivan Romanovitch, you are simply shameless!

CHEBUTIKIN. My dear good girl, you are the only thing, and the dearest thing I have in the world. I'll soon be sixty. I'm an old man, a lonely worthless old man. The only good thing in me is my love for you, and if it hadn't been for that, I would have been dead long ago.... *[To IRINA]* My dear little girl, I've known you since the day of your birth, I've carried you in my arms... I loved your dead mother....

MASHA. But your presents are so expensive!

CHEBUTIKIN. *[Angrily, through his tears]* Expensive presents.... You really, are!... *[To the orderly]* Take the samovar in there.... *[Teasing]* Expensive presents!

*[The orderly goes into the dining-room with the samovar.]*

ANFISA. *[Enters and crosses stage]* My dear, there's a strange Colonel come! He's taken off his coat already. Children, he's coming here. Irina darling, you'll be a nice and polite little girl, won't you.... Should have lunched a long time ago.... Oh, Lord.... *[Exit.]*

TUZENBACH. It must be Vershinin. *[Enter VERSHININ]* Lieutenant-Colonel Vershinin!

VERSHININ. *[To MASHA and IRINA]* I have the honour to introduce myself, my name is Vershinin. I am very glad indeed to be able to come at last. How you've grown! Oh! oh!

IRINA. Please sit down. We're very glad you've come.

VERSHININ. *[Gaily]* I am glad, very glad! But there are three sisters, surely. I remember—three little girls. I forget your faces, but your father, Colonel Prosorov, used to have three little girls, I remember that perfectly, I saw them with my own eyes. How time does fly! Oh, dear, how it flies!

TUZENBACH. Alexander Ignateyevitch comes from Moscow.

IRINA. From Moscow? Are you from Moscow?

VERSHININ. Yes, that's so. Your father used to be in charge of a battery there, and I was an officer in the same brigade. *[To MASHA]* I seem to remember your face a little.

MASHA. I don't remember you.

IRINA. Olga! Olga! *[Shouts into the dining-room]* Olga! Come along! *[OLGA enters from the dining-room]* Lieutenant Colonel Vershinin comes from Moscow, as it happens.

VERSHININ. I take it that you are Olga Sergeyevna, the eldest, and that you are Maria... and you are Irina, the youngest....

OLGA. So you come from Moscow?

VERSHININ. Yes. I went to school in Moscow and began my service there; I was there for a long time until at last I got my battery and moved over here, as you see. I don't really remember you, I only remember that there used to be three sisters. I remember your father well; I have only to shut my eyes to see him as he was. I used to come to your house in Moscow....

OLGA. I used to think I remembered everybody, but...

VERSHININ. My name is Alexander Ignateyevitch.

IRINA. Alexander Ignateyevitch, you've come from Moscow. That is really quite a surprise!

OLGA. We are going to live there, you see.

IRINA. We think we may be there this autumn. It's our native town, we were born there. In Old Basmanni Road.... *[They both laugh for joy.]*

MASHA. We've unexpectedly met a fellow countryman. *[Briskly]* I remember: Do you remember, Olga, they used to speak at home of a "lovelorn Major." You were only a Lieutenant then, and in love with somebody, but for some reason they always called you a Major for fun.

VERSHININ. *[Laughs]* That's it... the lovelorn Major, that's got it!

MASHA. You only wore moustaches then. You have grown older! *[Through her tears]* You have grown older!

VERSHININ. Yes, when they used to call me the lovelorn Major, I was young and in love. I've grown out of both now.

OLGA. But you haven't a single white hair yet. You're older, but you're not yet old.

VERSHININ. I'm forty-two, anyway. Have you been away from Moscow long?

IRINA. Eleven years. What are you crying for, Masha, you little fool.... *[Crying]* And I'm crying too.

MASHA. It's all right. And where did you live?

VERSHININ. Old Basmanni Road.

OLGA. Same as we.

VERSHININ. Once I used to live in German Street. That was when the Red Barracks were my headquarters. There's an ugly bridge in between, where the water rushes underneath. One gets melancholy when one is alone there. *[Pause]* Here the river is so wide and fine! It's a splendid river!

OLGA. Yes, but it's so cold. It's very cold here, and the midges....

VERSHININ. What are you saying! Here you've got such a fine healthy Russian climate. You've a forest, a river... and birches. Dear, modest birches, I like them more than any other tree. It's good to live here. Only it's odd that the railway station should be thirteen miles away.... Nobody knows why.

SOLENI. I know why. *[All look at him]* Because if it was near it wouldn't be far off, and if it's far off, it can't be near. *[An awkward pause.]*

TUZENBACH. Funny man.

OLGA. Now I know who you are. I remember.

VERSHININ. I used to know your mother.

CHEBUTIKIN. She was a good woman, rest her soul.

IRINA. Mother is buried in Moscow.

OLGA. At the Novo-Devichi Cemetery.

MASHA. Do you know, I'm beginning to forget her face. We'll be forgotten in just the same way.

VERSHININ. Yes, they'll forget us. It's our fate, it can't be helped. A time will come when everything that seems serious, significant, or very important to us will be forgotten, or considered trivial. *[Pause]* And the curious thing is that we can't possibly find out what will come to be regarded as great and important, and what will be feeble, or silly. Didn't the discoveries of Copernicus, or Columbus, say, seem unnecessary and ludicrous at first, while wasn't it thought that some rubbish written by a fool, held all the truth? And it may so happen that our present existence, with which we are so satisfied, will in time appear strange, inconvenient, stupid, unclean, perhaps even sinful....

TUZENBACH. Who knows? But on the other hand, they may call our life noble and honour its memory. We've abolished torture and capital punishment, we live in security, but how much suffering there is still!

SOLENI. *[In a feeble voice]* There, there.... The Baron will go without his dinner if you only let him talk philosophy.

TUZENBACH. Vassili Vassilevitch, kindly leave me alone. *[Changes his chair]* You're very dull, you know.

SOLENI. *[Feebly]* There, there, there.

TUZENBACH. *[To VERSHININ]* The sufferings we see to-day—there are so many of them!—still indicate a certain moral improvement in society.

VERSHININ. Yes, yes, of course.

CHEBUTIKIN. You said just now, Baron, that they may call our life noble; but we are very petty.... *[Stands up]* See how little I am. *[Violin played behind.]*

MASHA. That's Andrey playing—our brother.

IRINA. He's the learned member of the family. I expect he will be a professor some day. Father was a soldier, but his son chose an academic career for himself.

MASHA. That was father's wish.

OLGA. We ragged him to-day. We think he's a little in love.

IRINA. To a local lady. She will probably come here to-day.

MASHA. You should see the way she dresses! Quite prettily, quite fashionably too, but so badly! Some queer bright yellow skirt with a wretched little fringe and a red bodice. And such a complexion! Andrey isn't in love. After all he has taste, he's simply making fun of us. I heard yesterday that she was going to marry Protopopov, the chairman of the Local Council. That would do her nicely.... *[At the side door]* Andrey, come here! Just for a minute, dear! *[Enter ANDREY.]*

OLGA. My brother, Andrey Sergeyevitch.

VERSHININ. My name is Vershinin.

ANDREY. Mine is Prosorov. *[Wipes his perspiring hands]* You've come to take charge of the battery?

OLGA. Just think, Alexander Ignateyevitch comes from Moscow.

ANDREY. That's all right. Now my little sisters won't give you any rest.

VERSHININ. I've already managed to bore your sisters.

IRINA. Just look what a nice little photograph frame Andrey gave me to-day. *[Shows it]* He made it himself.

VERSHININ. *[Looks at the frame and does not know what to say]* Yes.... It's a thing that...

IRINA. And he made that frame there, on the piano as well. *[Andrey waves his hand and walks away.]*

OLGA. He's got a degree, and plays the violin, and cuts all sorts of things out of wood, and is really a domestic Admirable Crichton. Don't go away, Andrey! He's got into a habit of always going away. Come here!

*[MASHA and IRINA take his arms and laughingly lead him back.]*

MASHA. Come on, come on!

ANDREY. Please leave me alone.

MASHA. You are funny. Alexander Ignateyevitch used to be called the lovelorn Major, but he never minded.

VERSHININ. Not the least.

MASHA. I'd like to call you the lovelorn fiddler!

IRINA. Or the lovelorn professor!

OLGA. He's in love! little Andrey is in love!

IRINA. *[Applauds]* Bravo, Bravo! Encore! Little Andrey is in love.

CHEBUTIKIN. *[Goes up behind ANDREY and takes him round the waist with both arms]* Nature only brought us into the world that we should love! *[Roars with laughter, then sits down and reads a newspaper which he takes out of his pocket.]*

ANDREY. That's enough, quite enough.... *[Wipes his face]* I couldn't sleep all night and now I can't quite find my feet, so to speak. I read until four o'clock, then tried to sleep, but nothing happened. I thought about one thing and another, and then it dawned and the sun crawled into my bedroom. This summer, while I'm here, I want to translate a book from the English....

VERSHININ. Do you read English?

ANDREY. Yes father, rest his soul, educated us almost violently. It may seem funny and silly, but it's nevertheless true, that after his death I began to fill out and get rounder, as if my body had had some great pressure taken off it. Thanks to father, my sisters and I know French, German, and English, and Irina knows Italian as well. But we paid dearly for it all!

MASHA. A knowledge of three languages is an unnecessary luxury in this town. It isn't even a luxury but a sort of useless extra, like a sixth finger. We know a lot too much.

VERSHININ. Well, I say! *[Laughs]* You know a lot too much! I don't think there can really be a town so dull and stupid as to have no place for a clever, cultured person. Let us suppose even that among the hundred thousand inhabitants of this backward and uneducated town, there are only three persons like yourself. It stands to rcason that you won't be able to conquer that dark mob around you; little by little as you grow older you will be bound to give way and lose yourselves in this crowd of a hundred thousand human beings; their life will suck you up in itself, but still, you won't disappear having influenced nobody; later on, others like you will come, perhaps six of them, then twelve, and so on, until at last your sort will be in the majority. In two or three hundred years' time life on this earth will be unimaginably beautiful and wonderful. Mankind needs such a life, and if it is not ours to-day then we must look ahead for it, wait, think, prepare for it. We must see and know more than our fathers and grandfathers saw and knew. *[Laughs]* And you com-complain that you know too much.

MASHA. *[Takes off her hat]* I'll stay to lunch.

IRINA. *[Sighs]* Yes, all that ought to be written down.

*[ANDREY has gone out quietly.]*

TUZENBACH. You say that many years later on, life on this earth will be beautiful and wonderful. That's true. But to share in it now, even though at a distance, we must prepare by work....

VERSHININ. *[Gets up]* Yes. What a lot of flowers you have. *[Looks round]* It's a beautiful flat. I envy you! I've spent my whole life in rooms with two chairs, one sofa, and fires which always smoke. I've never had flowers like these in my life.... *[Rubs his hands]* Well, well!

TUZENBACH. Yes, we must work. You are probably thinking to yourself: the German lets himself go. But I assure you I'm a Russian, I can't even speak German. My father belonged to the Orthodox Church.... *[Pause.]*

VERSHININ. *[Walks about the stage]* I often wonder: suppose we could begin life over again, knowing what we were doing? Suppose we could use one life, already ended, as a sort of rough draft for another? I think that every one of us would try, more than anything else, not to repeat himself, at the very least he would rearrange his manner of life, he would make sure of rooms like these, with flowers and light... I have a wife and two daughters, my wife's health is delicate and so on and so on, and if I had to begin life all over again I would not marry.... No, no!

*[Enter KULIGIN in a regulation jacket.]*

KULIGIN. *[Going up to IRINA]* Dear sister, allow me to congratulate you on the day sacred to your good angel and to wish you, sincerely and from the bottom of my heart, good health and all that one can wish for a girl of your years. And then let me offer you this book as a present. *[Gives it to her]* It is the history of our High School during the last fifty years, written by myself. The book is worthless, and written because I had nothing to do, but read it all the same. Good day, gentlemen! *[To VERSHININ]* My name is Kuligin, I am a master of the local High School. *[Note: He adds that he is a Nadvorny Sovetnik (almost the same as a German Hofrat), an undistinguished civilian title with no English equivalent.] [To IRINA]* In this book you will find a list of all those who have taken the full course at our High School during these fifty years. *Feci quod potui, faciant meliora potentes. [Kisses MASHA.]*

IRINA. But you gave me one of these at Easter.

KULIGIN. *[Laughs]* I couldn't have, surely! You'd better give it back to me in that case, or else give it to the Colonel. Take it, Colonel. You'll read it some day when you're bored.

VERSHININ. Thank you. *[Prepares to go]* I am extremely happy to have made the acquaintance of...

OLGA. Must you go? No, not yet?

IRINA. You'll stop and have lunch with us. Please do.

OLGA. Yes, please!

VERSHININ. *[Bows]* I seem to have dropped in on your name-day. Forgive me, I didn't know, and I didn't offer you my congratulations. *[Goes with OLGA into the dining-room.]*

KULIGIN. To-day is Sunday, the day of rest, so let us rest and rejoice, each in a manner compatible with his age and disposition. The carpets will have to be taken up for the summer and put away till the winter... Persian powder or naphthaline.... The Romans were healthy because they knew both how to work and how to rest, they had *mens sana in corpore sano*. Their life ran along certain recognized patterns. Our director says: "The chief thing about each life is its pattern. Whoever loses his pattern is lost himself"—and it's just the same in our daily life. *[Takes MASHA by the waist, laughing]* Masha loves me. My wife loves me. And you ought to put the window curtains away with the carpets.... I'm feeling awfully pleased with life to-day. Masha, we've got to be at the director's at four. They're getting up a walk for the pedagogues and their families.

MASHA. I shan't go.

KULIGIN. *[Hurt]* My dear Masha, why not?

MASHA. I'll tell you later.... *[Angrily]* All right, I'll go, only please stand back.... *[Steps away.]*

KULIGIN. And then we're to spend the evening at the director's. In spite of his ill-health that man tries, above everything else, to be sociable. A splendid, illuminating personality. A wonderful man. After yesterday's committee he said to me: "I'm tired, Feodor Ilitch, I'm tired!" *[Looks at the clock, then at his watch]* Your clock is seven minutes fast. "Yes," he said, "I'm tired." *[Violin played off.]*

OLGA. Let's go and have lunch! There's to be a masterpiece of baking!

KULIGIN. Oh my dear Olga, my dear. Yesterday I was working till eleven o'clock at night, and got awfully tired. To-day I'm quite happy. *[Goes into dining-room]* My dear...

CHEBUTIKIN. *[Puts his paper into his pocket, and combs his beard]* A pie? Splendid!

MASHA. *[Severely to CHEBUTIKIN]* Only mind; you're not to drink anything to-day. Do you hear? It's bad for you.

CHEBUTIKIN. Oh, that's all right. I haven't been drunk for two years. And it's all the same, anyway!

MASHA. You're not to dare to drink, all the same. *[Angrily, but so that her husband should not hear]* Another dull evening at the Director's, confound it!

TUZENBACH. I shouldn't go if I were you.... It's quite simple.

CHEBUTIKIN. Don't go.

MASHA. Yes, "don't go...." It's a cursed, unbearable life.... *[Goes into dining-room.]*

CHEBUTIKIN. *[Follows her]* It's not so bad.

SOLENI. *[Going into the dining-room]* There, there, there....

TUZENBACH. Vassili Vassilevitch, that's enough. Be quiet!

SOLENI. There, there, there....

KULIGIN. *[Gaily]* Your health, Colonel! I'm a pedagogue and not quite at home here. I'm Masha's husband.... She's a good sort, a very good sort.

VERSHININ. I'll have some of this black vodka.... *[Drinks]* Your health! *[To OLGA]* I'm very comfortable here!

*[Only IRINA and TUZENBACH are now left in the sitting-room.]*

IRINA. Masha's out of sorts to-day. She married when she was eighteen, when he seemed to her the wisest of men. And now it's different. He's the kindest man, but not the wisest.

OLGA. *[Impatiently]* Andrey, when are you coming?

ANDREY. *[Off]* One minute. *[Enters and goes to the table.]*

TUZENBACH. What are you thinking about?

IRINA. I don't like this Soleni of yours and I'm afraid of him. He only says silly things.

TUZENBACH. He's a queer man. I'm sorry for him, though he vexes me. I think he's shy. When there are just the two of us he's quite all right and very good company; when other people are about he's rough and hectoring. Don't let's go in, let them have their meal without us. Let me stay with you. What are you thinking of? *[Pause]* You're twenty. I'm not yet thirty. How many years are there left to us, with their long, long lines of days, filled with my love for you....

IRINA. Nicolai Lvovitch, don't speak to me of love.

TUZENBACH. *[Does not hear]* I've a great thirst for life, struggle, and work, and this thirst has united with my love for you, Irina, and you're so beautiful, and life seems so beautiful to me! What are you thinking about?

IRINA. You say that life is beautiful. Yes, if only it seems so! The life of us three hasn't been beautiful yet; it has been stifling us as if it was weeds... I'm crying. I oughtn't.... *[Dries her tears, smiles]* We must work, work. That is why we are unhappy and look at the world so sadly; we don't know what work is. Our parents despised work....

*[Enter NATALIA IVANOVA; she wears a pink dress and a green sash.]*

NATASHA. They're already at lunch... I'm late... *[Carefully examines herself in a mirror, and puts herself straight]* I think my hair's done all right.... *[Sees IRINA]* Dear Irina Sergeyevna, I congratulate you! *[Kisses her firmly and at length]* You've so many visitors, I'm really ashamed.... How do you do, Baron!

OLGA. *[Enters from dining-room]* Here's Natalia Ivanovna. How are you, dear! *[They kiss.]*

NATASHA. Happy returns. I'm awfully shy, you've so many people here.

OLGA. All our friends. *[Frightened, in an undertone]* You're wearing a green sash! My dear, you shouldn't!

NATASHA. Is it a sign of anything?

OLGA. No, it simply doesn't go well... and it looks so queer.

NATASHA. *[In a tearful voice]* Yes? But it isn't really green, it's too dull for that. *[Goes into dining-room with OLGA.]*

*[They have all sat down to lunch in the dining-room, the sitting-room is empty.]*

KULIGIN. I wish you a nice fiancée, Irina. It's quite time you married.

CHEBUTIKIN. Natalia Ivanovna, I wish you the same.

KULIGIN. Natalia Ivanovna has a fiancé already.

MASHA. *[Raps with her fork on a plate]* Let's all get drunk and make life purple for once!

KULIGIN. You've lost three good conduct marks.

VERSHININ. This is a nice drink. What's it made of?

SOLENI. Blackbeetles.

IRINA. *[Tearfully]* Phoo! How disgusting!

OLGA. There is to be a roast turkey and a sweet apple pie for dinner. Thank goodness I can spend all day and the evening at home. You'll come in the evening, ladies and gentlemen....

VERSHININ. And please may I come in the evening!

IRINA. Please do.

NATASHA. They don't stand on ceremony here.

CHEBUTIKIN. Nature only brought us into the world that we should love! *[Laughs.]*

ANDREY. *[Angrily]* Please don't! Aren't you tired of it?

*[Enter FEDOTIK and RODE with a large basket of flowers.]*

FEDOTIK. They're lunching already.

RODE. *[Loudly and thickly]* Lunching? Yes, so they are....

FEDOTIK. Wait a minute! *[Takes a photograph]* That's one. No, just a moment.... *[Takes another]* That's two. Now we're ready!

*[They take the basket and go into the dining-room, where they have a noisy reception.]*

RODE. *[Loudly]* Congratulations and best wishes! Lovely weather to-day, simply perfect. Was out walking with the High School students all the morning. I take their drills.

FEDOTIK. You may move, Irina Sergeyevna! *[Takes a photograph]* You look well to-day. *[Takes a humming-top out of his pocket]* Here's a humming-top, by the way. It's got a lovely note!

IRINA. How awfully nice!

MASHA.

"There stands a green oak by the sea,

And a chain of bright gold is around it...
And a chain of bright gold is around it..."

*[Tearfully]* What am I saying that for? I've had those words running in my head all day....

KULIGIN. There are thirteen at table!

RODE. *[Aloud]* Surely you don't believe in that superstition? *[Laughter.]*

KULIGIN. If there are thirteen at table then it means there are lovers present. It isn't you, Ivan Romanovitch, hang it all.... *[Laughter.]*

CHEBUTIKIN. I'm a hardened sinner, but I really don't see why Natalia Ivanovna should blush....

*[Loud laughter; NATASHA runs out into the sitting-room, followed by ANDREY.]*

ANDREY. Don't pay any attention to them! Wait... do stop, please....

NATASHA. I'm shy... I don't know what's the matter with me and they're all laughing at me. It wasn't nice of me to leave the table like that, but I can't... I can't. *[Covers her face with her hands.]*

ANDREY. My dear, I beg you. I implore you not to excite yourself. I assure you they're only joking, they're kind people. My dear, good girl, they're all kind and sincere people, and they like both you and me. Come here to the window, they can't see us here.... *[Looks round.]*

NATASHA. I'm so unaccustomed to meeting people!

ANDREY. Oh your youth, your splendid, beautiful youth! My darling, don't be so excited! Believe me, believe me... I'm so happy, my soul is full of love, of ecstasy.... They don't see us! They can't! Why, why or when did I fall in love with you—Oh, I can't understand anything. My dear, my pure darling, be my wife! I love you, love you... as never before.... *[They kiss.]*

*[Two officers come in and, seeing the lovers kiss, stop in astonishment.]*

**Curtain.**

# ACT II

*[Scene as before. It is 8 p.m. Somebody is heard playing a concertina outside in' the street. There is no fire. NATALIA IVANOVNA enters in indoor dress carrying a candle; she stops by the door which leads into ANDREY'S room.]*

NATASHA. What are you doing, Andrey? Are you reading? It's nothing, only I.... *[She opens another door, and looks in, then closes it]* Isn't there any fire....

ANDREY. *[Enters with book in hand]* What are you doing, Natasha?

NATASHA. I was looking to see if there wasn't a fire. It's Shrovetide, and the servant is simply beside herself; I must look out that something doesn't happen. When I came through the dining-room yesterday midnight, there was a candle burning. I couldn't get her to tell me who had lighted it. *[Puts down her candle]* What's the time?

ANDREY. *[Looks at his watch]* A quarter past eight.

NATASHA. And Olga and Irina aren't in yet. The poor things are still at work. Olga at the teacher's council, Irina at the telegraph office.... *[Sighs]* I said to your sister this morning, "Irina, darling, you must take care of yourself." But she pays no attention. Did you say it was a quarter past eight? I am afraid little Bobby is quite ill. Why is he so cold? He was feverish yesterday, but today he is quite cold... I am so frightened!

ANDREY. It's all right, Natasha. The boy is well.

NATASHA. Still, I think we ought to put him on a diet. I am so afraid. And the entertainers were to be here after nine; they had better not come, Audrey.

ANDREY. I don't know. After all, they were asked.

NATASHA. This morning, when the little boy woke up and saw me he suddenly smiled; that means he knew me. "Good morning,

Bobby!" I said, "good morning, darling." And he laughed. Children understand, they understand very well. So I'll tell them, Andrey dear, not to receive the entertainers.

ANDREY. *[Hesitatingly]* But what about my sisters. This is their flat.

NATASHA. They'll do as I want them. They are so kind.... *[Going]* I ordered sour milk for supper. The doctor says you must eat sour milk and nothing else, or you won't get thin. *[Stops]* Bobby is so cold. I'm afraid his room is too cold for him. It would be nice to put him into another room till the warm weather comes. Irina's room, for instance, is just right for a child: it's dry and has the sun all day. I must tell her, she can share Olga's room. It isn't as if she was at home in the daytime, she only sleeps here.... *[A pause]* Andrey, darling, why are you so silent?

ANDREY. I was just thinking.... There is really nothing to say....

NATASHA. Yes... there was something I wanted to tell you.... Oh, yes. Ferapont has come from the Council offices, he wants to see you.

ANDREY. *[Yawns]* Call him here.

*[NATASHA goes out; ANDREY reads his book, stooping over the candle she has left behind. FERAPONT enters; he wears a tattered old coat with the collar up. His ears are muffled.]*

ANDREY. Good morning, grandfather. What have you to say?

FERAPONT. The Chairman sends a book and some documents or other. Here.... *[Hands him a book and a packet.]*

ANDREY. Thank you. It's all right. Why couldn't you come earlier? It's past eight now.

FERAPONT. What?

ANDREY. *[Louder]*. I say you've come late, it's past eight.

FERAPONT. Yes, yes. I came when it was still light, but they wouldn't let me in. They said you were busy. Well, what was I to do. If you're busy, you're busy, and I'm in no hurry. *[He thinks that ANDREY is asking him something]* What?

ANDREY. Nothing. *[Looks through the book]* To-morrow's Friday. I'm not supposed to go to work, but I'll come—all the same... and do some work. It's dull at home. *[Pause]* Oh, my dear old man, how strangely life changes, and how it deceives! To-day, out of sheer boredom, I took up this book—old university lectures, and I couldn't help laughing. My God, I'm secretary of the local district council, the council which has Protopopov for its chairman, yes, I'm the secretary, and the summit of my ambitions is—to become a member of the council! I to be a member of the local district council, I, who dream every night that I'm a professor of Moscow University, a famous scholar of whom all Russia is proud!

FERAPONT. I can't tell... I'm hard of hearing....

ANDREY. If you weren't, I don't suppose I should talk to you. I've got to talk to somebody, and my wife doesn't understand me, and I'm a bit afraid of my sisters—I don't know why unless it is that they may make fun of me and make me feel ashamed... I don't drink, I don't like public-houses, but how I should like to be sitting just now in Tyestov's place in Moscow, or at the Great Moscow, old fellow!

FERAPONT. Moscow? That's where a contractor was once telling that some merchants or other were eating pancakes; one ate forty pancakes and he went and died, he was saying. Either forty or fifty, I forget which.

ANDREY. In Moscow you can sit in an enormous restaurant where you don't know anybody and where nobody knows you, and you don't feel all the same that you're a stranger. And here you know everybody and everybody knows you, and you're a stranger... and a lonely stranger.

FERAPONT. What? And the same contractor was telling—perhaps he was lying—that there was a cable stretching right across Moscow.

ANDREY. What for?

FERAPONT. I can't tell. The contractor said so.

ANDREY. Rubbish. *[He reads]* Were you ever in Moscow?

FERAPONT. *[After a pause]* No. God did not lead me there. *[Pause]* Shall I go?

ANDREY. You may go. Good-bye. *[FERAPONT goes]* Good-bye. *[Reads]* You can come to-morrow and fetch these documents.... Go along.... *[Pause]* He's gone. *[A ring]* Yes, yes.... *[Stretches himself and slowly goes into his own room.]*

*[Behind the scene the nurse is singing a lullaby to the child. MASHA and VERSHININ come in. While they talk, a maidservant lights candles and a lamp.]*

MASHA. I don't know. *[Pause]* I don't know. Of course, habit counts for a great deal. After father's death, for instance, it took us a long time to get used to the absence of orderlies. But, apart from habit, it seems to me in all fairness that, however it may be in other towns, the best and most-educated people are army men.

VERSHININ. I'm thirsty. I should like some tea.

MASHA. *[Glancing at her watch]* They'll bring some soon. I was given in marriage when I was eighteen, and I was afraid of my husband because he was a teacher and I'd only just left school. He then seemed to me frightfully wise and learned and important. And now, unfortunately, that has changed.

VERSHININ. Yes... yes.

MASHA. I don't speak of my husband, I've grown used to him, but civilians in general are so often coarse, impolite, uneducated. Their rudeness offends me, it angers me. I suffer when I see that a man isn't quite sufficiently refined, or delicate, or polite. I simply suffer agonies when I happen to be among schoolmasters, my husband's colleagues.

VERSHININ. Yes.... It seems to me that civilians and army men are equally interesting, in this town, at any rate. It's all the same! If you listen to a member of the local intelligentsia, whether to civilian or military, he will tell you that he's sick of his wife, sick of his house, sick of his estate, sick of his horses.... We Russians are extremely gifted in the direction of thinking on an exalted plane, but, tell me, why do we aim so low in real life? Why?

MASHA. Why?

VERSHININ. Why is a Russian sick of his children, sick of his wife? And why are his wife and children sick of him?

MASHA. You're a little downhearted to-day.

VERSHININ. Perhaps I am. I haven't had any dinner, I've had nothing since the morning. My daughter is a little unwell, and when my girls are ill, I get very anxious and my conscience tortures me because they have such a mother. Oh, if you had seen her to-day! What a trivial personality! We began quarrelling at seven in the morning and at nine I slammed the door and went out. *[Pause]* I never speak of her, it's strange that I bear my complaints to you alone. *[Kisses her hand]* Don't be angry with me. I haven't anybody but you, nobody at all.... *[Pause.]*

MASHA. What a noise in the oven. Just before father's death there was a noise in the pipe, just like that.

VERSHININ. Are you superstitious?

MASHA. Yes.

VERSHININ. That's strange. *[Kisses her hand]* You are a splendid, wonderful woman. Splendid, wonderful! It is dark here, but I see your sparkling eyes.

MASHA. *[Sits on another chair]* There is more light here.

VERSHININ. I love you, love you, love you... I love your eyes, your movements, I dream of them.... Splendid, wonderful woman!

MASHA. *[Laughing]* When you talk to me like that, I laugh; I don't know why, for I'm afraid. Don't repeat it, please.... *[In an undertone]* No, go on, it's all the same to me.... *[Covers her face with her hands]* Somebody's coming, let's talk about something else.

*[IRINA and TUZENBACH come in through the dining-room.]*

TUZENBACH. My surname is really triple. I am called Baron Tuzenbach-Krone-Altschauer, but I am Russian and Orthodox, the same as you. There is very little German left in me, unless perhaps it is the patience and the obstinacy with which I bore you. I see you home every night.

IRINA. How tired I am!

TUZENBACH. And I'll come to the telegraph office to see you home every day for ten or twenty years, until you drive me away. *[He sees MASHA and VERSHININ; joyfully]* Is that you? How do you do.

IRINA. Well, I am home at last. *[To MASHA]* A lady came to-day to telegraph to her brother in Saratov that her son died to-day, and she couldn't remember the address anyhow. So she sent the telegram without an address, just to Saratov. She was crying. And for some reason or other I was rude to her. "I've no time," I said. It was so stupid. Are the entertainers coming to-night?

MASHA. Yes.

IRINA. *[Sitting down in an armchair]* I want a rest. I am tired.

TUZENBACH. *[Smiling]* When you come home from your work you seem so young, and so unfortunate.... *[Pause.]*

IRINA. I am tired. No, I don't like the telegraph office, I don't like it.

MASHA. You've grown thinner.... *[Whistles a little]* And you look younger, and your face has become like a boy's.

TUZENBACH. That's the way she does her hair.

IRINA. I must find another job, this one won't do for me. What I wanted, what I hoped to get, just that is lacking here. Labour without poetry, without ideas.... *[A knock on the floor]* The doctor is knocking. *[To TUZENBACH]* Will you knock, dear. I can't... I'm tired.... *[TUZENBACH knocks]* He'll come in a minute. Something ought to be done. Yesterday the doctor and Andrey played cards at the club and lost money. Andrey seems to have lost 200 roubles.

MASHA. *[With indifference]* What can we do now?

IRINA. He lost money a fortnight ago, he lost money in December. Perhaps if he lost everything we should go away from this town. Oh, my God, I dream of Moscow every night. I'm just like a lunatic. *[Laughs]* We go there in June, and before June there's still... February, March, April, May... nearly half a year!

MASHA. Only Natasha mustn't get to know of these losses.

IRINA. I expect it will be all the same to her.

*[CHEBUTIKIN, who has only just got out of bed—he was resting after dinner—comes into the dining-room and combs his beard. He then sits by the table and takes a newspaper from his pocket.]*

MASHA. Here he is.... Has he paid his rent?

IRINA. *[Laughs]* No. He's been here eight months and hasn't paid a copeck. Seems to have forgotten.

MASHA. *[Laughs]* What dignity in his pose! *[They all laugh. A pause.]*

IRINA. Why are you so silent, Alexander Ignateyevitch?

VERSHININ. I don't know. I want some tea. Half my life for a tumbler of tea: I haven't had anything since morning.

CHEBUTIKIN. Irina Sergeyevna!

IRINA. What is it?

CHEBUTIKIN. Please come here, Venez ici. *[IRINA goes and sits by the table]* I can't do without you. *[IRINA begins to play patience.]*

VERSHININ. Well, if we can't have any tea, let's philosophize, at any rate.

TUZENBACH. Yes, let's. About what?

VERSHININ. About what? Let us meditate... about life as it will be after our time; for example, in two or three hundred years.

TUZENBACH. Well? After our time people will fly about in balloons, the cut of one's coat will change, perhaps they'll discover a sixth sense and develop it, but life will remain the same, laborious, mysterious, and happy. And in a thousand years' time, people will still be sighing: "Life is hard!"—and at the same time they'll be just as afraid of death, and unwilling to meet it, as we are.

VERSHININ. *[Thoughtfully]* How can I put it? It seems to me that everything on earth must change, little by little, and is already changing under our very eyes. After two or three hundred years, after a thousand—the actual time doesn't matter—a new and happy age will begin. We, of course, shall not take part in it, but we live and work and even suffer to-day that it should come. We create it—and in that one object is our destiny and, if you like, our happiness.

*[MASHA laughs softly.]*

TUZENBACH. What is it?

MASHA. I don't know. I've been laughing all day, ever since morning.

VERSHININ. I finished my education at the same point as you, I have not studied at universities; I read a lot, but I cannot choose my books and perhaps what I read is not at all what I should, but the longer I love, the more I want to know. My hair is turning white, I am nearly an old man now, but I know so little, oh, so little! But I think I know the things that matter most, and that are most real. I know them well. And I wish I could make you understand that there is no happiness for us, that there should not and cannot be.... We must only work and work, and happiness is only for our distant posterity. *[Pause]* If not for me, then for the descendants of my descendants.

*[FEDOTIK and RODE come into the dining-room; they sit and sing softly, strumming on a guitar.]*

TUZENBACH. According to you, one should not even think about happiness! But suppose I am happy!

VERSHININ. No.

TUZENBACH. *[Moves his hands and laughs]* We do not seem to understand each other. How can I convince you? *[MASHA laughs quietly, TUZENBACH continues, pointing at her]* Yes, laugh! *[To VERSHININ]* Not only after two or three centuries, but in a million years, life will still be as it was; life does not change, it remains for ever, following its own laws which do not concern us, or which, at any rate, you will never find out. Migrant birds, cranes for example, fly and fly, and whatever thoughts, high or low, enter their heads, they will still fly and not know why or where. They fly and will continue to fly, whatever philosophers come to life among them; they may philosophize as much as they like, only they will fly....

MASHA. Still, is there a meaning?

TUZENBACH. A meaning.... Now the snow is falling. What meaning? *[Pause.]*

MASHA. It seems to me that a man must have faith, or must search for a faith, or his life will be empty, empty.... To live and not to know why the cranes fly, why babies are born, why there are stars in the sky.... Either you must know why you live, or everything is trivial, not worth a straw. *[A pause.]*

VERSHININ. Still, I am sorry that my youth has gone.

MASHA. Gogol says: life in this world is a dull matter, my masters!

TUZENBACH. And I say it's difficult to argue with you, my masters! Hang it all.

CHEBUTIKIN. *[Reading]* Balzac was married at Berdichev. *[IRINA is singing softly]* That's worth making a note of. *[He makes a note]* Balzac was married at Berdichev. *[Goes on reading.]*

IRINA. *[Laying out cards, thoughtfully]* Balzac was married at Berdichev.

TUZENBACH. The die is cast. I've handed in my resignation, Maria Sergeyevna.

MASHA. So I heard. I don't see what good it is; I don't like civilians.

TUZENBACH. Never mind.... *[Gets up]* I'm not handsome; what use am I as a soldier? Well, it makes no difference... I shall work. If only just once in my life I could work so that I could come home in the evening, fall exhausted on my bed, and go to sleep at once. *[Going into the dining-room]* Workmen, I suppose, do sleep soundly!

FEDOTIK. *[To IRINA]* I bought some coloured pencils for you at Pizhikov's in the Moscow Road, just now. And here is a little knife.

IRINA. You have got into the habit of behaving to me as if I am a little girl, but I am grown up. *[Takes the pencils and the knife, then, with joy]* How lovely!

FEDOTIK. And I bought myself a knife... look at it... one blade, another, a third, an ear-scoop, scissors, nail-cleaners.

RODE. *[Loudly]* Doctor, how old are you?

CHEBUTIKIN. I? Thirty-two. *[Laughter]*

FEDOTIK. I'll show you another kind of patience.... *[Lays out cards.]*

*[A samovar is brought in; ANFISA attends to it; a little later NATASHA enters and helps by the table; SOLENI arrives and, after greetings, sits by the table.]*

VERSHININ. What a wind!

MASHA. Yes. I'm tired of winter. I've already forgotten what summer's like.

IRINA. It's coming out, I see. We're going to Moscow.

FEDOTIK. No, it won't come out. Look, the eight was on the two of spades. *[Laughs]* That means you won't go to Moscow.

CHEBUTIKIN. *[Reading paper]* Tsitsigar. Smallpox is raging here.

ANFISA. *[Coming up to MASHA]* Masha, have some tea, little mother. *[To VERSHININ]* Please have some, sir... excuse me, but I've forgotten your name....

MASHA. Bring some here, nurse. I shan't go over there.

IRINA. Nurse!

ANFISA. Coming, coming!

NATASHA. *[To SOLENI]* Children at the breast understand perfectly. I said "Good morning, Bobby; good morning, dear!" And he looked at me in quite an unusual way. You think it's only the mother in me that is speaking; I assure you that isn't so! He's a wonderful child.

SOLENI. If he was my child I'd roast him on a frying-pan and eat him. *[Takes his tumbler into the drawing-room and sits in a corner.]*

NATASHA. *[Covers her face in her hands]* Vulgar, ill-bred man!

MASHA. He's lucky who doesn't notice whether it's winter now, or summer. I think that if I were in Moscow, I shouldn't mind about the weather.

VERSHININ. A few days ago I was reading the prison diary of a French minister. He had been sentenced on account of the Panama scandal. With what joy, what delight, he speaks of the birds he saw through the prison windows, which he had never noticed while he was a minister. Now, of course, that he is at liberty, he notices birds no more than he did before. When you go to live in Moscow you'll not notice it, in just the same way. There can be no happiness for us, it only exists in our wishes.

TUZENBACH. *[Takes cardboard box from the table]* Where are the pastries?

IRINA. Soleni has eaten them.

TUZENBACH. All of them?

ANFISA. *[Serving tea]* There's a letter for you.

VERSHININ. For me? *[Takes the letter]* From my daughter. *[Reads]* Yes, of course... I will go quietly. Excuse me, Maria Sergeyevna. I shan't have any tea. *[Stands up, excited]* That eternal story....

MASHA. What is it? Is it a secret?

VERSHININ. *[Quietly]* My wife has poisoned herself again. I must go. I'll go out quietly. It's all awfully unpleasant. *[Kisses MASHA'S hand]* My dear, my splendid, good woman... I'll go this way, quietly. *[Exit.]*

ANFISA. Where has he gone? And I'd served tea.... What a man.

MASHA. *[Angrily]* Be quiet! You bother so one can't have a moment's peace.... *[Goes to the table with her cup]* I'm tired of you, old woman!

ANFISA. My dear! Why are you offended!

ANDREY'S VOICE. Anfisa!

ANFISA. *[Mocking]* Anfisa! He sits there and... *[Exit.]*

MASHA. *[In the dining-room, by the table angrily]* Let me sit down! *[Disturbs the cards on the table]* Here you are, spreading your cards out. Have some tea!

IRINA. You are cross, Masha.

MASHA. If I am cross, then don't talk to me. Don't touch me!

CHEBUTIKIN. Don't touch her, don't touch her....

MASHA. You're sixty, but you're like a boy, always up to some beastly nonsense.

NATASHA. *[Sighs]* Dear Masha, why use such expressions? With your beautiful exterior you would be simply fascinating in good society, I tell you so directly, if it wasn't for your words. *Je vous prie, pardonnez moi, Marie, mais vous avez des manières un peu grossières.*

TUZENBACH. *[Restraining his laughter]* Give me... give me... there's some cognac, I think.

NATASHA. *Il parait, que mon Bobick déjà ne dort pas*, he has awakened. He isn't well to-day. I'll go to him, excuse me... *[Exit.]*

IRINA. Where has Alexander Ignateyevitch gone?

MASHA. Home. Something extraordinary has happened to his wife again.

TUZENBACH. *[Goes to SOLENI with a cognac-flask in his hands]* You go on sitting by yourself, thinking of something—goodness knows what. Come and let's make peace. Let's have some cognac. *[They drink]* I expect I'll have to play the piano all night, some rubbish most likely... well, so be it!

SOLENI. Why make peace? I haven't quarrelled with you.

TUZENBACH. You always make me feel as if something has taken place between us. You've a strange character, you must admit.

SOLENI. *[Declaims]* "I am strange, but who is not? Don't be angry, Aleko!"

TUZENBACH. And what has Aleko to do with it? *[Pause.]*

SOLENI. When I'm with one other man I behave just like everybody else, but in company I'm dull and shy and... talk all manner of rubbish. But I'm more honest and more honourable than very, very many people. And I can prove it.

TUZENBACH. I often get angry with you, you always fasten on to me in company, but I like you all the same. I'm going to drink my fill tonight, whatever happens. Drink, now!

SOLENI. Let's drink. *[They drink]* I never had anything against you, Baron. But my character is like Lermontov's *[In a low voice]* I even rather resemble Lermontov, they say.... *[Takes a scent-bottle from his pocket, and scents his hands.]*

TUZENBACH. I've sent in my resignation. Basta! I've been thinking about it for five years, and at last made up my mind. I shall work.

SOLENI. *[Declaims]* "Do not be angry, Aleko... forget, forget, thy dreams of yore...."

*[While he is speaking ANDREY enters quietly with a book, and sits by the table.]*

TUZENBACH. I shall work.

CHEBUTIKIN. *[Going with IRINA into the dining-room]* And the food was also real Caucasian onion soup, and, for a roast, some chehartma.

SOLENI. Cheremsha *[Note: A variety of garlic.]* isn't meat at all, but a plant something like an onion.

CHEBUTIKIN. No, my angel. Chehartma isn't onion, but roast mutton.

SOLENI. And I tell you, chehartma—is a sort of onion.

CHEBUTIKIN. And I tell you, chehartma—is mutton.

SOLENI. And I tell you, cheremsha—is a sort of onion.

CHEBUTIKIN. What's the use of arguing! You've never been in the Caucasus, and never ate any chehartma.

SOLENI. I never ate it, because I hate it. It smells like garlic.

ANDREY. *[Imploring]* Please, please! I ask you!

TUZENBACH. When are the entertainers coming?

IRINA. They promised for about nine; that is, quite soon.

TUZENBACH. *[Embraces ANDREY]*

"Oh my house, my house, my new-built house."

ANDREY. *[Dances and sings]* "Newly-built of maple-wood."

CHEBUTIKIN. *[Dances]*

"Its walls are like a sieve!" *[Laughter.]*

TUZENBACH. *[Kisses ANDREY]* Hang it all, let's drink. Andrey, old boy, let's drink with you. And I'll go with you, Andrey, to the University of Moscow.

SOLENI. Which one? There are two universities in Moscow.

ANDREY. There's one university in Moscow.

SOLENI. Two, I tell you.

ANDREY. Don't care if there are three. So much the better.

SOLENI. There are two universities in Moscow! *[There are murmurs and "hushes"]* There are two universities in Moscow, the old one and the new one. And if you don't like to listen, if my words annoy you, then I need not speak. I can even go into another room.... *[Exit.]*

TUZENBACH. Bravo, bravo! *[Laughs]* Come on, now. I'm going to play. Fun ny man, Soleni.... *[Goes to the piano and plays a waltz.]*

MASHA. *[Dancing solo]* The Baron's drunk, the Baron's drunk, the Baron's drunk!

*[NATASHA comes in.]*

NATASHA. *[To CHEBUTIKIN]* Ivan Romanovitch!

*[Says something to CHEBUTIKIN, then goes out quietly; CHEBUTIKIN touches TUZENBACH on the shoulder and whispers something to him.]*

IRINA. What is it?

CHEBUTIKIN. Time for us to go. Good-bye.

TUZENBACH. Good-night. It's time we went.

IRINA. But, really, the entertainers?

ANDREY. *[In confusion]* There won't be any entertainers. You see, dear, Natasha says that Bobby isn't quite well, and so.... In a word, I don't care, and it's absolutely all one to me.

IRINA. *[Shrugging her shoulders]* Bobby ill!

MASHA. What is she thinking of! Well, if they are sent home, I suppose they must go. *[To IRINA]* Bobby's all right, it's she herself.... Here! *[Taps her forehead]* Little bourgeoise!

*[ANDREY goes to his room through the right-hand door, CHEBUTIKIN follows him. In the dining-room they are saying good-bye.]*

FEDOTIK. What a shame! I was expecting to spend the evening here, but of course, if the little baby is ill... I'll bring him some toys to-morrow.

RODE. *[Loudly]* I slept late after dinner to-day because I thought I was going to dance all night. It's only nine o'clock now!

MASHA. Let's go into the street, we can talk there. Then we can settle things.

*(Good-byes and good nights are heard. TUZENBACH'S merry laughter is heard. [All go out] ANFISA and the maid clear the table, and put out the lights. [The nurse sings] ANDREY, wearing an overcoat and a hat, and CHEBUTIKIN enter silently.)*

CHEBUTIKIN. I never managed to get married because my life flashed by like lightning, and because I was madly in love with your mother, who was married.

ANDREY. One shouldn't marry. One shouldn't, because it's dull.

CHEBUTIKIN. So there I am, in my loneliness. Say what you will, loneliness is a terrible thing, old fellow.... Though really... of course, it absolutely doesn't matter!

ANDREY. Let's be quicker.

CHEBUTIKIN. What are you in such a hurry for? We shall be in time.

ANDREY. I'm afraid my wife may stop me.

CHEBUTIKIN. Ah!

ANDREY. I shan't play to-night, I shall only sit and look on. I don't feel very well.... What am I to do for my asthma, Ivan Romanovitch?

CHEBUTIKIN. Don't ask me! I don't remember, old fellow, I don't know.

ANDREY. Let's go through the kitchen. *[They go out.]*

*[A bell rings, then a second time; voices and laughter are heard.]*

IRINA. *[Enters]* What's that?

ANFISA. *[Whispers]* The entertainers! *[Bell.]*

IRINA. Tell them there's nobody at home, nurse. They must excuse us.

*[ANFISA goes out. IRINA walks about the room deep in thought; she is excited. SOLENI enters.]*

SOLENI. *[In surprise]* There's nobody here.... Where are they all?

IRINA. They've gone home.

SOLENI. How strange. Are you here alone?

IRINA. Yes, alone. *[A pause]* Good-bye.

SOLENI. Just now I behaved tactlessly, with insufficient reserve. But you are not like all the others, you are noble and pure, you can see the truth.... You alone can understand me. I love you, deeply, beyond measure, I love you.

IRINA. Good-bye! Go away.

SOLENI. I cannot live without you. *[Follows her]* Oh, my happiness! *[Through his tears]* Oh, joy! Wonderful, marvellous, glorious eyes, such as I have never seen before....

IRINA. *[Coldly]* Stop it, Vassili Vassilevitch!

SOLENI. This is the first time I speak to you of love, and it is as if I am no longer on the earth, but on another planet. *[Wipes his forehead]* Well, never mind. I can't make you love me by force, of course... but I don't intend to have any more-favoured rivals.... No... I swear to you by all the saints, I shall kill my rival.... Oh, beautiful one!

*[NATASHA enters with a candle; she looks in through one door, then through another, and goes past the door leading to her husband's room.]*

NATASHA. Here's Andrey. Let him go on reading. Excuse me, Vassili Vassilevitch, I did not know you were here; I am engaged in domesticities.

SOLENI. It's all the same to me. Good-bye! *[Exit.]*

NATASHA. You're so tired, my poor dear girl! *[Kisses IRINA]* If you only went to bed earlier.

IRINA. Is Bobby asleep?

NATASHA. Yes, but restlessly. By the way, dear, I wanted to tell you, but either you weren't at home, or I was busy... I think Bobby's present nursery is cold and damp. And your room would be so nice for the child. My dear, darling girl, do change over to Olga's for a bit!

IRINA. *[Not understanding]* Where?

*[The bells of a troika are heard as it drives up to the house.]*

NATASHA. You and Olga can share a room, for the time being, and Bobby can have yours. He's such a darling; to-day I said to him, "Bobby, you're mine! Mine!" And he looked at me with his dear little eyes. *[A bell rings]* It must be Olga. How late she is! *[The maid enters and whispers to NATASHA]* Protopopov? What a queer man to do such a thing. Protopopov's come and wants me to go for a drive with him in his troika. *[Laughs]* How funny these men are.... *[A bell rings]* Somebody has come. Suppose I did go and have half an hour's drive.... *[To the maid]* Say I shan't be long. *[Bell rings]* Somebody's ringing, it must be Olga. *[Exit.]*

*[The maid runs out; IRINA sits deep in thought; KULIGIN and OLGA enter, followed by VERSHININ.]*

KULIGIN. Well, there you are. And you said there was going to be a party.

VERSHININ. It's queer; I went away not long ago, half an hour ago, and they were expecting entertainers.

IRINA. They've all gone.

KULIGIN. Has Masha gone too? Where has she gone? And what's Protopopov waiting for downstairs in his troika? Whom is he expecting?

IRINA. Don't ask questions... I'm tired.

KULIGIN. Oh, you're all whimsies....

OLGA. My committee meeting is only just over. I'm tired out. Our chairwoman is ill, so I had to take her place. My head, my head is aching.... *[Sits]* Andrey lost 200 roubles at cards yesterday... the whole town is talking about it....

KULIGIN. Yes, my meeting tired me too. *[Sits.]*

VERSHININ. My wife took it into her head to frighten me just now by nearly poisoning herself. It's all right now, and I'm glad; I can rest now.... But perhaps we ought to go away? Well, my best wishes, Feodor Ilitch, let's go somewhere together! I can't, I absolutely can't stop at home.... Come on!

KULIGIN. I'm tired. I won't go. *[Gets up]* I'm tired. Has my wife gone home?

IRINA. I suppose so.

KULIGIN. *[Kisses IRINA'S hand]* Good-bye, I'm going to rest all day to-morrow and the day after. Best wishes! *[Going]* I should like some tea. I was looking forward to spending the whole evening in pleasant company and—o, fallacem hominum spem!... Accusative case after an interjection....

VERSHININ. Then I'll go somewhere by myself. *[Exit with KULIGIN, whistling.]*

OLGA. I've such a headache... Andrey has been losing money.... The whole town is talking.... I'll go and lie down. *[Going]* I'm free to-morrow.... Oh, my God, what a mercy! I'm free to-morrow, I'm free the day after.... Oh my head, my head.... *[Exit.]*

IRINA. *[alone]* They've all gone. Nobody's left.

*[A concertina is being played in the street. The nurse sings.]*

NATASHA. *[in fur coat and cap, steps across the dining-room, followed by the maid]* I'll be back in half an hour. I'm only going for a little drive. *[Exit.]*

IRINA. *[Alone in her misery]* To Moscow! Moscow! Moscow!

## Curtain.

# ACT III

*[The room shared by OLGA and IRINA. Beds, screened off, on the right and left. It is past 2 a.m. Behind the stage a fire-alarm is ringing; it has apparently been going for some time. Nobody in the house has gone to bed yet. MASHA is lying on a sofa dressed, as usual, in black. Enter OLGA and ANFISA.]*

ANFISA. Now they are downstairs, sitting under the stairs. I said to them, "Won't you come up," I said, "You can't go on like this," and they simply cried, "We don't know where father is." They said, "He may be burnt up by now." What an idea! And in the yard there are some people... also undressed.

OLGA. *[Takes a dress out of the cupboard]* Take this grey dress.... And this... and the blouse as well.... Take the skirt, too, nurse.... My God! How awful it is! The whole of the Kirsanovsky Road seems to have burned down. Take this... and this.... *[Throws clothes into her hands]* The poor Vershinins are so frightened.... Their house was nearly burnt. They ought to come here for the night.... They shouldn't be allowed to go home.... Poor Fedotik is completely burnt out, there's nothing left....

ANFISA. Couldn't you call Ferapont, Olga dear. I can hardly manage....

OLGA. *[Rings]* They'll never answer.... *[At the door]* Come here, whoever there is! *[Through the open door can be seen a window, red with flame: afire-engine is heard passing the house]* How awful this is. And how I'm sick of it! *[FERAPONT enters]* Take these things down.... The Kolotilin girls are down below... and let them have them. This, too.

FERAPONT. Yes'm. In the year twelve Moscow was burning too. Oh, my God! The Frenchmen were surprised.

OLGA. Go on, go on....

FERAPONT. Yes'm. *[Exit.]*

OLGA. Nurse, dear, let them have everything. We don't want anything. Give it all to them, nurse.... I'm tired, I can hardly keep on my legs.... The Vershinins mustn't be allowed to go home.... The girls can sleep in the drawing-room, and Alexander Ignateyevitch can go downstairs to the Baron's flat... Fedotik can go there, too, or else into our dining-room.... The doctor is drunk, beastly drunk, as if on purpose, so nobody can go to him. Vershinin's wife, too, may go into the drawing-room.

ANFISA. *[Tired]* Olga, dear girl, don't dismiss me! Don't dismiss me!

OLGA. You're talking nonsense, nurse. Nobody is dismissing you.

ANFISA. *[Puts OLGA'S head against her bosom]* My dear, precious girl, I'm working, I'm toiling away... I'm growing weak, and they'll all say go away! And where shall I go? Where? I'm eighty. Eighty-one years old....

OLGA. You sit down, nurse dear.... You're tired, poor dear.... *[Makes her sit down]* Rest, dear. You're so pale!

*[NATASHA comes in.]*

NATASHA. They are saying that a committee to assist the sufferers from the fire must be formed at once. What do you think of that? It's a beautiful idea. Of course the poor ought to be helped, it's the duty of the rich. Bobby and little Sophy are sleeping, sleeping as if nothing at all was the matter. There's such a lot of people here, the place is full of them, wherever you go. There's influenza in the town now. I'm afraid the children may catch it.

OLGA. *[Not attending]* In this room we can't see the fire, it's quiet here.

NATASHA. Yes... I suppose I'm all untidy. *[Before the looking-glass]* They say I'm growing stout... it isn't true! Certainly it isn't! Masha's asleep; the poor thing is tired out.... *[Coldly, to ANFISA]* Don't dare to be seated in my presence! Get up! Out of this! *[Exit ANFISA; a pause]* I don't understand what makes you keep on that old woman!

OLGA. *[Confusedly]* Excuse me, I don't understand either...

NATASHA. She's no good here. She comes from the country, she ought to live there.... Spoiling her, I call it! I like order in the house! We don't want any unnecessary people here. *[Strokes her cheek]* You're tired, poor thing! Our head mistress is tired! And when my little Sophie grows up and goes to school I shall be so afraid of you.

OLGA. I shan't be head mistress.

NATASHA. They'll appoint you, Olga. It's settled.

OLGA. I'll refuse the post. I can't... I'm not strong enough.... *[Drinks water]* You were so rude to nurse just now... I'm sorry. I can't stand it... everything seems dark in front of me....

NATASHA. *[Excited]* Forgive me, Olga, forgive me... I didn't want to annoy you.

*[MASHA gets up, takes a pillow and goes out angrily.]*

OLGA. Remember, dear... we have been brought up, in an unusual way, perhaps, but I can't bear this. Such behaviour has a bad effect on me, I get ill... I simply lose heart!

NATASHA. Forgive me, forgive me.... *[Kisses her.]*

OLGA. Even the least bit of rudeness, the slightest impoliteness, upsets me.

NATASHA. I often say too much, it's true, but you must agree, dear, that she could just as well live in the country.

OLGA. She has been with us for thirty years.

NATASHA. But she can't do any work now. Either I don't understand, or you don't want to understand me. She's no good for work, she can only sleep or sit about.

OLGA. And let her sit about.

NATASHA. *[Surprised]* What do you mean? She's only a servant. *[Crying]* I don't understand you, Olga. I've got a nurse, a wet-nurse, we've a cook, a housemaid... what do we want that old woman for as well? What good is she? *[Fire-alarm behind the stage.]*

OLGA. I've grown ten years older to-night.

NATASHA. We must come to an agreement, Olga. Your place is the school, mine—the home. You devote yourself to teaching, I, to the household. And if I talk about servants, then I do know what I am talking about; I do know what I am talking about... And to-morrow there's to be no more of that old thief, that old hag... *[Stamping]* that witch! And don't you dare to annoy me! Don't you dare! *[Stopping short]* Really, if you don't move downstairs, we shall always be quarrelling. This is awful.

*[Enter KULIGIN.]*

KULIGIN. Where's Masha? It's time we went home. The fire seems to be going down. *[Stretches himself]* Only one block has burnt down, but there was such a wind that it seemed at first the whole town was going to burn. *[Sits]* I'm tired out. My dear Olga... I often think that if it hadn't been for Masha, I should have married you. You are awfully nice.... I am absolutely tired out. *[Listens.]*

OLGA. What is it?

KULIGIN. The doctor, of course, has been drinking hard; he's terribly drunk. He might have done it on purpose! *[Gets up]* He seems to be coming here.... Do you hear him? Yes, here.... *[Laughs]* What a man... really... I'll hide myself. *[Goes to the cupboard and stands in the corner]* What a rogue.

OLGA. He hadn't touched a drop for two years, and now he suddenly goes and gets drunk....

*[Retires with NATASHA to the back of the room. CHEBUTIKIN enters; apparently sober, he stops, looks round, then goes to the wash-stand and begins to wash his hands.]*

CHEBUTIKIN. *[Angrily]* Devil take them all... take them all.... They think I'm a doctor and can cure everything, and I know absolutely nothing, I've forgotten all I ever knew, I remember nothing, absolutely nothing. *[OLGA and NATASHA go out, unnoticed by him]* Devil take it. Last Wednesday I attended a woman in Zasip—and she died, and it's my fault that she died. Yes... I used to know a certain amount five-and-twenty years ago, but I don't remember anything now. Nothing. Perhaps I'm not really a man, and am only pretending that I've got arms and legs and a head; perhaps I don't exist at all, and only imagine that I walk, and eat, and sleep. *[Cries]* Oh, if only I didn't exist! *[Stops crying; angrily]* The devil only knows.... Day before yesterday they were talking in the club; they said, Shakespeare, Voltaire... I'd never read, never read at all, and I put on an expression as if I had read. And so did the others. Oh, how beastly! How petty! And then I remembered the woman I killed on Wednesday... and I couldn't get her out of my mind, and everything in my mind became crooked, nasty, wretched.... So I went and drank....

*[IRINA, VERSHININ and TUZENBACH enter; TUZENBACH is wearing new and fashionable civilian clothes.]*

IRINA. Let's sit down here. Nobody will come in here.

VERSHININ. The whole town would have been destroyed if it hadn't been for the soldiers. Good men! *[Rubs his hands appreciatively]* Splendid people! Oh, what a fine lot!

KULIGIN. *[Coming up to him]* What's the time?

TUZENBACH. It's past three now. It's dawning.

IRINA. They are all sitting in the dining-room, nobody is going. And that Soleni of yours is sitting there. *[To CHEBUTIKIN]* Hadn't you better be going to sleep, doctor?

CHEBUTIKIN. It's all right... thank you.... *[Combs his beard.]*

KULIGIN. *[Laughs]* Speaking's a bit difficult, eh, Ivan Romanovitch! *[Pats him on the shoulder]* Good man! *In vino veritas*, the ancients used to say.

TUZENBACH. They keep on asking me to get up a concert in aid of the sufferers.

IRINA. As if one could do anything....

TUZENBACH. It might be arranged, if necessary. In my opinion Maria Sergeyevna is an excellent pianist.

KULIGIN. Yes, excellent!

IRINA. She's forgotten everything. She hasn't played for three years... or four.

TUZENBACH. In this town absolutely nobody understands music, not a soul except myself, but I do understand it, and assure you on my word of honour that Maria Sergeyevna plays excellently, almost with genius.

KULIGIN. You are right, Baron, I'm awfully fond of Masha. She's very fine.

TUZENBACH. To be able to play so admirably and to realize at the same time that nobody, nobody can understand you!

KULIGIN. *[Sighs]* Yes.... But will it be quite all right for her to take part in a concert? *[Pause]* You see, I don't know anything about it. Perhaps it will even be all to the good. Although I must admit that our Director is a good man, a very good man even, a very clever man, still he has such views.... Of course it isn't his business but still, if you wish it, perhaps I'd better talk to him.

*[CHEBUTIKIN takes a porcelain clock into his hands and examines it.]*

VERSHININ. I got so dirty while the fire was on, I don't look like anybody on earth. *[Pause]* Yesterday I happened to hear, casually, that they want to transfer our brigade to some distant place. Some said to Poland, others, to Chita.

TUZENBACH. I heard so, too. Well, if it is so, the town will be quite empty.

IRINA. And we'll go away, too!

CHEBUTIKIN. *[Drops the clock which breaks to pieces]* To smithereens!

*[A pause; everybody is pained and confused.]*

KULIGIN. *[Gathering up the pieces]* To smash such a valuable object—oh, Ivan Romanovitch, Ivan Romanovitch! A very bad mark for your misbehaviour!

IRINA. That clock used to belong to our mother.

CHEBUTIKIN. Perhaps.... To your mother, your mother. Perhaps I didn't break it; it only looks as if I broke it. Perhaps we only think that we exist, when really we don't. I don't know anything, nobody knows anything. *[At the door]* What are you looking at? Natasha has a little romance with Protopopov, and you don't see it.... There you sit and see nothing, and Natasha has a little romance with Protopovov.... *[Sings]* Won't you please accept this date.... *[Exit.]*

VERSHININ. Yes. *[Laughs]* How strange everything really is! *[Pause]* When the fire broke out, I hurried off home; when I get there I see the house is whole, uninjured, and in no danger, but my two girls are standing by the door in just their underclothes, their mother isn't there, the crowd is excited, horses and dogs are running about, and the girls' faces are so agitated, terrified, beseeching, and I don't know what else. My heart was pained when I saw those faces. My God, I thought, what these girls will have to put up with if they live long! I caught them up and ran, and still kept on thinking the one thing: what they will have to live through in this world! *[Fire-alarm; a pause]* I come here and find their mother shouting and angry. *[MASHA enters with a pillow and sits on the sofa]* And when my girls were standing by the door in just their underclothes, and the street was red from the fire, there was a dreadful noise, and I thought that something of the sort used to happen many years ago when an enemy made a sudden attack, and looted, and burned.... And at the same time what a difference there really is between the present and the past! And when a little more time has gone by, in two or three hundred years perhaps, people will look at our present life with just the same fear, and the same contempt, and the whole past will seem clumsy and dull, and very uncomfortable, and strange. Oh, indeed, what a life there will be, what a life! *[Laughs]* Forgive me, I've dropped into philosophy again. Please let me continue. I do awfully want to philosophize, it's just how I feel at present. *[Pause]* As if they are all asleep. As I was saying: what a life there will be! Only just imagine....

There are only three persons like yourselves in the town just now, but in future generations there will be more and more, and still more, and the time will come when everything will change and become as you would have it, people will live as you do, and then you too will go out of date; people will be born who are better than you.... *[Laughs]* Yes, to-day I am quite exceptionally in the vein. I am devilishly keen on living.... *[Sings.]*

"The power of love all ages know,
From its assaults great good does grow." *[Laughs.]*

MASHA. Trum-tum-tum...

VERSHININ. Tum-tum...

MASHA. Tra-ra-ra?

VERSHININ. Tra-ta-ta. *[Laughs.]*

*[Enter FEDOTIK. ]*

FEDOTIK. *[Dancing]* I'm burnt out, I'm burnt out! Down to the ground! *[Laughter.]*

IRINA. I don't see anything funny about it. Is everything burnt?

FEDOTIK. *[Laughs]* Absolutely. Nothing left at all. The guitar's burnt, and the photographs are burnt, and all my correspondence.... And I was going to make you a present of a note-book, and that's burnt too.

*[SOLENI comes in.]*

IRINA. No, you can't come here, Vassili Vassilevitch. Please go away.

SOLENI. Why can the Baron come here and I can't?

VERSHININ. We really must go. How's the fire?

SOLENI. They say it's going down. No, I absolutely don't see why the Baron can, and I can't? *[Scents his hands.]*

VERSHININ. Trum-tum-tum.

MASHA. Trum-tum.

VERSHININ. *[Laughs to SOLENI]* Let's go into the dining-room.

SOLENI. Very well, we'll make a note of it. "If I should try to make this clear, the geese would be annoyed, I fear." *[Looks at TUZENBACH]* There, there, there.... *[Goes out with VERSHININ and FEDOTIK.]*

IRINA. How Soleni smelt of tobacco.... *[In surprise]* The Baron's asleep! Baron! Baron!

TUZENBACH. *[Waking]* I am tired, I must say.... The brickworks.... No, I'm not wandering, I mean it; I'm going to start work soon at the brickworks... I've already talked it over. *[Tenderly, to IRINA]* You're so pale, and beautiful, and charming.... Your paleness seems to shine through the dark air as if it was a light.... You are sad, displeased with life.... Oh, come with me, let's go and work together!

MASHA. Nicolai Lvovitch, go away from here.

TUZENBACH. *[Laughs]* Are you here? I didn't see you. *[Kisses IRINA'S hand]* good-bye, I'll go... I look at you now and I remember, as if it was long ago, your name-day, when you, cheerfully and merrily, were talking about the joys of labour.... And how happy life seemed to me, then! What has happened to it now? *[Kisses her hand]* There are tears in your eyes. Go to bed now; it is already day... the morning begins.... If only I was allowed to give my life for you!

MASHA. Nicolai Lvovitch, go away! What business...

TUZENBACH. I'm off. *[Exit.]*

MASHA. *[Lies down]* Are you asleep, Feodor?

KULIGIN. Eh?

MASHA. Shouldn't you go home.

KULIGIN. My dear Masha, my darling Masha....

IRINA. She's tired out. You might let her rest, Fedia.

KULIGIN. I'll go at once. My wife's a good, splendid... I love you, my only one....

MASHA. *[Angrily]* Amo, amas, amat, amamus, amatis, amant.

KULIGIN. *[Laughs]* No, she really is wonderful. I've been your husband seven years, and it seems as if I was only married yesterday. On my word. No, you really are a wonderful woman. I'm satisfied, I'm satisfied, I'm satisfied!

MASHA. I'm bored, I'm bored, I'm bored.... *[Sits up]* But I can't got it out of my head.... It's simply disgraceful. It has been gnawing away at me... I can't keep silent. I mean about Andrey.... He has mortgaged this house with the bank, and his wife has got all the money; but the house doesn't belong to him alone, but to the four of us! He ought to know that, if he's an honourable man.

KULIGIN. What's the use, Masha? Andrey is in debt all round; well, let him do as he pleases.

MASHA. It's disgraceful, anyway. *[Lies down]*

KULIGIN. You and I are not poor. I work, take my classes, give private lessons... I am a plain, honest man... *Omnia mea mecum porto*, as they say.

MASHA. I don't want anything, but the unfairness of it disgusts me. *[Pause]* You go, Feodor.

KULIGIN. *[Kisses her]* You're tired, just rest for half an hour, and I'll sit and wait for you. Sleep.... *[Going]* I'm satisfied, I'm satisfied, I'm satisfied. *[Exit.]*

IRINA. Yes, really, our Andrey has grown smaller; how he's snuffed out and aged with that woman! He used to want to be a professor, and yesterday he was boasting that at last he had been made a member of the district council. He is a member, and Protopopov is chairman.... The whole town talks and laughs about it, and he alone knows and sees nothing.... And now everybody's gone to look at the fire, but he sits alone in his room and pays no attention, only just plays on his fiddle. *[Nervily]* Oh, it's awful, awful, awful. *[Weeps]* I can't, I can't bear it any longer!... I can't, I can't!... *[OLGA comes in and clears up at her little table. IRINA is sobbing loudly]* Throw me out, throw me out, I can't bear any more!

OLGA. *[Alarmed]* What is it, what is it? Dear!

IRINA. *[Sobbing]* Where? Where has everything gone? Where is it all? Oh my God, my God! I've forgotten everything, everything... I don't remember what is the Italian for window or, well, for ceiling... I forget everything, every day I forget it, and life passes and will never return, and we'll never go away to Moscow... I see that we'll never go....

OLGA. Dear, dear....

IRINA. *[Controlling herself]* Oh, I am unhappy... I can't work, I shan't work. Enough, enough! I used to be a telegraphist, now I work at the town council offices, and I have nothing but hate and contempt for all they give me to do... I am already twenty-three, I have already been at work for a long while, and my brain has dried up, and I've grown thinner, plainer, older, and there is no relief of any sort, and time goes and it seems all the while as if I am going away from the real, the beautiful life, farther and farther away, down some precipice. I'm in despair and

I can't understand how it is that I am still alive, that I haven't killed myself.

OLGA. Don't cry, dear girl, don't cry... I suffer, too.

IRINA. I'm not crying, not crying.... Enough.... Look, I'm not crying any more. Enough... enough!

OLGA. Dear, I tell you as a sister and a friend if you want my advice, marry the Baron. *[IRINA cries softly]* You respect him, you think highly of him.... It is true that he is not handsome, but he is so honourable and clean... people don't marry from love, but in order to do one's duty. I think so, at any rate, and I'd marry without being in love. Whoever he was, I should marry him, so long as he was a decent man. Even if he was old....

IRINA. I was always waiting until we should be settled in Moscow, there I should meet my true love; I used to think about him, and love him.... But it's all turned out to be nonsense, all nonsense....

OLGA. *[Embraces her sister]* My dear, beautiful sister, I understand everything; when Baron Nicolai Lvovitch left the army and came to us in evening dress, *[Note: I.e. in the correct dress for making a proposal of marriage.]* he seemed so bad-looking to me that I even started crying.... He asked, "What are you crying for?" How could I tell him! But if God brought him to marry you, I should be happy. That would be different, quite different.

*[NATASHA with a candle walks across the stage from right to left without saying anything.]*

MASHA. *[Sitting up]* She walks as if she's set something on fire.

OLGA. Masha, you're silly, you're the silliest of the family. Please forgive me for saying so. *[Pause.]*

MASHA. I want to make a confession, dear sisters. My soul is in pain. I will confess to you, and never again to anybody... I'll tell you this minute. *[Softly]* It's my secret but you must know everything... I can't be silent.... *[Pause]* I love, I love... I love that man.... You saw him only just now.... Why don't I say it... in one word. I love Vershinin.

OLGA. *[Goes behind her screen]* Stop that, I don't hear you in any case.

MASHA. What am I to do? *[Takes her head in her hands]* First he seemed queer to me, then I was sorry for him... then I fell in love with him... fell in love with his voice, his words, his misfortunes, his two daughters.

OLGA. *[Behind the screen]* I'm not listening. You may talk any nonsense you like, it will be all the same, I shan't hear.

MASHA. Oh, Olga, you are foolish. I am in love—that means that is to be my fate. It means that is to be my lot.... And he loves me.... It is all awful. Yes; it isn't good, is it? *[Takes IRINA'S hand and draws her to her]* Oh, my dear.... How are we going to live through our lives, what is to become of us.... When you read a novel it all seems so old and easy, but when you fall in love yourself, then you learn that nobody knows anything, and each must decide for himself.... My dear ones, my sisters... I've confessed, now I shall keep silence.... Like the lunatics in Gogol's story, I'm going to be silent... silent...

*[ANDREY enters, followed by FERAPONT.]*

ANDREY. *[Angrily]* What do you want? I don't understand.

FERAPONT. *[At the door, impatiently]* I've already told you ten times, Andrey Sergeyevitch.

ANDREY. In the first place I'm not Andrey Sergeyevitch, but sir. *[Note: Quite literally, "your high honour," to correspond to Andrey's rank as a civil servant.]*

FERAPONT. The firemen, sir, ask if they can go across your garden to the river. Else they go right round, right round; it's a nuisance.

ANDREY. All right. Tell them it's all right. *[Exit FERAPONT]* I'm tired of them. Where is Olga? *[OLGA comes out from behind the screen]* I came to you for the key of the cupboard. I lost my own. You've got a little key. *[OLGA gives him the key; IRINA goes behind her screen; pause]* What a huge fire! It's going down now. Hang it all, that Ferapont made me so angry that I talked nonsense to him.... Sir, indeed.... *[A pause]* Why are you so silent, Olga? *[Pause]* It's time you stopped all that nonsense and behaved as if you were properly alive.... You are here, Masha. Irina is here, well, since we're all here, let's come to a complete understanding, once and for all. What have you against me? What is it?

OLGA. Please don't, Audrey dear. We'll talk to-morrow. *[Excited]* What an awful night!

ANDREY. *[Much confused]* Don't excite yourself. I ask you in perfect calmness; what have you against me? Tell me straight.

VERSHININ'S VOICE. Trum-tum-tum!

MASHA. *[Stands; loudly]* Tra-ta-ta! *[To OLGA]* Goodbye, Olga, God bless you. *[Goes behind screen and kisses IRINA]* Sleep well.... Good-bye, Andrey. Go away now, they're tired... you can explain to-morrow.... *[Exit.]*

ANDREY. I'll only say this and go. Just now.... In the first place, you've got something against Natasha, my wife; I've noticed it since the very day of my marriage. Natasha is a beautiful and honest creature, straight and honourable—that's my opinion. I love and respect my wife; understand it, I respect her, and I insist that others should respect her too. I repeat, she's an honest and honourable person, and all your disapproval is simply silly... *[Pause]* In the second place, you seem to be annoyed because I am not a professor, and am not engaged in study. But I work for the zemstvo, I am a member of the district council, and I consider my service as worthy and as high as the service of science. I am a member of the district council, and I am proud of it, if you want to know. *[Pause]* In the third place, I have still this to say... that I have mortgaged the house without obtaining your permission.... For that I am to blame, and ask to be forgiven. My debts led me into doing it... thirty-five thousand... I do not play at cards any more, I stopped long ago, but the chief thing I have to say in my defence is that you girls receive a pension, and I don't... my wages, so to speak.... *[Pause.]*

KULIGIN. *[At the door]* Is Masha there? *[Excitedly]* Where is she? It's queer.... *[Exit.]*

ANDREY. They don't hear. Natasha is a splendid, honest person. *[Walks about in silence, then stops]* When I married I thought we should be happy... all of us.... But, my God.... *[Weeps]* My dear, dear sisters, don't believe me, don't believe me.... *[Exit.]*

*[Fire-alarm. The stage is clear.]*

IRINA. *[behind her screen]* Olga, who's knocking on the floor?

OLGA. It's doctor Ivan Romanovitch. He's drunk.

IRINA. What a restless night! *[Pause]* Olga! *[Looks out]* Did you hear? They are taking the brigade away from us; it's going to be transferred to some place far away.

OLGA. It's only a rumour.

IRINA. Then we shall be left alone.... Olga!

OLGA. Well?

IRINA. My dear, darling sister, I esteem, I highly value the Baron, he's a splendid man; I'll marry him, I'll consent, only let's go to Moscow! I implore you, let's go! There's nothing better than Moscow on earth! Let's go, Olga, let's go!

## Curtain

# ACT IV

*[The old garden at the house of the PROSOROVS. There is a long avenue of firs, at the end of which the river can be seen. There is a forest on the far side of the river. On the right is the terrace of the house: bottles and tumblers are on a table here; it is evident that champagne has just been drunk. It is midday. Every now and again passers-by walk across the garden, from the road to the river; five soldiers go past rapidly. CHEBUTIKIN, in a comfortable frame of mind which does not desert him throughout the act, sits in an armchair in the garden, waiting to be called. He wears a peaked cap and has a stick. IRINA, KULIGIN with a cross hanging from his neck and without his moustaches, and TUZENBACH are standing on the terrace seeing off FEDOTIK and RODE, who are coming down into the garden; both officers are in service uniform.]*

TUZENBACH. *[Exchanges kisses with FEDOTIK]* You're a good sort, we got on so well together. *[Exchanges kisses with RODE]* Once again.... Good-bye, old man!

IRINA. Au revoir!

FEDOTIK. It isn't au revoir, it's good-bye; we'll never meet again!

KULIGIN. Who knows! *[Wipes his eyes; smiles]* Here I've started crying!

IRINA. We'll meet again sometime.

FEDOTIK. After ten years—or fifteen? We'll hardly know one another then; we'll say, "How do you do?" coldly.... *[Takes a snapshot]* Keep still.... Once more, for the last time.

RODE. *[Embracing TUZENBACH]* We shan't meet again.... *[Kisses IRINA'S hand]* Thank you for everything, for everything!

FEDOTIK. *[Grieved]* Don't be in such a hurry!

TUZENBACH. We shall meet again, if God wills it. Write to us. Be sure to write.

RODE. *[Looking round the garden]* Good-bye, trees! *[Shouts]* Yo-ho! *[Pause]* Good-bye, echo!

KULIGIN. Best wishes. Go and get yourselves wives there in Poland.... Your Polish wife will clasp you and call you "kochanku!" *[Note: Darling.] [Laughs.]*

FEDOTIK. *[Looking at the time]* There's less than an hour left. Soleni is the only one of our battery who is going on the barge; the rest of us are going with the main body. Three batteries are leaving to-day, another three to-morrow and then the town will be quiet and peaceful.

TUZENBACH. And terribly dull.

RODE. And where is Maria Sergeyevna?

KULIGIN. Masha is in the garden.

FEDOTIK. We'd like to say good-bye to her.

RODE. Good-bye, I must go, or else I'll start weeping.... *[Quickly embraces KULIGIN and TUZENBACH, and kisses IRINA'S hand]* We've been so happy here....

FEDOTIK. *[To KULIGIN]* Here's a keepsake for you... a note-book with a pencil.... We'll go to the river from here.... *[They go aside and both look round.]*

RODE. *[Shouts]* Yo-ho!

KULIGIN. *[Shouts]* Good-bye!

*[At the back of the stage FEDOTIK and RODE meet MASHA; they say good-bye and go out with her.]*

IRINA. They've gone.... *[Sits on the bottom step of the terrace.]*

CHEBUTIKIN. And they forgot to say good-bye to me.

IRINA. But why is that?

CHEBUTIKIN. I just forgot, somehow. Though I'll soon see them again, I'm going to-morrow. Yes... just one day left. I shall be retired in a year, then I'll come here again, and finish my life near you. I've only one year before I get my pension.... *[Puts one newspaper into his pocket and takes another out]* I'll come here to you and change my life radically... I'll be so quiet... so agree... agreeable, respectable....

IRINA. Yes, you ought to change your life, dear man, somehow or other.

CHEBUTIKIN. Yes, I feel it. *[Sings softly.]* "Tarara-boom-deay...."

KULIGIN. We won't reform Ivan Romanovitch! We won't reform him!

CHEBUTIKIN. If only I was apprenticed to you! Then I'd reform.

IRINA. Feodor has shaved his moustache! I can't bear to look at him.

KULIGIN. Well, what about it?

CHEBUTIKIN. I could tell you what your face looks like now, but it wouldn't be polite.

KULIGIN. Well! It's the custom, it's modus vivendi. Our Director is clean-shaven, and so I too, when I received my inspectorship, had my moustaches removed. Nobody likes it, but it's all one to me. I'm satisfied. Whether I've got moustaches or not, I'm satisfied.... *[Sits.]*

*[At the back of the stage ANDREY is wheeling a perambulator containing a sleeping infant.]*

IRINA. Ivan Romanovitch, be a darling. I'm awfully worried. You were out on the boulevard last night; tell me, what happened?

CHEBUTIKIN. What happened? Nothing. Quite a trifling matter. *[Reads paper]* Of no importance!

KULIGIN. They say that Soleni and the Baron met yesterday on the boulevard near the theatre....

TUZENBACH. Stop! What right... *[Waves his hand and goes into the house.]*

KULIGIN. Near the theatre... Soleni started behaving offensively to the Baron, who lost his temper and said something nasty....

CHEBUTIKIN. I don't know. It's all bunkum.

KULIGIN. At some seminary or other a master wrote "bunkum" on an essay, and the student couldn't make the letters out—thought it was a Latin word "luckum." *[Laughs]* Awfully funny, that. They say that Soleni is in love with Irina and hates the Baron.... That's quite natural. Irina is a very nice girl. She's even like Masha, she's so thoughtful.... Only, Irina your character is gentler. Though Masha's character, too, is a very good one. I'm very fond of Masha. *[Shouts of "Yo-ho!" are heard behind the stage.]*

IRINA. *[Shudders]* Everything seems to frighten me today. *[Pause]* I've got everything ready, and I send my things off after dinner. The Baron and I will be married to-morrow, and to-morrow we go away to the brickworks, and the next day I go to the school, and the new life begins. God will help me! When I took my examination for the teacher's post, I actually wept for joy and gratitude.... *[Pause]* The cart will be here in a minute for my things....

KULIGIN. Somehow or other, all this doesn't seem at all serious. As if it was all ideas, and nothing really serious. Still, with all my soul I wish you happiness.

CHEBUTIKIN. *[With deep feeling]* My splendid... my dear, precious girl.... You've gone on far ahead, I won't catch up with you. I'm left behind like a migrant bird grown old, and unable to fly. Fly, my dear, fly, and God be with you! *[Pause]* It's a pity you shaved your moustaches, Feodor Ilitch.

KULIGIN. Oh, drop it! *[Sighs]* To-day the soldiers will be gone, and everything will go on as in the old days. Say what you will, Masha is a good, honest woman. I love her very much, and thank my fate for her. People have such different fates. There's a Kosirev who works in the excise department here. He was at school with me; he was expelled from the fifth class of the High School for being entirely unable to understand *ut consecutivum.* He's awfully hard up now and in very poor health, and when I meet him I say to him, "How do you do, *ut consecutivum.*" "Yes," he says, "precisely *consecutivum...*" and coughs. But I've been successful all my life, I'm happy, and I even have a Stanislaus Cross, of the second class, and now I myself teach others that *ut consecutivum.* Of course, I'm a clever man, much cleverer than many, but happiness doesn't only lie in that....

*["The Maiden's Prayer" is being played on the piano in the house.]*

IRINA. To-morrow night I shan't hear that "Maiden's Prayer" any more, and I shan't be meeting Protopopov.... *[Pause]* Protopopov is sitting there in the drawing-room; and he came to-day...

KULIGIN. Hasn't the head-mistress come yet?

IRINA. No. She has been sent for. If you only knew how difficult it is for me to live alone, without Olga.... She lives at the High School; she, a head-mistress, busy all day with her affairs and I'm alone, bored, with nothing to do, and hate the room I live in.... I've made up my mind: if I can't live in Moscow, then it must come to this. It's fate. It can't be helped. It's all the will of God, that's the truth. Nicolai Lvovitch made me a proposal.... Well? I thought it over and made up my mind. He's a good man... it's quite remarkable how good he is.... And suddenly my soul put out wings, I became happy, and light-hearted, and once again the desire for work, work, came over me.... Only something happened yesterday, some secret dread has been hanging over me....

CHEBUTIKIN. Luckum. Rubbish.

NATASHA. *[At the window]* The head-mistress.

KULIGIN. The head-mistress has come. Let's go. *[Exit with IRINA into the house.]*

CHEBUTIKIN. "It is my washing day.... Tara-ra... boom-deay."

*[MASHA approaches, ANDREY is wheeling a perambulator at the back.]*

MASHA. Here you are, sitting here, doing nothing.

CHEBUTIKIN. What then?

MASHA. *[Sits]* Nothing.... *[Pause]* Did you love my mother?

CHEBUTIKIN. Very much.

MASHA. And did she love you?

CHEBUTIKIN. *[After a pause]* I don't remember that.

MASHA. Is my man here? When our cook Martha used to ask about her gendarme, she used to say my man. Is he here?

CHEBUTIKIN. Not yet.

MASHA. When you take your happiness in little bits, in snatches, and then lose it, as I have done, you gradually get coarser, more bitter. *[Points to her bosom]* I'm boiling in here.... *[Looks at ANDREY with the perambulator]* There's our brother Andrey.... All our hopes in him have gone. There was once a great bell, a thousand persons were hoisting it, much money and labour had been spent on it, when it suddenly fell and was broken. Suddenly, for no particular reason.... Andrey is like that....

ANDREY. When are they going to stop making such a noise in the house? It's awful.

CHEBUTIKIN. They won't be much longer. *[Looks at his watch]* My watch is very old-fashioned, it strikes the hours.... *[Winds the watch and makes it strike]* The first, second, and fifth batteries are to leave at one o'clock precisely. *[Pause]* And I go to-morrow.

ANDREY. For good?

CHEBUTIKIN. I don't know. Perhaps I'll return in a year. The devil only knows... it's all one.... *[Somewhere a harp and violin are being played.]*

ANDREY. The town will grow empty. It will be as if they put a cover over it. *[Pause]* Something happened yesterday by the theatre. The whole town knows of it, but I don't.

CHEBUTIKIN. Nothing. A silly little affair. Soleni started irritating the Baron, who lost his temper and insulted him, and so at last Soleni had to challenge him. *[Looks at his watch]* It's about time, I think.... At half-past twelve, in the public wood, that one you can see from here across the river.... Piff-paff. *[Laughs]* Soleni thinks he's Lermontov, and even writes verses. That's all very well, but this is his third duel.

MASHA. Whose?

CHEBUTIKIN. Soleni's.

MASHA. And the Baron?

CHEBUTIKIN. What about the Baron? *[Pause.]*

MASHA. Everything's all muddled up in my head.... But I say it ought not to be allowed. He might wound the Baron or even kill him.

CHEBUTIKIN. The Baron is a good man, but one Baron more or less—what difference does it make? It's all the same! *[Beyond the garden somebody shouts "Co-ee! Hallo! "]* You wait. That's Skvortsov shouting; one of the seconds. He's in a boat. *[Pause.]*

ANDREY. In my opinion it's simply immoral to fight in a duel, or to be present, even in the quality of a doctor.

CHEBUTIKIN. It only seems so.... We don't exist, there's nothing on earth, we don't really live, it only seems that we live. Does it matter, anyway!

MASHA. You talk and talk the whole day long. *[Going]* You live in a climate like this, where it might snow any moment, and there you talk.... *[Stops]* I won't go into the house, I can't go there.... Tell me when Vershinin comes.... *[Goes along the avenue]* The migrant birds are already on the wing.... *[Looks up]* Swans or geese.... My dear, happy things.... *[Exit.]*

ANDREY. Our house will be empty. The officers will go away, you are going, my sister is getting married, and I alone will remain in the house.

CHEBUTIKIN. And your wife?

*[FERAPONT enters with some documents.]*

ANDREY. A wife's a wife. She's honest, well-bred, yes; and kind, but with all that there is still something about her that degenerates her into a petty, blind, even in some respects misshapen animal. In any case, she isn't a man. I tell you as a friend, as the only man to whom I can lay bare my soul. I love Natasha, it's true, but sometimes she seems extraordinarily vulgar, and then I lose myself and can't understand why I love her so much, or, at any rate, used to love her....

CHEBUTIKIN. *[Rises]* I'm going away to-morrow, old chap, and perhaps we'll never meet again, so here's my advice. Put on your cap, take a stick in your hand, go... go on and on, without looking round. And the farther you go, the better.

*[SOLENI goes across the back of the stage with two officers; he catches sight of CHEBUTIKIN, and turns to him, the officers go on.]*

SOLENI. Doctor, it's time. It's half-past twelve already. *[Shakes hands with ANDREY.]*

CHEBUTIKIN. Half a minute. I'm tired of the lot of you. *[To ANDREY]* If anybody asks for me, say I'll be back soon.... *[Sighs]* Oh, oh, oh!

SOLENI. "He didn't have the time to sigh. The bear sat on him heavily." *[Goes up to him]* What are you groaning about, old man?

CHEBUTIKIN. Stop it!

SOLENI. How's your health?

CHEBUTIKIN. *[Angry]* Mind your own business.

SOLENI. The old man is unnecessarily excited. I won't go far, I'll only just bring him down like a snipe. *[Takes out his scent-bottle and scents his hands]* I've poured out a whole bottle of scent to-day and they still smell... of a dead body. *[Pause]* Yes.... You remember the poem

"But he, the rebel seeks the storm,
As if the storm will bring him rest..."?

CHEBUTIKIN. Yes.

"He didn't have the time to sigh,
The bear sat on him heavily."

*[Exit with SOLENI.]*

*[Shouts are heard. ANDREY and FERAPONT come in.]*

FERAPONT. Documents to sign....

ANDREY. *[Irritated]*. Go away! Leave me! Please! *[Goes away with the perambulator.]*

FERAPONT. That's what documents are for, to be signed. *[Retires to back of stage.]*

*[Enter IRINA, with TUZENBACH in a straw hat; KULIGIN walks across the stage, shouting "Co-ee, Masha, co-ee!"]*

TUZENBACH. He seems to be the only man in the town who is glad that the soldiers are going.

IRINA. One can understand that. *[Pause]* The town will be empty.

TUZENBACH. My dear, I shall return soon.

IRINA. Where are you going?

TUZENBACH. I must go into the town and then... see the others off.

IRINA. It's not true... Nicolai, why are you so absentminded to-day? *[Pause]* What took place by the theatre yesterday?

TUZENBACH. *[Making a movement of impatience]* In an hour's time I shall return and be with you again. *[Kisses her hands]* My darling... *[Looking her closely in the face]* it's five years now since I fell in love with you, and still I can't get used to it, and you seem to me to grow more and more beautiful. What lovely, wonderful hair! What eyes! I'm going to take you away to-morrow. We shall work, we shall be rich, my dreams will come true. You will be happy. There's only one thing, one thing only: you don't love me!

IRINA. It isn't in my power! I shall be your wife, I shall be true to you, and obedient to you, but I can't love you. What can I do! *[Cries]* I have never been in love in my life. Oh, I used to think so much of love, I have been thinking about it for so long by day and by night, but my soul is like an expensive piano which is locked and the key lost. *[Pause]* You seem so unhappy.

TUZENBACH. I didn't sleep at night. There is nothing in my life so awful as to be able to frighten me, only that lost key torments my soul and does not let me sleep. Say something to me *[Pause]* say something to me....

IRINA. What can I say, what?

TUZENBACH. Anything.

IRINA. Don't! don't! *[Pause.]*

TUZENBACH. It is curious how silly trivial little things, sometimes for no apparent reason, become significant. At first you laugh at these things, you think they are of no importance, you go on and you feel that you haven't got the strength to stop yourself. Oh don't let's talk about it! I am happy. It is as if for the first time in my life I see these firs, maples, beeches, and they all look at me inquisitively and wait. What beautiful trees and how beautiful, when one comes to think of it, life must be near them! *[A shout of Co-ee! in the distance]* It's time I went.... There's a tree which has dried up but it still sways in the breeze with the others. And so it seems to me that if I die, I shall still take part in life in one way or another. Good-bye, dear.... *[Kisses her hands]* The papers which you gave me are on my table under the calendar.

IRINA. I am coming with you.

TUZENBACH. *[Nervously]* No, no! *[He goes quickly and stops in the avenue]* Irina!

IRINA. What is it?

TUZENBACH. *[Not knowing what to say]* I haven't had any coffee to-day. Tell them to make me some.... *[He goes out quickly.]*

*[IRINA stands deep in thought. Then she goes to the back of the stage and sits on a swing. ANDREY comes in with the perambulator and FERAPONT also appears.]*

FERAPONT. Andrey Sergeyevitch, it isn't as if the documents were mine, they are the government's. I didn't make them.

ANDREY. Oh, what has become of my past and where is it? I used to be young, happy, clever, I used to be able to think and frame clever ideas, the present and the future seemed to me full of hope. Why do we, almost before we have begun to live, become dull, grey, uninteresting, lazy, apathetic, useless, unhappy.... This town has already been in existence for two hundred years and it has a hundred thousand inhabitants, not one of whom is in any way different from the others. There has never been, now or at any other time, a single leader of men, a single scholar, an artist, a man of even the slightest eminence who might arouse envy or a passionate desire to be imitated. They only eat, drink, sleep, and then they die... more people are born and also eat, drink, sleep, and so as not to go silly from boredom, they try to make life many-sided with their beastly backbiting, vodka, cards, and litigation. The wives deceive their husbands, and the husbands lie, and pretend they see nothing and hear nothing, and the evil influence irresistibly oppresses the children and the divine spark in them is extinguished, and they become just as pitiful corpses and just as much like one another as their fathers and mothers.... *[Angrily to FERAPONT]* What do you want?

FERAPONT. What? Documents want signing.

ANDREY. I'm tired of you.

FERAPONT. *[Handing him papers]* The hall-porter from the law courts was saying just now that in the winter there were two hundred degrees of frost in Petersburg.

ANDREY. The present is beastly, but when I think of the future, how good it is! I feel so light, so free; there is a light in the distance, I see freedom. I see myself and my children freeing ourselves from vanities, from kvass, from goose baked with cabbage, from after-dinner naps, from base idleness....

FERAPONT. He was saying that two thousand people were frozen to death. The people were frightened, he said. In Petersburg or Moscow, I don't remember which.

ANDREY. *[Overcome by a tender emotion]* My dear sisters, my beautiful sisters! *[Crying]* Masha, my sister....

NATASHA. *[At the window]* Who's talking so loudly out here? Is that you, Andrey? You'll wake little Sophie. *Il ne faut pas faire du bruit, la Sophie est dormée deja. Vous êtes un ours. [Angrily]* If you want to talk, then give the perambulator and the baby to somebody else. Ferapont, take the perambulator!

FERAPONT. Yes'm. *[Takes the perambulator.]*

ANDREY. *[Confused]* I'm speaking quietly.

NATASHA. *[At the window, nursing her boy]* Bobby! Naughty Bobby! Bad little Bobby!

ANDREY. *[Looking through the papers]* All right, I'll look them over and sign if necessary, and you can take them back to the offices....

*[Goes into house reading papers; FERAPONT takes the perambulator to the back of the garden.]*

NATASHA. *[At the window]* Bobby, what's your mother's name? Dear, dear! And who's this? That's Aunt Olga. Say to your aunt, "How do you do, Olga!"

*[Two wandering musicians, a man and a girl, are playing on a violin and a harp. VERSHININ, OLGA, and ANFISA come out of the house and listen for a minute in silence; IRINA comes up to them.]*

OLGA. Our garden might be a public thoroughfare, from the way people walk and ride across it. Nurse, give those musicians something!

ANFISA. *[Gives money to the musicians]* Go away with God's blessing on you. *[The musicians bow and go away]* A bitter sort of people. You don't play on a full stomach. *[To IRINA]* How do you do, Arisha! *[Kisses her]* Well, little girl, here I am, still alive! Still alive! In the High School, together with little Olga, in her official apartments... so the Lord has appointed for my old age. Sinful woman that I am, I've never lived like that in my life before.... A large flat, government property, and I've a whole room and bed to myself. All government property. I wake up at nights and, oh God, and Holy Mother, there isn't a happier person than I!

VERSHININ. *[Looks at his watch]* We are going soon, Olga Sergeyevna. It's time for me to go. *[Pause]* I wish you every... every.... Where's Maria Sergeyevna?

IRINA. She's somewhere in the garden. I'll go and look for her.

VERSHININ. If you'll be so kind. I haven't time.

ANFISA. I'll go and look, too. *[Shouts]* Little Masha, co-ee! *[Goes out with IRINA down into the garden]* Co-ee, co-ee!

VERSHININ. Everything comes to an end. And so we, too, must part. *[Looks at his watch]* The town gave us a sort of farewell breakfast, we had champagne to drink and the mayor made a speech, and I ate and listened, but my soul was here all the time.... *[Looks round the garden]* I'm so used to you now.

OLGA. Shall we ever meet again?

VERSHININ. Probably not. *[Pause]* My wife and both my daughters will stay here another two months. If anything happens, or if anything has to be done...

OLGA. Yes, yes, of course. You need not worry. *[Pause]* To-morrow there won't be a single soldier left in the town, it will all be a memory, and, of course, for us a new life will begin.... *[Pause]* None of our plans are coming right. I didn't want to be a headmistress, but they made me one, all the same. It means there's no chance of Moscow....

VERSHININ. Well... thank you for everything. Forgive me if I've... I've said such an awful lot—forgive me for that too, don't think badly of me.

OLGA. *[Wipes her eyes]* Why isn't Masha coming...

VERSHININ. What else can I say in parting? Can I philosophize about anything? *[Laughs]* Life is heavy. To many of us it seems dull and hopeless, but still, it must be acknowledged that it is getting lighter and clearer, and it seems that the time is not far off when it will be quite clear. *[Looks at his watch]* It's time I went! Mankind used to be absorbed in wars, and all its existence was filled with campaigns, attacks, defeats, now we've outlived all that, leaving after us a great waste place, which there is nothing to fill with at present; but mankind is looking for something, and will certainly find it. Oh, if it only happened more quickly. *[Pause]* If only education could be added to industry, and industry to education. *[Looks at his watch]* It's time I went....

OLGA. Here she comes.

*[Enter MASHA.]*

VERSHININ. I came to say good-bye....

*[OLGA steps aside a little, so as not to be in their way.]*

MASHA. *[Looking him in the face]* Good-bye. *[Prolonged kiss.]*

OLGA. Don't, don't. *[MASHA is crying bitterly]*

VERSHININ. Write to me.... Don't forget! Let me go.... It's time. Take her, Olga Sergeyevna... it's time... I'm late...

*[He kisses OLGA'S hand in evident emotion, then embraces MASHA once more and goes out quickly.]*

OLGA. Don't, Masha! Stop, dear.... *[KULIGIN enters.]*

KULIGIN. *[Confused]* Never mind, let her cry, let her.... My dear Masha, my good Masha.... You're my wife, and I'm happy, whatever happens... I'm not complaining, I don't reproach you at all.... Olga is a witness to it. Let's begin to live again as we used to, and not by a single word, or hint...

MASHA. *[Restraining her sobs]*

"There stands a green oak by the sea,
And a chain of bright gold is around it....
And a chain of bright gold is around it...."

I'm going off my head...

"There stands... a green oak... by the sea."...

OLGA. Don't, Masha, don't... give her some water....

MASHA. I'm not crying any more....

KULIGIN. She's not crying any more... she's a good... *[A shot is heard from a distance.]*

MASHA

. "There stands a green oak by the sea,
And a chain of bright gold is around it...
An oak of green gold...."

I'm mixing it up.... *[Drinks some water]* Life is dull... I don't want anything more now... I'll be all right in a moment.... It doesn't matter.... What do those lines mean? Why do they run in my head? My thoughts are all tangled.

*[IRINA enters.]*

OLGA. Be quiet, Masha. There's a good girl.... Let's go in.

MASHA. *[Angrily]* I shan't go in there. *[Sobs, but controls herself at once]* I'm not going to go into the house, I won't go....

IRINA. Let's sit here together and say nothing. I'm going away to-morrow.... *[Pause.]*

KULIGIN. Yesterday I took away these whiskers and this beard from a boy in the third class.... *[He puts on the whiskers and beard]* Don't I look like the German master.... *[Laughs]* Don't I? The boys are amusing.

MASHA. You really do look like that German of yours.

OLGA. *[Laughs]* Yes. *[MASHA weeps.]*

IRINA. Don't, Masha!

KULIGIN. It's a very good likeness....

*[Enter NATASHA.]*

NATASHA. *[To the maid]* What? Mihail Ivanitch Protopopov will sit with little Sophie, and Andrey Sergeyevitch can take little Bobby out. Children are such a bother.... *[To IRINA]* Irina, it's such a pity you're going away to-morrow. Do stop just another week. *[Sees KULIGIN and screams; he laughs and takes off his beard and whiskers]* How you frightened me! *[To IRINA]* I've grown used to you and do you think it will be easy for me to part from you? I'm going to have Andrey and his violin put into your room—let him fiddle away in there!—and we'll put little Sophie into his room. The beautiful, lovely child! What a little girlie! To-day she looked at me with such pretty eyes and said "Mamma!"

KULIGIN. A beautiful child, it's quite true.

NATASHA. That means I shall have the place to myself to-morrow. *[Sighs]* In the first place I shall have that avenue of fir-trees cut down, then that maple. It's so ugly at nights.... *[To IRINA]* That belt doesn't suit you at all, dear.... It's an error of taste. And I'll give orders to have lots and lots of little flowers planted here, and they'll smell.... *[Severely]* Why is there a fork lying about here on the seat? *[Going towards the house, to the maid]* Why is there a fork lying about here on the seat, I say? *[Shouts]* Don't you dare to answer me!

KULIGIN. Temper! temper! *[A march is played off; they all listen.]*

OLGA. They're going.

*[CHEBUTIKIN comes in.]*

MASHA. They're going. Well, well.... Bon voyage! *[To her husband]* We must be going home.... Where's my coat and hat?

KULIGIN. I took them in... I'll bring them, in a moment.

OLGA. Yes, now we can all go home. It's time.

CHEBUTIKIN. Olga Sergeyevna!

OLGA. What is it? *[Pause]* What is it?

CHEBUTIKIN. Nothing... I don't know how to tell you.... *[Whispers to her.]*

OLGA. *[Frightened]* It can't be true!

CHEBUTIKIN. Yes... such a story... I'm tired out, exhausted, I won't say any more.... *[Sadly]* Still, it's all the same!

MASHA. What's happened?

OLGA. *[Embraces IRINA]* This is a terrible day... I don't know how to tell you, dear....

IRINA. What is it? Tell me quickly, what is it? For God's sake! *[Cries.]*

CHEBUTIKIN. The Baron was killed in the duel just now.

IRINA. *[Cries softly]* I knew it, I knew it....

CHEBUTIKIN. *[Sits on a bench at the back of the stage]* I'm tired.... *[Takes a paper from his pocket]* Let 'em cry.... *[Sings softly]* "Tarara-boom-deay, it is my washing day...." Isn't it all the same!

*[The three sisters are standing, pressing against one another.]*

MASHA. Oh, how the music plays! They are leaving us, one has quite left us, quite and for ever. We remain alone, to begin our life over again. We must live... we must live....

IRINA. *[Puts her head on OLGA's bosom]* There will come a time when everybody will know why, for what purpose, there is all this suffering, and there will be no more mysteries. But now we must live... we must work, just work! To-morrow, I'll go away alone, and I'll teach and give my whole life to those who, perhaps, need it. It's autumn now, soon it will be winter, the snow will cover everything, and I shall be working, working....

OLGA. *[Embraces both her sisters]* The bands are playing so gaily, so bravely, and one does so want to live! Oh, my God! Time will pass on, and we shall depart for ever, we shall be forgotten; they will forget our faces, voices, and even how many there were of us, but our sufferings will turn into joy for those who will live after us, happiness and peace will reign on earth, and people will remember with kindly words, and bless those who are living now. Oh dear sisters, our life is not yet at an end. Let us live. The music is so gay, so joyful, and, it seems that in a little while we shall know why we are living, why we are suffering.... If we could only know, if we could only know!

*[The music has been growing softer and softer; KULIGIN, smiling happily, brings out the hat and coat; ANDREY wheels out the perambulator in which BOBBY is sitting.]*

CHEBUTIKIN. *[Sings softly]* "Tara... ra-boom-deay.... It is my washing-day."... *[Reads a paper]* It's all the same! It's all the same!

OLGA. If only we could know, if only we could know!

## Curtain.

# THE CHERRY ORCHARD

## Translated by Julius West

### CHARACTERS

LUBOV ANDREYEVNA RANEVSKY (Mme. RANEVSKY), a land-owner
ANYA, her daughter, aged seventeen
VARYA (BARBARA), her adopted daughter, aged twenty-seven
LEONID ANDREYEVITCH GAEV, Mme. Ranevsky's brother
ERMOLAI ALEXEYEVITCH LOPAKHIN, a merchant
PETER SERGEYEVITCH TROFIMOV, a student
BORIS BORISOVITCH SIMEONOV-PISCHIN, a landowner
CHARLOTTA IVANOVNA, a governess
SIMEON PANTELEYEVITCH EPIKHODOV, a clerk
DUNYASHA (AVDOTYA FEDOROVNA), a maidservant
FIERS, an old footman, aged eighty-seven
YASHA, a young footman
A TRAMP
A STATION-MASTER
POST-OFFICE CLERK
GUESTS
A SERVANT

The action takes place on Mme. RANEVSKY'S estate

# ACT ONE

*[A room which is still called the nursery. One of the doors leads into ANYA'S room. It is close on sunrise. It is May. The cherry-trees are in flower but it is chilly in the garden. There is an early frost. The windows of the room are shut. DUNYASHA comes in with a candle, and LOPAKHIN with a book in his hand.]*

LOPAKHIN. The train's arrived, thank God. What's the time?

DUNYASHA. It will soon be two. *[Blows out candle]* It is light already.

LOPAKHIN. How much was the train late? Two hours at least. *[Yawns and stretches himself]* I have made a rotten mess of it! I came here on purpose to meet them at the station, and then overslept myself... in my chair. It's a pity. I wish you'd wakened me.

DUNYASHA. I thought you'd gone away. *[Listening]* I think I hear them coming.

LOPAKHIN. *[Listens]* No.... They've got to collect their luggage and so on.... *[Pause]* Lubov Andreyevna has been living abroad for five years; I don't know what she'll be like now.... She's a good sort—an easy, simple person. I remember when I was a boy of fifteen, my father, who is dead—he used to keep a shop in the village here—hit me on the face with his fist, and my nose bled.... We had gone into the yard together for something or other, and he was a little drunk. Lubov Andreyevna, as I remember her now, was still young, and very thin, and she took me to the washstand here in this very room, the nursery. She said, "Don't cry, little man, it'll be all right in time for your wedding." *[Pause]* "Little man" My father was a peasant, it's true, but here I am in a white waistcoat and yellow shoes... a pearl out of an oyster. I'm rich now, with lots of money, but just think about it and examine me, and you'll find I'm still a peasant down to the marrow of my bones. *[Turns over the pages of his book]* Here I've been reading this book, but I understood nothing. I read and fell asleep. *[Pause.]*

DUNYASHA. The dogs didn't sleep all night; they know that they're coming.

LOPAKHIN. What's up with you, Dunyasha...?

DUNYASHA. My hands are shaking. I shall faint.

LOPAKHIN. You're too sensitive, Dunyasha. You dress just like a lady, and you do your hair like one too. You oughtn't. You should know your place.

EPIKHODOV. *[Enters with a bouquet. He wears a short jacket and brilliantly polished boots which squeak audibly. He drops the bouquet as he enters, then picks it up]* The gardener sent these; says they're to go into the dining-room. *[Gives the bouquet to DUNYASHA.]*

LOPAKHIN. And you'll bring me some kvass.

DUNYASHA. Very well. *[Exit.]*

EPIKHODOV. There's a frost this morning—three degrees, and the cherry-trees are all in flower. I can't approve of our climate. *[Sighs]* I can't. Our climate is indisposed to favour us even this once. And, Ermolai Alexeyevitch, allow me to say to you, in addition, that I bought myself some boots two days ago, and I beg to assure you that they squeak in a perfectly unbearable manner. What shall I put on them?

LOPAKHIN. Go away. You bore me.

EPIKHODOV. Some misfortune happens to me every day. But I don't complain; I'm used to it, and I can smile. *[DUNYASHA comes in and brings LOPAKHIN some kvass]* I shall go. *[Knocks over a chair]* There.... *[Triumphantly]* There, you see, if I may use the word, what circumstances I am in, so to speak. It is even simply marvellous. *[Exit.]*

DUNYASHA. I may confess to you, Ermolai Alexeyevitch, that Epikhodov has proposed to me.

LOPAKHIN. Ah!

DUNYASHA. I don't know what to do about it. He's a nice young man, but every now and again, when he begins talking, you can't understand a word he's saying. I think I like him. He's madly in love with me. He's an unlucky man; every day something happens. We tease him about it. They call him "Two-and-twenty troubles."

LOPAKHIN. *[Listens]* There they come, I think.

DUNYASHA. They're coming! What's the matter with me? I'm cold all over.

LOPAKHIN. There they are, right enough. Let's go and meet them. Will she know me? We haven't seen each other for five years.

DUNYASHA. *[Excited]* I shall faint in a minute.... Oh, I'm fainting!

*[Two carriages are heard driving up to the house. LOPAKHIN and DUNYASHA quickly go out. The stage is empty. A noise begins in the next room. FIERS, leaning on a stick, walks quickly across the stage; he has just been to meet LUBOV ANDREYEVNA. He wears an old-fashioned livery and a tall hat. He is saying something to himself, but not a word of it can be made out. The noise behind the stage gets louder and louder. A voice is heard: "Let's go in there." Enter LUBOV ANDREYEVNA, ANYA, and CHARLOTTA IVANOVNA with a little dog on a chain, and all dressed in travelling clothes, VARYA in a long coat and with a kerchief on her head. GAEV, SIMEONOV-PISCHIN, LOPAKHIN, DUNYASHA with a parcel and an umbrella, and a servant with luggage—all cross the room.]*

ANYA. Let's come through here. Do you remember what this room is, mother?

LUBOV. *[Joyfully, through her tears]* The nursery!

VARYA. How cold it is! My hands are quite numb. *[To LUBOV ANDREYEVNA]* Your rooms, the white one and the violet one, are just as they used to be, mother.

LUBOV. My dear nursery, oh, you beautiful room.... I used to sleep here when I was a baby. *[Weeps]* And here I am like a little girl again. *[Kisses her brother, VARYA, then her brother again]* And Varya is just as she used to be, just like a nun. And I knew Dunyasha. *[Kisses her.]*

GAEV. The train was two hours late. There now; how's that for punctuality?

CHARLOTTA. *[To PISCHIN]* My dog eats nuts too.

PISCHIN. *[Astonished]* To think of that, now!

*[All go out except ANYA and DUNYASHA.]*

DUNYASHA. We did have to wait for you!

*[Takes off ANYA'S cloak and hat.]*

ANYA. I didn't get any sleep for four nights on the journey.... I'm awfully cold.

DUNYASHA. You went away during Lent, when it was snowing and frosty, but now? Darling! *[Laughs and kisses her]* We did have to wait for you, my joy, my pet.... I must tell you at once, I can't bear to wait a minute.

ANYA. *[Tired]* Something else now...?

DUNYASHA. The clerk, Epikhodov, proposed to me after Easter.

ANYA. Always the same.... *[Puts her hair straight]* I've lost all my hairpins.... *[She is very tired, and even staggers as she walks.]*

DUNYASHA. I don't know what to think about it. He loves me, he loves me so much!

ANYA. *[Looks into her room; in a gentle voice]* My room, my windows, as if I'd never gone away. I'm at home! To-morrow morning I'll get up and have a run in the garden....Oh, if I could only get to sleep! I didn't sleep the whole journey, I was so bothered.

DUNYASHA. Peter Sergeyevitch came two days ago.

ANYA. *[Joyfully]* Peter!

DUNYASHA. He sleeps in the bath-house, he lives there. He said he was afraid he'd be in the way. *[Looks at her pocket-watch]* I ought to wake him, but Barbara Mihailovna told me not to. "Don't wake him," she said.

*[Enter VARYA, a bunch of keys on her belt.]*

VARYA. Dunyasha, some coffee, quick. Mother wants some.

DUNYASHA. This minute. *[Exit.]*

VARYA. Well, you've come, glory be to God. Home again. *[Caressing her]* My darling is back again! My pretty one is back again!

ANYA. I did have an awful time, I tell you.

VARYA. I can just imagine it!

ANYA. I went away in Holy Week; it was very cold then. Charlotta talked the whole way and would go on performing her tricks. Why did you tie Charlotta on to me?

VARYA. You couldn't go alone, darling, at seventeen!

ANYA. We went to Paris; it's cold there and snowing. I talk French perfectly horribly. My mother lives on the fifth floor. I go to her, and find her there with various Frenchmen, women, an old abbé with a book, and everything in tobacco smoke and with no comfort at all. I suddenly became very sorry for mother—so sorry that I took her head in my arms and hugged her and wouldn't let her go. Then mother started hugging me and crying....

VARYA. *[Weeping]* Don't say any more, don't say any more....

ANYA. She's already sold her villa near Mentone; she's nothing left, nothing. And I haven't a copeck left either; we only just managed to get here. And mother won't understand! We had dinner at a station; she asked for all the expensive things, and tipped the waiters one rouble each. And Charlotta too. Yasha wants his share too—it's too bad. Mother's got a footman now, Yasha; we've brought him here.

VARYA. I saw the wretch.

ANYA. How's business? Has the interest been paid?

VARYA. Not much chance of that.

ANYA. Oh God, oh God...

VARYA. The place will be sold in August.

ANYA. O God....

LOPAKHIN. *[Looks in at the door and moos]* Moo!... *[Exit.]*

VARYA. *[Through her tears]* I'd like to.... *[Shakes her fist.]*

ANYA. *[Embraces VARYA, softly]* Varya, has he proposed to you? *[VARYA shakes head]* But he loves you.... Why don't you make up your minds? Why do you keep on waiting?

VARYA. I think that it will all come to nothing. He's a busy man. I'm not his affair... he pays no attention to me. Bless the man, I don't want to see him.... But everybody talks about our marriage, everybody congratulates me, and there's nothing in it at all, it's all like a dream. *[In another tone]* You've got a brooch like a bee.

ANYA. *[Sadly]* Mother bought it. *[Goes into her room, and talks lightly, like a child]* In Paris I went up in a balloon!

VARYA. My darling's come back, my pretty one's come back! *[DUNYASHA has already returned with the coffee-pot and is making the coffee, VARYA stands near the door]* I go about all day, looking after the house, and I think all the time, if only you could marry a rich man, then I'd be happy and would go away somewhere by myself, then to Kiev... to Moscow, and so on, from one holy place to another. I'd tramp and tramp. That would be splendid!

ANYA. The birds are singing in the garden. What time is it now?

VARYA. It must be getting on for three. Time you went to sleep, darling. *[Goes into ANYA'S room]* Splendid!

*[Enter YASHA with a plaid shawl and a travelling bag.]*

YASHA. *[Crossing the stage: Politely]* May I go this way?

DUNYASHA. I hardly knew you, Yasha. You have changed abroad.

YASHA. Hm... and who are you?

DUNYASHA. When you went away I was only so high. *[Showing with her hand]* I'm Dunyasha, the daughter of Theodore Kozoyedov. You don't remember!

YASHA. Oh, you little cucumber!

*[Looks round and embraces her. She screams and drops a saucer. YASHA goes out quickly.]*

VARYA. *[In the doorway: In an angry voice]* What's that?

DUNYASHA. *[Through her tears]* I've broken a saucer.

VARYA. It may bring luck.

ANYA. *[Coming out of her room]* We must tell mother that Peter's here.

VARYA. I told them not to wake him.

ANYA. *[Thoughtfully]* Father died six years ago, and a month later my brother Grisha was drowned in the river—such a dear little boy of seven! Mother couldn't bear it; she went away, away, without looking round.... *[Shudders]* How I understand her; if only she knew! *[Pause]* And Peter Trofimov was Grisha's tutor, he might tell her....

*[Enter FIERS in a short jacket and white waistcoat.]*

FIERS. *[Goes to the coffee-pot, nervously]* The mistress is going to have some food here.... *[Puts on white gloves]* Is the coffee ready? *[To DUNYASHA, severely]* You! Where's the cream?

DUNYASHA. Oh, dear me...! *[Rapid exit.]*

FIERS. *[Fussing round the coffee-pot]* Oh, you bungler.... *[Murmurs to himself]* Back from Paris... the master went to Paris once... in a carriage.... *[Laughs.]*

VARYA. What are you talking about, Fiers?

FIERS. I beg your pardon? *[Joyfully]* The mistress is home again. I've lived to see her! Don't care if I die now.... *[Weeps with joy.]*

*[Enter LUBOV ANDREYEVNA, GAEV, LOPAKHIN, and SIMEONOV-PISCHIN, the latter in a long jacket of thin cloth and loose trousers. GAEV, coming in, moves his arms and body about as if he is playing billiards.]*

LUBOV. Let me remember now. Red into the corner! Twice into the centre!

GAEV. Right into the pocket! Once upon a time you and I used both to sleep in this room, and now I'm fifty-one; it does seem strange.

LOPAKHIN. Yes, time does go.

GAEV. Who does?

LOPAKHIN. I said that time does go.

GAEV. It smells of patchouli here.

ANYA. I'm going to bed. Good-night, mother. *[Kisses her.]*

LUBOV. My lovely little one. *[Kisses her hand]* Glad to be at home? I can't get over it.

ANYA. Good-night, uncle.

GAEV. *[Kisses her face and hands]* God be with you. How you do resemble your mother! *[To his sister]* You were just like her at her age, Luba.

*[ANYA gives her hand to LOPAKHIN and PISCHIN and goes out, shutting the door behind her.]*

LUBOV. She's awfully tired.

PISCHIN. It's a very long journey.

VARYA. *[To LOPAKHIN and PISCHIN]* Well, sirs, it's getting on for three, quite time you went.

LUBOV. *[Laughs]* You're just the same as ever, Varya. *[Draws her close and kisses her]* I'll have some coffee now, then we'll all go. *[FIERS lays a cushion under her feet]* Thank you, dear. I'm used to coffee. I drink it day and night. Thank you, dear old man. *[Kisses FIERS.]*

VARYA. I'll go and see if they've brought in all the luggage. *[Exit.]*

LUBOV. Is it really I who am sitting here? *[Laughs]* I want to jump about and wave my arms. *[Covers her face with her hands]* But suppose I'm dreaming! God knows I love my own country, I love it deeply; I couldn't look out of the railway carriage, I cried so much. *[Through her tears]* Still, I must have my coffee. Thank you, Fiers. Thank you, dear old man. I'm so glad you're still with us.

FIERS. The day before yesterday.

GAEV. He doesn't hear well.

LOPAKHIN. I've got to go off to Kharkov by the five o'clock train. I'm awfully sorry! I should like to have a look at you, to gossip a little. You're as fine-looking as ever.

PISCHIN. *[Breathes heavily]* Even finer-looking... dressed in Paris fashions... confound it all.

LOPAKHIN. Your brother, Leonid Andreyevitch, says I'm a snob, a usurer, but that is absolutely nothing to me. Let him talk. Only I do wish you would believe in me as you once did, that your wonderful, touching eyes would look at me as they did before. Merciful God! My father was the serf of your grandfather and your own father, but you—you more than anybody else—did so much for me once upon a time that I've forgotten everything and love you as if you belonged to my family... and even more.

LUBOV. I can't sit still, I'm not in a state to do it. *[Jumps up and walks about in great excitement]* I'll never survive this happiness.... You can laugh at me; I'm a silly woman.... My dear little cupboard. *[Kisses cupboard]* My little table.

GAEV. Nurse has died in your absence.

LUBOV. *[Sits and drinks coffee]* Yes, bless her soul. I heard by letter.

GAEV. And Anastasius has died too. Peter Kosoy has left me and now lives in town with the Commissioner of Police. *[Takes a box of sugar-candy out of his pocket and sucks a piece.]*

PISCHIN. My daughter, Dashenka, sends her love.

LOPAKHIN. I want to say something very pleasant, very delightful, to you. *[Looks at his watch]* I'm going away at once, I haven't much time... but I'll tell you all about it in two or three words. As you already know, your cherry orchard is to be sold to pay your debts, and the sale is fixed for August 22; but you needn't be alarmed, dear madam, you may sleep in peace; there's a way out. Here's my plan. Please attend carefully! Your estate is only thirteen miles from the town, the railway runs by, and if the cherry orchard and the land by the river are broken up into building lots and are then leased off for villas you'll get at least twenty-five thousand roubles a year profit out of it.

GAEV. How utterly absurd!

LUBOV. I don't understand you at all, Ermolai Alexeyevitch.

LOPAKHIN. You will get twenty-five roubles a year for each dessiatin from the leaseholders at the very least, and if you advertise now I'm willing to bet that you won't have a vacant plot left by the autumn; they'll all go. In a word, you're saved. I congratulate you. Only, of course, you'll have to put things straight, and clean up.... For instance, you'll have to pull down all the old buildings, this house, which isn't any use to anybody now, and cut down the old cherry orchard....

LUBOV. Cut it down? My dear man, you must excuse me, but you don't understand anything at all. If there's anything interesting or remarkable in the whole province, it's this cherry orchard of ours.

LOPAKHIN. The only remarkable thing about the orchard is that it's very large. It only bears fruit every other year, and even then you don't know what to do with them; nobody buys any.

GAEV. This orchard is mentioned in the "Encyclopaedic Dictionary."

LOPAKHIN. *[Looks at his watch]* If we can't think of anything and don't make up our minds to anything, then on August 22, both the cherry orchard and the whole estate will be up for auction. Make up your mind! I swear there's no other way out, I'll swear it again.

FIERS. In the old days, forty or fifty years back, they dried the cherries, soaked them and pickled them, and made jam of them, and it used to happen that...

GAEV. Be quiet, Fiers.

FIERS. And then we'd send the dried cherries off in carts to Moscow and Kharkov. And money! And the dried cherries were soft, juicy, sweet, and nicely scented.... They knew the way....

LUBOV. What was the way?

FIERS. They've forgotten. Nobody remembers.

PISCHIN. *[To LUBOV ANDREYEVNA]* What about Paris? Eh? Did you eat frogs?

LUBOV. I ate crocodiles.

PISCHIN. To think of that, now.

LOPAKHIN. Up to now in the villages there were only the gentry and the labourers, and now the people who live in villas have arrived. All towns now, even small ones, are surrounded by villas. And it's safe to say that in twenty years' time the villa resident will be all over the place. At present he sits on his balcony and drinks tea, but it may well come to pass that he'll begin to cultivate his patch of land, and then your cherry orchard will be happy, rich, splendid....

GAEV. *[Angry]* What rot!

*[Enter VARYA and YASHA.]*

VARYA. There are two telegrams for you, little mother. *[Picks out a key and noisily unlocks an antique cupboard]* Here they are.

LUBOV. They're from Paris.... *[Tears them up without reading them]* I've done with Paris.

GAEV. And do you know, Luba, how old this case is? A week ago I took out the bottom drawer; I looked and saw figures burnt out in it. That case was made exactly a hundred years ago. What do you think of that? What? We could celebrate its jubilee. It hasn't a soul of its own, but still, say what you will, it's a fine bookcase.

PISCHIN. *[Astonished]* A hundred years.... Think of that!

GAEV. Yes... it's a real thing. *[Handling it]* My dear and honoured case! I congratulate you on your existence, which has already for more than a hundred years been directed towards the bright ideals of good and justice; your silent call to productive labour has not grown less in the hundred years *[Weeping]* during which you have upheld virtue and faith in a better future to the generations of our race, educating us up to ideals of goodness and to the knowledge of a common consciousness. *[Pause.]*

LOPAKHIN. Yes....

LUBOV. You're just the same as ever, Leon.

GAEV. *[A little confused]* Off the white on the right, into the corner pocket. Red ball goes into the middle pocket!

LOPAKHIN. *[Looks at his watch]* It's time I went.

YASHA. *[Giving LUBOV ANDREYEVNA her medicine]* Will you take your pills now?

PISCHIN. You oughtn't to take medicines, dear madam; they do you neither harm nor good.... Give them here, dear madam. *[Takes the pills, turns them out into the palm of his hand, blows on them, puts them into his mouth, and drinks some kvass]* There!

LUBOV. *[Frightened]* You're off your head!

PISCHIN. I've taken all the pills.

LOPAKHIN. Gormandizer! *[All laugh.]*

FIERS. They were here in Easter week and ate half a pailful of cucumbers.... *[Mumbles.]*

LUBOV. What's he driving at?

VARYA. He's been mumbling away for three years. We're used to that.

YASHA. Senile decay.

*[CHARLOTTA IVANOVNA crosses the stage, dressed in white: she is very thin and tightly laced; has a lorgnette at her waist.]*

LOPAKHIN. Excuse me, Charlotta Ivanovna, I haven't said "How do you do" to you yet. *[Tries to kiss her hand.]*

CHARLOTTA. *[Takes her hand away]* If you let people kiss your hand, then they'll want your elbow, then your shoulder, and then...

LOPAKHIN. My luck's out to-day! *[All laugh]* Show us a trick, Charlotta Ivanovna!

LUBOV ANDREYEVNA. Charlotta, do us a trick.

CHARLOTTA. It's not necessary. I want to go to bed. *[Exit.]*

LOPAKHIN. We shall see each other in three weeks. *[Kisses LUBOV ANDREYEVNA'S hand]* Now, good-bye. It's time to go. *[To GAEV]* See you again. *[Kisses PISCHIN]* Au revoir. *[Gives his hand to VARYA, then to FIERS and to YASHA]* I don't want to go away. *[To LUBOV ANDREYEVNA]*. If you think about the villas and make up your mind, then just let me know, and I'll raise a loan of 50,000 roubles at once. Think about it seriously.

VARYA. *[Angrily]* Do go, now!

LOPAKHIN. I'm going, I'm going.... *[Exit.]*

GAEV. Snob. Still, I beg pardon.... Varya's going to marry him, he's Varya's young man.

VARYA. Don't talk too much, uncle.

LUBOV. Why not, Varya? I should be very glad. He's a good man.

PISCHIN. To speak the honest truth... he's a worthy man.... And my Dashenka... also says that... she says lots of things. *[Snores, but wakes up again at once]* But still, dear madam, if you could lend me... 240 roubles... to pay the interest on my mortgage to-morrow...

VARYA. *[Frightened]* We haven't got it, we haven't got it!

LUBOV. It's quite true. I've nothing at all.

PISCHIN. I'll find it all right *[Laughs]* I never lose hope. I used to think, "Everything's lost now. I'm a dead man," when, lo and behold, a railway was built over my land... and they paid me for it. And something else will happen to-day or to-morrow. Dashenka may win 20,000 roubles... she's got a lottery ticket.

LUBOV. The coffee's all gone, we can go to bed.

FIERS. *[Brushing GAEV'S trousers; in an insistent tone]* You've put on the wrong trousers again. What am I to do with you?

VARYA. *[Quietly]* Anya's asleep. *[Opens window quietly]* The sun has risen already; it isn't cold. Look, little mother: what lovely trees! And the air! The starlings are singing!

GAEV. *[Opens the other window]* The whole garden's white. You haven't forgotten, Luba? There's that long avenue going straight, straight, like a stretched strap; it shines on moonlight nights. Do you remember? You haven't forgotten?

LUBOV. *[Looks out into the garden]* Oh, my childhood, days of my innocence! In this nursery I used to sleep; I used to look out from here into the orchard. Happiness used to wake with me every morning, and then it was just as it is now; nothing has changed. *[Laughs from joy]* It's all, all white! Oh, my orchard! After the dark autumns and the cold winters, you're young again, full of happiness, the angels of heaven haven't left you.... If only I could take my heavy burden off my breast and shoulders, if I could forget my past!

GAEV. Yes, and they'll sell this orchard to pay off debts. How strange it seems!

LUBOV. Look, there's my dead mother going in the orchard... dressed in white! *[Laughs from joy]* That's she.

GAEV. Where?

VARYA. God bless you, little mother.

LUBOV. There's nobody there; I thought I saw somebody. On the right, at the turning by the summer-house, a white little tree bent down, looking just like a woman. *[Enter TROFIMOV in a worn student uniform and spectacles]* What a marvellous garden! White masses of flowers, the blue sky....

TROFIMOV. Lubov Andreyevna! *[She looks round at him]* I only want to show myself, and I'll go away. *[Kisses her hand warmly]* I was told to wait till the morning, but I didn't have the patience.

*[LUBOV ANDREYEVNA looks surprised.]*

VARYA. *[Crying]* It's Peter Trofimov.

TROFIMOV. Peter Trofimov, once the tutor of your Grisha.... Have I changed so much?

*[LUBOV ANDREYEVNA embraces him and cries softly.]*

GAEV. *[Confused]* That's enough, that's enough, Luba.

VARYA. *[Weeps]* But I told you, Peter, to wait till to-morrow.

LUBOV. My Grisha... my boy... Grisha... my son.

VARYA. What are we to do, little mother? It's the will of God.

TROFIMOV. *[Softly, through his tears]* It's all right, it's all right.

LUBOV. *[Still weeping]* My boy's dead; he was drowned. Why? Why, my friend? *[Softly]* Anya's asleep in there. I am speaking so loudly, making such a noise.... Well, Peter? What's made you look so bad? Why have you grown so old?

TROFIMOV. In the train an old woman called me a decayed gentleman.

LUBOV. You were quite a boy then, a nice little student, and now your hair is not at all thick and you wear spectacles. Are you really still a student? *[Goes to the door.]*

TROFIMOV. I suppose I shall always be a student.

LUBOV. *[Kisses her brother, then VARYA]* Well, let's go to bed.... And you've grown older, Leonid.

PISCHIN. *[Follows her]* Yes, we've got to go to bed.... Oh, my gout! I'll stay the night here. If only, Lubov Andreyevna, my dear, you could get me 240 roubles to-morrow morning—

GAEV. Still the same story.

PISCHIN. Two hundred and forty roubles... to pay the interest on the mortgage.

LUBOV. I haven't any money, dear man.

PISCHIN. I'll give it back... it's a small sum....

LUBOV. Well, then, Leonid will give it to you.... Let him have it, Leonid.

GAEV. By all means; hold out your hand.

LUBOV. Why not? He wants it; he'll give it back.

*[LUBOV ANDREYEVNA, TROFIMOV, PISCHIN, and FIERS go out. GAEV, VARYA, and YASHA remain.]*

GAEV. My sister hasn't lost the habit of throwing money about. *[To YASHA]* Stand off, do; you smell of poultry.

YASHA. *[Grins]* You are just the same as ever, Leonid Andreyevitch.

GAEV. Really? *[To VARYA]* What's he saying?

VARYA. *[To YASHA]* Your mother's come from the village; she's been sitting in the servants' room since yesterday, and wants to see you....

YASHA. Bless the woman!

VARYA. Shameless man.

YASHA. A lot of use there is in her coming. She might have come to-morrow just as well. *[Exit.]*

VARYA. Mother hasn't altered a scrap, she's just as she always was. She'd give away everything, if the idea only entered her head.

GAEV. Yes.... *[Pause]* If there's any illness for which people offer many remedies, you may be sure that particular illness is incurable, I think. I work my brains to their hardest. I've several remedies, very many, and that really means I've none at all. It would be nice to inherit a fortune from somebody, it would be nice to marry our Anya to a rich man, it would be nice to go to Yaroslav and try my luck with my aunt the Countess. My aunt is very, very rich.

VARYA. *[Weeps]* If only God helped us.

GAEV. Don't cry. My aunt's very rich, but she doesn't like us. My sister, in the first place, married an advocate, not a noble.... *[ANYA appears in the doorway]* She not only married a man who was not a noble, but she behaved herself in a way which cannot be described as proper. She's nice and kind and charming, and I'm very fond of her, but say what you will in her favour and you still have to admit that she's wicked; you can feel it in her slightest movements.

VARYA. *[Whispers]* Anya's in the doorway.

GAEV. Really? *[Pause]* It's curious, something's got into my right eye... I can't see properly out of it. And on Thursday, when I was at the District Court...

*[Enter ANYA.]*

VARYA. Why aren't you in bed, Anya?

ANYA. Can't sleep. It's no good.

GAEV. My darling! *[Kisses ANYA'S face and hands]* My child.... *[Crying]* You're not my niece, you're my angel, you're my all.... Believe in me, believe...

ANYA. I do believe in you, uncle. Everybody loves you and respects you... but, uncle dear, you ought to say nothing, no more than that. What were you saying just now about my mother, your own sister? Why did you say those things?

GAEV. Yes, yes. *[Covers his face with her hand]* Yes, really, it was awful. Save me, my God! And only just now I made a speech before a bookcase... it's so silly! And only when I'd finished I knew how silly it was.

VARYA. Yes, uncle dear, you really ought to say less. Keep quiet, that's all.

ANYA. You'd be so much happier in yourself if you only kept quiet.

GAEV. All right, I'll be quiet. *[Kisses their hands]* I'll be quiet. But let's talk business. On Thursday I was in the District Court, and a lot of us met there together, and we began to talk of this, that, and the other, and now I think I can arrange a loan to pay the interest into the bank.

VARYA. If only God would help us!

GAEV. I'll go on Tuesday. I'll talk with them about it again. *[To VARYA]* Don't howl. *[To ANYA]* Your mother will have a talk to Lopakhin; he, of course, won't refuse... And when you've rested you'll go to Yaroslav to the Countess, your grandmother. So you see, we'll have three irons in the fire, and we'll be safe. We'll pay up the interest. I'm certain. *[Puts some sugar-candy into his mouth]* I swear on my honour, on anything you will, that the estate will not be sold! *[Excitedly]* I swear on my happiness! Here's my hand. You may call me a dishonourable wretch if I let it go to auction! I swear by all I am!

ANYA. *[She is calm again and happy]* How good and clever you are, uncle. *[Embraces him]* I'm happy now! I'm happy! All's well!

*[Enter FIERS.]*

FIERS. *[Reproachfully]* Leonid Andreyevitch, don't you fear God? When are you going to bed?

GAEV. Soon, soon. You go away, Fiers. I'll undress myself. Well, children, bye-bye...! I'll give you the details to-morrow, but let's go to bed now. *[Kisses ANYA and VARYA]* I'm a man of the eighties.... People don't praise those years much, but I can still say that I've suffered for my beliefs. The peasants don't love me for nothing, I assure you. We've got to learn to know the peasants! We ought to learn how....

ANYA. You're doing it again, uncle!

VARYA. Be quiet, uncle!

FIERS. *[Angrily]* Leonid Andreyevitch!

GAEV. I'm coming, I'm coming.... Go to bed now. Off two cushions into the middle! I turn over a new leaf.... *[Exit. FIERS goes out after him.]*

ANYA. I'm quieter now. I don't want to go to Yaroslav, I don't like grandmother; but I'm calm now; thanks to uncle. *[Sits down.]*

VARYA. It's time to go to sleep. I'll go. There's been an unpleasantness here while you were away. In the old servants' part of the house, as you know, only the old people live—little old Efim and Polya and Evstigney, and Karp as well. They started letting some tramps or other spend the night there—I said nothing. Then I heard that they were saying that I had ordered them to be fed on peas and nothing else; from meanness, you see.... And it was all Evstigney's doing.... Very well, I thought, if that's what the matter is, just you wait. So I call Evstigney.... *[Yawns]* He comes. "What's this," I say, "Evstigney, you old fool."... *[Looks at ANYA]* Anya dear! *[Pause]* She's dropped off.... *[Takes ANYA'S arm]* Let's go to bye-bye.... Come along!... *[Leads her]* My darling's gone to sleep! Come on.... *[They go. In the distance, the other side of the orchard, a shepherd plays his pipe. TROFIMOV crosses the stage and stops on seeing VARYA and ANYA]* Sh! She's asleep, asleep. Come on, dear.

ANYA. *[Quietly, half-asleep]* I'm so tired... all the bells... uncle, dear! Mother and uncle!

VARYA. Come on, dear, come on! *[They go into ANYA'S room.]*

TROFIMOV. *[Moved]* My sun! My spring!

**Curtain.**

# ACT TWO

*[In a field. An old, crooked shrine, which has been long abandoned; near it a well and large stones, which apparently are old tombstones, and an old garden seat. The road is seen to GAEV'S estate. On one side rise dark poplars, behind them begins the cherry orchard. In the distance is a row of telegraph poles, and far, far away on the horizon are the indistinct signs of a large town, which can only be seen on the finest and clearest days. It is close on sunset. CHARLOTTA, YASHA, and DUNYASHA are sitting on the seat; EPIKHODOV stands by and plays on a guitar; all seem thoughtful. CHARLOTTA wears a man's old peaked cap; she has unslung a rifle from her shoulders and is putting to rights the buckle on the strap.]*

CHARLOTTA. *[Thoughtfully]* I haven't a real passport. I don't know how old I am, and I think I'm young. When I was a little girl my father and mother used to go round fairs and give very good performances and I used to do the *salto mortale* and various little things. And when papa and mamma died a German lady took me to her and began to teach me. I liked it. I grew up and became a governess. And where I came from and who I am, I don't know.... Who my parents were—perhaps they weren't married—I don't know. *[Takes a cucumber out of her pocket and eats]* I don't know anything. *[Pause]* I do want to talk, but I haven't anybody to talk to... I haven't anybody at all.

EPIKHODOV. *[Plays on the guitar and sings]*

"What is this noisy earth to me,
What matter friends and foes?"
I do like playing on the mandoline!

DUNYASHA. That's a guitar, not a mandoline. *[Looks at herself in a little mirror and powders herself.]*

EPIKHODOV. For the enamoured madman, this is a mandoline. *[Sings]*

"Oh that the heart was warmed,
By all the flames of love returned!"

*[YASHA sings too.]*

CHARLOTTA. These people sing terribly.... Foo! Like jackals.

DUNYASHA. *[To YASHA]* Still, it must be nice to live abroad.

YASHA. Yes, certainly. I cannot differ from you there. *[Yawns and lights a cigar.]*

EPIKHODOV. That is perfectly natural. Abroad everything is in full complexity.

YASHA. That goes without saying.

EPIKHODOV. I'm an educated man, I read various remarkable books, but I cannot understand the direction I myself want to go—whether to live or to shoot myself, as it were. So, in case, I always carry a revolver about with me. Here it is. *[Shows a revolver.]*

CHARLOTTA. I've done. Now I'll go. *[Slings the rifle]* You, Epikhodov, are a very clever man and very terrible; women must be madly in love with you. Brrr! *[Going]* These wise ones are all so stupid. I've nobody to talk to. I'm always alone, alone; I've nobody at all... and I don't know who I am or why I live. *[Exit slowly.]*

EPIKHODOV. As a matter of fact, independently of everything else, I must express my feeling, among other things, that fate has been as pitiless in her dealings with me as a storm is to a small ship. Suppose, let us grant, I am wrong; then why did I wake up this morning, to give an example, and behold an enormous spider on my chest, like that. *[Shows with both hands]* And if I do drink some kvass, why is it that there is bound to be something of the most indelicate nature in it, such as a beetle? *[Pause]* Have you read Buckle? *[Pause]* I should like to trouble you, Avdotya Fedorovna, for two words.

DUNYASHA. Say on.

EPIKHODOV. I should prefer to be alone with you. *[Sighs.]*

DUNYASHA. *[Shy]* Very well, only first bring me my little cloak.... It's by the cupboard. It's a little damp here.

EPIKHODOV. Very well... I'll bring it.... Now I know what to do with my revolver. *[Takes guitar and exits, strumming.]*

YASHA. Two-and-twenty troubles! A silly man, between you and me and the gatepost. *[Yawns.]*

DUNYASHA. I hope to goodness he won't shoot himself. *[Pause]* I'm so nervous, I'm worried. I went into service when I was quite a little girl, and now I'm not used to common life, and my hands are white, white as a lady's. I'm so tender and so delicate now; respectable and afraid of everything.... I'm so frightened. And I don't know what will happen to my nerves if you deceive me, Yasha.

YASHA. *[Kisses her]* Little cucumber! Of course, every girl must respect herself; there's nothing I dislike more than a badly behaved girl.

DUNYASHA. I'm awfully in love with you; you're educated, you can talk about everything. *[Pause.]*

YASHA. *[Yawns]* Yes. I think this: if a girl loves anybody, then that means she's immoral. *[Pause]* It's nice to smoke a cigar out in the open air.... *[Listens]* Somebody's coming. It's the mistress, and people with her. *[DUNYASHA embraces him suddenly]* Go to the house, as if you'd been bathing in the river; go by this path, or they'll meet you and will think I've been meeting you. I can't stand that sort of thing.

DUNYASHA. *[Coughs quietly]* My head's aching because of your cigar.

*[Exit. YASHA remains, sitting by the shrine. Enter LUBOV ANDREYEVNA, GAEV, and LOPAKHIN.]*

LOPAKHIN. You must make up your mind definitely—there's no time to waste. The question is perfectly plain. Are you willing to let the land for villas or no? Just one word, yes or no? Just one word!

LUBOV. Who's smoking horrible cigars here? *[Sits.]*

GAEV. They built that railway; that's made this place very handy. *[Sits]* Went to town and had lunch... red in the middle! I'd like to go in now and have just one game.

LUBOV. You'll have time.

LOPAKHIN. Just one word! *[Imploringly]* Give me an answer!

GAEV. *[Yawns]* Really!

LUBOV. *[Looks in her purse]* I had a lot of money yesterday, but there's very little to-day. My poor Varya feeds everybody on milk soup to save money, in the kitchen the old people only get peas, and I spend recklessly. *[Drops the purse, scattering gold coins]* There, they are all over the place.

YASHA. Permit me to pick them up. *[Collects the coins.]*

LUBOV. Please do, Yasha. And why did I go and have lunch there?... A horrid restaurant with band and tablecloths smelling of soap.... Why do you drink so much, Leon? Why do you eat so much?

Why do you talk so much? You talked again too much to-day in the restaurant, and it wasn't at all to the point—about the seventies and about decadents. And to whom? Talking to the waiters about decadents!

LOPAKHIN. Yes.

GAEV. *[Waves his hand]* I can't be cured, that's obvious.... *[Irritably to YASHA]* What's the matter? Why do you keep twisting about in front of me?

YASHA. *[Laughs]* I can't listen to your voice without laughing.

GAEV. *[To his sister]* Either he or I...

LUBOV. Go away, Yasha; get out of this....

YASHA. *[Gives purse to LUBOV ANDREYEVNA]* I'll go at once. *[Hardly able to keep from laughing]* This minute.... *[Exit.]*

LOPAKHIN. That rich man Deriganov is preparing to buy your estate. They say he'll come to the sale himself.

LUBOV. Where did you hear that?

LOPAKHIN. They say so in town.

GAEV. Our Yaroslav aunt has promised to send something, but I don't know when or how much.

LOPAKHIN. How much will she send? A hundred thousand roubles? Or two, perhaps?

LUBOV. I'd be glad of ten or fifteen thousand.

LOPAKHIN. You must excuse my saying so, but I've never met such frivolous people as you before, or anybody so unbusinesslike and peculiar. Here I am telling you in plain language that your estate will be sold, and you don't seem to understand.

LUBOV. What are we to do? Tell us, what?

LOPAKHIN. I tell you every day. I say the same thing every day. Both the cherry orchard and the land must be leased off for villas and at once, immediately—the auction is staring you in the face: Understand! Once you do definitely make up your minds to the villas, then you'll have as much money as you want and you'll be saved.

LUBOV. Villas and villa residents—it's so vulgar, excuse me.

GAEV. I entirely agree with you

LOPAKHIN. I must cry or yell or faint. I can't stand it! You're too much for me! *[To GAEV]* You old woman!

GAEV. Really!

LOPAKHIN. Old woman! *[Going out.]*

LUBOV. *[Frightened]* No, don't go away, do stop; be a dear. Please. Perhaps we'll find some way out!

LOPAKHIN. What's the good of trying to think!

LUBOV. Please don't go away. It's nicer when you're here.... *[Pause]* I keep on waiting for something to happen, as if the house is going to collapse over our heads.

GAEV. *[Thinking deeply]* Double in the corner... across the middle....

LUBOV. We have been too sinful....

LOPAKHIN. What sins have you committed?

GAEV. *[Puts candy into his mouth]* They say that I've eaten all my substance in sugar-candies. *[Laughs.]*

LUBOV. Oh, my sins.... I've always scattered money about without holding myself in, like a madwoman, and I married a man who made nothing but debts. My husband died of champagne—he drank terribly—and to my misfortune, I fell in love with another man and went off with him, and just at that time—it was my first punishment, a blow that hit me right on the head—here, in the river... my boy was drowned, and I went away, quite away, never to return, never to see this river again...I shut my eyes and ran without thinking, but *he* ran after me... without pity, without respect. I bought a villa near Mentone because *he* fell ill there, and for three years I knew no rest either by day or night; the sick man wore me out, and my soul dried up. And last year, when they had sold the villa to pay my debts, I went away to Paris, and there he robbed me of all I had and threw me over and went off with another woman. I tried to poison myself.... It was so silly, so shameful.... And suddenly I longed to be back in Russia, my own land, with my little girl.... *[Wipes her tears]* Lord, Lord be merciful to me, forgive me my sins! Punish me no more! *[Takes a telegram out of her pocket]* I had this to-day from Paris.... He begs my forgiveness, he implores me to return.... *[Tears it up]* Don't I hear music? *[Listens.]*

GAEV. That is our celebrated Jewish band. You remember—four violins, a flute, and a double-bass.

LUBOV So it still exists? It would be nice if they came along some evening.

LOPAKHIN. *[Listens]* I can't hear.... *[Sings quietly]* "For money will the Germans make a Frenchman of a Russian." *[Laughs]* I saw such an awfully funny thing at the theatre last night.

LUBOV. I'm quite sure there wasn't anything at all funny. You oughtn't to go and see plays, you ought to go and look at yourself. What a grey life you lead, what a lot you talk unnecessarily.

LOPAKHIN. It's true. To speak the straight truth, we live a silly life. *[Pause]* My father was a peasant, an idiot, he understood nothing, he didn't teach me, he was always drunk, and always used a stick on me. In point of fact, I'm a fool and an idiot too. I've never learned anything, my handwriting is bad, I write so that I'm quite ashamed before people, like a pig!

LUBOV. You ought to get married, my friend.

LOPAKHIN. Yes... that's true.

LUBOV. Why not to our Varya? She's a nice girl.

LOPAKHIN. Yes.

LUBOV. She's quite homely in her ways, works all day, and, what matters most, she's in love with you. And you've liked her for a long time.

LOPAKHIN. Well? I don't mind... she's a nice girl. *[Pause.]*

GAEV. I'm offered a place in a bank. Six thousand roubles a year.... Did you hear?

LUBOV. What's the matter with you! Stay where you are....

*[Enter FIERS with an overcoat.]*

FIERS. *[To GAEV]* Please, sir, put this on, it's damp.

GAEV. *[Putting it on]* You're a nuisance, old man.

FIERS It's all very well.... You went away this morning without telling me. *[Examining GAEV.]*

LUBOV. How old you've grown, Fiers!

FIERS. I beg your pardon?

LOPAKHIN. She says you've grown very old!

FIERS. I've been alive a long time. They were already getting ready to marry me before your father was born.... *[Laughs]* And when the Emancipation came I was already first valet. Only I didn't agree with the Emancipation and remained with my people.... *[Pause]* I remember everybody was happy, but they didn't know why.

LOPAKHIN. It was very good for them in the old days. At any rate, they used to beat them.

FIERS. *[Not hearing]* Rather. The peasants kept their distance from the masters and the masters kept their distance from the peasants, but now everything's all anyhow and you can't understand anything.

GAEV. Be quiet, Fiers. I've got to go to town tomorrow. I've been promised an introduction to a General who may lend me money on a bill.

LOPAKHIN. Nothing will come of it. And you won't pay your interest, don't you worry.

LUBOV. He's talking rubbish. There's no General at all.

*[Enter TROFIMOV, ANYA, and VARYA.]*

GAEV. Here they are.

ANYA. Mother's sitting down here.

LUBOV. *[Tenderly]* Come, come, my dears.... *[Embracing ANYA and VARYA]* If you two only knew how much I love you. Sit down next to me, like that. *[All sit down.]*

LOPAKHIN. Our eternal student is always with the ladies.

TROFIMOV. That's not your business.

LOPAKHIN. He'll soon be fifty, and he's still a student.

TROFIMOV. Leave off your silly jokes!

LOPAKHIN. Getting angry, eh, silly?

TROFIMOV. Shut up, can't you.

LOPAKHIN. *[Laughs]* I wonder what you think of me?

TROFIMOV. I think, Ermolai Alexeyevitch, that you're a rich man, and you'll soon be a millionaire. Just as the wild beast which eats everything it finds is needed for changes to take place in matter, so you are needed too.

*[All laugh.]*

VARYA. Better tell us something about the planets, Peter.

LUBOV ANDREYEVNA. No, let's go on with yesterday's talk!

TROFIMOV. About what?

GAEV. About the proud man.

TROFIMOV. Yesterday we talked for a long time but we didn't come to anything in the end. There's something mystical about the proud man, in your sense. Perhaps you are right from your point of view, but if you take the matter simply, without complicating it, then what pride can there be, what sense can there be in it, if a man is imperfectly made, physiologically speaking, if in the vast majority of cases he is coarse and stupid and deeply unhappy? We must stop admiring one another. We must work, nothing more.

GAEV. You'll die, all the same.

TROFIMOV. Who knows? And what does it mean—you'll die? Perhaps a man has a hundred senses, and when he dies only the five known to us are destroyed and the remaining ninety-five are left alive.

LUBOV. How clever of you, Peter!

LOPAKHIN. *[Ironically]* Oh, awfully!

TROFIMOV. The human race progresses, perfecting its powers. Everything that is unattainable now will some day be near at hand and comprehensible, but we must work, we must help with all our strength those who seek to know what fate will bring. Meanwhile in Russia only a very few of us work. The vast majority of those intellectuals whom I know seek for nothing, do nothing, and are at present incapable of hard work. They call themselves intellectuals, but they use "thou" and "thee" to their servants, they treat the peasants like animals, they learn badly, they read nothing seriously, they do absolutely nothing, about science they only talk, about art they understand little. They are all serious, they all have severe faces, they all talk about important things. They philosophize, and at the same time, the vast majority of us, ninety-nine out of a hundred, live like savages, fighting and cursing at the slightest opportunity, eating filthily, sleeping in the dirt, in stuffiness, with fleas, stinks, smells, moral filth, and so on... And it's obvious that all our nice talk is only carried on to distract ourselves and others. Tell me, where are those créches we hear so much of? and where are those reading-rooms? People only write novels about them; they don't really exist. Only dirt, vulgarity, and Asiatic plagues really exist.... I'm afraid, and I don't at all like serious faces; I don't like serious conversations. Let's be quiet sooner.

LOPAKHIN. You know, I get up at five every morning, I work from morning till evening, I am always dealing with money—my own and other people's—and I see what people are like. You've only got to begin to do anything to find out how few honest, honourable people there are. Sometimes, when I can't sleep, I think: "Oh Lord, you've given us huge forests, infinite fields, and endless horizons, and we, living here, ought really to be giants."

LUBOV. You want giants, do you?... They're only good in stories, and even there they frighten one. *[EPIKHODOV enters at the back of the stage playing his guitar. Thoughtfully:]* Epikhodov's there.

ANYA. *[Thoughtfully]* Epikhodov's there.

GAEV. The sun's set, ladies and gentlemen.

TROFIMOV. Yes.

GAEV *[Not loudly, as if declaiming]* O Nature, thou art wonderful, thou shinest with eternal radiance! Oh, beautiful and indifferent one, thou whom we call mother, thou containest in thyself existence and death, thou livest and destroyest....

VARYA. *[Entreatingly]* Uncle, dear!

ANYA. Uncle, you're doing it again!

TROFIMOV. You'd better double the red into the middle.

GAEV. I'll be quiet, I'll be quiet.

*[They all sit thoughtfully. It is quiet. Only the mumbling of FIERS is heard. Suddenly a distant sound is heard as if from the sky, the sound of a breaking string, which dies away sadly.]*

LUBOV. What's that?

LOPAKHIN. I don't know. It may be a bucket fallen down a well somewhere. But it's some way off.

GAEV. Or perhaps it's some bird... like a heron.

TROFIMOV. Or an owl.

LUBOV. *[Shudders]* It's unpleasant, somehow. *[A pause.]*

FIERS. Before the misfortune the same thing happened. An owl screamed and the samovar hummed without stopping.

GAEV. Before what misfortune?

FIERS. Before the Emancipation. *[A pause.]*

LUBOV. You know, my friends, let's go in; it's evening now. *[To ANYA]* You've tears in your eyes.... What is it, little girl? *[Embraces her.]*

ANYA. It's nothing, mother.

TROFIMOV. Some one's coming.

*[Enter a TRAMP in an old white peaked cap and overcoat. He is a little drunk.]*

TRAMP. Excuse me, may I go this way straight through to the station?

GAEV. You may. Go along this path.

TRAMP. I thank you from the bottom of my heart. *[Hiccups]* Lovely weather.... *[Declaims]* My brother, my suffering brother.... Come out on the Volga, you whose groans... *[To VARYA]* Mademoiselle, please give a hungry Russian thirty copecks....

*[VARYA screams, frightened.]*

LOPAKHIN. *[Angrily]* There's manners everybody's got to keep!

LUBOV. *[With a start]* Take this... here you are.... *[Feels in her purse]* There's no silver.... It doesn't matter, here's gold.

TRAMP. I am deeply grateful to you! *[Exit. Laughter.]*

VARYA. *[Frightened]* I'm going, I'm going.... Oh, little mother, at home there's nothing for the servants to eat, and you gave him gold.

LUBOV. What is to be done with such a fool as I am! At home I'll give you everything I've got. Ermolai Alexeyevitch, lend me some more!...

LOPAKHIN. Very well.

LUBOV. Let's go, it's time. And Varya, we've settled your affair; I congratulate you.

VARYA. *[Crying]* You shouldn't joke about this, mother.

LOPAKHIN. Oh, feel me, get thee to a nunnery.

GAEV. My hands are all trembling; I haven't played billiards for a long time.

LOPAKHIN. Oh, feel me, nymph, remember me in thine orisons.

LUBOV. Come along; it'll soon be supper-time.

VARYA. He did frighten me. My heart is beating hard.

LOPAKHIN. Let me remind you, ladies and gentlemen, on August 22 the cherry orchard will be sold. Think of that!... Think of that!...

*[All go out except TROFIMOV and ANYA.]*

ANYA. *[Laughs]* Thanks to the tramp who frightened Barbara, we're alone now.

TROFIMOV. Varya's afraid we may fall in love with each other and won't get away from us for days on end. Her narrow mind won't allow her to understand that we are above love. To escape all the petty and deceptive things which prevent our being happy and free, that is the aim and meaning of our lives. Forward! We go irresistibly on to that bright star which burns there, in the distance! Don't lag behind, friends!

ANYA. *[Clapping her hands]* How beautifully you talk! *[Pause]* It is glorious here to-day!

TROFIMOV. Yes, the weather is wonderful.

ANYA. What have you done to me, Peter? I don't love the cherry orchard as I used to. I loved it so tenderly, I thought there was no better place in the world than our orchard.

TROFIMOV. All Russia is our orchard. The land is great and beautiful, there are many marvellous places in it. *[Pause]* Think, Anya, your grandfather, your great-grandfather, and all your ancestors were serf-owners, they owned living souls; and now, doesn't something human look at you from every cherry in the orchard, every leaf and every stalk? Don't you hear voices...? Oh, it's awful, your orchard is terrible; and when in the evening or at night you walk through the orchard, then the old bark on the trees sheds a dim light and the old cherry-trees seem to be dreaming of all that was a hundred, two hundred years ago, and are oppressed by their heavy visions. Still, at any rate, we've left those two hundred years behind us. So far we've gained nothing at all—we don't yet know what the past is to be to us—we only philosophize, we complain that we are dull, or we drink vodka. For it's so clear that in order to begin to live in the present we must first redeem the past, and that can only be done by suffering, by strenuous, uninterrupted labour. Understand that, Anya.

ANYA. The house in which we live has long ceased to be our house; I shall go away. I give you my word.

TROFIMOV. If you have the housekeeping keys, throw them down the well and go away. Be as free as the wind.

ANYA. *[Enthusiastically]* How nicely you said that!

TROFIMOV. Believe me, Anya, believe me! I'm not thirty yet, I'm young, I'm still a student, but I have undergone a great deal! I'm as hungry as the winter, I'm ill, I'm shaken. I'm as poor as a beggar, and where haven't I been—fate has tossed me everywhere! But my soul is always my own; every minute of the day and the night it is filled with unspeakable presentiments. I know that happiness is coming, Anya, I see it already....

ANYA. *[Thoughtful]* The moon is rising.

*[EPIKHODOV is heard playing the same sad song on his guitar. The moon rises. Somewhere by the poplars VARYA is looking for ANYA and calling, "Anya, where are you?"]*

TROFIMOV. Yes, the moon has risen. *[Pause]* There is happiness, there it comes; it comes nearer and nearer; I hear its steps already. And if we do not see it we shall not know it, but what does that matter? Others will see it!

THE VOICE OF VARYA. Anya! Where are you?

TROFIMOV. That's Varya again! *[Angry]* Disgraceful!

ANYA. Never mind. Let's go to the river. It's nice there.

TROFIMOV Let's go. *[They go out.]*

THE VOICE OF VARYA. Anya! Anya!

## Curtain.

# ACT THREE

*[A reception-room cut off from a drawing-room by an arch. Chandelier lighted. A Jewish band, the one mentioned in Act II, is heard playing in another room. Evening. In the drawing-room the grand rond is being danced. Voice of SIMEONOV PISCHIN "Promenade a une paire!" Dancers come into the reception-room; the first pair are PISCHIN and CHARLOTTA IVANOVNA; the second, TROFIMOV and LUBOV ANDREYEVNA; the third, ANYA and the POST OFFICE CLERK; the fourth, VARYA and the STATION-MASTER, and so on. VARYA is crying gently and wipes away her tears as she dances. DUNYASHA is in the last pair. They go off into the drawing-room, PISCHIN shouting, "Grand rond, balancez:" and "Les cavaliers à genou et remerciez vos dames!" FIERS, in a dress-coat, carries a tray with seltzer-water across. Enter PISCHIN and TROFIMOV from the drawing-room.]*

PISCHIN. I'm full-blooded and have already had two strokes; it's hard for me to dance, but, as they say, if you're in Rome, you must do as Rome does. I've got the strength of a horse. My dead father, who liked a joke, peace to his bones, used to say, talking of our ancestors, that the ancient stock of the Simeonov-Pischins was descended from that identical horse that Caligula made a senator.... *[Sits]* But the trouble is, I've no money! A hungry dog only believes in meat. *[Snores and wakes up again immediately]* So I... only believe in money....

TROFIMOV. Yes. There is something equine about your figure.

PISCHIN. Well... a horse is a fine animal... you can sell a horse.

*[Billiard playing can be heard in the next room. VARYA appears under the arch.]*

TROFIMOV. *[Teasing]* Madame Lopakhin! Madame Lopakhin!

VARYA. *[Angry]* Decayed gentleman!

TROFIMOV. Yes, I am a decayed gentleman, and I'm proud of it!

VARYA. *[Bitterly]* We've hired the musicians, but how are they to be paid? *[Exit.]*

TROFIMOV. *[To PISCHIN]* If the energy which you, in the course of your life, have spent in looking for money to pay interest had been used for something else, then, I believe, after all, you'd be able to turn everything upside down.

PISCHIN. Nietzsche... a philosopher... a very great, a most celebrated man... a man of enormous brain, says in his books that you can forge bank-notes.

TROFIMOV. And have you read Nietzsche?

PISCHIN. Well... Dashenka told me. Now I'm in such a position, I wouldn't mind forging them... I've got to pay 310 roubles the day after to-morrow... I've got 130 already.... *[Feels his pockets, nervously]* I've lost the money! The money's gone! *[Crying]* Where's the money? *[Joyfully]* Here it is behind the lining... I even began to perspire.

*[Enter LUBOV ANDREYEVNA and CHARLOTTA IVANOVNA.]*

LUBOV. *[Humming a Caucasian dance]* Why is Leonid away so long? What's he doing in town? *[To DUNYASHA]* Dunyasha, give the musicians some tea.

TROFIMOV. Business is off, I suppose.

LUBOV. And the musicians needn't have come, and we needn't have got up this ball.... Well, never mind.... *[Sits and sings softly.]*

CHARLOTTA. *[Gives a pack of cards to PISCHIN]* Here's a pack of cards, think of any one card you like.

PISCHIN. I've thought of one.

CHARLOTTA. Now shuffle. All right, now. Give them here, oh my dear Mr. Pischin. *Ein, zwei, drei*! Now look and you'll find it in your coat-tail pocket.

PISCHIN. *[Takes a card out of his coat-tail pocket]* Eight of spades, quite right! *[Surprised]* Think of that now!

CHARLOTTA. *[Holds the pack of cards on the palm of her hand. To TROFIMOV]* Now tell me quickly. What's the top card?

TROFIMOV. Well, the queen of spades.

CHARLOTTA. Right! *[To PISCHIN]* Well now? What card's on top?

PISCHIN. Ace of hearts.

CHARLOTTA. Right! *[Claps her hands, the pack of cards vanishes]* How lovely the weather is to-day. *[A mysterious woman's voice answers her, as if from under the floor, "Oh yes, it's lovely weath-weather, madam."]* You are so beautiful, you are my ideal. *[Voice, "You, madam, please me very much too."]*

STATION-MASTER. *[Applauds]* Madame ventriloquist, bravo!

PISCHIN. *[Surprised]* Think of that, now! Delightful, Charlotte Ivanovna... I'm simply in love....

CHARLOTTA. In love? *[Shrugging her shoulders]* Can you love? Guter Mensch aber schlechter Musikant.

TROFIMOV. *[Slaps PISCHIN on the shoulder]* Oh, you horse!

CHARLOTTA. Attention please, here's another trick. *[Takes a shawl from a chair]* Here's a very nice plaid shawl, I'm going to sell it.... *[Shakes it]* Won't anybody buy it?

PISCHIN. *[Astonished]* Think of that now!

CHARLOTTA. Ein, zwei, drei.

*[She quickly lifts up the shawl, which is hanging down. ANYA is standing behind it; she bows and runs to her mother, hugs her and runs back to the drawing-room amid general applause.]*

LUBOV. *[Applauds]* Bravo, bravo!

CHARLOTTA. Once again! *Ein, zwei, drei*!

*[Lifts the shawl. VARYA stands behind it and bows.]*

PISCHIN. *[Astonished]* Think of that, now.

CHARLOTTA. The end!

*[Throws the shawl at PISCHIN, curtseys and runs into the drawing-room.]*

PISCHIN. *[Runs after her]* Little wretch.... What? Would you? *[Exit.]*

LUBOV. Leonid hasn't come yet. I don't understand what he's doing so long in town! Everything must be over by now. The estate must be sold; or, if the sale never came off, then why does he stay so long?

VARYA. *[Tries to soothe her]* Uncle has bought it. I'm certain of it.

TROFIMOV. *[Sarcastically]* Oh, yes!

VARYA. Grandmother sent him her authority for him to buy it in her name and transfer the debt to her. She's doing it for Anya. And I'm certain that God will help us and uncle will buy it.

LUBOV. Grandmother sent fifteen thousand roubles from Yaroslav to buy the property in her name—she won't trust us—and that wasn't even enough to pay the interest. *[Covers her face with her hands]* My fate will be settled to-day, my fate....

TROFIMOV. *[Teasing VARYA]* Madame Lopakhin!

VARYA. *[Angry]* Eternal student! He's already been expelled twice from the university.

LUBOV. Why are you getting angry, Varya? He's teasing you about Lopakhin, well what of it? You can marry Lopakhin if you want to, he's a good, interesting man.... You needn't if you don't want to; nobody wants to force you against your will, my darling.

VARYA. I do look at the matter seriously, little mother, to be quite frank. He's a good man, and I like him.

LUBOV. Then marry him. I don't understand what you're waiting for.

VARYA. I can't propose to him myself, little mother. People have been talking about him to me for two years now, but he either says nothing, or jokes about it. I understand. He's getting rich, he's busy, he can't bother about me. If I had some money, even a little, even only a hundred roubles, I'd throw up everything and go away. I'd go into a convent.

TROFIMOV. How nice!

VARYA. *[To TROFIMOV]* A student ought to have sense! *[Gently, in tears]* How ugly you are now, Peter, how old you've grown! *[To LUBOV ANDREYEVNA, no longer crying]* But I can't go on without working, little mother. I want to be doing something every minute.

*[Enter YASHA.]*

YASHA. *[Nearly laughing]* Epikhodov's broken a billiard cue! *[Exit.]*

VARYA. Why is Epikhodov here? Who said he could play billiards? I don't understand these people. *[Exit.]*

LUBOV. Don't tease her, Peter, you see that she's quite unhappy without that.

TROFIMOV. She takes too much on herself, she keeps on interfering in other people's business. The whole summer she's given no peace to me or to Anya, she's afraid we'll have a romance all to ourselves. What has it to do with her? As if I'd ever given her grounds to believe I'd stoop to such vulgarity! We are above love.

LUBOV. Then I suppose I must be beneath love. *[In agitation]* Why isn't Leonid here? If I only knew whether the estate is sold or not! The disaster seems to me so improbable that I don't know what to think, I'm all at sea... I may scream... or do something silly. Save me, Peter. Say something, say something.

TROFIMOV. Isn't it all the same whether the estate is sold to-day or isn't? It's been all up with it for a long time; there's no turning back, the path's grown over. Be calm, dear, you shouldn't deceive yourself, for once in your life at any rate you must look the truth straight in the face.

LUBOV. What truth? You see where truth is, and where untruth is, but I seem to have lost my sight and see nothing. You boldly settle all important questions, but tell me, dear, isn't it because you're young, because you haven't had time to suffer till you settled a single one of your questions? You boldly look forward, isn't it because you cannot foresee or expect anything terrible, because so far life has been hidden from your young eyes? You are bolder, more honest, deeper than we are, but think only, be just a little magnanimous, and have mercy on me. I was born here, my father and mother lived here, my grandfather too, I love this house. I couldn't understand my life without that cherry orchard, and if it really must be sold, sell me with it! *[Embraces TROFIMOV, kisses his forehead]*. My son was drowned here.... *[Weeps]* Have pity on me, good, kind man.

TROFIMOV. You know I sympathize with all my soul.

LUBOV. Yes, but it ought to be said differently, differently.... *[Takes another handkerchief, a telegram falls on the floor]* I'm so sick at heart to-day, you can't imagine. Here it's so noisy, my soul shakes at every sound. I shake all over, and I can't go away by myself, I'm afraid of the silence. Don't judge me harshly, Peter... I loved you, as if you belonged to my family. I'd gladly let Anya marry you, I swear it, only dear, you ought to work, finish your studies. You don't do anything, only fate throws you about from place to place, it's so odd.... Isn't it true? Yes? And you ought to do something to your beard to make it grow better *[Laughs]* You are funny!

TROFIMOV. *[Picking up telegram]* I don't want to be a Beau Brummel.

LUBOV. This telegram's from Paris. I get one every day. Yesterday and to-day. That wild man is ill again, he's bad again.... He begs for forgiveness, and implores me to come, and I really ought to go to Paris to be near him. You look severe, Peter, but what can I do, my dear, what can I do; he's ill, he's alone, unhappy, and who's to look after him, who's to keep him away from his errors, to give him his medicine punctually? And why should I conceal it and say nothing about it; I love him, that's plain, I love him, I love him.... That love is a stone round my neck; I'm going with it to the bottom, but I love that stone and can't live without it. *[Squeezes TROFIMOV'S hand]* Don't think badly of me, Peter, don't say anything to me, don't say...

TROFIMOV. *[Weeping]* For God's sake forgive my speaking candidly, but that man has robbed you!

LUBOV. No, no, no, you oughtn't to say that! *[Stops her ears.]*

TROFIMOV. But he's a wretch, you alone don't know it! He's a petty thief, a nobody....

LUBOV. *[Angry, but restrained]* You're twenty-six or twenty-seven, and still a schoolboy of the second class!

TROFIMOV. Why not!

LUBOV. You ought to be a man, at your age you ought to be able to understand those who love. And you ought to be in love yourself, you must fall in love! *[Angry]* Yes, yes! You aren't pure, you're just a freak, a queer fellow, a funny growth...

TROFIMOV. *[In horror]* What is she saying!

LUBOV. "I'm above love!" You're not above love, you're just what our Fiers calls a bungler. Not to have a mistress at your age!

TROFIMOV. *[In horror]* This is awful! What is she saying? *[Goes quickly up into the drawing-room, clutching his head]* It's awful... I can't stand it, I'll go away. *[Exit, but returns at once]* All is over between us! *[Exit.]*

LUBOV. *[Shouts after him]* Peter, wait! Silly man, I was joking! Peter! *[Somebody is heard going out and falling downstairs noisily. ANYA and VARYA scream; laughter is heard immediately]* What's that?

*[ANYA comes running in, laughing.]*

ANYA. Peter's fallen downstairs! *[Runs out again.]*

LUBOV. This Peter's a marvel.

*[The STATION MASTER stands in the middle of the drawing-room and recites "The Magdalen" by Tolstoy. He is listened to, but he has only delivered a few*

*lines when a waltz is heard from the front room, and the recitation is stopped. Everybody dances. TROFIMOV, ANYA, VARYA, and LUBOV ANDREYEVNA come in from the front room.]*

LUBOV. Well, Peter... you pure soul... I beg your pardon... let's dance.

*[She dances with PETER. ANYA and VARYA dance. FIERS enters and stands his stick by a side door. YASHA has also come in and looks on at the dance.]*

YASHA. Well, grandfather?

FIERS. I'm not well. At our balls some time back, generals and barons and admirals used to dance, and now we send for post-office clerks and the Station-master, and even they come as a favour. I'm very weak. The dead master, the grandfather, used to give everybody sealing-wax when anything was wrong. I've taken sealing-wax every day for twenty years, and more; perhaps that's why I still live.

YASHA. I'm tired of you, grandfather. *[Yawns]* If you'd only hurry up and kick the bucket.

FIERS. Oh you... bungler! *[Mutters.]*

*[TROFIMOV and LUBOV ANDREYEVNA dance in the reception-room, then into the sitting-room.]*

LUBOV. *Merci*. I'll sit down. *[Sits]* I'm tired.

*[Enter ANYA.]*

ANYA. *[Excited]* Somebody in the kitchen was saying just now that the cherry orchard was sold to-day.

LUBOV. Sold to whom?

ANYA. He didn't say to whom. He's gone now. *[Dances out into the reception-room with TROFIMOV.]*

YASHA. Some old man was chattering about it a long time ago. A stranger!

FIERS. And Leonid Andreyevitch isn't here yet, he hasn't come. He's wearing a light, *demi-saison* overcoat. He'll catch cold. Oh these young fellows.

LUBOV. I'll die of this. Go and find out, Yasha, to whom it's sold.

YASHA. Oh, but he's been gone a long time, the old man. *[Laughs.]*

LUBOV. *[Slightly vexed]* Why do you laugh? What are you glad about?

YASHA. Epikhodov's too funny. He's a silly man. Two-and-twenty troubles.

LUBOV. Fiers, if the estate is sold, where will you go?

FIERS. I'll go wherever you order me to go.

LUBOV. Why do you look like that? Are you ill? I think you ought to go to bed....

FIERS. Yes... *[With a smile]* I'll go to bed, and who'll hand things round and give orders without me? I've the whole house on my shoulders.

YASHA. *[To LUBOV ANDREYEVNA]* Lubov Andreyevna! I want to ask a favour of you, if you'll be so kind! If you go to Paris again, then please take me with you. It's absolutely impossible for me to stop here. *[Looking round; in an undertone]* What's the good of talking about it, you see for yourself that this is an uneducated country, with an immoral population, and it's so dull. The food in the kitchen is beastly, and here's this Fiers walking about mumbling various inappropriate things. Take me with you, be so kind!

*[Enter PISCHIN.]*

PISCHIN. I come to ask for the pleasure of a little waltz, dear lady.... *[LUBOV ANDREYEVNA goes to him]* But all the same, you wonderful woman, I must have 180 little roubles from you... I must.... *[They dance]* 180 little roubles.... *[They go through into the drawing-room.]*

YASHA. *[Sings softly]*

"Oh, will you understand
My soul's deep restlessness?"

*[In the drawing-room a figure in a grey top-hat and in baggy check trousers is waving its hands and jumping about; there are cries of "Bravo, Charlotta Ivanovna!"]*

DUNYASHA. *[Stops to powder her face]* The young mistress tells me to dance—there are a lot of gentlemen, but few ladies—and my head goes round when I dance, and my heart beats, Fiers Nicolaevitch; the Post-office clerk told me something just now which made me catch my breath. *[The music grows faint.]*

FIERS. What did he say to you?

DUNYASHA. He says, "You're like a little flower."

YASHA. *[Yawns]* Impolite.... *[Exit.]*

DUNYASHA. Like a little flower. I'm such a delicate girl; I simply love words of tenderness.

FIERS. You'll lose your head.

*[Enter EPIKHODOV.]*

EPIKHODOV. You, Avdotya Fedorovna, want to see me no more than if I was some insect. *[Sighs]* Oh, life!

DUNYASHA. What do you want?

EPIKHODOV. Undoubtedly, perhaps, you may be right. *[Sighs]* But, certainly, if you regard the matter from the aspect, then you, if I may say so, and you must excuse my candidness, have absolutely reduced me to a state of mind. I know my fate, every day something unfortunate happens to me, and I've grown used to it a long time ago, I even look at my fate with a smile. You gave me your word, and though I...

DUNYASHA. Please, we'll talk later on, but leave me alone now. I'm meditating now. *[Plays with her fan.]*

EPIKHODOV. Every day something unfortunate happens to me, and I, if I may so express myself, only smile, and even laugh.

*[VARYA enters from the drawing-room.]*

VARYA. Haven't you gone yet, Simeon? You really have no respect for anybody. *[To DUNYASHA]* You go away, Dunyasha. *[To EPIKHODOV]* You play billiards and break a cue, and walk about the drawing-room as if you were a visitor!

EPIKHODOV. You cannot, if I may say so, call me to order.

VARYA. I'm not calling you to order, I'm only telling you. You just walk about from place to place and never do your work. Goodness only knows why we keep a clerk.

EPIKHODOV. *[Offended]* Whether I work, or walk about, or eat, or play billiards, is only a matter to be settled by people of understanding and my elders.

VARYA. You dare to talk to me like that! *[Furious]* You dare? You mean that I know nothing? Get out of here! This minute!

EPIKHODOV. *[Nervous]* I must ask you to express yourself more delicately.

VARYA. *[Beside herself]* Get out this minute. Get out! *[He goes to the door, she follows]* Two-and-twenty troubles! I don't want any sign of you here! I don't want to see anything of you! *[EPIKHODOV has gone out; his voice can be heard outside: "I'll make a complaint against you."]* What, coming back? *[Snatches up the stick left by FIERS by the door]* Go... go... go,

I'll show you.... Are you going? Are you going? Well, then take that. *[She hits out as LOPAKHIN enters.]*

LOPAKHIN. Much obliged.

VARYA. *[Angry but amused]* I'm sorry.

LOPAKHIN. Never mind. I thank you for my pleasant reception.

VARYA. It isn't worth any thanks. *[Walks away, then looks back and asks gently]* I didn't hurt you, did I?

LOPAKHIN. No, not at all. There'll be an enormous bump, that's all.

VOICES FROM THE DRAWING-ROOM. Lopakhin's returned! Ermolai Alexeyevitch!

PISCHIN. Now we'll see what there is to see and hear what there is to hear... *[Kisses LOPAKHIN]* You smell of cognac, my dear, my soul. And we're all having a good time.

*[Enter LUBOV ANDREYEVNA.]*

LUBOV. Is that you, Ermolai Alexeyevitch? Why were you so long? Where's Leonid?

LOPAKHIN. Leonid Andreyevitch came back with me, he's coming....

LUBOV. *[Excited]* Well, what? Is it sold? Tell me?

LOPAKHIN. *[Confused, afraid to show his pleasure]* The sale ended up at four o'clock.... We missed the train, and had to wait till half-past nine. *[Sighs heavily]* Ooh! My head's going round a little.

*[Enter GAEV; in his right hand he carries things he has bought, with his left he wipes away his tears.]*

LUBOV. Leon, what's happened? Leon, well? *[Impatiently, in tears]* Quick, for the love of God....

GAEV. *[Says nothing to her, only waves his hand; to FIERS, weeping]* Here, take this.... Here are anchovies, herrings from Kertch.... I've had no food to-day.... I have had a time! *[The door from the billiard-room is open; the clicking of the balls is heard, and YASHA'S voice, "Seven, eighteen!" GAEV'S expression changes, he cries no more]* I'm awfully tired. Help me change my clothes, Fiers.

*[Goes out through the drawing-room; FIERS after him.]*

PISCHIN. What happened? Come on, tell us!

LUBOV. Is the cherry orchard sold?

LOPAKHIN. It is sold.

LUBOV. Who bought it?

LOPAKHIN. I bought it.

*[LUBOV ANDREYEVNA is overwhelmed; she would fall if she were not standing by an armchair and a table. VARYA takes her keys off her belt, throws them on the floor, into the middle of the room and goes out.]*

LOPAKHIN. I bought it! Wait, ladies and gentlemen, please, my head's going round, I can't talk.... *[Laughs]* When we got to the sale, Deriganov was there already. Leonid Andreyevitch had only fifteen thousand roubles, and Deriganov offered thirty thousand on top of the mortgage to begin with. I saw how matters were, so I grabbed hold of him and bid forty. He went up to forty-five, I offered fifty-five. That means he went up by fives and I went up by tens.... Well, it came to an end. I bid ninety more than the mortgage; and it stayed with me. The cherry orchard is mine now, mine! *[Roars with laughter]* My God, my God, the cherry orchard's mine! Tell me I'm drunk, or mad, or dreaming.... *[Stamps his feet]* Don't laugh at me! If my father and grandfather rose from their graves and looked at the whole affair, and saw how their Ermolai, their beaten and uneducated Ermolai, who used to run barefoot in the winter, how that very Ermolai has bought an estate, which is the most beautiful thing in the world! I've bought the estate where my grandfather and my father were slaves, where they weren't even allowed into the kitchen. I'm asleep, it's only a dream, an illusion.... It's the fruit of imagination, wrapped in the fog of the unknown.... *[Picks up the keys, nicely smiling]* She threw down the keys, she wanted to show she was no longer mistress here.... *[Jingles keys]* Well, it's all one! *[Hears the band tuning up]* Eh, musicians, play, I want to hear you! Come and look at Ermolai Lopakhin laying his axe to the cherry orchard, come and look at the trees falling! We'll build villas here, and our grandsons and great-grandsons will sec a new life here.... Play on, music! *[The band plays. LUBOV ANDREYEVNA sinks into a chair and weeps bitterly. LOPAKHIN continues reproachfully]* Why then, why didn't you take my advice? My poor, dear woman, you can't go back now. *[Weeps]* Oh, if only the whole thing was done with, if only our uneven, unhappy life were changed!

PISCHIN. *[Takes his arm; in an undertone]* She's crying. Let's go into the drawing-room and leave her by herself... come on.... *[Takes his arm and leads him out.]*

LOPAKHIN. What's that? Bandsmen, play nicely! Go on, do just as I want you to! *[Ironically]* The new owner, the owner of the cherry orchard is coming! *[He accidentally knocks up against a little table and nearly upsets the candelabra]* I can pay for everything! *[Exit with PISCHIN]*

*[In the reception-room and the drawing-room nobody remains except LUBOV ANDREYEVNA, who sits huddled up and weeping bitterly. The band plays softly. ANYA and TROFIMOV come in quickly. ANYA goes up to her mother and goes on her knees in front of her. TROFIMOV stands at the drawing-room entrance.]*

ANYA. Mother! mother, are you crying? My dear, kind, good mother, my beautiful mother, I love you! Bless you! The cherry orchard is sold, we've got it no longer, it's true, true, but don't cry mother, you've still got your life before you, you've still your beautiful pure soul... Come with me, come, dear, away from here, come! We'll plant a new garden, finer than this, and you'll see it, and you'll understand, and deep joy, gentle joy will sink into your soul, like the evening sun, and you'll smile, mother! Come, dear, let's go!

**Curtain.**

# ACT FOUR

*[The stage is set as for Act I. There are no curtains on the windows, no pictures; only a few pieces of furniture are left; they are piled up in a corner as if for sale. The emptiness is felt. By the door that leads out of the house and at the back of the stage, portmanteaux and travelling paraphernalia are piled up. The door on the left is open; the voices of VARYA and ANYA can be heard through it. LOPAKHIN stands and waits. YASHA holds a tray with little tumblers of champagne. Outside, EPIKHODOV is tying up a box. Voices are heard behind the stage. The peasants have come to say good-bye. The voice of GAEV is heard: "Thank you, brothers, thank you."]*

YASHA. The common people have come to say good-bye. I am of the opinion, Ermolai Alexeyevitch, that they're good people, but they don't understand very much.

*[The voices die away. LUBOV ANDREYEVNA and GAEV enter. She is not crying but is pale, and her face trembles; she can hardly speak.]*

GAEV. You gave them your purse, Luba. You can't go on like that, you can't!

LUBOV. I couldn't help myself, I couldn't! *[They go out.]*

LOPAKHIN. *[In the doorway, calling after them]* Please, I ask you most humbly! Just a little glass to say good-bye. I didn't remember to bring any from town and I only found one bottle at the station. Please, do! *[Pause]* Won't you really have any? *[Goes away from the door]* If I only knew—I wouldn't have bought any. Well, I shan't drink any either. *[YASHA carefully puts the tray on a chair]* You have a drink, Yasha, at any rate.

YASHA. To those departing! And good luck to those who stay behind! *[Drinks]* I can assure you that this isn't real champagne.

LOPAKHIN. Eight roubles a bottle. *[Pause]* It's devilish cold here.

YASHA. There are no fires to-day, we're going away. *[Laughs]*

LOPAKHIN. What's the matter with you?

YASHA. I'm just pleased.

LOPAKHIN. It's October outside, but it's as sunny and as quiet as if it were summer. Good for building. *[Looking at his watch and speaking through the door]* Ladies and gentlemen, please remember that it's only forty-seven minutes till the train goes! You must go off to the station in twenty minutes. Hurry up.

*[TROFIMOV, in an overcoat, comes in from the grounds.]*

TROFIMOV. I think it's time we went. The carriages are waiting. Where the devil are my goloshes? They're lost. *[Through the door]* Anya, I can't find my goloshes! I can't!

LOPAKHIN. I've got to go to Kharkov. I'm going in the same train as you. I'm going to spend the whole winter in Kharkov. I've been hanging about with you people, going rusty without work. I can't live without working. I must have something to do with my hands; they hang about as if they weren't mine at all.

TROFIMOV. We'll go away now and then you'll start again on your useful labours.

LOPAKHIN. Have a glass.

TROFIMOV. I won't.

LOPAKHIN. So you're off to Moscow now?

TROFIMOV Yes. I'll see them into town and to-morrow I'm off to Moscow.

LOPAKHIN. Yes.... I expect the professors don't lecture nowadays; they're waiting till you turn up!

TROFIMOV. That's not your business.

LOPAKHIN. How many years have you been going to the university?

TROFIMOV. Think of something fresh. This is old and flat. *[Looking for his goloshes]* You know, we may not meet each other again, so just let me give you a word of advice on parting: "Don't wave your hands about! Get rid of that habit of waving them about. And then, building villas and reckoning on their residents becoming freeholders in time—that's the same thing; it's all a matter of waving your hands about.... Whether I want to or not, you know, I like you. You've thin, delicate fingers, like those of an artist, and you've a thin, delicate soul...."

LOPAKHIN. *[Embraces him]* Good-bye, dear fellow. Thanks for all you've said. If you want any, take some money from me for the journey.

TROFIMOV. Why should I? I don't want it.

LOPAKHIN. But you've nothing!

TROFIMOV. Yes, I have, thank you; I've got some for a translation. Here it is in my pocket. *[Nervously]* But I can't find my goloshes!

VARYA. *[From the other room]* Take your rubbish away! *[Throws a pair of rubber goloshes on to the stage.]*

TROFIMOV. Why are you angry, Varya? Hm! These aren't my goloshes!

LOPAKHIN. In the spring I sowed three thousand acres of poppies, and now I've made forty thousand roubles net profit. And when my poppies were in flower, what a picture it was! So I, as I was saying, made forty thousand roubles, and I mean I'd like to lend you some, because I can afford it. Why turn up your nose at it? I'm just a simple peasant....

TROFIMOV. Your father was a peasant, mine was a chemist, and that means absolutely nothing. *[LOPAKHIN takes out his pocket-book]* No, no.... Even if you gave me twenty thousand I should refuse. I'm a free man. And everything that all you people, rich and poor, value so highly and so dearly hasn't the least influence over me; it's like a flock of down in the wind. I can do without you, I can pass you by. I'm strong and proud. Mankind goes on to the highest truths and to the highest happiness such as is only possible on earth, and I go in the front ranks!

LOPAKHIN. Will you get there?

TROFIMOV. I will. *[Pause]* I'll get there and show others the way. *[Axes cutting the trees are heard in the distance.]*

LOPAKHIN. Well, good-bye, old man. It's time to go. Here we stand pulling one another's noses, but life goes its own way all the time. When I work for a long time, and I don't get tired, then I think more easily, and I think I get to understand why I exist. And there are so many people in Russia, brother, who live for nothing at all. Still, work goes on without that. Leonid Andreyevitch, they say, has accepted a post in a bank; he will get sixty thousand roubles a year.... But he won't stand it; he's very lazy.

ANYA. *[At the door]* Mother asks if you will stop them cutting down the orchard until she has gone away.

TROFIMOV. Yes, really, you ought to have enough tact not to do that. *[Exit.]*

LOPAKHIN. All right, all right... yes, he's right. *[Exit.]*

ANYA. Has Fiers been sent to the hospital?

YASHA. I gave the order this morning. I suppose they've sent him.

ANYA. *[To EPIKHODOV, who crosses the room]* Simeon Panteleyevitch, please make inquiries if Fiers has been sent to the hospital.

YASHA. *[Offended]* I told Egor this morning. What's the use of asking ten times!

EPIKHODOV. The aged Fiers, in my conclusive opinion, isn't worth mending; his forefathers had better have him. I only envy him. *[Puts a trunk on a hat-box and squashes it]* Well, of course. I thought so! *[Exit.]*

YASHA. *[Grinning]* Two-and-twenty troubles.

VARYA. *[Behind the door]* Has Fiers been taken away to the hospital?

ANYA. Yes.

VARYA. Why didn't they take the letter to the doctor?

ANYA. It'll have to be sent after him. *[Exit.]*

VARYA. *[In the next room]* Where's Yasha? Tell him his mother's come and wants to say good-bye to him.

YASHA. *[Waving his hand]* She'll make me lose all patience!

*[DUNYASHA has meanwhile been bustling round the luggage; now that YASHA is left alone, she goes up to him.]*

DUNYASHA. If you only looked at me once, Yasha. You're going away, leaving me behind.

*[Weeps and hugs him round the neck.]*

YASHA. What's the use of crying? *[Drinks champagne]* In six days I'll be again in Paris. To-morrow we get into the express and off we go. I can hardly believe it. Vive la France! It doesn't suit me here, I can't live here... it's no good. Well, I've seen the uncivilized world; I have had enough of it. *[Drinks champagne]* What do you want to cry for? You behave yourself properly, and then you won't cry.

DUNYASHA. *[Looks in a small mirror and powders her face]* Send me a letter from Paris. You know I loved you, Yasha, so much! I'm a sensitive creature, Yasha.

YASHA. Somebody's coming.

*[He bustles around the luggage, singing softly. Enter LUBOV ANDREYEVNA, GAEV, ANYA, and CHARLOTTA IVANOVNA.]*

GAEV. We'd better be off. There's no time left. *[Looks at YASHA]* Somebody smells of herring!

LUBOV. We needn't get into our carriages for ten minutes.... *[Looks round the room]* Good-bye, dear house, old grandfather. The winter will go, the spring will come, and then you'll exist no more, you'll be pulled down. How much these walls have seen! *[Passionately kisses her daughter]* My treasure, you're radiant, your eyes flash like two jewels! Are you happy? Very?

ANYA. Very! A new life is beginning, mother!

GAEV. *[Gaily]* Yes, really, everything's all right now. Before the cherry orchard was sold we all were excited and we suffered, and then, when the question was solved once and for all, we all calmed down, and even became cheerful. I'm a bank official now, and a financier... red in the middle; and you, Luba, for some reason or other, look better, there's no doubt about it.

LUBOV Yes. My nerves are better, it's true. *[She puts on her coat and hat]* I sleep well. Take my luggage out, Yasha. It's time. *[To ANYA]* My little girl, we'll soon see each other again.... I'm off to Paris. I'll live there on the money your grandmother from Yaroslav sent along to buy the estate—bless her!—though it won't last long.

ANYA. You'll come back soon, soon, mother, won't you? I'll get ready, and pass the exam at the Higher School, and then I'll work and help you. We'll read all sorts of books to one another, won't we? *[Kisses her mother's hands]* We'll read in the autumn evenings; we'll read many books, and a beautiful new world will open up before us.... *[Thoughtfully]* You'll come, mother....

LUBOV. I'll come, my darling. *[Embraces her.]*

*[Enter LOPAKHIN. CHARLOTTA is singing to herself.]*

GAEV. Charlotta is happy; she sings!

CHARLOTTA. *[Takes a bundle, looking like a wrapped-up baby]* My little baby, bye-bye. *[The baby seems to answer, "Oua! Oua!"]* Hush, my nice little boy. *["Oua! Oua!"]* I'm so sorry for you!

*[Throws the bundle back]* So please find me a new place. I can't go on like this.

LOPAKHIN. We'll find one, Charlotta Ivanovna, don't you be afraid.

GAEV. Everybody's leaving us. Varya's going away... we've suddenly become unnecessary.

CHARLOTTA. I've nowhere to live in town. I must go away. *[Hums]* Never mind.

*[Enter PISCHIN.]*

LOPAKHIN. Nature's marvel!

PISCHIN. *[Puffing]* Oh, let me get my breath back.... I'm fagged out... My most honoured, give me some water....

GAEV. Come for money, what? I'm your humble servant, and I'm going out of the way of temptation. *[Exit.]*

PISCHIN. I haven't been here for ever so long... dear madam. *[To LOPAKHIN]* You here? Glad to see you... man of immense brain... take this... take it.... *[Gives LOPAKHIN money]* Four hundred roubles.... That leaves 840....

LOPAKHIN. *[Shrugs his shoulders in surprise]* As if I were dreaming. Where did you get this from?

PISCHIN. Stop... it's hot.... A most unexpected thing happened. Some Englishmen came along and found some white clay on my land.... *[To LUBOV ANDREYEVNA]* And here's four hundred for you... beautiful lady.... *[Gives her money]* Give you the rest later.... *[Drinks water]* Just now a young man in the train was saying that some great philosopher advises us all to jump off roofs. "Jump!" he says, and that's all. *[Astonished]* To think of that, now! More water!

LOPAKHIN. Who were these Englishmen?

PISCHIN. I've leased off the land with the clay to them for twenty-four years.... Now, excuse me, I've no time.... I must run off.... I must go to Znoikov and to Kardamonov... I owe them all money.... *[Drinks]* Good-bye. I'll come in on Thursday.

LUBOV. We're just off to town, and to-morrow I go abroad.

PISCHIN. *[Agitated]* What? Why to town? I see furniture... trunks.... Well, never mind. *[Crying]* Never mind. These Englishmen are men of immense intellect.... Never mind.... Be happy.... God will help you.... Never mind.... Everything in this world comes to an end.... *[Kisses LUBOV ANDREYEVNA'S hand]* And if you should happen to hear that my end has come, just remember this old... horse and say: "There was one such and such a Simeonov-Pischin, God bless his soul...." Wonderful weather... yes.... *[Exit deeply moved, but returns at once and says in the door]* Dashenka sent her love! *[Exit.]*

LUBOV. Now we can go. I've two anxieties, though. The first is poor Fiers *[Looks at her watch]* We've still five minutes....

ANYA. Mother, Fiers has already been sent to the hospital. Yasha sent him off this morning.

LUBOV. The second is Varya. She's used to getting up early and to work, and now she's no work to do she's like a fish out of water. She's grown thin and pale, and she cries, poor thing.... *[Pause]* You know very well, Ermolai Alexeyevitch, that I used to hope to marry her to you, and I suppose you are going to marry somebody? *[Whispers to ANYA, who nods to CHARLOTTA, and they both go out]* She loves you, she's your sort, and I don't understand, I really don't, why you seem to be keeping away from each other. I don't understand!

LOPAKHIN. To tell the truth, I don't understand it myself. It's all so strange.... If there's still time, I'll be ready at once... Let's get it over, once and for all; I don't feel as if I could ever propose to her without you.

LUBOV. Excellent. It'll only take a minute. I'll call her.

LOPAKHIN. The champagne's very appropriate. *[Looking at the tumblers]* They're empty, somebody's already drunk them. *[YASHA coughs]* I call that licking it up....

LUBOV. *[Animated]* Excellent. We'll go out. Yasha, allez. I'll call her in.... *[At the door]* Varya, leave that and come here. Come! *[Exit with YASHA.]*

LOPAKHIN. *[Looks at his watch]* Yes.... *[Pause.]*

*[There is a restrained laugh behind the door, a whisper, then VARYA comes in.]*

VARYA. *[Looking at the luggage in silence]* I can't seem to find it....

LOPAKHIN. What are you looking for?

VARYA. I packed it myself and I don't remember. *[Pause.]*

LOPAKHIN. Where are you going to now, Barbara Mihailovna?

VARYA. I? To the Ragulins.... I've got an agreement to go and look after their house... as housekeeper or something.

LOPAKHIN. Is that at Yashnevo? It's about fifty miles. *[Pause]* So life in this house is finished now....

VARYA. *[Looking at the luggage]* Where is it?... perhaps I've put it away in the trunk.... Yes, there'll be no more life in this house....

LOPAKHIN. And I'm off to Kharkov at once... by this train. I've a lot of business on hand. I'm leaving Epikhodov here... I've taken him on.

VARYA. Well, well!

LOPAKHIN. Last year at this time the snow was already falling, if you remember, and now it's nice and sunny. Only it's rather cold.... There's three degrees of frost.

VARYA. I didn't look. *[Pause]* And our thermometer's broken.... *[Pause.]*

VOICE AT THE DOOR. Ermolai Alexeyevitch!

LOPAKHIN. *[As if he has long been waiting to be called]* This minute. *[Exit quickly.]*

*[VARYA, sitting on the floor, puts her face on a bundle of clothes and weeps gently. The door opens. LUBOV ANDREYEVNA enters carefully.]*

LUBOV. Well? *[Pause]* We must go.

VARYA. *[Not crying now, wipes her eyes]* Yes, it's quite time, little mother. I'll get to the Ragulins to-day, if I don't miss the train....

LUBOV. *[At the door]* Anya, put on your things. *[Enter ANYA, then GAEV, CHARLOTTA IVANOVNA. GAEV wears a warm overcoat with a cape. A servant and drivers come in. EPIKHODOV bustles around the luggage]* Now we can go away.

ANYA. *[Joyfully]* Away!

GAEV. My friends, my dear friends! Can I be silent, in leaving this house for evermore?—can I restrain myself, in saying farewell, from expressing those feelings which now fill my whole being...?

ANYA. *[Imploringly]* Uncle!

VARYA. Uncle, you shouldn't!

GAEV. *[Stupidly]* Double the red into the middle.... I'll be quiet.

*[Enter TROFIMOV, then LOPAKHIN.]*

TROFIMOV. Well, it's time to be off.

LOPAKHIN. Epikhodov, my coat!

LUBOV. I'll sit here one more minute. It's as if I'd never really noticed what the walls and ceilings of this house were like, and now I look at them greedily, with such tender love....

GAEV. I remember, when I was six years old, on Trinity Sunday, I sat at this window and looked and saw my father going to church....

LUBOV. Have all the things been taken away?

LOPAKHIN. Yes, all, I think. *[To EPIKHODOV, putting on his coat]* You see that everything's quite straight, Epikhodov.

EPIKHODOV. *[Hoarsely]* You may depend upon me, Ermolai Alexeyevitch!

LOPAKHIN. What's the matter with your voice?

EPIKHODOV. I swallowed something just now; I was having a drink of water.

YASHA. *[Suspiciously]* What manners....

LUBOV. We go away, and not a soul remains behind.

LOPAKHIN. Till the spring.

VARYA. *[Drags an umbrella out of a bundle, and seems to be waving it about. LOPAKHIN appears to be frightened]* What are you doing?... I never thought...

TROFIMOV. Come along, let's take our seats... it's time! The train will be in directly.

VARYA. Peter, here they are, your goloshes, by that trunk. *[In tears]* And how old and dirty they are....

TROFIMOV. *[Putting them on]* Come on!

GAEV. *[Deeply moved, nearly crying]* The train... the station.... Cross in the middle, a white double in the corner....

LUBOV. Let's go!

LOPAKHIN. Are you all here? There's nobody else? *[Locks the side-door on the left]* There's a lot of things in there. I must lock them up. Come!

ANYA. Good-bye, home! Good-bye, old life!

TROFIMOV. Welcome, new life! *[Exit with ANYA.]*

*[VARYA looks round the room and goes out slowly. YASHA and CHARLOTTA, with her little dog, go out.]*

LOPAKHIN. Till the spring, then! Come on... till we meet again! *[Exit.]*

*[LUBOV ANDREYEVNA and GAEV are left alone. They might almost have been waiting for that. They fall into each other's arms and sob restrainedly and quietly, fearing that somebody might hear them.]*

GAEV. *[In despair]* My sister, my sister....

LUBOV. My dear, my gentle, beautiful orchard! My life, my youth, my happiness, good-bye! Good-bye!

ANYA'S VOICE. *[Gaily]* Mother!

TROFIMOV'S VOICE. *[Gaily, excited]* Coo-ee!

LUBOV. To look at the walls and the windows for the last time.... My dead mother used to like to walk about this room....

GAEV. My sister, my sister!

ANYA'S VOICE. Mother!

TROFIMOV'S VOICE. Coo-ee!

LUBOV. We're coming! *[They go out.]*

*[The stage is empty. The sound of keys being turned in the locks is heard, and then the noise of the carriages going away. It is quiet. Then the sound of an axe against the trees is heard in the silence sadly and by itself. Steps are heard. FIERS comes in from the door on the right. He is dressed as usual, in a short jacket and white waistcoat; slippers on his feet. He is ill. He goes to the door and tries the handle.]*

FIERS. It's locked. They've gone away. *[Sits on a sofa]* They've forgotten about me.... Never mind, I'll sit here.... And Leonid Andreyevitch will have gone in a light overcoat instead of putting on his fur coat.... *[Sighs anxiously]* I didn't see.... Oh, these young people! *[Mumbles something that cannot be understood]* Life's gone on as if I'd never lived. *[Lying down]* I'll lie down.... You've no strength left in you, nothing left at all.... Oh, you... bungler!

*[He lies without moving. The distant sound is heard, as if from the sky, of a breaking string, dying away sadly. Silence follows it, and only the sound is heard, some way away in the orchard, of the axe falling on the trees.]*

**Curtain.**

**Mourning Becomes Electra**
**Eugene O'Neill**
Oxford City Press, 2011
210 pages
ISBN: 978-1-84902-448-8

Available from www.amazon.com, www.amazon.co.uk

Mourning Becomes Electra is a play written by the American playwright Eugene O'Neill. It premiered on Broadway in 1931 and ran for 150 performances.

The story is an updated Greek tragedy and features murder, adultery, incestuous love and revenge. O'Neill's characters have motivations that are influenced by the psychological theories of the 1930s. Hence, it can be understood from a Freudian perspective, with characters displaying Oedipus and Electra complexes.

Mourning Becomes Electra is divided into three plays entitled Homecoming, The Hunted, and The Haunted, with themes corresponding to The Oresteia trilogy by Aeschylus. These plays are normally shown together and, as they each have four or five acts, it is extraordinarily lengthy, often being cut down when produced.

**Six Characters in Search of an Author**
**Luigi Pirandello**
Benediction Classics, 2011
104 pages
ISBN: 978-1-84902-461-7
Available from www.amazon.com, www.amazon.co.uk

'Six Characters in search of an Author' is a is a satirical tragicomedy play. First performed in 1921 at the Teatro Valle in Rome, it had a very mixed reception, with the audience shouting "Manicomio!" ("Madhouse!"). However, the reception improved significantly and in 1922 it played on Broadway at the Princess Theatre. The play starts with a group of actors preparing to rehearse for a Pirandello play. The rehearsal is interrupted by the arrival of six characters. One of then informs the manager that they are looking for an author. He explains that the author who created them did not finish their story, and that they therefore are unrealized characters who have not been fully brought to life. Initially, the manager goes to throw them out of the theatre, but becomes more intrigued when they start to describe their story.

**The Complete Plays of George Bernard Shaw (1893-1921), 34 Complete and Unabridged plays including: Mrs. Warren's Profession, Caesar and Cleopatra, Man and Superman, Major Barbara, Heartbreak House, Pygmalion, Arms and the Man, Misalliance, The Doctor's Dilemma and Candida**
**George Bernard Shaw**
Oxford City Press, 2012
1076 pages
ISBN: 978-1-78139-348-2

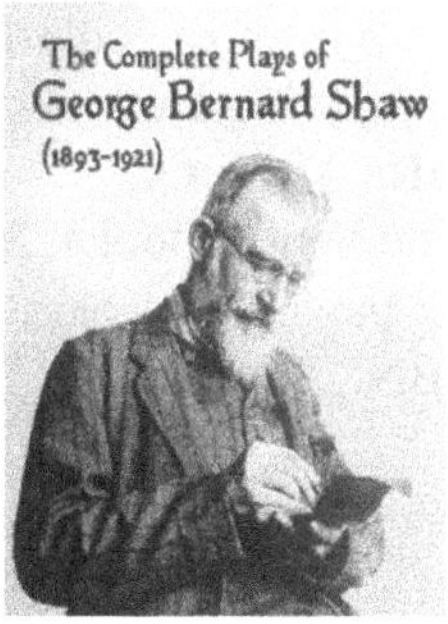


Available from www.amazon.com, www.amazon.co.uk

George Bernard Shaw was a satirical genius, ruthlessly exposing hypocrisy, and creating moral dilemmas for the reader to mull on. These are biting, witty, sometimes rude, highly intelligent plays. This collection of thirty-four of his plays is an Omnibus that will give hours of pleasure to the reader.

**The New Hudson Shakespeare: Julius Caesar - with footnotes and Indexes**
**William Shakespeare**
Benediction Classics, 2011
246 pages
ISBN: 978-1-84902-411-2

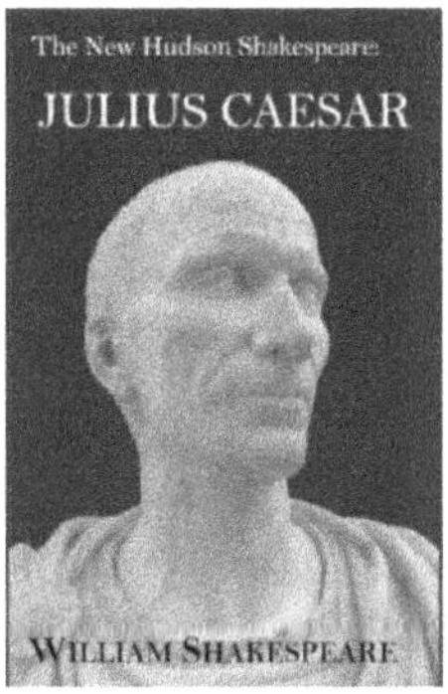


Available from www.amazon.com, www.amazon.co.uk

This book is based on an edition first published in 1908 and contains not only the play written by William Shakespeare, but a wealth of other information. There is an extensive introduction by Henry Hudson, explaining, amongst other things: the sources that Shakespeare drew on, the date of composition, early editions of the play, analysis by act and scene, the versification and diction, the characters and a chronological chart of Shakespeare's life. The text itself is presented with copious numbers of footnotes, some show text variants and others are editors notes. This edition also contains two indexes, the first referencing words and phrases in the text, and the second referencing quotations from Plutarch, who was thought to be the main source that Shakespeare used for this play. This book is a great resource for the reader intent on gaining a detailed understanding of this great work by Shakespeare.

Also from Benediction Books …
**Wandering Between Two Worlds: Essays on Faith and Art**
**Anita Mathias**
Benediction Books, 2007
152 pages
ISBN: 0955373700

Available from www.amazon.com, www.amazon.co.uk

In these wide-ranging lyrical essays, Anita Mathias writes, in lush, lovely prose, of her naughty Catholic childhood in Jamshedpur, India; her large, eccentric family in Mangalore, a sea-coast town converted by the Portuguese in the sixteenth century; her rebellion and atheism as a teenager in her Himalayan boarding school, run by German missionary nuns, St. Mary's Convent, Nainital; and her abrupt religious conversion after which she entered Mother Teresa's convent in Calcutta as a novice. Later rich, elegant essays explore the dualities of her life as a writer, mother, and Christian in the United States-- Domesticity and Art, Writing and Prayer, and the experience of being "an alien and stranger" as an immigrant in America, sensing the need for roots.

**About the Author**

Anita Mathias is the author of *Wandering Between Two Worlds: Essays on Faith and Art.* She has a B.A. and M.A. in English from Somerville College, Oxford University, and an M.A. in Creative Writing from the Ohio State University, USA. Anita won a National Endowment of the Arts fellowship in Creative Non-fiction in 1997. She lives in Oxford, England with her husband, Roy, and her daughters, Zoe and Irene.

Anita's website:
http://www.anitamathias.com, and
Anita's blog Dreaming Beneath the Spires:
http://dreamingbeneaththespires.blogspot.com

**The Church That Had Too Much**
**Anita Mathias**
Benediction Books, 2010
52 pages
ISBN: 9781849026567

Available from www.amazon.com, www.amazon.co.uk

The Church That Had Too Much was very well-intentioned. She wanted to love God, she wanted to love people, but she was both hampered by her muchness and the abundance of her possessions, and beset by ambition, power struggles and snobbery. Read about the surprising way The Church That Had Too Much began to resolve her problems in this deceptively simple and enchanting fable.

**About the Author**

Anita Mathias is the author of *Wandering Between Two Worlds: Essays on Faith and Art*. She has a B.A. and M.A. in English from Somerville College, Oxford University, and an M.A. in Creative Writing from the Ohio State University, USA. Anita won a National Endowment of the Arts fellowship in Creative Non-fiction in 1997. She lives in Oxford, England with her husband, Roy, and her daughters, Zoe and Irene.

Anita's website:
    http://www.anitamathias.com, and
Anita's blog Dreaming Beneath the Spires:
    http://dreamingbeneaththespires.blogspot.com

www.ingramcontent.com/pod-product-compliance
Lightning Source LLC
Chambersburg PA
CBHW050400110426
42812CB00006BA/1753
* 9 7 8 1 7 8 1 3 9 4 0 4 5 *